MONOGRAPHS ON SOIL AND RESOURCES SURVEY

General Editor: P. H. T. Beckett

MONOGRAPHS ON SOIL AND RESOURCES SURVEY

Principles of Geographical Information Systems for Land Resources Assessment

P. A. BURROUGH

Professor of Physical Geography, University of Utrecht, the Netherlands

CLARENDON PRESS · OXFORD

Oxford University Press, Walton Street, Oxford OX2 6DP

Oxford New York Toronto
Delhi Bombay Calcutta Madras Karachi
Petaling Jaya Singapore Hong Kong Tokyo
Nairobi Dar es Salaam Cape Town
Melbourne Auckland
and associated companies in
Berlin Ibadan

Oxford is a trade mark of Oxford University Press

Published in the United States
by Oxford University Press, New York

British Library Cataloguing in Publication Data
Burrough, P. A.
Principles of geographical information systems
for land resources assessment.—(Monographs
on soil and resources survey)
1. Information storage and retrieval systems—
Land use
I. Title II. Series
333.73'028'5574 HD108.15
ISBN 0–19–854563–0
ISBN 0–19–854592–4 (pbk.)

Library of Congress Cataloging in Publication Data
Burrough, P. A.
Principles of geographical information systems
for land resources assessment.
(Monographs on soil and resources survey)
Bibliography: p.
Includes index.
1. Land use—Data processing. 2. Land use—Maps.
3. Digital mapping. I. Title. II. Series: Monographs
on soil and resources survey.
HD108.15.B87 1986 333'.0028'5 85–24661
ISBN 0–19–854563–0
ISBN 0–19–854592–4 (pbk.)

Printed and bound in Great Britain by
Butler and Tanner Ltd, Frome, Somerset

To Joy, Alexander, and Nicholas

Preface

This book describes and explains the principles of geographical information systems that are important for most applications in environmental and natural resource inventory and analysis. It describes the major components of geographical information systems, including raster and vector data structures, modules for data input, verification, storage, and output, digital terrain models, methods of spatial analysis and modelling, and methods of classification and interpolation. Besides discussing the latest developments in these fields, there is also a critical review of the sources and propagation of error in geographical information processing, a subject that has received less than its due share of attention.

The material presented here is based on material developed for courses for undergraduates and postgraduates at the Agricultural University, Wageningen, and more recently at the Geographical Institute, Utrecht University. It also includes experience and material gathered while I was working on the development of geographical information systems at the Netherlands Soil Survey Institute. Although the text makes reference to many results derived by using geographical information systems, this book is *not* intended to be a review of current applications, but rather an explanation of the principles behind many systems now in common use. The reader wishing to learn more about specific applications of geographical information systems is referred to publications, among many others, by Teicholz and Berry (1983), Tomlinson *et al.* (1976), Salmen *et al.* (1976), Knapp and Rider (1979), Nagy and Wagle (1979), Marble *et al.* (1981), Dueker (1979), Burrough and de Veer (1984), Fabos and Caswell (1977), Fraser-Taylor (1980), the publications of the Laboratory for Computer Graphics and Spatial Analysis, Harvard University, the International Cartographical Union 'AUTOCARTO' Congress Proceedings, and the publications of the Working Group on Soil Information Systems (Moore *et al.* 1981; Burrough and Bie 1984).

The maps used to accompany the text have not necessarily been chosen for their high technical quality, but rather for their suitability for illustrating various aspects of the techniques explained. Nevertheless, there has been an attempt to include a range of technical quality in the figures from results from some of the best modern film scanners to simple raster maps drawn on a graphics matrix printer driven by a personal computer.

The literature on geographical information systems is vast and is spread over a large number of journals representative of many disciplines. There is also a huge 'grey' literature of conference papers, internal reports, and theses. I have selected what I have found to be the most useful sources for the material presented in this book, and have taken from them only the essentials. The extensive bibliography should provide readers with the means to follow any particular topic further, should they desire.

Although technical principles are important, it is also essential that if geographical information systems are to be properly used then they must be properly accommodated in the organization in which they are to be used. Although the costs of computer hardware are falling steadily in relation to the power of the systems available, computer software remains a considerable investment. It is essential that the software and hardware are properly matched to an organization's needs, and the last chapter attempts to provide some guidelines about how a geographical information system can best be chosen. This chapter will undoubtedly date quickly as technology advances, but it is hoped that the principles discussed will remain valid for some time.

Utrecht, May 1985   P. A. B.

References

Burrough, P. A. and Bie, S. W. (ed.) (1984). *Soil data technology. Proc. 6th Meeting of the International Society of Soil Science Working Group on Soil Information Systems,* Bolkesjø, Norway. 28 Feb.–4 March 1983. PUDOC, Wageningen.

—— and de Veer, A. A. (1984). Automatic production of

landscape maps for physical planning in The Netherlands. *Landsc. Plan.* **11**, 205-26.

Dueker, K. J. (1979). Land resource information systems: a review of fifteen years experience. *GeoProcessing* **1**, 105-28.

Fabos, J. G. and Caswell, S. J. (1977). Composite landscape assessment: metropolitan landscape planning model MET-LAND. Massachusetts Agricultural Experimental Station, University of Massachusetts at Amherst, Research Bulletin No. 637.

Fraser-Taylor, D. R. (1980). *The computer in contemporary cartography*. Wiley, Chichester, UK.

Knapp, E. M. and Rider, D. (1979). Automated geographic information systems and LANDSAT data: a survey. Harvard Library of Computer Graphics Mapping Collection, pp. 57-69.

Marble, D. F., Calkins, H., Peuquet, D. J., Brassel, K., and Wasilenko, M. (1981). *Computer software for spatial data handling* (3 Vols). Prepared by the International Geographical Union, Commission on Geographical Data Sensing and Processing for the US Department of the Interior, Geological Survey. IGU, Ottawa, Canada.

Moore, A. W., Cook, B. G. and Lynch, L. G., ed. (1981). Information systems for soil and related data. *Proc. 2nd Australian Meeting of the International Soil Science Society Working Group on Soil Information Systems*, Canberra, Australia, 19-21 February 1980. PUDOC, Wageningen.

Nagy, G. and Wagle, S. (1979). Geographic data processing. *Comput. Surv.* **11**, 139-181.

Salmen, L., Gropper, J., Hamil, J., and Reed, C. (1977). Comparison of selected operational capabilities of 54 geographic information systems. Ft. Collins, Western Governor's Policy Office.

Teicholz, E. and Berry, B. J. L. (1983). *Computer graphics and environmental planning*. Prentice-Hall, Englewood Cliffs, NJ.

Tomlinson, R. F., Calkins, H. W., and Marble, D. F. (1976). *Computer handling of geographical data*. UNESCO, Geneva.

Acknowledgements

Much of the material in this book results from contacts and discussions with many people at various times during the last eight years. I am especially grateful to the Netherlands Soil Survey Institute, and my colleagues Dr J. Schelling (now retired), Dr J. Bouma, Dr A. A. de Veer, and Ir A. Bregt for the intensive cooperation we have had for developing geographical information systems for soil and landscape mapping. I thank Dr R. Webster for suggesting improvements to Chapter 8 and Mr J. van den Berg and Ir W. H. E. de Man for reading and suggesting improvements to Chapter 9, and Ir G. Oerlemans, Mr R. P. L. Legis, and Dr M. Kilic for the use of data. I wish to thank Professor Carl Steinitz and Dr C. D. Tomlin of Harvard University for their stimulating introduction to the use of the Map Analysis Package and Ir A. van den Berg, Ir R. Blom, Mrs J. van Lith, and Mrs J. Roos of the Netherlands Institute for Forest and Landscape Research, 'De Dorschkamp', for their cooperation in making the package available for students and our colleagues in the Netherlands. I also thank the following authors and publishers for permission to reproduce figures and plates: Professor C. Steinitz and Mr D. White (Harvard University) Plates 9–12; Professor T. Poiker for Fig. 3.4; Professor B. K. Horn (M.I.T.), Elsevier, and the Institute of Electrical and Electronics Engineers for Fig. 3.15; Professor G. McGrath, Ir T. Bouw and Ir E. van der Zee from the I.T.C. Enschede for discussions, supply of relevant literature, and Plate 7; Dr R. Ross, US Forest Service, and Mr B. Evans for Fig. 3.9; Dr J. van Genderen of I²S Incorporated for permission to use Plates 1–6 and 13–14; Versatec BV and The Netherlands Soil Survey Institute for Fig. 4.12; The Netherlands Soil Survey and Elsevier for Figs 3.11 and 3.12; The Netherlands Soil Survey and Geoabstracts for Fig. 5.5; SYSSCAN, Norway for Fig 4.11; Dr H. Floor and Dr T. de Jong for Fig 3.7; and Computervision Europe for Plate 8. I am also extremely grateful to the Agricultural University, Wageningen, and Utrecht University for the time and the facilities they have made available to me, and to I.B.M. Nederland for the generous provision of a personal computer which, apart from many other tasks, was used to prepare parts of the manuscript. To Ing J. van Keulen and Drs L. Hazelhoff my thanks for assisting with some of the computing, and to Mrs E. Gelderman for typing part of the manuscript.

Contents

Plates

(*Plates fall between pp. 66 and 67 of the text.*)

Plates 1 and 2. Overlaying a geological interpretation of a LANDSAT image correctly with the topographic map. The latter has been digitized using a video camera device. By varying the contrasts of the two images a 'light table' effect has been created.

Plates 3–6. Land-use classification of Hungry Horse reservoir in the Flathead National Forest, Montana, USA, showing superposition and projection of the thematic information on a digital elevation model.

Plate 7. Very high quality raster image of part of the digital database of the City of Rotterdam showing utilities, cadastral information, and ownership details (in colours green and magenta).

Plate 8. Three-dimensional view of a choropleth map revealing the 'stepped' character of this land-use classification. Hidden line removal would greatly improve the appearance of this image.

Plates 9–12. Images showing thematic information concerning the Monadnock area, New Hampshire, USA, projected over a shaded relief image created from a digital elevation model.

Plate 13. Three-dimensional image of the Grand Canyon obtained from LANDSAT data and a digital elevation model showing the present situation, and a simulation of the canyon dammed full of water.

Plate 14. Digital elevation model of Hungry Horse reservoir showing trail lines superimposed on a digital elevation model.

1. Geographical Information Systems

Introduction—maps and spatial information

The collation of data about the spatial distribution of significant properties of the earth's surface has long been an important part of the activities of organized societies. From the earliest civilizations to modern times, spatial data have been collected by navigators, geographers, and surveyors and rendered into pictorial form by the map makers or cartographers. Originally, maps were used to describe far-off places, as an aid for navigation and for military strategists (Hodgkiss 1981). In Roman times, the agrimensores, or land surveyors, were an important part of the government, and the results of their work may still be seen in vestigial form in the landscapes of Europe today (Dilke 1971). The decline of the Roman Empire led to the decline of surveying and map making. Only in the eighteenth century did European civilization once again reach a state of organization such that many governments realized the value of systematic mapping of their lands. National government bodies were commissioned to produce topographical maps of whole countries. These highly disciplined institutes have continued to this day to render the spatial distribution of the features of the earth's surface, or topography, into map form. During the last 200 years many individual styles of map have been developed, but there has been a long, unbroken tradition of high cartographic standards that has continued until the present.

As the European powers increased their influence over the globe, they spread their ideas and methods of map making to the countries that fell under their sway. As scientific study of the earth advanced, so new material needed to be mapped. The developments in the assessment and understanding of natural resources—geology, geomorphology, soil science, ecology, and land—that began in the nineteenth century and have continued to this day, provided new material to be mapped. Whereas topographical maps can be regarded as general purpose because they do not set out to fulfil any specific aim (i.e. they can be interpreted for many different purposes), maps of the distribution of rock types, soil series or land use are made for more limited purposes. These specific-purpose maps are often referred to as 'thematic' maps because they contain information about a single subject or theme. To make the thematic data easy to understand, thematic maps are commonly drawn over a simplified topographic base by which users can orient themselves.

The term 'thematic map' is very widely and loosely applied (see for example, Fisher 1978; Hodgkiss 1981) and is used not only for maps showing a general purpose theme such as 'soil' or 'landform', but for much more specific properties such as the distribution of the value of the soil pH over an experimental field, the variation of the incidence of a given disease in a city, or the variation of air pressure shown on a meteorological chart. The theme may be qualitative (as in the case of land-use classes) or quantitative (as in the case of the variation of the depth to the phreatic zone). Both quantitative and qualitative information can be expressed as a choropleth map—that is, areas of equal value separated by boundaries—and typical examples are soil maps, land-use maps or maps showing the results of censuses (Fig. 1.1).† Quantitative data can also be mapped by assuming that the data can be modelled by a continuous surface that is capable of mathematical description. The variations are then shown by isolines or contours—that is, lines connecting points of equal value. Typical examples are the

† The term 'choropleth map' is used in this book in a very general sense. Some cartographers prefer to use the term only for maps displaying census tracts or administrative areas. They prefer the term 'chorochromatic' for maps of soil or geology in which the boundaries have been defined by field or aerial photo survey and the units are distinguished by different colours. Other cartographers (e.g. Campbell 1984) use the term 'dasymetric map' for maps resulting from combining administrative districts with maps differentiating land use, soil type or other phenomena. In each case, the data structure is similar: boundaries define polygons enclosing areas that are assumed to be uniform, or to which a single description can be applied. Because all data structures are the same, the term 'choropleth' is used throughout, to include all these variants.

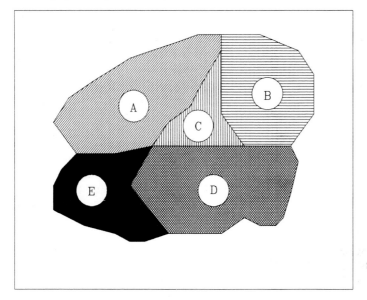

Fig. 1.1 An example of a choropleth map.

elevation contours on a topographic map, lines of equal groundwater level, and the isobars on a weather chart (Fig. 1.2).

In the twentieth century, the demand for maps of the topography and specific themes of the earth's surface, such as natural resources, has accelerated greatly. Stereo aerial photography and remotely sensed imagery have allowed photogrammetrists to map large areas with great accuracy. The same technology has also given the earth resource scientists—the geologist, the soil scientist, the ecologist, the land-use specialist—

enormous advantages for reconnaissance and semi-detailed mapping (e.g. American Society of Photogrammetry 1960). The resulting thematic maps have been a source of useful information for resource exploitation and management. The study of land evaluation arose through the need to match the land requirements for producing food and supporting populations to the resources of climate, soil, water, and available technology (e.g. Brinkman and Smyth 1973; Beek 1978; FAO 1976).

The study of the spatial distribution of rocks or soil,

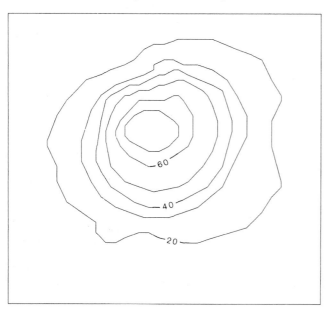

Fig. 1.2 An example of an isoline map.

of plant communities or people, started in a qualitative way. As in many new sciences, the first aim of many surveys was *inventory*—to observe, classify, and record. Qualitative methods of classification and mapping were unavoidable given the huge quantities of complex data that most environmental surveys generate. Quantitative description was hindered not only by data volume, but also by the lack of quantitative observation. Further, there was a lack of appropriate mathematical tools for describing spatial variation quantitatively. The first developments in appropriate mathematics for spatial problems began to be developed in the 1930s and 1940s in parallel with developments in statistical methods and time series analysis. Effective practical progress was completely blocked, however, by the lack of suitable computing tools. It is only since the 1960s, with the availability of the digital computer, that both the conceptual methods for spatial analysis and the actual possibilities for quantitative thematic mapping and spatial analysis have been able to blossom (e.g. Cliff and Ord 1981; Journel and Huijbregts 1978; Ripley 1981; Webster 1977).

The need for spatial data and spatial analysis has not been restricted to earth scientists. Urban planners and cadastral agencies need detailed information about the distribution of land and resources in towns and cities. Civil engineers need to plan the routes of roads and canals and to estimate construction costs, including those of cutting away hillsides and filling in valleys. Police departments need to know the spatial distribution of various kinds of crime, medical organizations the distribution of sickness and disease, commercial interests the distribution of sales outlets, and potential markets. The enormous infrastructure of what are collectively known as 'utilities'—i.e. water, gas, electricity, telephone lines, sewerage systems—all need to be recorded and manipulated in map form.

Until computers were applied to mapping, all kinds of mapping had one point in common. The spatial database was a drawing on a piece of paper or film. The information was encoded in the form of points, lines or areas. These basic geographical entities were displayed using various visual artifices, such as diverse symbolism or colour or text codes, the meaning of which is explained in a legend; where more information was available than could be printed in the legend on the map, then it was given in an accompanying memoir.

Because the paper map, and its accompanying memoir, was *the* database, there were several very important consequences for the collection, coding, and use of the information it contained. First, the original data had to be greatly reduced in volume, or classified, in order to make them understandable and representable; consequently, many local details were often filtered away and lost. Second, the map had to be drawn extremely accurately and the presentation, particularly of complex themes, had to be very clear. Third, the sheer volume of information meant that areas that are large with respect to the map scale could only be represented by a number of map sheets. It is a common experience that one's area of interest is frequently near the junction of two, if not more, map sheets! Fourth, once data had been put into a map, it was not cheap or easy to retrieve them in order to combine them with other spatial data. Fifth, the printed map is a static, qualitative document. It is extremely difficult to attempt quantitative spatial analysis within the units delineated on a thematic map without resorting to collecting new information for the specific purpose in hand.

The collection and compilation of data and the publication of a printed map is a costly and time-consuming business. Consequently, the extraction of single themes from a general purpose map can be prohibitively expensive if the map must be redrawn by hand. It was not important that initial mapping costs were large when a map could be thought of as being relevant for a period of 20 years or more. But there is now such a need for information about how the earth's surface is changing that conventional map-making techniques are totally inadequate. For example, for some kinds of mapping, such as weather charts or the distribution net of a telephone company, there can be a daily, or even hourly need for the spatial database to be brought up to date, which is just simply not possible by hand.

Essentially, the hand-drawn map or the map in a resource inventory is a snapshot of the situation seen through the particular filter of a given surveyor in a given discipline at a certain moment in time. More recently, the aerial photograph, but more especially the satellite image, have made it possible to see how landscapes change over time, to follow the slow march of desertification or erosion or the swifter progress of forest fires, floods, locust swarms or weather systems. But the products of airborne and space sensors are not maps, in the original meaning of the word, but photographic images or streams of data on magnetic tapes. The digital data are not in the familiar form of points, lines and areas representing the already recognized and classified features of the earth's surface, but are coded in picture elements—pixels—cells in a two-dimensional matrix that contain merely a number indicating the strength of reflected electromagnetic radiation in a given band. New tools were needed to turn these streams of numbers into pictures and to identify meaningful patterns. The cartographers, initially, did not possess the skills to use these new tools and so the fledgling sciences of remote sensing, image analysis, and pattern recognition were nursed into being, not by the traditional custodians of spatial data, but by mathematicians, physicists, and computer scientists (with, it must be said, much support from military authorities). These new practitioners of the art of making images of the earth have taken a very different approach to that of the conventional field scientists, surveyors, and cartographers. In the beginning, they often made exaggerated claims about the abilities of remote sensing and image analysis to recognize and map the properties of the earth's surface without expensive ground surveys. Gradually it has come to be realized that the often very striking images produced from remotely sensed data only have a real value if they can be linked to ground truth—a certain amount of field survey is essential for proper interpretation. And to facilitate calibration, the images have to be located properly with respect to a proper geodetic grid, otherwise the information cannot be related to a definite place. The need for a marriage between remote sensing, earthbound survey, and cartography arose, which has been made possible by the class of mapping tools known as Geographical Information Systems, or GIS.

Computer-assisted mapping and map analysis

During the 1960s and 1970s, new trends arose in the ways in which mapped data were being used for resource assessment, land evaluation, and planning. Owing to the realization that the different aspects of the earth's surface did not function independently of each other, people began to want to evaluate them in an integrated, multidisciplinary way. There are two ways to do this. The first, which Hopkins (1977) terms the 'gestalte' method (see also Hills 1961) attempts to find 'naturally occurring' environmental units that can be recognized, described, and mapped in terms of the total interaction of the attributes under study. Within these 'natural units' there is supposed to be a recognizable, unique, and interdependent combination of the environmental characteristics of landform, geology, soil, vegetation, and water—what Vink (1981) terms the 'correlative complex'.

The same basic idea was adopted for integrated resource surveys—classic examples come from the Australia integrated resource or land systems surveys (Christian and Stewart 1968) or from the UK Land Resources Division (now the Land Resources Development Centre; e.g. Brunt 1967) or the MEXE work (Webster and Beckett 1970) and work at the ITC in Enschede in The Netherlands.

The main problem with using the results of integrated surveys is that for many purposes they are too general and it is often very difficult to retrieve specific information from them about particular attributes of a landscape. So there has remained a ready market for the more conventional monodisciplinary surveys, such as those of geology, landform, soil, vegetation, and land use, particularly as surveys have tended towards larger and larger scales as development has proceeded.

When a wide range of monodisciplinary resource maps is available, the user must, and indeed may well prefer to, seek ways in which the available information can be combined to give an integrated overview, or a reclassification or a generalization as needed. In particular, planners and landscape architects, particularly in the USA, have realized that, in principle, data from several monodisciplinary resource surveys can be combined and integrated simply by overlaying transparent copies of the resource maps on a light table and looking for the places where the boundaries on the several maps coincide. One of the best-known exponents of this simple technique was the American landscape architect, Ian McHarg (McHarg 1969). It was another American architect and city planner, Howard T. Fisher, who in 1963 elaborated Edgar M. Horwood's idea of using the computer to make simple maps by printing statistical values on a grid of plain paper (Sheehan 1979). Fisher's program SYMAP, short for SYnagraphic MAPping system (the name has its origin in the Greek word synagein, meaning to bring together), includes a set of modules for analysing data, manipulating them to produce choropleth or isoline interpolations, and allows the results to be displayed in many ways using the overprinting of lineprinter characters to produce suitable grey scales.

Fisher became director of the Harvard Graduate School of Design's Laboratory for Computer Graphics, and SYMAP was the first in a line of mapping programs that was produced by an enthusiastic, internationally known and able staff. Among these programs were the well-known grid-cell (or raster) mapping programs GRID and IMGRID that allowed the user to do in the computer what McHarg had done with transparent overlays. Naturally, the Harvard group was not alone in this new field and many other workers developed programs with similar capabilities (e.g. Duffield and Coppock 1975; Steiner and Matt 1972; Fabos and Caswell 1977, to name but a few). All these overlay programs at first did not in principle allow the user to do anything that McHarg could not do, but they allowed it to be done more quickly and reproducibly. In addition to the simple overlay, users then began to realize that with little extra effort they could do other kinds of spatial and logical analysis on mapped data, such as planning studies (e.g. Steinitz and Brown 1981) or ecological studies (Luder 1980) that had previously been extremely difficult to do by hand. We may note in passing, that although the terminology and the sources of the data are quite different, many of the image analysis methods used in these raster map analysis programs are little different from those first adopted for processing remotely sensed data.

Because SYMAP, GRID, IMGRID, GEOMAP, and many of these other relatively simple programs were designed for quick cheap analysis of gridded data and initially their results could only be displayed by using crude lineprinter graphics, many cartographers refused to accept the results they produced as maps. Cartographers had begun to adopt computer techniques in the 1960s, but these were until recently largely limited to aids for the automated drafting and preparation of masters for printed maps. For traditional cartography the new computer technology did not change fundamental attitudes to map making— the high quality paper map remained the principal data store and end product alike.

By 1977, however, the experience of using computers in map making had advanced so far that Rhind (1977) was able to present the following cogent list of reasons for using computers in cartography:

1. To make existing maps more quickly.
2. To make existing maps more cheaply.
3. To make maps for specific user needs.
4. To make map production possible in situations where skilled staff are unavailable.
5. To allow experimentation with different graphical representations of the same data.
6. To facilitate map making and updating when the data are already in digital form.
7. To facilitate analyses of data that demand interaction between statistical analyses and mapping.
8. To minimize the use of the printed map as a data store and thereby to minimize the effects of classification and generalization on the quality of the data.
9. To create maps that are difficult to make by hand, e.g. 3-D maps or stereoscopic maps.
10. To create maps in which selection and generalization procedures are explicitly defined and consistently executed.
11. Introduction of automation can lead to a review of the whole map-making process, which can also lead to savings and improvements.

By the late 1970s there had been considerable investments in the development and application of computer-assisted cartography, particularly in North America by government and private agencies (e.g. Tomlinson *et al.* 1976; Teicholz and Berry 1983). Literally hundreds of computer programs and systems were developed for various mapping applications (e.g. Marble *et al.* 1981). There are estimated to be approximately 1000 geographical information systems now installed in North America with a prognosis of 4000 systems by 1990 (Tomlinson 1984). In Europe the developments proceeded on a smaller scale than in North America but major strides in using and developing computer-assisted cartography have been made by several nations, notably Sweden, Norway, Denmark, France, The Netherlands, The United Kingdom, and West Germany.

The introduction of computer-assisted cartography did not always immediately lead to a direct saving in costs as had been hoped. The acquisition and development of the new tools was often extremely expensive (e.g. Burrough 1980) and there was (and there still is) a shortage of trained staff. The computer-assisted mapping market was seen by many manufacturers of computer-aided design and computer graphics systems as being so diverse that the major investments needed to develop the software were unlikely to reap returns from a mass market. Consequently, many purchasers of expensive systems were forced to hire programming staff to adapt a particular system to their needs. There were many uncertainties in many mapping organizations about just what the new tools were supposed to do—were they merely for doing existing work more quickly, or were they for providing the users of spatial data with a much wider range of products? In some organizations the new technology was not given a fair try. That is to say that the new computer-assisted mapping tools were introduced into an organization without the necessary structural changes in work flow and practices that would allow the new technology to work efficiently. Technological development, particularly in the computer hardware, continued so fast that it outstripped the ability of managers to keep up. Under these circumstances it was difficult for them to remain objective and to think of how the new technology was really addressing the fundamental problems of mapping. So, in organizations geared for map production, automation was usually applied in areas that were 'safe'—accurate drafting, scanning contours, preparing films for printing. Many cartographers seemed not to realize that having mapped data in digital form presented them with an enormously powerful database that could be used for the analysis of many important spatial problems. We find Poiker (1982) commenting that 'computer cartography is like a person with the body of an athlete in his prime time and the mind of a child', and the President of the Canadian Cartographic Association complaining that 'Cartographers still have the belief that the only use of computer-assisted cartography is as an aid to the "pen-pushing" copying of maps' (Boyle 1981).

These remarks of Boyle and Poiker point to a common problem in the automation of existing manual techniques without a parallel conceptual development of the subject matter itself that has been identified by the computer scientist Joseph Weizenbaum. Weizenbaum (1976) noted that 'strengthening a particular technique [i.e. introducing automation]—putting muscles on it—contributes nothing to its validity. ... The poverty of the technique, if it is indeed impotent to deal with its presumed subject matter, is hidden behind a mountain of effort ... the harder the sub-problems were to solve, and the more technical success was gained in solving them, the more is the original technique fortified'. For computer cartography Weizenbaum's comments ring true. It was extremely difficult to solve the topological and computational problems of coding spatial data, of building cartographic databases and ensuring that the computer could reproduce faithfully that which a skilled cartographer could do. Indeed, computer cartography has been a costly technological development that has cost many hundreds of computer-programmer years. And, with certain exceptions that will be discussed in this book, most development has been directed to automating existing manual methods, rather than exploring new ways of handling spatial data.

So, during the 1960s and 1970s there were two main trends in the application of computer methods to mapping—one was the automation of existing tasks, with an accent on cartographic accuracy and visual quality, and the other with the accent on spatial analysis but at the expense of good graphical results. As we shall see, this development to a very large extent mirrored the technical possibilities of the times and further progress has been largely assisted by new developments in computer technology made in the last few years.

Geographical information systems

The history of using computers for mapping and spatial analysis shows that there have been parallel developments in automated data capture, data analysis, and presentation in several broadly related fields. These fields are cadastral and topographical mapping, thematic cartography, civil engineering, geography, mathematical studies of spatial variation, soil science, surveying and photogrammetry, rural and urban planning, utility networks, and remote sensing and image analysis. Military applications have overlapped and even dominated several of these monodisciplinary fields. Consequently there has been much duplication of effort and a multiplication of discipline-specific jargon for different applications in different lands. This multiplicity of effort in several initially separate but closely related fields is now resulting in the possibility of linking many kinds of spatial data processsing together into truly general-purpose geographical information systems, as technical and conceptual problems are overcome (Fig. 1.3).

Essentially, all these disciplines are attempting the same sort of operation—namely to develop a powerful set of tools for collecting, storing, retrieving at will, transforming, and displaying spatial data from the real world for a particular set of purposes. This set of tools constitutes a '*Geographical Information System*' (sometimes a Geographic Information System—*sic*). Geo-

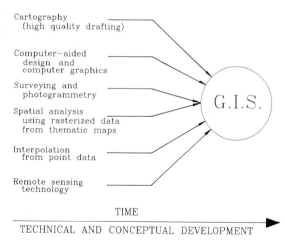

Fig. 1.3 Geographical information systems are the result of linking parallel developments in many separate spatial data processing disciplines.

graphical data describe objects from the real world in terms of (a) their position with respect to a known coordinate system, (b) their attributes that are unrelated to position (such as colour, cost, pH, incidence of disease, etc.) and (c) their spatial interrelations with each other (topological relations), which describe how they are linked together or how one can travel between them.

Geographical information systems differ from computer graphics because the latter are largely concerned with the display and manipulation of visible material. Computer graphics systems do not to pay much attention to the non-graphic attributes that the visible entities might or might not have, and which might be useful data for analysis. Good computer graphics are essential for a modern geographical information system but a graphics package is by itself not sufficient for performing the tasks expected, nor are such drawing packages necessarily a good basis for developing such a system.

Geographical information systems do have a lot in common with computer-aided design (CAD) systems used for drafting a wide range of technical objects, from aeroplanes to the layout of a microchip. Both GIS and CAD systems need to be able to relate objects to a frame of reference, both need to handle non-graphic attributes and both need to be able to describe topological relations. The major differences between GIS and CAD systems are the much greater volume and diversity of the data input to GIS systems and the specialized nature of the analysis methods used. These differences can be so large that an efficient system for CAD may be quite unsuitable for GIS and vice versa.

Geographical information systems should be thought of as being very much more than means of coding, storing, and retrieving data about aspects of the earth's surface. In a very real sense the data in a geographical information system, whether they are coded on the surface of a piece of paper or as invisible marks on the surface of a magnetic tape, should be thought of as representing a model of the real world (eg. Bouillé 1978). Because these data can be accessed, transformed, and manipulated interactively in a geographical information system, they can serve as a test bed for studying environmental processes or for analysing the results of trends, or of anticipating the possible results of planning decisions. By using the GIS in a similar way that a trainee pilot uses a flight simulator, it is, in principle, possible for planners and decision-makers to explore a range of possible scenarios and to obtain an idea of the consequences of a

course of action before the mistakes have been irrevocably made in the landscape itself.

The components of a geographical information system

Geographical information systems have three important components—computer hardware, sets of application software modules, and a proper organizational context. These three components need to be in balance if the system is to function satisfactorily.

Computer hardware

The general hardware components of a geographical information system are presented in Fig. 1.4. The computer or central processing unit (CPU) is linked to a disk drive storage unit, which provides space for storing data and programs. A digitizer or other device is used to convert data from maps and documents into digital form and send them to the computer. A plotter or other kind of display device is used to present the results of the data processing, and a tape drive is used for storing data or programs on magnetic tape, or for communicating with other systems. Inter-computer communication can also take place via a networking system over special data lines, or over telephone lines using a device known as a 'modem'. The user controls the computer and the peripherals (a general term for plotters, printers, digitizers, and other apparatus linked to the computer) via a visual display unit (VDU), otherwise known as a terminal. The user's terminal might itself be a microcomputer, or it might incorporate special hardware to allow maps to be displayed quickly. There is a very wide range of devices that can be used to fill these general hardware requirements and they are described more fully in Chapter 4.

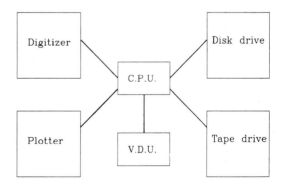

Fig. 1.4 The major hardware components of a geographical information system.

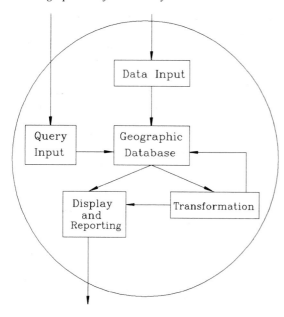

Fig. 1.5 The main software components of a geographical information system.

GIS software modules

The software package for a geographical information system consists of five basic technical modules (Fig. 1.5). These basic modules are sub-systems for:

(a) Data input and verification;
(b) Data storage and database management;
(c) Data output and presentation;
(d) Data transformation;
(e) Interaction with the user.

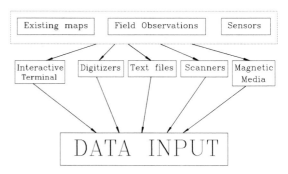

Fig. 1.6 Data input.

Data input (Fig. 1.6) covers all aspects of transforming data captured in the form of existing maps, field observations, and sensors (including aerial photography, satellites, and recording instruments) into a compatible digital form. A wide range of computer tools is available for this purpose, including the interactive terminal or visual display device (VDU), the digitizer, lists of data in text files, scanners (in satellites or aeroplanes for direct recording of data or for converting maps and photographic images) and the devices necessary for recording data already written on magnetic media such as tapes, drums, and disks. Data input, and the verification of data needed to build a geographical database, is the subject of Chapter 4.

Data storage and database management (Fig. 1.7) concerns the way in which the data about the position, linkages (topology), and attributes of geographical elements (points, lines, and areas representing objects on the earth's surface) are structured and organized,

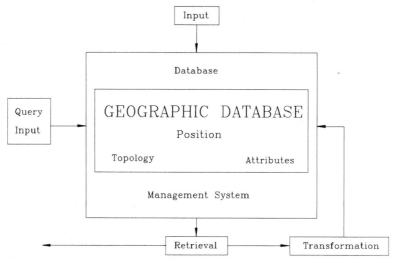

Fig. 1.7 The components of the geographical database.

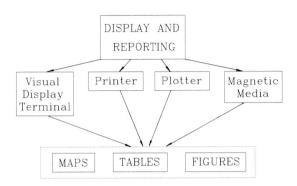

Fig. 1.8 Data output.

both with respect to the way they must be handled in the computer and how they are perceived by the users of the system. The computer program used to organize the database is known as a Database Management System (DBMS). Database structures and methods of data organization are discussed in Chapters 2 and 3.

Data output and presentation (Fig. 1.8) concerns the ways the data are displayed and the results of analyses are reported to the users. Data may be presented as maps, tables, and figures (graphs and charts) in a variety of ways, ranging from the ephemeral image on a cathode ray tube (CRT) through hard-copy output drawn on printer or plotter to information recorded on magnetic media in digital form. Methods of display and reporting are also discussed in Chapter 4.

Data transformation (Fig. 1.9) embraces two classes of operation, namely (a) transformations needed to remove errors from the data or to bring them up to date or to match them to other data sets, and (b) the large array of analysis methods that can be applied to the data in order to achieve answers to the questions

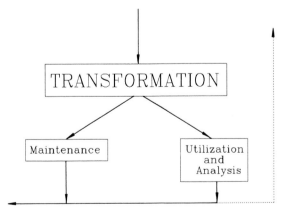

Fig. 1.9 Data transformation.

asked of the GIS. Transformations can operate on the spatial and the non-spatial aspects of the data, either separately or in combination. Many of these transformations, such as those associated with scale-changing, fitting data to new projections, logical retrieval of data, and calculation of areas and perimeters, are of such a general nature that one should expect to find them in every kind of GIS in one form or another. Other kinds of manipulation may be extremely application-specific, and their incorporation into a particular GIS may be only to satisfy the particular users of that system. The kinds of transformation method available, their optimum use and misuse, the ways in which sets of simple transformations can be combined in order to achieve certain types of geographical or spatial modelling, are the major subject of this book, being covered by Chapters 5, 6, 7, and 8; certain spatial transformations and transformations necessary to ensure the integrity of a database are discussed in Chapter 4.

The designer of a GIS should expect that a user will want to ask an almost unlimited number of questions that will need to be answered by using certain combinations of data retrieval and transformation options. Although the range of actual questions will be unlimited, there are several broad types of question that need to be catered for. Some of these general questions are the following:

(a) Where is object A?
(b) Where is A in relation to place B?
(c) How many occurrences of type A are there within distance D of B?
(d) What is the value of function Z at position X?
(e) How large is B (area, perimeter, count of inclusions)?
(f) What is the result of intersecting various kinds of spatial data?
(g) What is the path of least cost, resistance, or distance along the ground from X to Y along pathway P?
(h) What is at points XI, X2, ...?
(i) What objects are next to objects having certain combinations of attributes?
(j) Reclassify objects having certain combinations of attributes.
(k) Using the digital database as a model of the real world, simulate the effect of process P over time T for a given scenario S.

Many of these general questions are difficult to answer using conventional methods (for example calculating the proportion of different kinds of soil mapped requires either extensive work with a plani-meter or that the map units drawn on the paper should be cut out individually and weighed!), and some are still difficult and time consuming using computer-assisted methods. There is a real danger, however, when using a powerful geographical information system, that the user may unwittingly create or propagate errors that render the work valueless—these aspects of GIS are considered in Chapter 6. Alternatively, standard GIS techniques may lead to unacceptably large errors that could be reduced by using other methods of analysis, and some of these methods are discussed in Chapter 8.

The last module in the list for geographical information systems mentioned above, that of interaction with the user—query input—is absolutely essential for the acceptance and use of any information system. Certainly it is an aspect that until relatively recently has received less attention than it deserves. It is only in the last few years that the average user has been able to make direct contact with the computer other than via the impersonal and unforgiving media of punched paper tapes and cards handed in to the computing centre. The widespread introduction of the personal computer and of programs that are operated by commands chosen from a menu (a list), or that are initiated by a response to requests in an English-like command language of verbs, nouns, and modifiers has broken down the barriers that once frightened many a would-be computer user away for life. We shall assume in this book that all user interaction with the GIS proceeds via menu-driven command systems or via English-like command languages simply because the old methods of punched cards and tape are now so infrequently used.

The organizational aspects of GIS

The five technical sub-systems of GIS govern the way in which geographical information can be processed but they do not of themselves guarantee that any particular GIS will be used effectively. In order to be used effectively, the GIS needs to be placed in an appropriate organizational context (Fig. 1.10). It is simply not sufficient for an organization to purchase a computer and some software and to hire or retrain one or two enthusiastic individuals and then to expect instant success. Just as in all organizations dealing with complex products, as in manufacturing industry, new tools can only be used effectively if they are properly integrated into the whole work process and not tacked on as an afterthought. To do this properly requires not only the

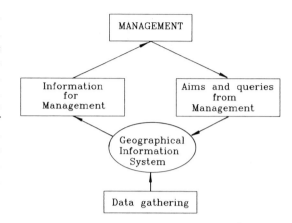

Fig. 1.10 Organizational aspects of geographical information systems.

necessary investments in hardware and software, but also in the retraining of personnel and managers to use the new technology in the proper organizational context. In the 1970s the high price of many commercial systems sold for geographical information processing made managers cautious of making expensive investments in the then new and untried technology. In recent years the falling hardware prices have encouraged automation, but skilled personnel and good, reasonably priced software have remained scarce. There are still many choices open to an organization wishing to invest in geographical information systems, and Chapter 9 attempts to present an overview of the factors involved and the decisions that need to be taken to set up an effective system for a reasonable investment.

Future directions and trends in GIS

Until not so very long ago, most geographical information systems were set up for local applications, or for work on a limited project area. There are now strong indications that many users, particularly major government agencies, are following a desire that has been with us from the earliest years in computer-assisted mapping, namely to set up comprehensive countrywide systems. For example, the US Geological Survey is envisioning a cartographic database containing all information from 55 000 $7\frac{1}{2}$-min map sheets covering the entire United States (Peuquet 1984). It is estimated that a single layer or attribute (e.g. topography or hydrology) mapped at usual cartographic precision will have a data volume of 10^{15} bits.

One of the greatest problems with geographical information processing, compared with computer-aided design or computer graphics, has always been the problem of sheer data volume generated by the surveying sciences. This is partly a result of the complexity of the earth's surface, but it is also largely because geographical 'entities' or phenomena can rarely be so well defined or are rarely as reproducible as the components of a computer or of an automobile. Different scientists tend to describe the same area in different ways. Even if they stem from the same discipline they tend to draw boundaries around geographical 'objects' in different ways and these boundaries are usually convoluted and highly irregular. Consequently, geographical phenomena, at least as described by current generations of earth scientists, cannot be described economically. Further problems arise because, as is shown in Chapter 6, digital geographical data are prone to be imprecise, highly variable or of uncertain quality. Finally, the ways in which spatial relationships between geographical objects can be described are often highly application-specific.

The range of topics covered in this book does not go so far as to be able to suggest answers to all these problems; the question of data volumes is scarcely touched upon. But the problems of errors and data description arise largely as a consequence of the imprecision of the world in general, coupled with the requirement of current conceptual models to be able to represent natural spatial variation in terms of compartmentalized models and watertight logic. The latest directions in research in geographical information processing suggest that we should be looking for better ways in which to describe the vagaries of the world, and new methods for dealing with the imprecision of qualitative judgements that are an integral part of human thought processes. These directions suggest that we should be looking seriously at the new ideas afforded by fractals, fuzzy logic, and methods of artificial intelligence, if only to attempt to cope with the technical problems that have arisen as a result of our present conceptual shortcomings. These new directions are hinted at in various places in this book, but it will take another volume and another generation of research before these new ideas join the body of principles that have been covered here. It is clear that even with the present shortcomings of GIS technology, more and more people are wanting to have access to geographical information systems, and they are not prepared to pay the very high prices for systems that must be currently paid. With hardware prices still declining in terms of processing power available, (the largest computer in 1963 cost $600 000 [$2 million in

1984 dollars], had 16 kbcd memory and could process 1000 instructions per second) and demand increasing, there seems certain to be a trend towards small, decentralized systems that can be used for specific projects, or as entry points to larger, country-wide geographical databases. But for this all to work smoothly there have to be enough trained personnel who know what GIS is all about, which is why this book was written.

References

American Society of Photogrammetry (1960). *Manual of aerial photo interpretation*. Washington DC.

Beek, K. J. (1978). Land evaluation for agricultural development. International Institute for Land Reclamation and Improvement, Publication No. 23, Wageningen.

Bouillé, F. 1978. Structuring cartographic data and spatial processes with the hypergraph-based data structure. In *First International Advanced Study Symposium on Topological Data Structures for Geographic Information Systems* (ed. G. Dutton) Vol. 5. Laboratory for Computer Graphics and Spatial Analysis, Harvard.

Boyle, A. R. (1981). Concerns about the present applications of computer-assisted cartography. *Cartographica* **18**, 31–3.

Brinkman, R. and Smyth, A. J. (1973). Land evaluation for rural purposes. Summary of an expert consultation, Wageningen, The Netherlands, 6–12 October 1972. International Institute for Land Reclamation and Improvement, Wageningen, Publication no. 17.

Brunt, M. (1967). The methods employed by the Directorate of Overseas Surveys in the assessment of land resources. *Actes du 2me Symp. Intil. de Photo Interpretation*, Paris, 1966.

Burrough, P. A. (1980). The development of a landscape information system in The Netherlands, based on a turn-key graphics system. *GeoProcessing* **1**, 257–74.

Campbell, J. (1984). *Introductory cartography*. Prentice-Hall, Englewood Cliffs, NJ.

Christian, C. S. and Stewart, G. A. (1968). Aerial surveys and integrated studies. In *Proc. Toulouse Conference*, 21–28 September 1964. Natural Resources Research VI, UNESCO, Paris.

Cliff, A. D. and Ord, J. K. (1981). *Spatial processes: models and applications*. Pion, London.

Dilke, O. A. W. (1971) *The Roman land surveyors. An introduction to the agrimensores*. David and Charles, Newton Abbot, UK.

Duffield, B. S. and Coppock, J. T. (1975). The delineation of recreational landscapes: the role of a computer-based information system. *Trans. Inst. Br. Geogrs* **661**, 141–8.

Fabos, J. G. and Caswell, S. J. (1977). Composite landscape assessment: metropolitan landscape planning model MET-LAND. Massachusetts Agricultural Experimental Station, University of Massachusetts at Amherst Research Bulletin No. 637.

FAO (1976). A framework for land evaluation. Soils, Bulletin No. 32. FAO Rome and International Institution for Land Reclamation and Improvement, Publication No. 22.

Fisher, H. T. (1978). Thematic cartography—what it is and what is different about it. *Harvard papers in theoretical cartography*. Laboratory for Computer Graphics and Spatial Analysis, Harvard.

Hills, G. A. (1961). The ecological basis for land use planning. Research Report No. 46, Ontario Department of Lands and Forests, Ontario, Canada.

Hodgkiss, A. G. (1981) *Understanding maps*. Dawson, Folkestone, UK.

Hopkins, L. D. (1977). Methods for generating land suitability maps: a comparative evaluation. *Am. Inst. Plan. J.* October, 386–400.

Journel, A. G. and Huijbregts, Ch. J. (1978) *Mining geostatistics*. Academic Press, London.

Luder, P. (1980). Das ökologische ausgleichspotential der landschaft. *Basler Beiträge zur Physiogeografie*. Geografisches Institut der Universität Basel.

McHarg, I. L. (1969). *Design with nature*. Doubleday/Natural History Press, New York.

Marble, D. F., Calkins, H., Peuquet, D. J., Brassel, K. and Wasilenko, M. (1981). *Computer software for spatial data handling* (3 Vols). Prepared by the International Geographical Union, Commission on Geographical Data Sensing and Processing for the US Department of the Interior, Geological Survey. IGU, Ottawa, Canada.

Peuquet, D. J. (1984). Data structures for a knowledge-based geographic information system. In *Proc. Int. Symp. on Spatial Data Handling*, 20–24 August, Zurich, pp. 372–91.

Poiker, T. K. (formerly Peuker) (1982). Looking at computer cartography. *GeoJournal* **6**, 241–9.

Rhind, D. (1977). Computer-aided cartography. *Trans. Inst. Br. Geogrs* (N.S.) **2**, 71–96.

Ripley, B. D. (1981). *Spatial statistics*. Wiley, New York.

Sheehan, D. E. (1979). A discussion of the SYMAP program. Harvard Library of Computer Graphics (1979), mapping collection Vol. 2: mapping software and cartographic databases, pp. 167–79.

Steiner, D. and Matt, O. F. (1972). Computer program for the production of shaded cloropleth and isarithmic maps on a line printer. User's manual. Waterloo, Ontario.

Steinitz, C. and Brown, H. J. (1981). A computer modelling approach to managing urban expansion. *GeoProcessing* **1**, 341–75.

Teicholz, E. and Berry, B. J. L. (1983). *Computer graphics and environmental planning*. Prentice-Hall, Englewood Cliffs, NJ.

Tomlinson, R. F. (1984). Geographic information systems— a new frontier. In *Proc. Int. Symp. on Spatial Data Handling*. 20–24 August, Zurich, pp. 1–14.

Tomlinson, R. F., Calkins, H. W., and Marble, D. F. (1976). *Computer handling of geographic data*. UNESCO, Geneva.

Vink, A. P. A. (1981). *Landschapsecologie en landgebruik*. Scheltema en Holkema, Amsterdam.

Webster, R. (1977). *Quantitative and numerical methods for soil survey and classification*. Oxford University Press, Oxford.

—— and Beckett, P. H. T. (1970). Terrain classification and evaluation using air photography: a review of recent work at Oxford. *Photogrammetrica* **26**, 51–75.

Weizenbaum, J. (1976). *Computer power and human reason*. W. H. Freeman, San Francisco.

2. Data Structures for Thematic Maps

Data structures for geographical information systems

Unlike many other kinds of data handled routinely by modern information systems, geographical data are complicated by the fact that they must include information about position, possible topological connections, and attributes of the objects recorded. The topological and spatial aspects of geographical data processing distinguish systems designed for graphics and mapping from those other modern data processing systems such as those used for banking, library searches, airline bookings or medical records.

Geographical data are referenced to locations on the earth's surface by using a standard system of coordinates. The coordinate system may be purely local, as in the case of a study of a limited area, or it may be that of a national grid or an internationally accepted projection such as the Universal Transverse Mercator Coordinate System (UTM). Geographical data are very often recognized and described in terms of well-established geographical 'objects', or phenomena. All geographical studies have used phenomenological concepts such as 'town', 'river', 'floodplain', 'ecotope', 'soil association' as fundamental building blocks for analysing and synthesizing complex information. These phenomenological building blocks are very often grouped or divided into units at other scales according to hierarchically defined taxonomies, for example the hierarchy of country–province–town–district, or the hierarchy of most soil classification systems or of plants and animals. We should note, in passing, that although many of these perceived geographical phenomena are described by scientists as though they were explicit objects (such as 'table', or 'chair') their exact form and extent may be debatable, or may change with time. The implications of this are discussed in Chapter 6 on data quality and errors.

Points, lines, and areas

All geographical data can be reduced to three basic topological concepts—the point, the line, and the area.

Every geographical phenomenon can in principle be represented by a point, line or area plus a label saying what it is. So an oil well could be represented by a point entity consisting of a single XY coordinate pair and the label 'oil well'; a section of railway line could be represented by a line entity consisting of a starting XY coordinate and an end XY coordinate and the label 'railway'; a floodplain could be represented by an area entity covering a set of XY coordinates plus the label 'floodplain'. The labels could be the actual names as given here, or they could be numbers that cross-reference with a legend, or they could be special symbols. All these techniques are used in conventional mapping.

Definition of a map

A *map* is a set of *points*, *lines*, and *areas* that are defined both by their location in space with reference to a coordinate system and by their non-spatial attributes (Fig. 2.1 (a–c)). A map is usually represented in two dimensions but there is no reason to exclude higher dimensions except through the difficulty of portraying them on a flat piece of paper.

The *map legend* is the key linking the non-spatial attributes to the spatial entities. Non-spatial attributes may be indicated visually by colours, symbols or shading, the meaning of which is defined in the legend. For geographical information systems, non-spatial attributes need to be coded in a form in which they can be used for data analysis. A *region* is a set of pixels, areas or polygons that are described by a single legend unit. A region may be made up of several discrete occurrences (Fig. 2.1.(d)), which may be uniform or which may contain polygons belonging to regions of another kind (Fig. 2.1(e)). Although the eye can easily distinguish the topological relationships between the regions in Fig. 2.1(d–f), these relationships must be explicitly built into any digital representation.

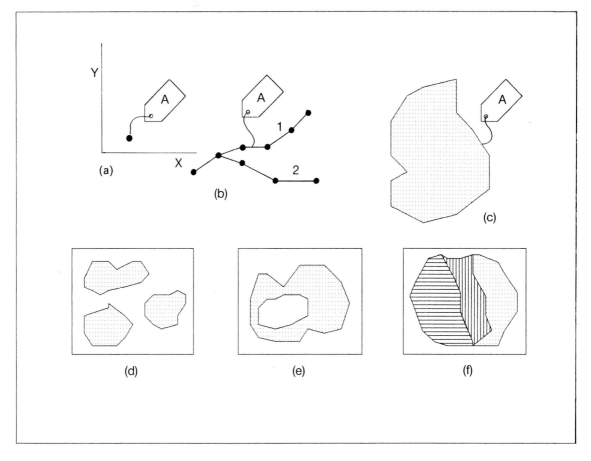

Fig. 2.1 A map is a set of points, lines, and areas defined both by position with reference to a coordinate system and by their non-spatial attributes (a,b,c). A region is a set of loci on a map that belong to the same class or have the same attribute (d,e,f). (d) is a disjoint region, (e) a perforated region; (f) shows three different regions.

Geographical data in the computer

When geographical data are entered into a computer the user will be most at ease if the geographical information system can accept the phenomenological data structures that he has always been accustomed to using. But computers are not organized like human minds and must be programmed to represent phenomenological structures appropriately. Moreover, the way the geographical data are visualized by the user is frequently not the most efficient way to structure the computer database. Finally, the data have to be written and stored on magnetic devices that need to be addressed in a specific way. We can represent these four stages as follows:

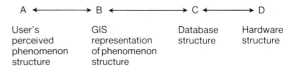

A	B	C	D
User's perceived phenomenon structure	GIS representation of phenomenon structure	Database structure	Hardware structure

We shall consider stages A, B, and C here; hardware aspects fall outside the scope of this discussion and the interested reader should consult a text on computer architecture.

Database structures: data organization in the computer

Before considering in detail the ways in which geographical data can be stored in the computer, we must first consider the ways in which data can be organized for storage and access in general. Although it is not essential for a user of a geographical information system to understand in detail how the data can be ordered inside the computer, any more than the driver of a car needs to know about the workings of the internal combustion engine, a little knowledge of data structuring methods will help him to understand better how the systems work, and what their limitations and advantages might be. The following section presents only a brief introduction. Readers interested in a more thorough treatment should consult a standard work in information storage and retrieval such as Salton and McGill (1983), Giloi (1978), CODASYL (1971), Gersting (1984), Kroenke (1977), Date (1981), Ullman (1980) or Wirth (1976).

The essential features of any data storage system are that they should be able to allow data to be accessed and cross-referenced quickly. There are several ways of achieving this, some of which are more efficient than others. Unfortunately, there seems to be no one 'best' method that can be used for all situations. This explains in part the massive investment in labour and money in effective *database management systems*, which are the computer programs that control data input, output, storage, and retrieval from a digital database.

Files and data access

Simple lists

The simplest form of database is a simple list of all the items. As each new item is added to the database, it is simply placed at the end of the file, which gets longer and longer. It is very easy to add data to such a system, but retrieving data is inefficient. For a list containing n items, it takes an average of $(n+1)/2$ search operations to find the item you want. So, for an information system containing 10 000 soil profiles on cards, given that it takes 1 s to read the card name or number, it would take an average of $(10\,000+1)/2$ s or about an hour and a half to find the card you want.

Most people know that searching through unstructured lists trying to find 'the needle in the haystack' is very inefficient. It is thus an obvious step to order or structure the data and to provide a key to that structure in order to speed up data retrieval.

Ordered sequential files

Words in a dictionary, or names in a telephone book are structured alphabetically. Addition of a new item

means that extra room must be created to insert it, but the advantage is that stored items can be reached very much faster. Very often, ordered sequential files are accessed by binary search procedures. Instead of beginning the search at the beginning of the list, the record in the middle is examined first. If the key value (e.g. the sequence of letters in a word) matches, then the middle record is the one being sought. If the values do not match, a simple test is made to see whether the required item occurs before or after the middle element. The appropriate half of the file is retained and the search repeated, until the item has been located. Binary search requires $\log_2 (n+1)$ steps. If the file is 10 000 items long, and the search time per item is 1 s, the average time to find an item is approximately 14 s, compared with the 1.5 h previously!

Indexed files

Simple sequential and ordered sequential files require that data be retrieved according to a key attribute. In the case of a dictionary, the key attribute is the spelling. But in many applications, particularly in geographical information, the individual items (pixels, points, lines or areas) will have not only a key attribute such as an identification number or a name, but will also carry information about associated attributes. Very often it is the information about the associated attributes that is required, not just the name. For example, we may have an ordered list of soil profiles that has been structured by soil series name, but we would like to retrieve information about soil depth, drainage, pH, texture or erosion. Unless we adopt another database strategy, our search procedures revert to those of the simple sequential list.

With indexed files, access to the original data file can be speeded up in two ways. If the data items in the files themselves provide the main order of the file, then the files are known as *direct files*. The location of items in the main file can also be specified according to topic, which is given in a second file, known as an *inverted file*. Just as in a book, examination of the index can determine the items (pages) which satisfy the search request.

In the direct file, the record for each item contains sufficient information for the search to jump over unnecessary items. For example, consider a data file containing soil series names that have been ordered alphabetically. Each item contains not only the series name and other information but also a number indicating the storage location of series names beginning with that letter. The search for a particular record is then made much simpler by constructing a simple index file that lists the correspondence between first letter of series name and storage location. The search proceeds by a sequential search of the index, followed by a sequential search of the appropriate data block. The average number of search steps is then $(n_1+1)/2+(n_2+1)/2$, where n_1 is the number of steps in the index and n_2 is the number of items in the data block referenced by the index.

The use of the inverted file index requires first that it be constructed by performing an initial sequential search on the data for each topic. The results are then assembled in the inverted file or index, which provides the key for further data access (Table 2.1).

Indexed files permit rapid access to databases. Un-

Table 2.1 Indexed files

Direct files

Index		File
Item key	Record No.	item
A	1	A_1
B	n_a+1	A_2
C	n_a+n_b+1	:
.	.	B_1
.	.	:
.	.	C_1
		:

Inverted files

Soil profile number	Attributes					
	S	pH	De	Dr	T	E
1	A	4	deep	good	sandy	—
2	B	5	shallow	good	clay	yes
3	C	6	shallow	poor	sandy	no
4	D	7	deep	good	clay	yes
5	E	4	deep	poor	clay	no
6	F	5	shallow	poor	clay	no

S = Series, De = Depth, Dr = Drainage, T = Texture, E = Erosion.

Index (inverted file)

Topic	Profiles (sequential numbers in original file)					
Deep	1			4	5	
Shallow		2	3			6
Good drainage	1	2		4		
Poor drainage			3		5	6
Sandy	1		3			
Clay		2		4	5	6
Eroded		2		4		

fortunately, they have inherent problems when used with files in which records are continually being added or deleted, such as often happens with interactive mapping systems. Addition or deletion of a record in a direct file means that both the file and its index must be modified. When new records are written to a file accessed by an inverted file index, the new record does not have to be placed at a special position; it can be simply added to the end of the file, but the index must be updated. File modification can be an expensive undertaking with large data files, particularly in an interactive environment. A further disadvantage of indexed files is that very often data can only be accessed via the key contained in the index files; other information may only be retrievable using sequential search methods.

Database structures

A database consists of data in many files. In order to be able to access data from one or more files easily, it is necessary to have some kind of structure or organization. Three main kinds of database structure are commonly recognized, termed hierarchical, network, and relational.

Hierarchical data structure

When the data have a parent/child or one-to-many relation, such as soil series within a soil family, or pixels within a region, hierarchical methods provide quick and convenient means of data access. Hierarchical systems of data organization are well-known, of course, to environmental science, being the methods used for plant and animal taxonomies, soil classification, and so on. Hierarchical systems assume that each part of the hierarchy can be reached using a key (a set of discriminating criteria) that fully describes the data structure. Hierarchical systems assume that there is a good correlation between the key attributes (discriminating criteria) and the associated attributes that the items may possess. Hierarchical systems have the advantage that they are easy to understand and they are easy to update and expand. Data access via the keys is easy for key attributes, but unfortunately is very difficult for associated attributes. Consequently, hierarchical systems are good for data retrieval if the structure of all possible queries can be known beforehand. This is commonly the case with bibliographic, bank or airline retrieval systems. For environmental data, however, the exploratory nature of many retrieval requests cannot be accommodated by the rigid hierarchy and the critical user may reject the system as

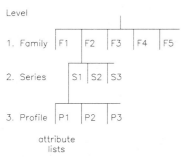

Fig. 2.2 Hierarchical database structure commonly used in soil science.

impossibly inflexible. For example, Beyer (1984) reports that the Royal Botanical Gardens in Kew initially set up a hierarchical database based on the rules of plant taxonomy for their herbarium collection of more than a million items. This seemed sensible until the Director wished to make a trip to Mexico to gather new material for the herbarium and asked the database which plants that Kew already had from that land. Unfortunately for the suppliers and the users of the database, the director received no answer because the attribute 'place of collection' is not part of the plant taxonomy key!

Further disadvantages of hierarchical database structures are that large index files have to be maintained, and certain attribute values may have to be repeated many times, leading to data redundancy, which increases storage and access costs (Fig. 2.2).

Network systems

In hierarchical systems, travel within the database is restricted to the paths up and down the taxonomic pathways. In many situations much more rapid linkage is required, particularly in data structures for graphics features where adjacent items in a map or figure need to be linked together even though the actual data about their coordinates may be written in very different parts of the database. Network systems fulfil this need.

Consider Fig. 2.3(a), which consists of a simple map of two polygons. Figure. 2.3(a) shows the map as it appears to the human brain; that is the two polygons are defined by a set of lines, one of which is common to both. The lines, in turn, are defined by coordinate pairs, with each coordinate pair common to two lines. Clearly, a hierarchical data structure for the map would result in a clumsy representation involving much redundancy (Fig. 2.3(b, e)). Each coordinate pair would have to repeated twice, and coordinates 3 and 4 would have to be repeated four times because

line c has to be repeated twice. The structure is not only wasteful of space; it is clumsy, for if an operation were made to give polygons I and II the same name there is no easy way to suppress the display of line c, which would become unnecessary. These problems are avoided by the compact network structure shown in Fig. 2.3(c), in which each line and each coordinate need appear only once. With this structure it is a simple matter to suppress the printing of line c when-

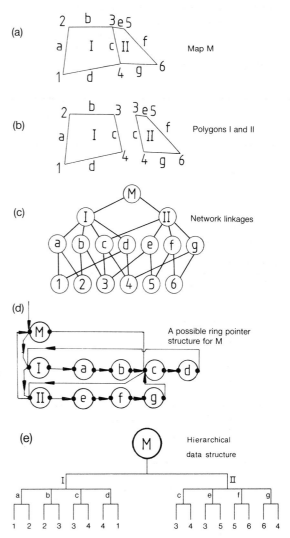

Fig. 2.3 Network data structures for simple polygons. (a) The map M. (b) The two component polygons I and II. (c) A network structure linking all polygons, lines, and points. (d) A ring pointer structure for M. (e) A hierarchical data structure for M.

ever it is referenced by polygons having the same name, thus making map generalization easier.

Very often in graphics, network structures are used that have a ring pointer structure. Ring pointer structures (Fig. 2.3(d)) are very useful ways of navigating around complex topological structures. Network systems are very useful when the relations or linkages can be specified beforehand. They avoid data redundancy and make good use of available data. The disadvantages are that the database is enlarged by the overhead of the pointers, which in complex systems can become quite a substantial part of the database. These pointers must be updated/maintained every time a change is made to the database and the building and maintenance of pointer structures can be a considerable overhead for the database system.

Relational database structures

The relational database structure in its simplest form stores no pointers and has no hierarchy. Instead, the data are stored in simple records, known as *tuples*, containing an ordered set of attribute values that are

Map	M	I	II

Polygon	I	a	b	c	d
	II	c	e	f	g

Lines	I	a	1	2
	I	b	2	3
	I	c	3	4
	I	d	4	1
	II	e	3	5
	II	f	5	6
	II	g	6	4
	II	c	4	3

Fig. 2.4 A relational data structure for the map M.

grouped together in two-dimensional tables, known as *relations*. Each table or relation is usually a separate file. The pointer structures in network models and the keys in hierarchical structures are replaced by data redundancy in the form of identification codes that are used as unique keys to identify the records in each file (Fig. 2.4).

Data are extracted from a relational database through a procedure in which the user defines the relation that is appropriate for the query. This relation is not necessarily already present in the existing files, so the controlling program uses the methods of relational algebra to construct the new tables.

Relational databases have the great advantage that their structure is very flexible and can meet the demands of all queries that can be formulated using the rules of Boolean logic and of mathematical operations. They allow different kinds of data to be searched, combined, and compared. Addition or removal of data is easy too, because this just involves adding or removing a tuple. The disadvantage of relational databases is that many of the operations involve sequential searches through the files to find the right data to satisfy the specified relations. This can involve a considerable amount of time with large databases, even on fast computers. Consequently commercial relational database systems have to be very skilfully designed in order to support the search capabilities with reasonable speed, which is why they are so expensive. They are just beginning to be applied to geographical information systems (Abel 1983; Lorie and Meier 1984; van Roessel and Fosnight 1984).

Record structures

In all kinds of database structures, the data are written in the form of records. The simplest kind of record is a one-dimensional array of fixed length, divided into a number of equal partitions (Fig. 2.5(a)). This record is ideal when all items have the same number of attributes, for example when a number of soil profiles have been sampled and analysed for a standard range of cations. Fixed length records are inconvenient, however, when the attributes are of variable length, and when the set of attributes measured is not common to all items. For example, not all soil profiles have the same number of horizons, and not all polygon boundaries have the same number of coordinates. In these situations variable length records are used. Each record has a 'header', an extra attribute that contains information about the type of information in the sub-record and the amount of space it takes up (Fig. 2.5(b)).

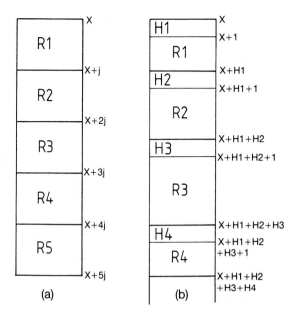

Fig. 2.5 Two kinds of sequential list: (a) fixed length records; (b) variable length records including a 'header' H to record data about the record itself.

Perceived structures and computer representations of geographical data

The human eye is highly efficient at recognizing shapes and forms, but the computer needs to be instructed exactly how spatial patterns should be handled and displayed. Essentially there are two contrasting, but complementary ways of representing spatial data in the computer that we shall refer to as explicit and implicit ways of describing spatial entities.

Figure 2.6 shows the two different ways in which a chair can be explicitly or implicitly represented in a computer. Explicit representation means that the form of the chair is built up from a set of points on a grid or *raster*. So that the computer knows that this set of points represents a chair and not a table, each cell is given the same code value 'C'. In practice, the C's would not be themselves displayed but would be represented by a numerical value or a colour or grey scale. We would then have the following simple data structure for the chair:

chair attribute→symbol/colour→cell X

The implicit representation makes use of a set of lines, defined by starting and end points and some form of connectivity. The starting and end points of the lines define *vectors* that represent the form of the chair;

pointers between the lines indicate to the computer how the lines link together to form the chair. The data structure is:

chair attribute→set of vectors→ connectivity.

Figure 2.6 also demonstrates several other differences between the two representations. First, the implicit representation requires fewer numbers, implying fewer storage spaces, to store the information about the chair (the vector representation uses 11XY pairs and 14 connecting pointers and the raster representation uses 60 cells). Second, the vector representation is aesthetically more pleasing than the raster image—to produce an equivalent resolution the raster image would need to be based on a 0.5 mm grid, thereby requiring 470 XY pairs. Third, the connectivity information allows directed spatial searches to be made over the chair. On the other hand, if the shape or size of the chair has to be changed, this can be done much quicker and easier in the raster representation than in the vector. In a raster representation data update merely involves deleting certain values and writing in new ones. In vector representation, not only must the coordinates be updated but the connectivity must also be rebuilt.

We see that there are at least two fundamental ways of representing topological data which can be summarized as follows:

Raster representation—set of cells located by co-

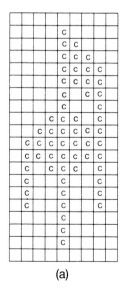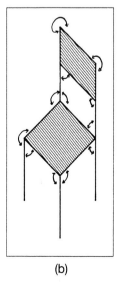

(a)　　　　　　　　　(b)

Fig. 2.6 An image of a chair in (a) raster or grid-cell and (b) vector format.

ordinates; each cell is independently addressed with the value of an attribute.

Vector representation—three main geographical entities, points, lines and areas: points are similar to cells, except they do not cover areas; lines and areas are sets of interconnected coordinates that can be linked to given attributes.

Note that there is no necessary or unique connection between the raster or vector structure of the geographical database and the raster or vector structure of the devices used to display the data, although this is very often the case. For example, most modern interactive computer-aided design and mapping systems work with vector-structured databases but use colour raster displays and vector plotters (see Chapter 4).

Raster data structures

The simplest raster data structures consist of an array of grid cells (sometimes termed pixels or picture elements). Each grid cell is referenced by a row and column number and it contains a number representing the type or value of the attribute being mapped. In raster structures a point is represented by a single grid cell; a line by a number of neighbouring cells strung out in a given direction and an area by an agglomeration of neighbouring cells. This type of data structure is easy to handle in the computer, particularly with programming languages such as FORTRAN, because of the ease with which arrays of rows and columns can be stored, manipulated, and displayed. This data structure also means that the two-dimensional surface upon which the geographical data are represented is not continuous, but quantized, which can have an important effect on the estimation of lengths and areas when grid cell sizes are large with respect to the features being represented. For example, Fig. 2.7(a) shows that the (Euclidean) distance between a and c is 5 units, while on Fig. 2.7(b), the distance between a and c could be 7 or 4 units depending on whether one counts cell edges or whole cells that must be traversed. The area of Fig. 2.7(a) is 6 units^2; the area of Fig. 2.7(b) is 7 units^2. We shall return to this problem of errors in Chapter 6. Because of the discrepancies that can arise in this way through the loss of precision associated with the cell size, many fields such as digital image processing often assume that the quantized surface can be treated as continuous, so that mathematical functions having derivatives that exist can be used (e.g. Castleman 1979).

Raster representation assumes that the geographical space can be treated as though it were a flat Cartesian surface. Each pixel or grid cell is then by implication

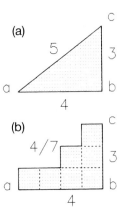

Fig. 2.7 Raster coding can affect estimates of distance and area because of the quantizing effect of the cells.

associated with a square parcel of land. The resolution, or scale of the raster data is then the relation between the cell size in the database and the size of the cell on the ground.

Map overlays

Because each cell in a two-dimensional array can only hold one number, different geographical attributes

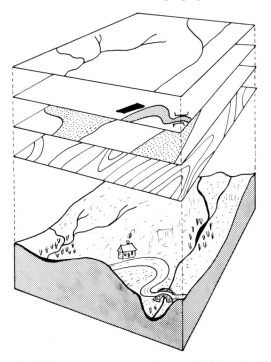

Fig. 2.8 The 'overlay' concept; the real world is portrayed by a series of overlays in each of which one aspect of reality has been recorded (e.g. topography, soil type, roads, rivers, etc.).

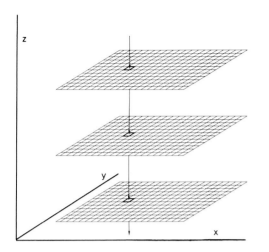

Fig. 2.9 Three-dimensional arrays used for coding map overlays in raster database structures.

must be represented by separate sets of Cartesian arrays, known as 'overlays'. The overlay idea for separating data is not restricted to computer cartography, having been used by cartographers for preparing printed maps and by landscape planners (e.g. McHarg 1969) for a very long time. Figure. 2.8 illustrates the overlay concept in which each separate attribute is described and mapped separately.

In its simplest form, the overlay concept is realized in raster data structures by stacking two-dimensional arrays. This results in a three-dimensional structure as shown in Fig. 2.9. The overlay concept is essentially equivalent to the 'picture function' in digital image processing (Duda and Hart 1973), a 'data plane' in remote sensing (Tom *et al.* 1978) or 'image-based' storage (O'Callaghan and Graetz 1981), and it is fundamental to most raster image processing.

Referencing pixels in raster overlay structures

Given that a raster map file is built up from what the user perceives as a number of Cartesian overlays, the question arises as to how these data can best be organized in the computer to optimize data access and to minimize storage and processing requirements. If each cell on each overlay is assumed to be an independent unit in the database (one-to-one relation between data value, pixel, and location) three basic and equivalent methods of organization are possible (Tomlin 1983). These are shown in Fig. 2.10. Figure 2.10(a) represents the structure used in the GRID program (Sinton and Steinitz 1969), the LUNR system (New York State Office of Planning Services 1972), and the MAGI sys-

tem (Dangermond and Atenucci 1974). Each point on a map is represented as a vertical array in which each array position carries the value of the attribute associated with that overlay. Figure 2.10(b) represents the alternative method of representing each overlay as a two-dimensional matrix of points carrying the value of a single attribute. This method was used in IMGRID (Sinton 1977).

Figure 2.10(c) shows the hierarchical structure used by the Map Analysis Package (Tomlin 1983), which though formally equivalent to the other structures, has several advantages. Because of the many-to-one relation between attribute value and the set of points, for example, recoding a map requires rewriting only one number per mapping unit (the value). This is in contrast to the large number of recoding operations required when the other two structures are used.

Compact methods for storing raster data

When each cell has a unique value it takes a total of n rows $\times m$ columns $\times 3$ values (X, Y coordinates and attribute value) to encode each overlay. This is the situation with the altitude matrices used for digital terrain models. If sets of cells within a polygon or a mapping unit all have the same value, however, it is possible to effect considerable savings in the data storage requirements for the raster data, providing of course that the data structures are properly designed. The data structures described in Fig. 2.10(a, b) use the coordinates to reduce the actual quantity of numbers stored, with the limitation that all spatial operations must be carried out in terms of array row and column numbers. Because these systems do not encode the data in the form of a one-to-many relation between mapping unit value and cell coordinates, compact methods for encoding cannot be used. The third structure given in Fig. 2.10(c) references the sets of points per region (or mapping unit) and allows a variety of methods of compact storage to be used. There are four main ways in which compact storage can be achieved: these are by using chain codes, run-length codes, block codes, and quadtrees.

Chain codes. Consider Fig. 2.11. The boundary of the region can be given in terms of its origin and a sequence of unit vectors in the cardinal directions. These directions can be numbered (east = 0, north = 1, west = 2, south = 3). For example, if we start at cell row = 10, column = 1, the boundary of the region is coded clockwise by:

$0, 1, 0^2, 3, 0^2, 1, 0, 3, 0, 1, 0^3, 3^2, 2, 3^3, 0^2, 1, 0^5, 3^2,$
$2^2, 3, 2^3, 3, 2^3, 1, 2^2, 1, 2^2, 1, 2^2, 1, 2^2, 1^3$

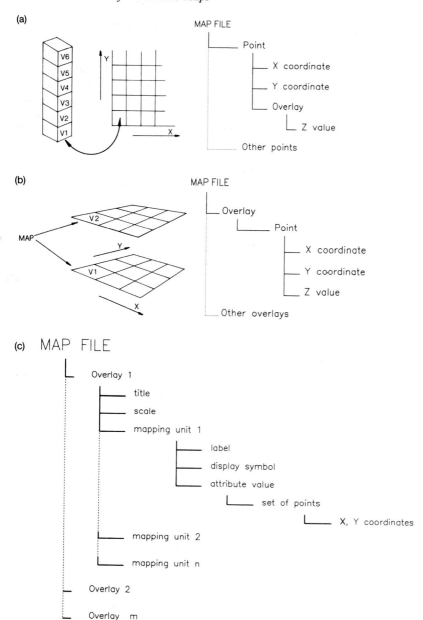

Fig. 2.10 Three kinds of raster database structure. (a) Each cell is referenced directly. (b) Each overlay is referenced directly. (c) Each mapping unit or 'region' is referenced directly.

where the number of steps (pixels) in each direction is given by the superscripted number.

Chain codes provide a very compact way of storing a region representation and they allow certain operations such as estimation of areas and perimeters, or detection of sharp turns and concavities to be carried out easily. On the other hand, overlay operations such as union and intersection are difficult to perform without returning to a full grid representation. Another disadvantage is the redundancy introduced because all boundaries between regions must be stored twice. Freeman (1974) gives further details.

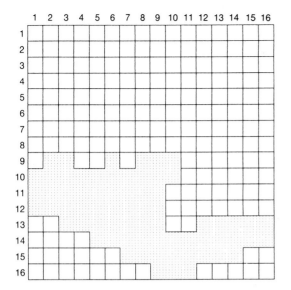

Fig. 2.11 A simple region on a rasterized map.

Run-length codes. Run-length codes allow the points in each mapping unit to be stored per row in terms, from left to right, of a begin cell and an end cell. For the area shown in Fig. 2.11 the codes would be as follows:

Row 9	2,3	6,6	8,10
Row 10	1,10		
Row 11	1,9		
Row 12	1,9		
Row 13	3,9	12,16	
Row 14	5,16		
Row 15	7,14		
Row 16	9,11		

In this example, the 69 cells of Fig. 2.11 have been completely coded by 22 numbers, thereby effecting a considerable reduction in the space needed to store the data.

Clearly, run-length coding is a considerable improvement in storage requirements over conventional methods whenever the many-to-one relations are present. It is especially suitable for use in small computers (e.g. Giltrap 1984) and where total volumes of data must be kept limited. On the other hand, too much data compression may lead to increased processing requirements during cartographic processing and manipulation.

Run-length codes are also useful in reducing the volume of data that need to be input to a simple raster database (see Chapter 4).

Block codes. The idea of run-length codes can be extended to two dimensions by using square blocks to tile the area to be mapped. Figure. 2.12 shows how this can be done for the raster map of Fig. 2.11. The data structure consists of just three numbers, the origin (the centre or bottom left) and radius of each square. This is called a *medial axis transformation* or MAT (Rosenfeld 1980). The region shown in Fig. 2.11 can be stored by 17 unit squares + 9 4-squares + 1 16-square. Given that two coordinates are needed for each square the region can be stored using 57 numbers (54 for coordinates and 3 for cell sizes). Clearly, the larger the square that can be fitted in any given region and the simpler the boundary, the more efficient block coding becomes. Both run-length and block codes are clearly most efficient for large simple shapes and least so for small complicated areas that are only a few times larger than the basic cell. Medial axis transformation has advantages for performing union and intersection of regions and for detecting properties such as elongation (Rosenfeld 1980).

For some operations, data stored in block or run-length codes must be converted to simple raster format.

Quadtrees. The fourth method of more compact representation is based on successive division of the $2^n \times 2^n$

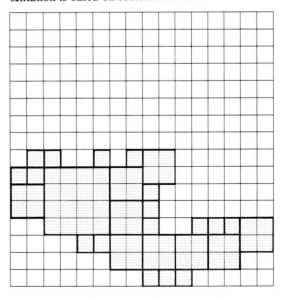

Fig. 2.12 The simple region described by a medial axis transformation block coding.

1	2	3	4
5	6	7	8

Fig. 2.13 The simple region as a quadtree.

'in' at the current level (↑↓) or a node 'out' at the current level (↓↑). So the region in Fig. 2.11 can be coded in 92 bits or 6×16-bit words.

Rosenfeld (1980), Klinger and Dyer (1976) and Hunter and Steiglitz (1979a, b) describe the use of quadtrees for region representation, and applications in soil and resource information systems are described by Abel (1983). Detailed descriptions of the algorithms used for computing perimeters and areas, and for converting from raster to quadtree and other representations have been described in a series of papers by Samet (1980, 1984), Dyer *et al.* (1980) and Pavlidis (1982). Quadtrees have many interesting advantages over other methods of raster representation. Standard region properties can be easily and efficiently computed. Quadtrees are 'variable resolution' arrays in which detail is represented only when available without requiring excessive storage for parts where detail is lacking (Figs. 2.15(a–d), and 2.16.) The largest problems associated with quadtrees appear to be that the tree representation is not translation-invariant—two regions of the same shape and size may have quite different quadtrees, so consequently shape analysis and pattern recognition are not straightforward. Quadtree representation does allow a region to be split up into parts, or to contain holes, however, without difficulty. There is a growing interest in the use of quadtrees in geographical information systems (Samet *et al.* 1984; Martin 1982; Mark and Lauzon 1984) and it is clearly an elegant technique that has much to offer.

array into quadrants. A region is tiled by subdividing the array step by step into quadrants and noting which quadrants are wholly contained with the region. The lowest limit of division is the single pixel. Figure. 2.13 shows the successive division of the one region of Fig. 2.11 intro quadrant blocks. This block structure can be described by a tree of degree 4, known as *a quadtree*; the quadtree representation of Fig. 2.11 is given in Fig. 2.14.

The entire array of $2^n \times 2^n$ points is the root node of the tree, and the height of the tree is at most n levels. Each node has four branches, respectively the NW, NE, SW, and SE quadrants. Leaf nodes correspond to those quadrants for which no further subdivision is necessary. Each node in the quadtree can be represented by 2 bits, which define whether it is a terminator 'in' (↑↑), a terminator 'out' (↓↓) or node

Summary—raster data structures

If each cell represents a potentially different value, then the simple $N \times N$ array structure is difficult to improve upon. Its limitations are largely related to the

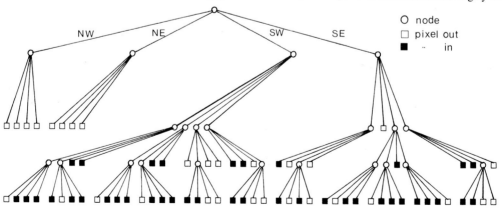

Fig. 2.14 The quadtree structure of the simple region of Fig. 2.11.

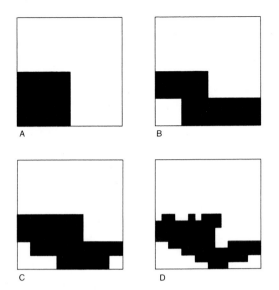

area of the regions being displayed and sorted; as resolution improves and pixel numbers per region increase, however, block codes and quadtrees become increasingly attractive. The quadtree representation has the added advantage of variable resolution. The ease of subsequent processing varies with the data structure used.

Fig. 2.15 The visual appearance of the simple region at each of the four levels of the quadtree hierarchy.

volume of data and size of memory required. When 'regions' (i.e. areas of uniform value) are present, as is assumed to be the case in many thematic maps, data storage requirements can be considerably reduced by using *chain codes, run-length codes, block codes,* or *quadtrees*. Run-length codes appear to be most efficient when the pixel size is large with respect to the

Vector data structures for geographical entities

As we saw earlier in this chapter, the vector representation of an object is an attempt to represent the object as exactly as possible. The coordinate space is assumed to be continuous, not quantized as with the raster space, allowing all positions, lengths, and dimensions to be defined precisely. In fact this is not exactly possible because of the limitations of the length of a computer word on the exact representation of a coordinate and because all vector display devices have a basic step size, albeit very much smaller than the resolution of most raster devices. Besides the assumption of mathematically exact coordinates, vector methods of data storage use implicit relations that allow complex data to be stored in a minimum of space. There is no single, preferred method, however. This section explains a range of vector structures used in geographical information systems for the storage of points, lines, and areas.

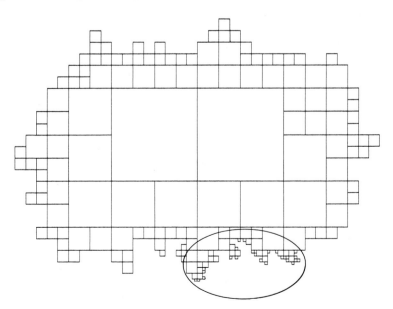

Fig. 2.16 A region divided by a quadtree structure. The area within the ellipse has detail shown to six levels of branching; the rest four.

'POINT'

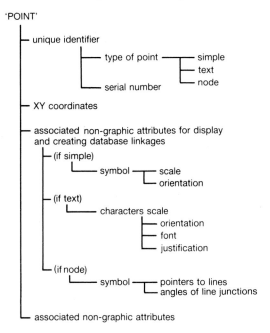

Fig. 2.17 Vector data structure of simple 'point' entities.

Point entities

Point entities can be considered to embrace all geographical and graphical entities that are positioned by a single *XY* coordinate pair. Besides the *XY* coordinates, other data must be stored to indicate what kind of 'point' it is, and the other information associated with it. For example, a 'point' could be a symbol unrelated to any other information. The data record would have to include information about the symbol. and the display size and orientation of the symbol. If the 'point' were a text entity, the data record would have to include information about the text characters to be displayed, the text font (style), the justification (right, left, centre), the scale, and the orientation, as well as ways of associating other non-graphic attributes with the 'point'. Figure 2.17 illustrates a possible data structure for 'point' entities.

Line entities

Line entities can be defined as all linear features built up of straight line segments made up of two or more coordinates. The simplest line requires the storage of a begin point and an end point (two *XY* coordinate pairs) plus a possible record indicating the display symbol to be used. For example, the display symbol parameter could be used to call up solid or dashed lines on the display device even though all the seg-

ments of the dashed display had not been stored in the database.

An 'arc', a 'chain' or a 'string' is a set of *n XY* coordinate pairs describing a continuous complex line. The shorter the line segments, and the larger the number of *XY* coordinate pairs, the closer the chain will approximate a complex curve. Data storage space can be saved at the expense of processing time by storing a number that indicates that the display driver routines should fit a mathematical interpolation function (e.g. B-splines) to the stored coordinates when the line data are sent to the display device.

As with 'points' and simple lines, chains can be stored with data records indicating the type of display line symbol to be used.

Networks: simple lines and chains carry no inherent spatial information about connectivity such as might be required for drainage network analysis or for road and transport sites. To achieve a line network that can be traced by the computer from line to line it is necessary to build 'pointers' into the data structure. The pointer structure is often built up with the help of nodes. Figure 2.18 illustrates the sort of data structure

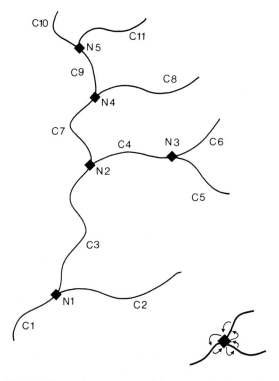

Fig. 2.18 Vector data structure of line networks using nodes to carry the connectivity information.

that would be necessary to establish connectivity between all branches of a stream network. Besides carrying pointers to the chains, the nodes would probably also carry data records indicating the angle at which each chain joins the node, thereby fully defining the topology of the network. This simple linkage structure incorporates some data redundancy because coordinates at each node are recorded a total of ($n \times$ chains + 1) times, where n is the number of chains joining a node.

Area entities

Areas of polygons (sometimes called 'regions') can be represented in various ways in a vector database. Because most kinds of thematic mapping used in geographical information systems have to do with polygons, the way in which these entities can be represented and manipulated has received considerable attention. The following discussion is largely based on the work of Peuker and Chrisman (1975), Cook (1978, 1983), Weber (1978), and Burrough (1980), and covers several well-known and frequently used methods of structuring polygon data.

The aim of a polygon data structure is to be able to describe the topological properties of areas (that is their shapes, neighbours, and hierarchy) in such a way that the associated properties of these basic spatial building blocks can be displayed and manipulated as thematic map data. Before describing the ways in which a polygon data structure can be constructed it would be as well to state the requirements of polygon networks that geographical data impose.

First, each component polygon (or region) on a map will have a unique shape, perimeter, and area. There is no single standard basic unit as is the case in raster systems. Even for the most regular or regularly laid out American street plan it will be unwise to assume that all or even some of the blocks have exactly the same shape and size. For soil and geological maps uniformity of space and size is clearly most unlikely. Second, geographical analyses require that the data structure be able to record the neighbours of each polygon in the same way that the stream network required connectivity. Third, polygons on thematic maps are not all at the same level—islands occur in lakes that are themselves on large islands, and so on.

Simple polygons

The simplest way to represent a polygon is an extension of the simple chain, i.e. to represent each polygon as a set of *XY* coordinates on the boundary (Fig. 2.19). The names or symbols used to tell the user what each

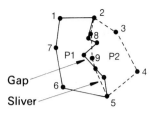

Fig. 2.19 Simple polygon structures have the disadvantage that boundary lines between two polygons have to be digitized and stored twice. This can lead to topological errors known as 'slivers' and 'gaps'.

polygon is are then held as a set of simple text entities. While this method has the advantages of simplicity it has many disadvantages. These are:

1. Lines between adjacent polygons must be digitized and stored twice. This can lead to serious errors in matching, giving rise to slivers and gaps along the common boundary.

2. There is no neighbourhood information.

3. Islands are impossible except as purely graphical constructions.

4. There are no easy ways to check if the topology of the boundary is correct or whether it is incomplete ('dead-end') or makes topologically inadmissable loops ('weird polygons')—see Fig. 2.20.

The simple polygon structure can be extended such that each polygon is represented by a number of chains, but this does not avoid the basic problems.

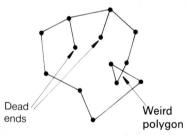

Fig. 2.20 Topological errors in the boundary of a simple polygon. Incomplete linkages ('dead ends') and topologically inadmissible loops ('weird polygons') must be removed from the data.

Polygons with point dictionaries

All coordinate pairs are numbered sequentially and are referenced by a dictionary that records which points are associated with each polygon (Fig. 2.21(a)). This system is used by the Harvard Laboratory for Computer Graphics CALFORM program.

The point dictionary database has the advantage that boundaries between adjacent polygons are unique, but the problem of neighbourhood functions

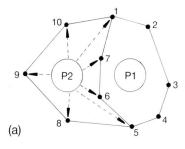

(a)

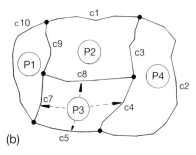

(b)

Fig. 2.21 (a) Polygon data structure in which all coordinates of a polygon are referenced directly from the polygon record. (b) The same, but all chains (arcs or boundary lines) are referenced directly from the polygon record.

still exists. Also, the structure does not easily allow boundaries between adjacent polygons to be suppressed or dissolved if a renumbering or reclassification should result in them both being allocated to the same class. The problem of island polygons still exists, as do the problems of checking for weird polygons and dead ends. As with simple polygons, polygons can be used with chain dictionaries (Fig. 2.21(b)). An advantage of using chain dictionaries is that over-defined chains (resulting from stream digitizing) can be reduced in size by weeding algorithms (see Chapter 4) without having to modify the dictionary.

Polygon systems with explicit topological structures

Islands and neighbours can only be properly handled by incorporating explicit topological relationships into the data structure. The topological structure can be built up in one of two ways—by creating the topological links during data input, or by using software to create the topology from a set of interlinked chains or strings. In the first case, the burden of creating the topology is thrust on the operator; the second relies on often considerable amounts of computing power.

Both methods result in an increase in the amount of data that needs to be stored to describe the full polygon structure.

One of the first attempts to build explicit topological relationships into a geographical data structure is the Dual Independent Map Encoding (DIME) system of the US Bureau of the Census. The basic element of the DIME data file is a simple line segment defined by two end points; complex lines are represented by a series of segments. The segment has two pointers to the nodes, and codes for the polygon on each side of the segment. Because nodes do not point back to segments, or segments to adjacent segments, laborious searches are needed to assemble the outlines of polygons. Moreover, the simple segment structure makes the handling of complex lines very cumbersome because of the large data redundancy.

A simple, effective approach has been developed at the Netherlands Soil Survey Institute, Wageningen for distributing polygonal data sets in such a way that they can be processed by a small computer (van Kuilenburg 1981). The polygon map is stored as a segment or chain file in which each chain is stored as a list of *XY* coordinate pairs and two pointers that refer to the adjacent map areas (Fig. 2.22). The names of the polygons are stored in a separate table that also includes the same pointers. The data structure is specially designed for producing simple derivative maps from the basic polygon network. When a derived map is needed, the polygon names in the table are recoded. The plotter subroutines only allow a chain to be plotted or used for area calculations if its pointers refer-

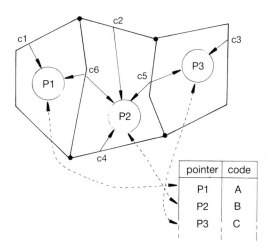

Fig. 2.22 Polygon data structure in which all polygons are referenced from the chains (arcs or boundary lines).

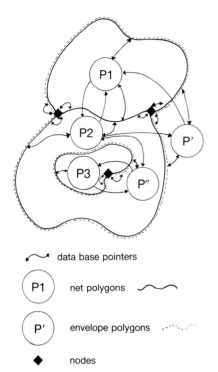

⌐⌐ data base pointers

(P1) net polygons ⌐⌐⌐

(P') envelope polygons ⌐⌐⌐

◆ nodes

Fig. 2.23 A full topological network for polygons.

ence different polygon names, thereby leading to a simplification of the original polygon network. Areas of polygons that contain islands are computed using a 'point-in-polygon' search algorithm, to be described in more detail below. This data structure does not allow any more sophisticated neighbourhood searches to be made, nor does it allow error checks for weird polygons or dead ends, so it can best be derived from a fully topologically structured database.

In order to establish a proper topological polygon data structure in which island polygons, area calculations, neighbourhood operations such as recoding and merging, and error checks for weird polygons and dead ends are all possible, the data structure shown schematically in Fig. 2.23 must be built up. Many experimental and production mapping systems have been designed in which the operator has been required to build the topological links into the database while digitizing the line pattern. These systems often require the operator to digitize all polygons in a strict clockwise or counter-clockwise order, to associate each line with the polygon on both right and left of the line and to digitize virtual lines to link 'islands' with their surrounding 'lakes'. The developers of these systems have clearly never spent long hours at a digitizing table nor

have they given much thought to how error-prone such a system may be. Cook (1978) documents some of the topological problems arising from the virtual line, such as with the calculation of areas and perimeters. Moreover, when highly detailed polygon maps have been produced by vectorizing a scanned raster image (see Chapter 4) it is clearly absurd that an operator should have to go over every part of the map by hand just to establish the topology. As White (1983) has complained, an elementary knowledge of topology can eliminate all the problems stated so far, but it must be fair to add that this has to be accompanied by an increase in the complexity of the software and of the resulting database.

A fully topological polygon network structure

The following section describes how the fully integrated topologically linked polygon network structure shown in Fig. 2.23 can be built up from a set of boundary chains or strings that have been digitized in any order and in any direction. The system allows islands and lakes to be nested to any level; it allows automatic checks for weird polygons and dead ends and automated or semi-automated association of non-spatial attributes with the resulting polygons. Neighbourhood searches are fully supported. Although differing in details, the system that is about to be described is similar to systems used in the Harvard Polyvrt program (Peuker and Chrisman 1975), in CSIRO (Cook 1978) by Baxter (1980), Burrough (1980), and the CODASYL model (Weber 1978).

The simple polygon systems described so far often require data input methods to meet the requirements of the data structure. This leads to problems with data input and to sub-optimal data structures. It is more efficient to treat data input and data structure as two separate and independent processes. The procedures used to build the data structure should need only to make two assumptions of the input data, namely that the polygon boundaries have been encoded in the form of chains or arcs, and that the polygon names or other records used to link the graphical to the attribute data are digitized in the form of identifiable point entities somewhere within each polygon boundary.

Stage 1. Linking chains into a boundary network. The chains are first sorted according to their extents (minimum and maximum *X* and *Y* coordinates occupied by the chain) so that chains topologically close to one another are also close together in the data file. This is to save time when searching for adjacent chains. The chains are then examined to see which other chains they intersect. Junction points are built at the end of all chains that join, and the chain data records are extended to contain chain pointers and angles. Chains that cross at places other than the end points are automatically cut into new chains and the chain pointers are built. To handle minor digitizing errors such as overshoots and small gaps, a tolerance window can be built into the searching routine. The final end coordinates are then rewritten in all chain-end records as the average of all points found.

(Note: in some systems the nodes must be entered manually. Although this practice decreases processing times it results in extra work for data input, a non-standard data format and redundancy in the database.)

Stage 2. Checking polygons for closure. The resulting network can easily be checked for closure by scanning the modified chain records to see if they all have pointers to and from at least another chain. The other chain may be the chain itself, in the case of single islands defined by a single chain. All chains failing to pass the test can be 'flagged' (i.e. brought to the attention of the operator) by causing them to be displayed in a particular way, or otherwise be removed from the subset of chains to be used for the polygon network.

Stage 3. Linking the lines into polygons. The first step in linking lines into polygons is to create a new 'envelope' polygon from the outer boundary of the map. This envelope entity consists of records containing:

(a) a unique identifier;
(b) a code that identifies it as an envelope polygon;
(c) a ring pointer;
(d) a list of pointers to the bounding chains;
(e) its area;
(f) its extent (minimum and maximum *XY* coordinates of bounding rectangle).

Note that the envelope polygon will not be seen by the user—its sole purpose is in building the topological structure of the network. The envelope polygon is created by following chains around the outer boundary by proceeding in a clockwise direction and choosing the most left-hand chain at each junction. The unique identifier of every chain is recorded and stored along with the other data and a flag is set to indicate that each chain has been traversed once.

Once the outer, or envelope, polygon has been built, each individual polygon can be created. This is done by starting at the same place as before, but this time

the clockwise searches involve choosing the most right-hand chain at each junction. A tally must be kept of the number of times a chain has been traversed—once it has been traversed twice it falls out of the search. Arriving back at the starting point, one has identified all the component lines. At the same time, a check is made on the cumulative turning angle (Fig. 2.20). If this is not 360° there has been a digitizing fault and the polygon is weird. (NB weird polygons should have been filtered out by the intersection-seeking step in Stage 1, but if the chains must be linked to manually entered nodes then this check is essential.) As with the envelope polygon, each polygon entity receives several sets of information:

(a) a unique identifier;
(b) an ordinary polygon code;
(c) a ring pointer *from* the envelope polygon (at the same time the identifier of this polygon is written in the ring pointer of the envelope polygon);
(d) a list of all bounding chains (at the same time, the polygon's unique identifier is written into the record of the line);
(e) a ring pointer *to* the adjacent polygon in the network;
(f) minimum and maximum *XY* coordinates (extents) of the bounding rectangle.

The search proceeds to the next polygon in the same network at the same level in the hierarchy, and so on until all individual polygons have been built up. When the last polygon in the net has been traced, its ring pointer (e) is set pointing back to the envelope polygon. Note that this ensures that all bounding lines are associated with *two* polygons.

The same procedure is followed for all 'islands' and 'unconnected sub-continents'. Once all bounding chains

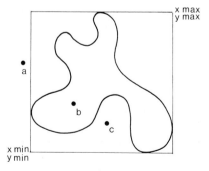

Fig. 2.24 Solving the point-in-polygon problem. Point a is easily excluded because it is outside the extents (*XY*-min, *XY*-max). Points b and c need further processing.

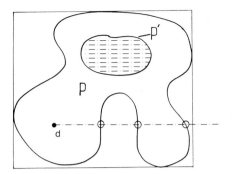

Fig. 2.25 If a horizontal line drawn from a point, d, makes an odd number of intersections with the polygon boundary then the point is 'in'. For polygons, the whole of the area of the small polygon must be scanned for enclosure.

have been linked into polygons, the 'islands' and the 'sub-continents' must be arranged in the proper topological hierarchy. This can be done by first sorting them into increasing area, and then testing to see if an 'island' falls within an 'envelope' of the next largest size. A quick test can be made by comparing the extents of the two envelope polygons. Once a match has been found, the problem is to locate the exact polygon in which the island lies. The matching of extents is then repeated for each component polygon in the 'continent'. Once a match has been found, a 'point-in-polygon' routine is used to see if the island is totally within the polygon (see Figs. 2.24 and 2.25). If an overlap is found, it signals an error in the database or the intersection procedures (Stage 1) and indicates that the operator must take remedial action. If there is no overlap, then a pointer is written from the network polygon to the envelope polygon of the enclosed island. If no overlap and no matching is found, it means that the two polygon networks are independent of each other. Note that the ring pointer structure of envelope polygons–network polygons–island envelope polygons–island network polygons allows an infinite amount of nesting. Moreover, the nesting only needs to be worked out once; thereafter the network can be traversed easily by following the pointers.

Stage 4. Computing polygon areas. The next stage involves computing the area of the individual polygons by the trapezoidal rule. Because in geographical data, polygons may have many hundreds of coordinates in the bounding chains and many island polygons (imagine the geological map of an area with lakes and drumlins), it is usually more efficient to compute areas once, subtracting the areas of enclosed islands as

necessary, and then to store these areas as an associated attribute.

Stage 5. Associating non-graphic attributes to the polygons. The last stage of building the database is to link the polygons to the associated attributes that describe what they represent. This can be done in several ways. The first is to digitize a unique text entity within each polygon area, either as part of the data entry, or interactively after polygons have been formed. This text can then be used as a pointer to the associated attributes that may or may not be stored with the graphic data. The text can be used for visual display; it is linked to the polygon by the use of a point-in-polygon search (see above, Fig. 2.25). The second is to get the computer to write the unique identifier of each polygon at the centre of each polygon; at the same time the computer prints a list of all polygon identifiers. This list can then be merged with a file containing the other non-graphic attributes of the polygons which can then be cross-referenced through the unique polygon identifiers.

The reader will appreciate that considerable computing power and complex software is needed to construct the topologically sound polygon network described above. The resulting data structure has the following advantages, however:

(a) the polygon network is fully integrated and is free from gaps, slivers, and excessive amounts of redundant coordinates;

(b) all polygons, chains, and associated attributes are part of an interlinked unit so that all kinds of neighbourhood analyses are possible (note that the system just described also allows the chains to have non-graphic attributes associated with them as well);

(c) the number of continent–island nestings is unlimited;

(d) the locational accuracy of the database is limited only by the accuracy of the digitizer and the length of the computer word;

(e) the data structure has few implications for data gathering and entry.

Point-in-polygon search

Figures 2.24 and 2.25 show two aspects of point-in-polygon algorithms. In Fig. 2.24, a quick comparison of the coordinates of the point with the polygon extents quickly reveals whether a point is likely to be in or not. So point a can easily be excluded but c cannot.

To check if point d is in the polygon in Fig. 2.25, a horizontal line is extended from the point. If the number of intersections is odd, the point is *inside* the polygon.

To check if an island polygon, P′ is inside P, first check the extents. P′ is then divided into a number of horizontal bands and the first and last points of each band are treated as the point c above. If the number of points for each line is odd, then the polygon P′ is completely enclosed. (NB Problems may occur if any segment of a boundary is exactly horizontal and has exactly the same *Y* coordinate as the point *X*, but these can be easily filtered out.)

Haralick (1980) lists an alternative procedure for finding the polygon containing a point that is based on a binary search of monotone chains—that is, sequences of arcs in which the order of the vertices in the chain is the same as the order of the vertices projected onto a line.

Other features of vector database structures

Layers. When discussing raster database structures it was noted how each attribute could be mapped as a separate overlay, giving rise to a three-dimensional data matrix. In principle, the number of layers is un-limited, restrictions being imposed only by storage space. The overlay concept is so natural to cartographers and designers that it is also frequently built into vector systems, particularly those that are used for computer-aided design (CAD). Unlike raster systems, where each new attribute in the database means a new overlay, the overlay/layer system used in CAD vector systems is used to separate major classes of spatial entities, mainly for purposes of drawing and display.

The layer information is usually added to the graphic data by coding a bit sequence in a header that is attached to the data record of each graphic entity. Depending on the system, the bit sequences may allow 64 or 256 different layers for display; alternatively, the headers may be even more flexibly coded in terms of major non-graphic attributes that the user can define, such as railways, major roads, streams or soil boundaries (Fig. 2.26). The layer system makes it very easy to count, flag, and selectively display graphic entities. The landscape information system developed at The Netherlands Soil Survey Institute (Burrough 1980) uses Boolean selection rules to identify chosen graphic entities that can be isolated and displayed separately simply by changing the layer address.

Lists and sequential searches. All the vector structures described up to now have only been concerned with relations between the points, chains, and polygons that go to make up the thematic map. The reader will have noted that in every case the basic entity, be it point, line or polygon, has been uniquely identified by a pointer or a label. The topological structures discussed can only be traversed by means of these unique labels.

These labels, sometimes called master index pointers, are often held in a sequential list that is the key to accessing the rest of the database (Fig. 2.27(a)). This list has two major problems associated with it. First, it is rarely fully consecutive—during editing, gaps may appear, or it may be increased in length, which means that non-pointer searches almost invariably have to be of a sequential nature. Second, the search times increase sharply with the length of the table, which often means that map processing times increase non-linearly with the size of the database. This is not least the result of the master index table being distributed over a disk. Consequently, procedures that work well on small, demonstration databases may become very slow on production-size maps.

There are two fundamentally different ways to tackle the problem of an increasingly large database. One is to use 'brute-force' computing methods to scan the pointer arrays quickly, or to concentrate the mas-

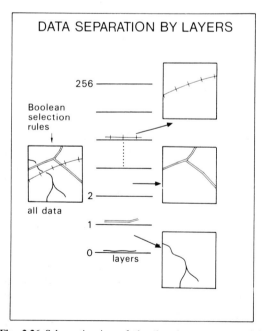

Fig. 2.26 Schematic view of the 'layer' structures used in many vector mapping systems to separate different map themes. Each layer can be used to carry a separate theme. Different maps can be made by viewing layers singly, or in combination. Numbers refer to the 'position' of the layers.

(a)

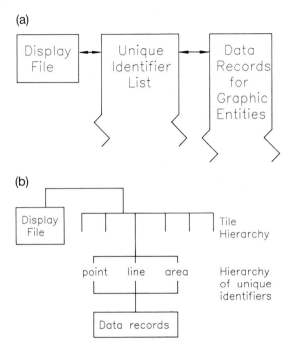

(b)

Fig. 2.27 (a) Simple sequential data structure used for vector graphics. (b) Better design that splits database up into tiles (separate areas) and geographical entities.

ter index array onto a small, contiguous area of disk or core storage. While this approach can undoubtedly effect some improvements, it is at best a palliative and does little to resolve the underlying problems. Another approach involves structuring the master index pointers not only according to entity type, but also to spatial location (Fig. 2.27(b)). The database is considered to consist of an (in theory) infinite set of tiles reaching in both directions. Each tile (or page as it is sometimes called) can reference a certain amount of information; extra details can be accommodated by dividing each main tile into sub-tiles, in a manner similar to that used in quadtree structures (see Cook 1978). Tiling introduces an extra complication in that all chains must automatically be terminated and begun at tile boundaries, and topological pointers must not only reference other entities, but other tiles as well. The costs are thus a larger database, but one in which searching times can be kept very low by virtue of the positional hierarchy.

In principle, tiling allows limitless maps to be created and stored, as only data from a few tiles need be referenced at any one time, the rest being stored on disk. In practice, the sheer volume of data will exceed the financially allowable disk space (it does not take

many map sheets of soil polygons to fill 150 Mbyte) so that for countrywide mapping great reliance must be placed on magnetic tape for storing much of the total database until it is required.

Data structures for thematic maps—the choice between raster and vector

The raster and vector methods for spatial data structures are distinctly different approaches to modelling geographical information, but are they mutually exclusive? Only a few years ago, the conventional wisdom was that raster and vector data structures were irreconcilable alternatives. They were then irreconcilable because raster methods required huge computer memories to store and process images at the level of spatial resolution obtained by vector structures. Certain kinds of data manipulation, such as polygon intersection or spatial averaging presented enormous technical problems with vector methods. The user was faced with the choice of raster methods that allowed easy spatial analysis but resulted in ugly maps, or vector methods that could provide databases of manageable size and elegant graphics but in which spatial analysis was extremely difficult.

In recent years it has become clear that what until recently was seen as an important conceptual problem is, in fact, a technological problem. When punched cards were the main medium of data storage, it was clearly an enormous task to code a 1:50 000 scale soil series map measuring 400×500 mm at a resolution of 0.2 mm (the line width on the printed map) because there would be 5×10^6 pixels. These data would require something like 500 000 punched cards, assuming that each card could carry 10 coordinate pairs or pixels, which would occupy a volume of between two and three cubic metres! Today, it is commonplace for a good graphics colour screen to have an addressable raster array of 1024×1024 pixels within an area of some 300×300 mm, a resolution of 0.3 mm.

The quality of the graphics was not the only technological limitation. Most early technical developments were done in vector processing, simply because vector structures were the most familiar form of graphic expression. In the late 1970s, several workers, notably Peuquet (1977, 1979) and Nagy and Wagle (1979) showed that many of the algorithms that had been developed for vector data structures of polygonal data not only had raster alternatives, but that in some cases the raster alternatives were more efficient. For example, the calculation of polygon perimeters and areas, sums, averages, and other operations within a defined radius from a point are all reduced to simple counting operations in the raster mode. Because of the presorted and regular coordinate structure, windowing and clipping and the retrieval of items on the basis of location is easier in raster than in vector data structures. On the other hand, linked networks are really only feasible in the vector mode, so this is the preferred data structure for utility mapping or for analysing transport networks. Also, recent developments in faster algorithms for some vector-based operations have shown that there are more efficient ways to solve some problems than had previously been thought (Haralick 1980).

The gigantic storage volumes required for raster formats can also be greatly reduced by means of some of the compact raster data structures mentioned earlier in this chapter, such as run length codes or quadtrees. Conversely, the inclusion of a large amount of topological information in a vector network structure, or the redundancy in a relational data structure can seriously increase the size of vector-structured databases.

The problem of raster *or* vector disappears once it is realized that both are valid methods for representing spatial data, and that both structures are interconvertible. Conversion from vector to raster is the simplest and there are many well-known algorithms (e.g. Pavlidis 1982). Vector to raster conversions are now performed automatically in many display screens by inbuilt microprocessors. The reverse operation, raster to vector, is also well understood (Pavlidis lists four algorithms for thinning bands of pixels to lines), but it is a much more complex operation that is complicated by the need to reduce the numbers of coordinates in the resulting lines by a process known as weeding.

The original method of reducing the number of points in a digitized curve is due to Douglas and Peuker (1973); more recently Opheim (1982) has published a faster method. The point here is that whereas vector to raster conversion is a single-stage process, the converse is at best a two-stage process.

Haralick (1980), Shapiro (1980), and Shapiro and Haralick (1980) have shown in recent papers how a relational database structure for points, lines, and polygons can be established that treats the raster and vector approaches to modelling the topology as equivalent alternatives. The following discussion of this idea is based on Haralick's and on Shapiro's work, but includes a number of extensions to relate it to the material already discussed.

The idea rests ón the understanding that attribute data and topological data should be kept separate from each other, but can be easily linked. The attribute data that describe what the entity represents may include data about its real world attributes, and also about how the entity must be managed within the database. This last can also include information that governs the kinds of relations that a given spatial entity may have; for example, a point entity should not possess a record indicating its area, and a polygon entity should be defined in terms of records including information about the entities (boundaries or pixels) that describe it spatially.

The idea will be made clearer by an example. Consider Fig. 2.28. The polygon P1 is a part of a polygon network that we shall call 'soil map'. P1 contains two small inclusions (P2 and P3) and is surrounded by polygons P4, P5, and P7. There are At_n attributes that refer to the properties of the space described by P1. In vector notation, the space described by P1 is circum-

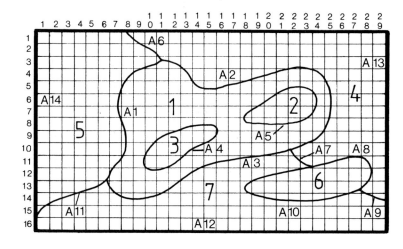

Fig. 2.28 A simple map that can be represented in vector (arc–polygon) or raster form.

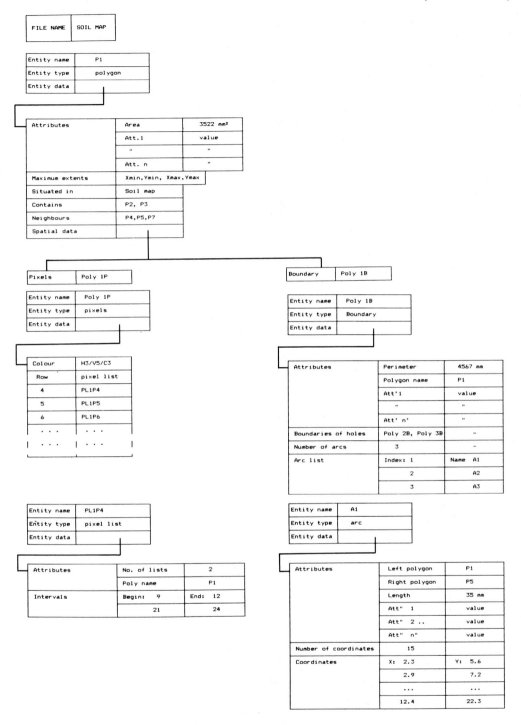

Fig. 2.29 A possible relational database structure of Fig. 2.28 for combined vector and raster representation.

scribed by a boundary. It is part of Haralick and Shapiro's scheme that the boundary is an entity in its own right. The boundary consists of a number of arcs (A_1–A_{14}) (chains or strings in the notation used earlier in the chapter) that are themselves also entities. For both boundaries and arcs the *entity data* can be described by a set of relations. The permissible set of relations is governed by the *entity type*. In addition, each entity has an *entity name* in order to identify it uniquely.

In raster notation, the space described by P1 can be defined in terms of sets of pixels. As we have already seen there are several ways of defining pixel sets in raster mapping—in this example we shall use the compact run length code method to describe the space defined by P1. This method requires that the polygon be defined by an entity here called 'pixels' containing the lists of rows that have pixels within the polygon; each pixel list is then an entity containing the begin and end indices of the sets of pixels in each row that form a part of the space of P1.

Figure 2.29 shows how the polygon P1 can be represented fully in either raster or vector form. At the highest level, the polygon is described by a simple set of relations listing the *entity name*, the *entity type*, and the *entity data*. Whereas the name and type are simple records, the *entity data* is a set of relations including *attributes*, *spatial relations*, *extents*, and *spatial description*. Note that the entity data are identical in all respects for raster and vector notation, except for the set of relations referenced in the spatial description record.

In the vector notation, the boundary entity type is set up in a similar way to that of the polygon. The entity data relation contains attributes of the boundary, a list of the arcs making up that boundary and a list of the boundary entities of the holes within that boundary. The data structure for the arcs includes attributes indicating the polygons to their left and right, the boundary in which they belong, and a list of their coordinates.

This scheme contains a considerable amount of data redundancy in order to provide the linkages that are carried by pointers in the vector structures discussed earlier in the chapter.

In order to represent polygon P1 in raster notation, it is only necessary to change the entry in the record describing spatial description from 'boundary' to 'pixels'. The pixel set is described in terms equivalent to those used for boundaries and arcs, except the pixel entities refer to sets of pixel lists on rows and to contiguous sets of pixels within rows (pixel lists).

Clearly, the main data structure of polygon P1 is

Table 2.2 Comparison of vector and raster methods

Vector methods

Advantages
  Good representation of phenomenological data structure
  Compact data structure
  Topology can be completely described with network linkages
  Accurate graphics
  Retrieval, updating and generalization of graphics and attributes are possible
Disadvantages
  Complex data structures
  Combination of several vector polygon maps or polygon and raster maps through overlay creates difficulties
  Simulation is difficult because each unit has a different topological form
  Display and plotting can be expensive, particularly for high quality, colour and cross-hatching
  The technology is expensive, particularly for the more sophisticated software and hardware
  Spatial analysis and filtering within polygons are impossible

Raster methods

Advantages
  Simple data structures
  The overlay and combination of mapped data with remotely sensed data is easy
  Various kinds of spatial analysis are easy
  Simulation is easy because each spatial unit has the same size and shape
  The technology is cheap and is being energetically developed
Disadvantages
  Volumes of graphic data
  The use of large cells to reduce data volumes means that phenomenologically recognizable structures can be lost and there can be a serious loss of information
  Crude raster maps are considerably less beautiful than maps drawn with fine lines
  Network linkages are difficult to establish
  Projection transformation are time consuming unless special algorithms or hardware are used.

unchanged by the way in which the space it occupies is described. Both the raster and vector representations of that space are equally valid data structures. If routines are available for the speedy conversion from one spatial structure to another, data retrieval and analysis routines can be programmed to choose the structure that is most efficient for solving a given problem without the user having to intervene (Table 2.2). In some circumstances it may be advantageous to have spatial data present in both raster and vector form, particularly when line or boundary data need to be represented by connected networks or drawn in a particular style and the spaces between must be filled with a print raster of a given symbolism or colour.

Bickmore (1984) describes an experimental coloured map of ecological zones in the Dolgellau area of North Wales made for the UK Nature Conservancy Council by the IGN in Paris that was made using combined raster and vector techniques. While this experiment referred only to making a map, we may expect that the use of vector and raster spatial data structures as complementary components of a geographical information system will increase in importance as demands for high resolution, compact data structures and the power of flexible data analyses increase.

References

Abel, D. J. (1983). Towards a relational database for geographic information systems. Workshop on Databases in the Natural Sciences. CSIRO Division of Computing Research, 7–9 Sept 1983. Cunningham Laboratory, Brisbane, Queensland, Australia.

Baxter, R. (1980). A computer file and data structure for manipulating digital outlines of polygons. *GeoProcessing* 1 (3), 243–56.

Beyer, R. I. (1984). A database for a botanical plant collection. In *Computer-aided landscape design: principles and practice* (ed. B. M. Evans) pp. 134–41. The Landscape Institute, Scotland.

Bickmore, D. (1984). Computer aided soil cartography: some recent Franco-British projects. In *Soil data technology; Proc. 6th Meeting of the International Society of Soil Science Working Group on Soil Information Systems*, Bolkesjø, Norway, 28 Feb.–4 March 1983 (ed. P. A. Burrough and S. W. Bie). PUDOC, Wageningen.

Burrough, P. A. (1980). The development of a landscape information system in The Netherlands, based on a turn-key graphics system. *GeoProcessing* 1 (3), 257–74.

CODASYL (1971). *Database task group report*. ACM, New York.

Castleman, K. R. (1979). *Digital image processing*. Prentice Hall, Englewood Cliffs, NJ.

Cook, B. G. (1978). The structural and algorithmic basis of a geographic data base. *Harvard papers on geographic information systems: First International Advanced Study Symposium on Topological Data Structures for Geographic Information systems* (ed. G. Dutton) Vol. 4. Laboratory for Computer Graphics and Spatial Analysis, Graduate School of Design, Harvard University.

Cook, B. G. (1983). An introduction to the design of geographic databases. In *Proc. Workshop on Databases in the Natural Sciences*, CSIRO Division of Computing Research, 7–9 Sept. 1983, pp. 175–186. Cunningham Laboratory, Brisbane, Queensland.

Dangermond, J. and Antenucci, J. (1974). *Maryland automated geographic information system (MAGI)*. Maryland Department of State Planning, Baltimore, Maryland.

Date, C. J. (1981). *An introduction to database systems*. (3rd edn). Addison-Wesley, Reading, Mass.

Douglas, D. H. and Peuker, T. K. (1973). Algorithms for the reduction of the number of points required to represent a digitised line or its caricature. *Can. Cartogr.* **10**, 112–22.

Duda, R. and Hart, P. (1973). *Pattern classification and scene analysis*. Wiley, New York.

Dyer, C. R., Rosenfeld, A., and Samet, H. (1980). Region representation: boundary codes from quadtrees. *Comm. Ass. Comput. Mach.* **23**, 171–9.

Freeman, H. (1974). Computer processing of line-drawing images. *Comput. Surv.* **6**, 54–97.

Gersting, J. L. (1984). *Mathematical Structures for computer science*. W. H. Freeman, New York.

Giloi, W. K. (1978). *Interactive computer graphics*. Prentice-Hall, Englewood Cliffs, NJ.

Giltrap, D. (1984). MIDGE—a microcomputer for soil mapping. In *Proc. 6th Meeting ISSS Working Group of Soil Information Systems*, Bolkesjø, Norway, 28 Feb–4 March 1983 (ed. P. A. Burrough and S. W. Bie). pp. 112–19. PUDOC, Wageningen.

Haralick, R. M. (1980). A spatial data structure for geographic information systems. In *Map data processing* (ed. H. Freeman and G. G. Pieroni). Academic Press, New York.

Hunter, G. M. and Steiglitz, K. (1979a). Operations on images using quadtrees. *IEEE Trans. Pattern Anal. Mach. Intell.* **1**, 145–153.

—— and Steiglitz, K. (1979b). Linear transformations of pictures represented by quadtrees. *Comput. Graph. Image Process.* **10**, 289–96.

Klinger, A. and Dyer, C. R. (1976). Experiments in picture representation using regular decomposition. *Comput. Graph. Image Process.* **5**, 68–105.

Kroenke, D. (1977). *Database processing: fundamental modeling, applications*. Science Research Associates, Chicago.

Lorie, R. A. and Meier, A. (1984). Using a relational DBMS for geographical databases. *GeoProcessing* **2**, 243–57.

Mark, D. M. and Lauzon, J. P. (1984). Linear quadtrees for geographic information systems. In *Proc. IGU Int. Symp. on Spatial Data Handling*, Zurich, 20–24 Aug. 1984, pp. 412–431.

Martin, J. J. 1982. Organization of geographical data with quadtrees and least squares approximation. In *Proc. Symp. on Pattern Recognition and Image Processing (PRIP)*, Las Vegas, Nevada, pp. 458–465. IEEE Computer Society.

McHarg, I. L. 1969. *Design with nature*. Natural History Press, Garden City-Doubleday, New York.

Nagy, G. and Wagle, S. G. (1979). Approximation of polygonal maps by cellular maps. *Comm. Ass. Comput. Mach.* **22**, 518–25.

New York State Office of Planning Services (1972). PLAN-MAP II. New York State office of Planning Services, Albany, NY.

O'Callaghan, J. F. and Graetz, R. D. (1981). Software for image-based information systems: its application to integrating LANDSAT imagery and land tenure data for rangeland management. In *Information systems for soil and related data* (ed. A. W. Moore, B. G. Cook, and L. G. Lynch). *Proc. 2nd Australian Meeting of the ISSS Working Group on Soil Information Systems*, Canberra, Australia 19–21 Feb. 1980. PUDOC, Wageningen.

Opheim, H. (1982). Fast data reduction of a digitized curve. *GeoProcessing* **2**, 33–40.

Pavlidis, T. (1982). *Algorithms for graphics and image processing*. Springer, Berlin.

Peuker, T. K. (now Poiker) and Chrisman, N. (1975). Cartographic data structures. *Am. Cartogr.* **2** (1), 55–69.

Peuquet, D. J. (1977). Raster data handling in geographic information systems. In *Proc. 1st Int. Advanced Study Symposium on Topological Data Structures* (ed. G. Dutton). Laboratory for Computer Graphics, and Spatial Analysis, Harvard.

—— (1979). Raster processing: an alternative approach to automated cartographic data handling. *Am. Cartogr.* **6**, 129–39.

Rosenfeld, A. (1980) Tree structures for region representation. In *Map data processing* (ed. H. Freeman and G. G. Pieroni) pp. 137–50. Academic Press, New York.

Salton, G. and McGill, M. J. (1983). *Introduction to modern information retrieval*. McGraw-Hill, New York.

Samet, H. (1980). Region representation: quadtrees from boundary codes. Comm. Ass. Comput. Mach. ACM **23**, 163–170.

—— (1984). The quadtree and related heirarchical data structures. ACM *Comput. Surv.* **16** (2).

——, Rosenfeld, A., Schaffer, C.A. and Weber R.E.(1984). Use of hierarchical data structures in geographical information systems. In *Proc. IGU Int. Symp. on Spatial Data Handling,* Zurich, 20–24 Aug. 1984, pp. 392–411.

Shapiro, L. G. (1980). Design of a spatial information system. In *Map data processing* (ed. H. Freeman and G. G. Pieroni). Academic Press, New York.

——, and Haralick, R. M. (1980). A spatial data structure. *GeoProcessing* **1**, 313–97.

Sinton, D. F. (1977). *The user's guide to IMGRID: an information system for grid cell data structures*. Department of Landscape Architecture, Graduate School of Design, Harvard University.

——, and Steinitz, C. F. (1969). *GRID: a user's manual*. Laboratory for Computer Graphics and Spatial Analysis, Graduate School of Design, Harvard University.

Tom, C., Miller, L. D., and Christenson, J. W. (1978). Spatial land use inventory, modelling and projection. Denver metropolitan area, Technical memo. N.79710. National Aeronautics and Space Administration. NSTL Station, Mississippi.

Tomlin, C. D. (1983). Digital cartographic modelling techniques in environmental planning. Unpublished Ph.D. dissertation, Yale University, Connecticut.

Ullman, J. D. (1980). *Principles of database systems*. Computer Science Press, Potomac, Maryland.

Van Kuilenburg, J. (1981) Segment encoding for the production of low-cost interpretation maps. *ISSS Working Group on Soil Information Systems Newsletter*, No. 8 (Sept. 1981), p. 5.

Van Roessel, J. W. and Fosnight, E. A. (1984). A relational approach to vector data structure conversion. In *Proc. IGU Int. Symp. on Spatial Data Handling*, 20–24 August, Zürich, pp. 78–95.

Weber, W. (1978). Three types of map data structures, their ANDs and NOTs, and a possible OR. *Harvard papers on geographic information systems. First International Advanced Study Symposium on Topological Data Structures for Geographic Information Systems* (ed. G. Dutton). Laboratory for Computer Graphics and Spatial Analysis, Graduate School of Design, Harvard.

White, M. (1983). Tribulations of automated cartography and how mathematics helps. *Proc. AUTOCARTO 6,* Ottawa, October 1983, pp. 408–18.

Wirth, N. (1976). *Algorithms + data = structures*. Prentice-Hall, Englewood Cliffs, NJ.

3. Digital Elevation Models /CONTINUOUS SFC.

Unlike land-use, soil series, or geological units, the landform is usually perceived as a continually varying surface that cannot be modelled appropriately by the choropleth map model. Although abrupt steps and cliffs may occur, these changes are thought usually to be the exception rather than the rule.

A continually varying surface can be represented by isolines (contours), and these contours can be effectively regarded as sets of closed, nested polygons. Consequently, contour sets do not require a method of digitizing or of storage that is different from that described for choropleth maps in Chapter 2. Although sets of isolines are very suitable for the *display* of a continually varying surface, they are not particularly suitable for numerical analysis or modelling. So other methods have been developed in order to be able to represent and to use effectively information about the continuous variation of an attribute (usually altitude) over space.

Any digital representation of the continuous variation of relief over space is known as a digital elevation model (DEM). The term digital terrain model (DTM) is also commonly used. Because the term 'terrain' often implies attributes of a landscape other than the altitude of the landsurface, the term DEM is preferred for models containing only elevation data. Although DEMs were originally developed for modelling relief, they can of course be used to model the continuous variation of any other attribute Z over a two-dimensional surface.

The need for DEMs

Digital elevation models have many uses. Among the most important are the following:

1. Storage of elevation data for digital topographic maps in national databases.

2. Cut-and-fill problems in road design and other civil and military engineering projects.

3. Three-dimensional display of landforms for military purposes (weapon guidance systems, pilot train-

ing) and for landscape design and planning (landscape architecture).

4. For analysis of cross-country visibility (also for military and for landscape planning purposes).

5. For planning routes of roads, locations of dams, etc.

6. For statistical analysis and comparison of different kinds of terrain.

7. For computing slope maps, aspect maps, and slope profiles that can be used to prepare shaded relief maps, assist geomorphological studies, or estimate erosion and run-off.

8. As a background for displaying thematic information or for combining relief data with thematic data such as soils, land-use or vegetation.

9. Provide data for image simulation models of landscapes and landscape processes.

10. By replacing altitude by any other continuously varying attribute, the DEM can represent surfaces of travel time, cost, population, indices of visual beauty, levels of pollution, groundwater levels, and so on.

This chapter describes the various methods of representation that can be used for digital elevation models, how data are obtained (sources and sampling techniques), and finally the kinds of products that can be derived from them.

Methods of representing DEMs

The variation of surface elevation over an area can be modelled in many ways. DEMs can be represented either by mathematically defined surfaces or by point or line images as shown in Table 3.1 (adapted from Mark 1978).

Mathematical patch methods

Mathematical methods of surface fitting rely on continuous three-dimensional functions that are capable of representing complex forms with a very high degree of smoothness. The local methods split a complete surface into square cells or irregularly shaped patches

Table 3.1 Methods of representing terrain surfaces

A. Mathematical methods
    A.1 Global—Fourier series
                Multiquadratic polynomials
    A.2 Local—Regular patches
              Irregular patches

B. Image methods
B.1 Using point data
        Regular—uniform density
              —variable density
       Irregular—triangulation
              —proximal networks
    Critical features—peaks
              —pits
              —passes
              —boundaries
B.2 Using line data
        Horizontal slices (contours)
        Vertical slices (profiles)
        Critical lines
              —ridges
              —stream courses
              —shorelines
              —breaks in slope

Fig. 3.1 Contour plot made using patch methods. Patches with missing data can clearly be seen, as can the joins between the patches. (Courtesy Department of Landscape Architecture, Agricultural University, Wageningen.)

of roughly equal area and the surfaces are fitted to the point observations within the patch. Weighting functions are used to ensure that the surface patches match at the edges, though the surface does not always seem to be continuous in slope at the borders (Schut 1976). Mathematical functions using piecewise approximations have found little favour in cartography (Fig. 3.1 shows why) but they are widely used in computer-aided design systems for modelling complex surfaces. More recently, piecewise approximations have been used for interpolating surfaces showing the variation of groundwater or soil properties or other kinds of environmental data: these methods are compared with other interpolation techniques in Chapter 8.

Image methods

Line models. The most common line model of terrain is given by the set of contour lines that describe the hypsometric curve. Profiles are usually a derived product used for slope analysis, the construction of ortho-photomaps or for block diagrams. Because contours are drawn on most existing maps they are a ready source of data for digital terrain models and great efforts have been made to capture them automatically using scanners (see Chapter 4). This is in spite of arguments that digitizing existing contours produces poorer quality DEMs than direct photogrammetric measurements (e.g. Yoeli 1982). Unfortunately, digi-

tized contours are not especially suitable for computing slopes or for making shaded relief models and so they are usually converted to a point model such as a discrete altitude matrix (see below). Ceruti (1980) and Yoeli (1984) describe algorithms for interpolating contour lines to altitude matrices. Oswald and Raetzsch (1984) describe a system for generating discrete altitude matrices from sets of polygons representing contours that have been digitized either manually or by raster scanning supplemented by drainage and ridge lines. This system is known as 'The Graz Terrain Model' and operates in conjunction with the turn-key mapping system supplied by the Norwegian firm SYS-SCAN. This sytem can be considered to be represen-

we don't have SYSSCAN!

tative of modern methods for converting digitized contour envelopes to altitude matrices.

The Graz Terrain Model generates an altitude matrix in several steps. First, a grid of an appropriate cell size is overlaid on the digital image of the contour envelopes (contour polygons) and the ridge and drainage lines. All cells lying on or immediately next to a contour line are assigned the height value of that contour. All other cells are assigned a value of -1. These other cells are assigned a height value in the following step, which is a linear interpolation procedure working within rectangular subsets or windows of the raster database. Interpolation usually takes place along four search lines oriented N–S, E–W, NE–SW, and NW–SE. The interpolation proceeds by computing the local steepest slope for the window as a simple function of the difference between the heights of cells that already have a height value assigned. For each window the slopes are grouped in four classes. Beginning with the class of steepest slope, unassigned cells within the window are assigned a height; the procedure is repeated for the other slope classes excepting flat areas, which are computed separately after all steep parts of the DEM have been computed. Oswald and Raetzsch (1984) claim that this interpolation method, the 'sequential steepest slope algorithm' is a robust and useful technique. Contrary to reports by others (e.g. Clarke *et al.* 1982) they suggest that non-linear interpolation methods were 'utterly unsatisfactory'. Schut (1976) and Tempfli and Makarovic (1979) have also recently reviewed interpolation methods for DEMs.

Point models. (a) *Altitude matrices.* The most common form of DEM is the altitude matrix or regular rectangular grid that is obtained from quantitative measurements from stereoscopic aerial photographs made on analytical stereo-plotters such as the GESTALT GPM-II (Kelly *et al.* 1977). Alternatively, the altitude matrix can be produced by interpolation from irregularly or regularly spaced data points.

Because of the ease with which matrices can be handled in the computer, in particular in raster-based geographical information systems, the altitude matrix has become the most available form of DEM. Britain and the United States of America are completely covered by coarse matrices (grid cell sides of 63.5 m for the USA) derived from 1:250 000 scale topographic maps, and higher resolution matrices based on 1:50 000 or 1:25 000 maps and aerial photography are becoming increasingly available for these and other countries.

Although altitude matrices are useful for calculating contours, slope angles and aspects, hill shading, and automatic basin delineation (see below), the regular grid system is not without its disadvantages. These disadvantages are:

(a) the large amount of data redundancy in areas of uniform terrain;

(b) the inability to adapt to areas of differing relief complexity without changing the grid size;

(c) the exaggerated emphasis along the axes of the grid for certain kinds of computation such as line of sight calculations.

The problem of data redundancy when sampling has been largely solved by the practice of 'progressive sampling' (Makarovic 1973) in which stereo photographs are automatically scanned at grids of increasing fineness in areas of complex relief (see next section). The data redundancy persists in data storage, however, because the continuously changing altitude surface cannot be coded easily in any of the compact forms for storing rasterized data that can be used with choropleth maps (see Chapter 2). As with all grid cell data structures, the altitude matrix may be too coarse to be able to represent all the critical features of terrain such as peaks, pits, passes, ridge lines, and stream courses. The misrepresentation of these features may lead to problems when attempting quantitative geomorphometric analyses. The orientation of the axes allows all computations along bearings parallel to the grid lines to be reduced to a simple row or column search, while computations at other angles require trigonometric calculations to locate the correct distances and angles. Nevertheless, in spite of these disadvantages, the altitude matrix is the most easily obtainable form of DEM.

Irregularly spaced point samples can be used in two ways to generate a DEM. The first is to overlay a regular grid over the points and then use an interpolation technique to generate a derived altitude matrix. Interpolation techniques can also be used to generate a finer matrix from a coarser one, though naturally, not without loss of information. The second method is to use the data on the irregularly spaced points as the basis of a system of triangulation.

(b) *The Triangulated Irregular Network* (TIN). The Triangulated Irregular Network (or TIN) is a system designed by Peuker and his co-workers (Peuker *et al.* 1978) for digital elevation modelling that avoids the redundancies of the altitude matrix and which at the same time would also be more efficient for many types of computation (such as slope) than systems that are based only on digitized contours. A TIN is a terrain model that uses a sheet of continuous, connected triangular facets based on a Delaunay triangulation of irregularly spaced nodes or observation points (Fig. 3.2). Unlike the altitude matrices, the TIN allows extra information to be gathered in areas of complex relief without the need for huge amounts of redundant data to be gathered from areas of simple relief. Consequently, the data capture process for a TIN can specifically follow ridges, stream lines, and other important topological features that can be digitized to the accuracy required.

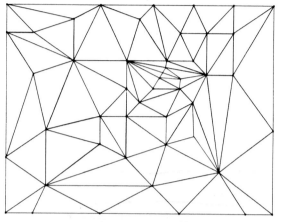

Fig. 3.2 An example of a triangulated irregular network structure for a DEM based on a Delaunay Triangulation.

The TIN model is a vector topological structure similar in concept to the fully topologically defined structures for representing polygon networks (Chapter 2) with the exception that the TIN does not have to make provision for islands or holes. The TIN model regards the nodes of the network as primary entities in the database. The topological relations are built into the database by constructing pointers from each node to each of its neighbouring nodes. The neighbour list is sorted clockwise around each node starting at north. The world outside the area modelled by the TIN is represented by a dummy node on the 'reverse side' of the topological sphere on to which the TIN is projected. This dummy node assists with describing the topology of the border points and simplifies their processing.

Figure 3.3 shows a part of the network data structure used to define a TIN. The figure shows the details for three nodes and two triangles at the edge of an area. The database consists of three sets of records called a node list, a pointer list and a trilist (triangle list). The node list consist of records identifying each node and containing its coordinates, the number of neighbouring nodes and the start location of the identifiers of these neighbouring nodes in the pointer list. Nodes on the edge of the area have a dummy pointer set to −32 000 to indicate that they border the outside world.

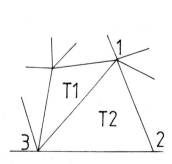

Fig. 3.3 Data structure of a TIN (detail).

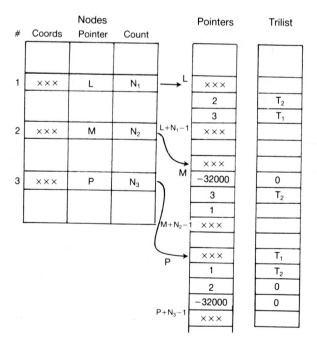

Because the node list and pointer list contain all the essential altitude information and linkages they are sufficient for many applications. For other applications, such as slope mapping, hill shading or associating other attributes with the triangles, it is necessary to be able to reference the triangle directly. This is done by using the trilist to associate each directed edge with the triangle to its right. In Fig. 3.3., triangle T2 is associated with three directed edges held in the pointer list, namely from node 1 to 2, from node 2 to 3 and from node 3 to 1.

Peuker *et al.* (1978) have demonstrated that the TIN structure can be built up from data captured by manual digitizing or from automated point selection and triangulation of dense raster data gathered by automated orthophoto machines. They have also shown that the TIN structure can be used to generate slope maps, maps showing shaded relief, contour maps, profiles, horizons, block diagrams (e.g. Fig. 3.4) and line of sight maps, though the final map images retain an imprint of the Delaunay triangulation. Information about surface cover can be incorporated by overlaying and intersecting the TIN structure with the topological polygon structure used for many thematic maps of discrete variables. The TIN structure has been adopted for at least one commercially available geographical information system.

Recently Dutton (1984) has proposed an interesting alternative compact method for modelling planetary relief based on a recursive tesselation (tiling) of a regular octahedron or icosahedron into equilateral triangular facets. The method is known as the Geodesic Elevation Model of Planetary Relief because it attempts to bring the whole of the earth's surface into one system. Horizontal coordinates are implicit in the hierarchy of nested triangles and only elevations are stored, using single bit flags to quantize height changes. It is claimed that an entire terrain can be coded using less than one bit of data for each triangular facet.

Data sources and sampling methods for DEMs

Data about the elevation of the earth's surface are usually obtained from stereoscopic aerial photographs using suitable photogrammetric instruments. Alternatively, data may be obtained from ground survey, from sonar or from radar scanning devices.

Makarovic (1976) distinguishes several methods of photogrammetric sampling for DEMs. Selective sampling is when sample points are selected prior to or during the sampling process, adaptive sampling is

CANOE VALLEY

(a)

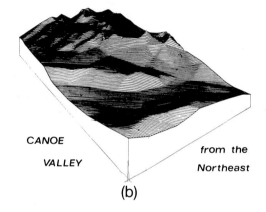

CANOE VALLEY   from the Northeast

(b)

Fig. 3.4 Contour map and block diagram of Canoe Valley generated from a TIN elevation model. (Courtesy T. Poiker.)

when redundant sample points may be rejected during the sampling process on the grounds that they carry too little extra information. Progressive sampling is when sampling and data analysis are carried out together, the results of the data analysis dictating how the sampling should proceed. Sampling can be manual—i.e. a human operator guides the stereoplotter. This is a slow process and liable to error. Semi-automatic systems have been developed to guide the operator and these result in improved speeds and accuracy; they are considered to be better than fully automated systems, which though fast, may be insufficiently accurate.

Sampling may proceed in various modes, depending on the product required. Purposive sampling is carried out to digitize contour lines, form lines, profiles, and morphological lines. For many purposes, however, a more general DEM based on an altitude matrix is required, and so area sampling is carried out, usually based on a regular or irregular grid. In this respect, sampling aerial photographs for spot heights does not differ greatly from the sampling techniques used for sampling any other spatial property (e.g. random, stratified random, or regular grid—see Ayeni 1982, Cochran 1963, or Ripley 1981). With elevation as expressed on aerial photographs, however, we have the distinct advantage that the operator can see when a sampling point is returning useful information or not. A regular sampling grid has a low adaptability to the scale of the variation of the surface; in areas of low variation too many points may be sampled, and in areas of large variation the number of sample points may be too small. If the operator is given the freedom to make observations at will, the sampling can be highly subjective. Makarovic (1973) has proposed a method called 'progressive sampling' that provides an objective and automatable method for sampling terrain of varying complexity in order to produce an altitude matrix.

Progressive sampling involves a series of successive runs, beginning first with a coarse grid, and then proceeding to grids of higher densities (Fig. 3.5). The grid density is doubled on each successive sampling run, and the points to be sampled are determined by a computer analysis of the data obtained on the preceding run.

The computer analysis proceeds as follows: a square patch of nine points on the coarsest grid is selected and the height differences between each adjacent pair of points along the rows and columns is calculated. The second differences are then calculated. These carry information about the terrain curvature. If the estimated curvature exceeds a certain threshold, then it is desirable to increase the sampling density and sample points at the next level of grid density on the next run.

Progressive sampling works well when there are no anomalous areas on the photographs, such as cloud regions, or man-made objects; it is best for regular or semi-regular terrain with horizontal, slightly tilted or smoothly undulating surfaces. Moderately rough terrain with distinct morphological features and some anomalous areas can be better handled by a modification of progressive sampling called composite sampling (Makarovic 1977). In composite sampling, abrupt steps in the terrain or the boundaries of natural or anomalous objects are first delineated by hand before sampling within these areas. Rough terrain types with many abrupt changes may not be efficiently covered by any semi-automated progressive or composite sampling approach, and all data may have to be gathered by selective sampling.

Finally, the data collected by progressive and composite sampling must be automatically converted to fill the whole altitude matrix uniformly (Makarovic 1984).

Data registration and geocoding

The coordinates obtained from digitizing stereo aerial photographs do not refer to any regular system of coordinates and have to be corrected for distortions caused by variations in altitude over the area, aircraft tilt, and so on. The data must be brought to a common coordinate system so that they can be drawn to an accurate scale and so that they can be interfaced with other spatial data from the same area. The simplest coordinate system is the regular square grid—this is suitable for small areas. For larger areas, certain approved cartographic projections such as the Universal Transverse Mercator Projection (UTM) are commonly used (see for example Maling 1973). Once data have been referenced to one coordinate system, they can be changed to any other by use of the appropriate mathematical transformation. For large sets of raster data this can be a very time-consuming operation even on

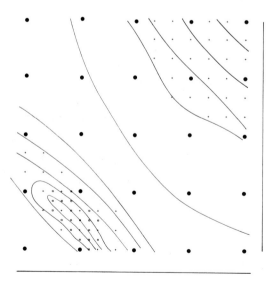

Fig. 3.5 In progressive sampling, the density of the sample grid is automatically adjusted to the complexity of the terrain.

large computers unless special hardware is available (e.g. Chapter 4, p. 68).

Products that can be derived from a DEM

Various derived products can be obtained from DEMs whether the latter are in the form of altitude matrices, sets of irregular point data or triangulated networks (Table 3.2).

Table 3.2 Products derived from DEMs

Block diagrams, profiles, and horizons
Volume estimation by numerical integration
Contour maps
Line of sight maps
Maps of slope, convexity, concavity, and aspect
Shaded relief maps
Drainage network and drainage basin delineation

Block diagrams, profiles, and horizons

The block diagram is one of the most familiar forms of digital terrain model because it is a visually appealing method of showing the variation of the value of a quantitative variable (not necessarily altitude) over an area. There are many standard programs such as SYMVU and ASPEX (Laboratory for Computer Graphics and Spatial Analysis 1978) available for rendering regular and irregular sets of *X*, *Y*, and *Z* data in three-dimensional or even stereoscopic form as line drawings or as shaded raster displays. Figures 3.6 to 3.8 present some examples. Block diagrams are useful for displaying many kinds of landscape information and can be used as a basis for landscape design or for simulating forest cover (e.g. Fig. 3.9 (a, b, c, d)): Ross and Evans 1984; Myklestad and Wagar 1977) or for displaying classified remotely sensed data (Plates 3–6). The computation of the block diagram usually requires that the observer specify a viewing point and scale factors for the vertical exaggeration. Inclusion of perspective in the computations improves the acceptability of the resulting model. The computations need to

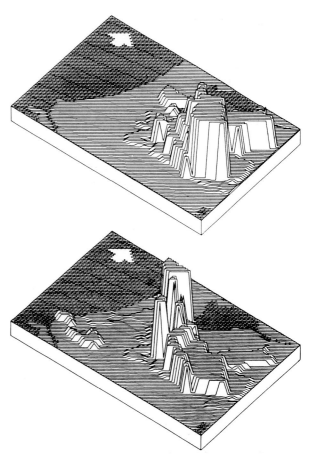

Fig. 3.7 Data from choropleth maps can also be represented by block diagrams. Here the source and destination areas of commuters in the 'Oostrand' research area of The Netherlands are displayed. (Courtesy H. Floor; source Floor and de Jong 1981).

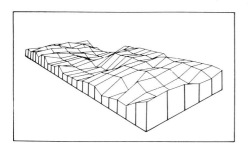

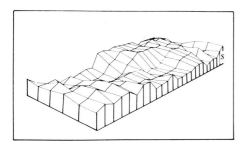

Fig. 3.6 Block diagram of first Principal Component Scores from a set of 6 × 25 soil profiles on a 125 m grid from Follonica, Italy. Data from Kilic (1979).

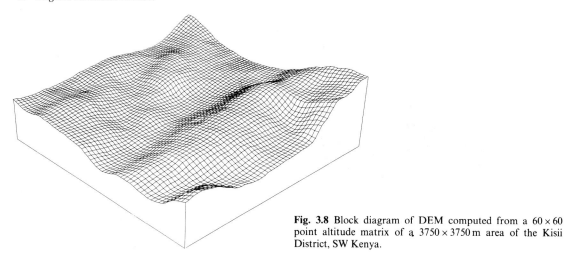

Fig. 3.8 Block diagram of DEM computed from a 60 × 60 point altitude matrix of a 3750 × 3750 m area of the Kisii District, SW Kenya.

include methods to solve the hidden line problem (Sutherland *et al.* 1974); Pavlidis (1982) gives a hidden line algorithm for quadtree data and a raster line scan hidden surface algorithm for solving the visibility problem while generating the display line by line.

Volume estimation in cut-and-fill problems

In many civil engineering problems it is necessary to model a landform in order to be able to estimate the volume of material needed to be removed or to be brought in to make the site ready for the proposed development. Accurate estimates of this material are required for accurate costing. The most usual procedure is to construct a DEM of the site by surveying

before the work begins, and then to create a second DEM that has been modified to show the proposed changes. The DEM obtained by differencing is that of the material removed or added, and its volume can be obtained by numerical integration.

Contour maps

Contour maps can easily be obtained from altitude matrices by reclassifying the cells into the appropriate height classes and printing the classes with different colours or grey tones (Fig. 3.10). The resulting contours, although considered sufficient for colour graphics displays and simple environmental mapping, are often considered to be too coarse for cartographic pur-

(a)

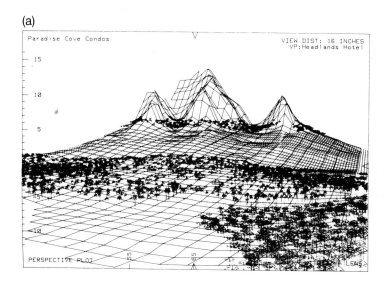

(b)

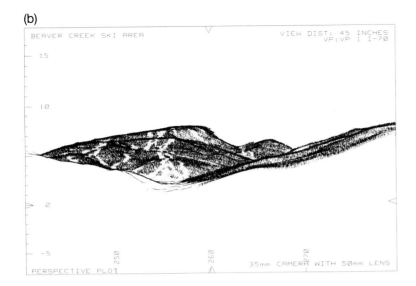

(c)

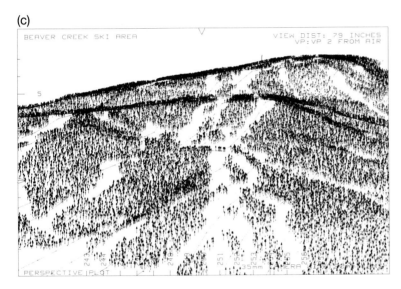

(d)

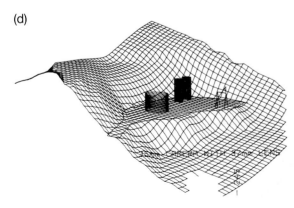

Fig. 3.9 Example of use of block diagrams for displaying landscape detail. (Courtesy R. Ross, U.S. Forest Service.) (a) Perspective simulation showing mixture of tropical hardwoods, coconut palms, pineapple plantations, and planned condominium structures as would be visible from the Headland House Hotel in Paradise Cove, Hawaii. (b) and (c) Perspective plots showing overview and detail of the Beaver Creek Ski Area in Central Colorado, USA (d) Simulation of oil and gas structures in the landscape.

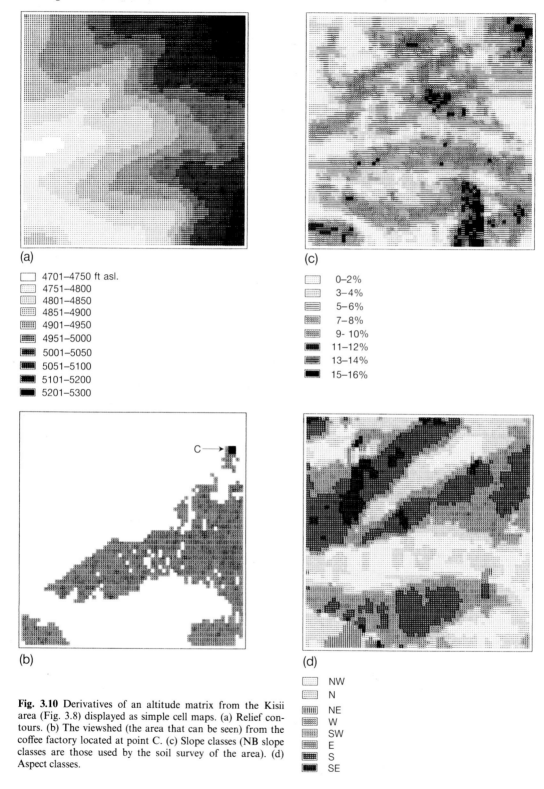

(a)

☐ 4701–4750 ft asl.
▫ 4751–4800
▫ 4801–4850
▦ 4851–4900
▦ 4901–4950
▦ 4951–5000
▦ 5001–5050
▦ 5051–5100
▦ 5101–5200
■ 5201–5300

(b)

(c)

▫ 0–2%
▫ 3–4%
▭ 5–6%
▦ 7–8%
▦ 9- 10%
■ 11–12%
▬ 13–14%
■ 15–16%

(d)

▫ NW
▫ N
▥ NE
▦ W
▦ SW
▦ E
■ S
■ SE

Fig. 3.10 Derivatives of an altitude matrix from the Kisii area (Fig. 3.8) displayed as simple cell maps. (a) Relief contours. (b) The viewshed (the area that can be seen) from the coffee factory located at point C. (c) Slope classes (NB slope classes are those used by the soil survey of the area). (d) Aspect classes.

poses and so special algorithms are used to thread the contour lines through the points on the altitude matrix. If the original data are irregularly or too widely spaced the contour threading may be preceded by interpolation to a still finer grid. The resulting lines are then drawn accurately with a pen plotter.

Contour maps are generated from TIN models by intersecting horizontal planes with the network. The secondary data structure of ridges and channels is used as a guide to the starting points of each contour envelope. The contour envelopes may need secondary processing to remove artifacts resulting from the edges of the triangles (Peuker *et al.* 1978).

Line of sight maps

The ability to determine the intervisibility of points in a landscape is important for military operations, planning microwave communication networks, and for recreational studies. Determining intervisibility from conventional contour maps is not easy because of the large number of profiles that must be extracted and compared.

Intervisibility maps can be prepared from altitude matrices and TINs using tracking procedures that are variants of the hidden line algorithms already mentioned. The site from which the viewshed needs to be calculated is identified on the DEM and rays are sent out from this point to all points in the model. Points

(cells) that are found not to be hidden by other cells are coded accordingly to give a simple map (Fig. 3.10(b)). Because DEMs are often encoded directly from aerial photographs, the heights recorded may not take into account features such as woods or buildings and the true landform, and the results may need to be interpreted with care. In some cases the heights of landscape elements may be built into a DEM in order to model their effect on intervisiblity in the landscape. Burrough and De Veer (1984) designed a method for mapping the visibility of high buildings in The Netherlands where the relief is so flat that it is totally subordinate to lines of trees and other large landscape elements. Their databases for mapping the visible landscape include estimated heights for all lines of trees and buildings. This information was used for mapping the visibility of existing high buildings and for estimating the areas where planned new buildings would be visible (Figs 3.11–3.13).

Maps of slope, convexity, concavity, and aspect

Before digital elevation models were available, geomorphologists adopted a wide variety of qualitative and semi-quantitative techniques to describe and compare terrain (Evans 1980). Quantitative analysis was made difficult by the huge labour of collecting data, either in the field or from aerial photographs. Once the elevation data have been gathered and transformed

A	high building
B, D	dense line elements taller than 1.5 m
C, E	observer
H	height of building A
h	height of line element B
o	eye height of the observer (1.5 m)
T	topographic height of building A
t	topographic height of element B
tw	topographic height of observer C
V, V^1	zones with visual impact
S, S^1	zones with no visual impact (shadow)

Length of path where
building cannot be seen
$$S = \frac{[V \times (h+t) - (0+tw)]}{[(H+T) - (h+t)]}$$

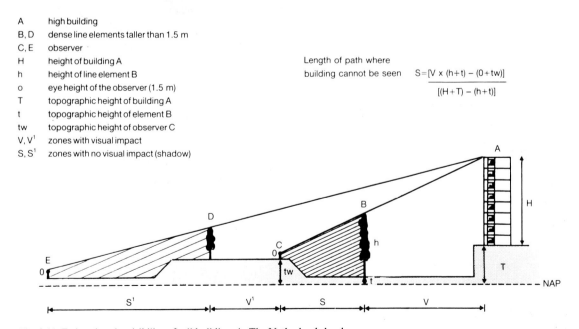

Fig. 3.11 Estimating the visibility of tall buildings in The Netherlands landscape.

's-GRAVENHAGE LANDSCAPE STUDY

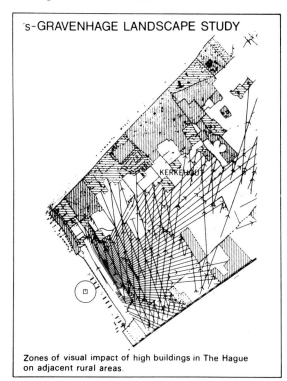

KERKEHOUT

Zones of visual impact of high buildings in The Hague
on adjacent rural areas.

Fig. 3.12 Estimating zones in rural fringe area north-west of
The Hague where high buildings can be seen (Courtesy The
Netherlands Soil Survey Institute). The radial shading shows
areas from which high buildings just outside the mapped area
can be seen.

into an altitude matrix or a TIN, several standard
procedures suffice to allow production of maps showing the slope and other features of the terrain.

Slope is defined by a plane tangent to the surface as
modelled by the DEM at any given point and comprises two components namely, *gradient*, the maximum rate of change of altitude, and *aspect*, the compass direction of this maximum rate of change. The
terms just used follow the terminology of Evans
(1980); many authors use 'slope' to mean 'gradient' as
just defined (e.g. Peuker *et al.* 1978, Marks *et al.* 1984)
and 'exposure' for 'aspect' (e.g. Marks *et al.* 1984).
Gradient and aspect are sufficient for many purposes,
being the first two derivatives of the altitude surface
or hypsometric curve, but for geomorphological
analysis, the second differentials *convexity*—the rate of
change of slope, expressed as *plan convexity* and *profile
convexity*—and *concavity* (i.e. negative convexity) are
also useful (Evans 1980). Gradient is usually measured
in per cent or degrees, aspect in degrees (converted to
a compass bearing), while convexity is measured in
degrees per unit of distance (e.g. degrees per 100 m).

The derivatives of the hypsometric curve are usually
derived locally for each cell on the altitude matrix by
computations made within a 3×3 cell kernel or 'window' that is successively moved over the map (Fig.
3.14).

The gradient is given by

$$\tan G = [(\delta Z/\delta X)^2 + (\delta Z/\delta Y)^2]^{\frac{1}{2}} \qquad (3.1)$$

where Z is altitude and X and Y are the coordinate
axes.

The aspect is given by

$$\tan A = \frac{-\delta Z/\delta Y}{\delta Z/\delta X} \qquad (-\pi < A < \pi). \qquad (3.2)$$

The convexity and concavity are similarly defined.
Evans (1980) estimates gradient, aspect, convexity,
and concavity from a six-parameter quadratic equation fitted to the data in the kernel; the quadratic coefficients are determined without the use of least
squares, presumably to speed the calculations. Most
other authors, particularly those working in image
analysis, show most interest in gradient and aspect,
which are computed by finite differences. The simplest
finite difference estimate of gradient in the X direction
at point i, j is

$$[\delta Z/\delta X]_{i,j} = (Z_{i+1,j} - Z_{i-1,j})/2\delta x \qquad (3.3)$$

where δx is the distance between cell centres. (Note
that for comparisons along diagonals the $\sqrt{2}$ correction to δX should be applied!)

This estimator has the disadvantage that local errors
in terrain elevation contribute heavily to errors in
slope. A better estimator given by methods of numerical analysis (Horn 1981) is for the east–west gradient,

$$[\delta Z/\delta X]_{i,j} = [(Z_{i+1,j+1} + 2Z_{i+1,j} + Z_{i+1,j-1}) -$$
$$(Z_{i-1,j+1} + 2Z_{i-1,j} + Z_{i-1,j-1})]/8\delta x$$

and for the south–north gradient

$$[\delta Z/\delta Y]_{i,j} = [(Z_{i+1,j+1} + 2Z_{i,j+1} + Z_{i-1,j+1}) -$$
$$(Z_{i+1,j-1} + 2Z_{i,j-1} + Z_{i-1,j-1})]/8\delta y. \qquad (3.4)$$

Mapping slopes. After the appropriate derivative has
been calculated for each cell in the altitude matrix, the
results may need to be classified in order to display
them on a map. This is very often achieved by means
of a look-up table in which the appropriate classes and
their colour or grey scale representation have been
defined. The value in each cell is compared with the
look-up table, and the appropriate grey tone or colour

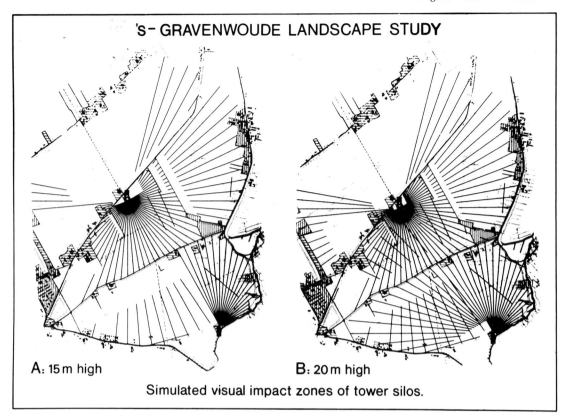

'S- GRAVENWOUDE LANDSCAPE STUDY

A: 15 m high   B: 20 m high

Simulated visual impact zones of tower silos.

Fig. 3.13 Simulation of the zones where future tower silos might be seen. (Courtesy The Netherlands Soil Survey Institute). The radial shading shows where the silos would be seen.

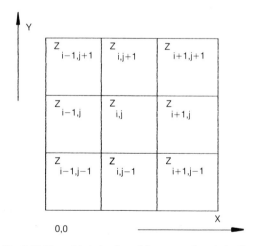

Fig. 3.14 Kernel (window) used for computing derivatives of altitude matrices.

is sent to the output device. Aspect maps usually have nine classes—one for each of the main compass directions N, NE, E, SE, S, SW, W, NW, and one for flat terrain. Gradient often varies differently in different regions and although adherents of standard classification systems usually want to apply uniform class definitions, the best maps are produced by calibrating the class limits to the mean and standard deviation of the frequency distribution at hand. Six classes, with class limits at the mean, the mean ± 0.6 standard deviations, the mean ± 1.2 standard deviations usually give very satisfactory results (Evans 1980). Evans also shows a map drawn by a pen plotter which displays both gradient and aspect by the length and direction of arrows.

It is a general feature of maps derived from altitude matrices that the images are more noisy than the original surface—in general, roughness increases with the order of the derivative. The images can be improved by drawing them as shaded or coloured maps on a laser plotter (Clarke *et al.* 1980) or the original derivatives can be smoothed using a local moving average before the results are plotted. It is unwise (Horn 1981), particularly in systems using integer arithmetic, to interpolate the altitude matrix to too fine a grid because the problem of quantization noise in the data (rounding off) may lead to numerical problems when estimating the slopes. If necessary, the output could be smoothed by interpolating between the results obtained on the original grid and displaying them on a finer grid.

Gradient maps are prepared from TIN DEMs by computing the slope for each triangular facet separately and then shading the facet according to the gradient class.

Shaded relief maps

Cartographers have developed many techniques for improving the visual qualities of maps, particularly with respect to portraying relief differences in hilly and mountainous areas. One of the most successful of these is the method of relief shading that was developed largely by the Austrian and Swiss schools of cartography and which has its roots in chiaroscuro, the technique developed by Renaissance artists for using light and shade to portray three-dimensional objects. These hand methods relied on hand shading and airbrush techniques to produce the effect desired; consequently the end product, though often visually very striking, was very expensive and was very dependent on the skills of the cartographer who, one suspects, was often also something of a mountaineer.

As digital maps became a possibility, many cartographers realized that it might be possible to produce shaded relief maps automatically, accurately, and reproducibly. Horn (1981) has given an extensive and thorough review of the developments and methods that have been tried.

The principle of automated shaded relief mapping is based on a model of what the terrain might look like were it to be made of an ideal material, illuminated from a given position. The final results (e.g. Fig. 3.15) resemble an aerial photograph because of the use of grey scales and continuous tone techniques for portrayal, but the shaded relief map computed from an altitude matrix differs from aerial photographs in many ways. First, the shaded relief map does not display terrain cover, only the digitized land surface. Second, the light source is usually chosen as being at an angle of 45° above the horizon in the north-west, a position that has much more to do with human faculties for perception than with astronomical reality. Third, the terrain model is usually smoothed and

generalized because of the data gathering process and will not show fine details present in the aerial photograph.

The shaded relief map can be produced very simply. All that is required are the estimates of the orientation of a given surface element (i.e. the components of slope) and a model of how the surface element will reflect light when illuminated by a light source placed 45° high to the north-west. The apparent brightness of a surface element depends largely on its orientation with respect to the light source and also on the material. Glossy surfaces will reflect more light than porous or matt surfaces. Most discussion in the development of computed shaded relief maps seems to have been generated by the problem of how to estimate reflectance (Horn 1981).

According to Horn (1981), the following method is sufficient to generate shaded relief maps of reasonable quality. The first step is to compute the slopes p, q at each cell in the x (east–west) and y (south–north) directions, as given in eqn (3.4) above. These values are then converted to a reflectance value using an appropriate 'reflectance map'. This is a graph relating reflectance to the slopes p, q for the given reflectance model used. Horn suggests that the following formulations for reflectance give good results:

(i) $R(p, q) = \frac{1}{2} + \frac{1}{2}(p' + a)/b$ (3.5)

where $p' = (p_0 p + q_0 q)/\sqrt{(p^2{}_0 + q^2{}_0)}$ is the slope in the direction away from the light source. For a light source in the 'standard cartographic position' (45° NW), $p_0 = 1/\sqrt{2}$ and $q_0 = -1/\sqrt{2}$. The parameters a and b allow the choice of grey values for horizontal surfaces and the rate of change of grey with surface inclination: $a = 0$, and $b = 1/\sqrt{2}$ are recommended.

(ii) $R(p, q) = \frac{1}{2} + \frac{1}{2}(p' + a)/\sqrt{(b^2 + (p' + a)^2)}$ (3.6)

maps all possible slopes in the range 0–1.

Some formulations for reflectance are computationally complex and it may be more efficient to create a look-up table for converting slopes to reflectance. The reflectance value for each cell is then converted to a grey or colour scale and sent to the output device (e.g. Fig. 3.15). The computations for shaded relief are not complex and do not require large memories, except for the display, because all calculations proceed using no more data from the altitude matrix than is necessary to fill the kernel.

Shaded relief maps are produced from TIN DEMs in a similar way to that described above, with the exception that the reflectance is determined for each triangular facet instead of every cell. The facets are

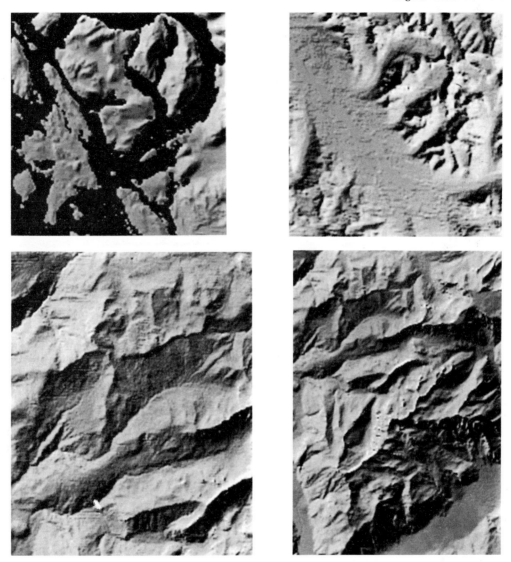

Fig. 3.15 Shaded relief maps produced from dense altitude matrices using a high quality film printer. (Courtesy B. K. Horn, Massachusetts Institute of Technology. Original data: K. Brassel, Zurich © I.E.E.E.)

shaded by hatching the triangles with parallel lines oriented along the surface gradient whose separation varies with the intensity of the reflected light. The results strongly retain the structure of the triangular net and in the author's opinion give less realistic images than those produced from altitude matrices, though this is largely dependent on both the resolution of the database and the output device.

Applications of shaded relief maps

Shaded relief maps can be extremely useful by them-

selves for presenting a single image of terrain in which the three-dimensional aspects are accurately portrayed. Not only have they been extremely useful for giving three-dimensional images of the bodies of the solar system, they are finding a growing application in quantitative landform analysis. When used in combination with thematic information they can greatly enhance the realism of the final map in a way that was impossible before computers were available.

The technique of overlaying thematic information from satellite imagery or rasterized thematic maps onto shaded relief maps is available in several commercial GIS packages now, but was developed initially by Dennis White of the Laboratory of Computer Graphics in Harvard. White used a display device that was capable of displaying an array of 512×512 pixels using eight-bit planes (see Chapter 4, output devices). His experimental program IMAGO MUNDI (White, personal communication) split the bit planes of the display device between the shaded grey information of the DEM and the coloured information from the thematic map (Plates 9–12). The resulting combined image is a pleasing combination that enhances the visual attractiveness and acceptability of the results of the data analyses.

Dutton (1982) has pointed out that the grey scale information obtained from slope alone is insufficient to convey to the viewer all he needs to be able to interpret the relief unambiguously. He has suggested that this can be improved by modifying the grey scales used for output to relate to elevation. In an experimental study, he showed that more realistic shaded relief images could be made on colour display terminals in which square sets of four pixels were used to code four separate parts of the information present for each cell of the altitude matrix. Dutton used the NW pixel of the four to code elevation in terms of shades of red; the SE codes reflectance in yellow; the NE slope in blue and the SW flatness in green. The results are an improvement on the simple relief map but although the computations are little more than for the simple shaded relief maps they are dependent on the user having a colour display device of sufficient resolution, otherwise the results are rather grainy.

Automated landform delineation from DEMs

When drainage and ridge lines have not been separately digitized it may be necessary or desirable to derive them from the altitude matrix using an automated procedure. For example, it may be necessary to outline a catchment area on a satellite image that has been overlaid on a DEM (Marks *et al.* 1984) so that the remotely sensed data can be related to a specific landscape unit. Proponents of TINs will claim that this model should contain all the necessary ridge and stream information, which should have been entered accurately when digitizing, and that all one needs to do is to recall the specific features required. On the other hand, 'altitude matrices' are used for other numerical quantities such as costs, travel times or concentrations, and it is useful to have general methods that can help delineate linear and area features. Also

if the DEM is initially in the form of an altitude matrix, automated methods of detecting ridges and streams are necessary to generate the complementary TIN.

Until recently, before drainage basins and drainage networks could be analysed quantitatively, they had to be laboriously copied from aerial photographs or printed topographical maps. Besides being tedious, this work inevitably led to an increase in the errors in the data. In areas of gentle relief in particular, it is not always easy to judge by eye where the boundary of a catchment should be. Also, even on very detailed topographical maps, the drainage network as represented by the drawn blue lines may seriously underestimate the actual pattern of all potential water courses. It could be useful, for example, to be able to separate water-carrying channels from dry channels at different times of the year, with the information about water coming from remote sensing and the channels from a DEM.

The biggest common problem in using altitude matrices for detecting linear features is that of 'pits' in the digital surface caused by noise. The noise may result from short range variations on the digitized land surface (e.g. resulting from a cleared patch in a forest or a mined area) or as a result of the quantization of the original data. Ridges and drainage courses may be missed because the grid is too coarse. Rounding errors may result in flattish areas having an incoherent drainage pattern.

As with the estimators of slope, pits can be detected using a kernel of 3×3 cells. A cell is defined as a 'pit' if its elevation is less than or equal to that of all of its eight neighbours (Mark 1984), i.e.

$$Z_{i,j} \leq Z_{i,j}(i = 1, 3; j = 1, 3; i \neq j) \qquad (3.7)$$

Finding out the point where a pit should overflow is not a trivial problem, so it is best to preprocess the DEM to remove pits before attempting a structural analysis.

Detecting ridges and stream lines

In order to detect ridges it is necessary to locate all convex-downward ($\cap$) places; for stream lines the reverse. Peuker and Douglas (1975) provide a simple, local algorithm that uses a kernel of four cells. This kernel is moved over the altitude matrix for each set of four cells at a time. To estimate the drainage network, the square with the highest elevation is flagged. To estimate the ridges, the square with the lowest elevation is flagged. At the end of the flagging process, the cells remaining unflagged represent the drainage or

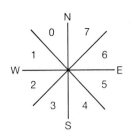

4 or 5	3 or 4	3 or 2
6 or 5	this point is in	1 or 2
6 or 7	0 or 7	0 or 1

Fig. 3.16 The estimation of aspect classes and the determination of which points relative to the centre point are 'up-stream' and thus 'in'.

ridge pattern respectively. The next stage of the processing is to join up the non-flagged cells to make a line pattern.

Although this simple algorithm works well, it is not based on any understanding of fluvial processes, and Mark (1984) decided to investigate whether for geomorphological studies it might not be better to have an algorithm that could follow the simulated flow of water over the DEM. Such an algorithm would resemble that defined by the Cauchy theorem, which states that the shortest distance between any point on a curved surface and the lowest point is the line of steepest descent. The relation to the Cauchy theorem is important because if the altitude surface is replaced by a cost surface, the line of steepest descent then represents a minimum cost path.

Algorithms of the type proposed by Mark require the outlet of the drainage network and the location of the starting cell. For each cell, except the outlet, its altitude is compared with its eight neighbours within the 3×3 kernel. The lowest neighbour is flagged, and the amount of water (which is expressed as a function of the number of cells traversed and the area of the cell) is carried over to that cell. The kernel is moved to the lowest neighbour, and the process is repeated. The drainage lines can be grey-scale coded according to the 'volume' of water that that passes over them.

Although this algorithm is realistic, it is computationally very demanding, both in terms of time and memory, and is approximately 20 times slower than the local Peuker and Douglas algorithm (Mark 1984). The method is very sensitive for pits in the data.

Determining the boundary of a catchment

This is a corollary to finding all ridges, but in this case only the boundaries of a single catchment need to be found in order to isolate it from the rest of the database. Marks *et al.*, (1984) have proposed the following algorithm. They start by computing the local gradient and aspect for every cell as described above. They then identify the outlet of the catchment interactively. The computer then searches for all cells that are 'upstream' of the catchment outlet and in the same catchment by using the following algorithm. As before, they work with a kernel of 3×3 cells. Starting at the outlet, they define a cell to be upstream of the centre point in the kernel if its aspect faces towards the centre point. The aspect is estimated as usual in eight quantized levels (Fig. 3.16).

The algorithm works through the database recursively, starting at the outlet. At each current 'in' point it checks the eight neighbours sequentially, allowing for grid edges and corners. If a neighbour has already been flagged as 'in' it is ignored, otherwise a neighbour that is found to be 'upstream' or nearly horizontal (within a threshold depending on the database) is chosen as the new centre for the kernel. The algorithm travels over the DEM until it finds a ridge or the edge of the data. It then backtracks and repeats until the whole basin has been marked. The method visits each cell once and ignores cells outside the current drainage basin.

Marks *et al.* present their algorithm in a form suitable for programming in the C language. They also note the problem with pits and pre-process the elevation data to remove them as much as possible. They present applications for the results of basin identification such as making catchment maps, comparing basin characteristics, and masking satellite data.

References

Ayeni, O. O. (1982). Optimum sampling for digital terrain models: a trend towards automation. *Photogramm. Engng Rem. Sens.* XLVIII (11), 1687–94

Burrough, P. A. and De Veer, A. A. (1984). Automated production of landscape maps for physical planning in The Netherlands. *Landsc. Plan.* 11, 205–26.

Ceruti, A. (1980). A method for drawing slope maps from contour maps by automatic data acquisition and processing. *Comput. Geosci.* 6, 289–97.

Clarke, J. I., Dewdney, J. C., Evans, I. S., Rhind, D. W. and Visvalingam, M. (1980). *People in Britain: a census atlas.* HMSO for OPCS, London.

Clarke, A. L., Green, A., and Loon, J. L. (1982). A contour specific interpolation algorithm for DEM generation. In *Proc. Symp. on Mathematical Models, Accuracy Aspects and Quality Control*, 7-11 June, Helsinki University of Technology, Finland, pp. 68-81. International Society for Photogrammetry and Remote Sensing (ISP).

Cochran, W. G. (1963). *Sampling techniques* (2nd edn). Wiley, New York.

Dutton, G. (1982). Land alive. *Perspect. Comput.* (IBM) **2** (1), 26-39.

——(1984) Geodesic modelling of planetary relief. *Cartographica* **21**, 188-207.

Evans, I. S. (1980). An integrated system of terrain analysis and slope mapping. *Z. Geomorphol. Suppl.* **36**, 274-95.

Floor, H. and de Jong, T. (1981). Ontwikkling en toetsing van een woonallocatiemodel. *Utrechtse Geografische Studies 22.* Geografisch Instituut, Rijksuniversiteit, Utrecht, The Netherlands.

Horn, B. K. P., (1981). Hill shading and the reflectance map. *Proc. IEEE* **69** (1), 14-47.

Kelly, R. E., McConnell, P. R. H., and Mildenberger, S. J. (1977). The Gestalt photomapping system. *Photogramm. Engng Rem. Sens.* **43**, (11), 1407-17.

Kilic, M. (1979). Soil science and water management. Unpublished M.Sc. thesis, Agricultural University, Wageningen.

Laboratory for Computer Graphics and Spatial Analysis (1978). User's manuals for ASPEX and SYMVU.

Makarovic, B. (1973). Progressive sampling for digital terrain models. *ITCJ.* **1973-3**, 397-416.

——(1976). A digital terrain model system. *ITCJ.* **1976-1**, 57-83.

——(1977). Composite sampling for digital terrain models. *ITCJ.* **1977-3**, 406-33.

——(1984). Automated production of DTM data using digital off-line techniques. *ITCJ.* **1984-2**, 135-41.

Maling, D. H. (1973) *Coordinate systems and map projections.* George Phillip, London.

Mark, D. M. (1978). Concepts of data structure for digital terrain models. In *Proc. DTM Symp. American Society of Photogrammetry*-American Congress on Survey and Mapping, St Louis, Missouri, pp. 24-31.

——(1984). Automated detection of drainage networks from digital elevation models. *Cartographica* **21**, 168-178.

Marks, D., Dozier, J., and Frew, J. (1984). Automated basin delineation from digital elevation data. *GeoProcessing* **2**, 299-311.

Myklestad, E. and Wagar, J. A. (1977). PREVIEW: computer assistance for visual management of forested landscapes. *Landsc. Plan.* **4**, 313-32.

Oswald, H. and Raetzsch, H. (1984). A system for generation and display of digital elevation models. *GeoProcessing* **2**, 197-218.

Pavlidis, T. (1982). *Algorithms for graphics and image processing.* Springer-Verlag, Berlin.

Peuker, T. K., (1977). Data structures for digital terrain models: discussion and comparison. In *Proc. Advanced Study Symp. on Topological Data Structures for Geographic Information Systems*, Harvard University, Cambridge, Massachusetts.

——and Douglas, D. H. (1975). Detection of surface-specific points by local parallel processing of discrete terrain elevation data. *Comput. Graph. Image Process.* **4**, 375-87.

——Fowler, R. J., Little, J. J., and Mark, D. M. (1978). The triangulated irregular network. In *Proc. of the DTM Symp. American Society of Photogrammetry-American Congress on Survey and Mapping*, St Louis, Missouri, pp. 24-31.

Ripley, B., (1981). *Spatial statistics.* Wiley, New York.

Ross, R. and Evans, B. M. (1984). The development of visual resources management and computer aided design in the United States Forest Service. In *Computer-aided landscape design: principles and practice* (ed. B. M. Evans) pp. 85-105. The Landscape Institute, Scotland.

Schut, G. (1976). Review of interpolation methods for digital terrain models. In *Archives of the International Society for Photogrammetry*, 13th Congress, Helsinki, Finland. Vol. 21, Part 3. Also published in *Can. Surv.* **30**, 389-412.

Sutherland, I. E.. Sproull, R. F., and Schumacker, R. A. (1974). A characterisation of ten hidden-surface algorithms. *Comput. Surv.* **6**(1), 1-55.

Tempfli, K. and Makarovic, B. (1979). Transfer functions of interpolation methods. *GeoProcessing* **1**, 1-26.

Yoeli, P. (1982). Ueber digitale Geländemodelle und deren computergestützte kartographische und kartometrische Auswertung. *Vermess., Photogramm. Kulturtech.* **2/82**, 34-9.

——(1984). Cartographic contouring with computer and plotter. *Am. Cartogr.* **11**, 139-55.

4. Data Input, Verification, Storage, and Output

Data input

Data input is the operation of encoding the data and writing them to the database. The creation of a clean, digital database is a most important and complex task upon which the usefulness of the GIS depends. Two aspects of the data need to be considered separately for geographical information systems; these are first the positional or geographical data necessary to define where the graphic or cartographic features occur, and second, the associated attributes that record what the cartographic features represent. It is this ability to process the cartographic features in terms of their spatial and non-spatial attributes that is the main distinguishing criterion between automated cartography (where the non-spatial data relate mainly to colour, line type, symbolism, etc.) and geographical information processing (where the non-spatial data may record land use, soil properties, ownership, vegetation types, disease, and so on).

Data input to a geographical information system can be best described under three headings:

(a) entering the spatial data (digitizing);
(b) entering the non-spatial, associated attributes; and
(c) linking the spatial to the non-spatial data.

At each stage there should be necessary and proper data verification and checking procedures to ensure that the resultant database is as free as possible from error.

(a) *Entering the spatial data*

There is no single method of entering the spatial data to a GIS. Rather, there are several, mutually compatible methods that can be used singly or in combination. The choice of method is governed largely by the application, the available budget, and the type of data being input. The types of data encountered are existing maps, including field sheets and hand-drawn documents, aerial photographs, remotely-sensed data from satellite or airborne scanners, point-sample data

(e.g. soil profiles), and data from censuses or other surveys in which the spatial nature of the data is more implicit than explicit.

The actual method of data input is also dependent on the structure of the database of the geographical system. Although in an ideal system the user should not have to worry about whether the data are stored and processed in raster or vector form, such flexibility is still far from generally available, particularly in low-budget systems. So, the following discussion is couched in terms of various combinations of data input method and whether the database has a vector or grid data structure.

(i) *Manual input to a vector system*

The source data are envisaged as points, lines or areas. The coordinates of the data are obtained from the reference grid already on the map, or from reference to a graticule or overlaid grid. They can then be simply typed into a file or input to a program.

(ii) *Manual input to a grid system*

For a grid system, all points, lines, and areas are envisaged as sets of cells. The simplest, and most tedious, method of inputting the data is as follows. First, a grid cell (raster) size is chosen. Second, a transparent grid of that size is laid over the map. The value of a single map attribute for each cell is then written down and typed into a text file on the computer. For example, consider the following simple map to be input by gridding (Fig. 4.1). To enter this map in grid form, not only must we decide on the resolution of the grid (here 5 mm) but on how the various soil units will be coded. If the data are to be stored in an integer matrix, for example, it will first be necessary to replace the As, Bs, and Cs of the original legend by numbers. It will also be necessary, either implicitly or explicitly, to designate the gridded area outside the mapped area of interest in such a way as to distinguish it from the map. These numbers used to represent the mapped units can be thought of as colours or grey shades, but

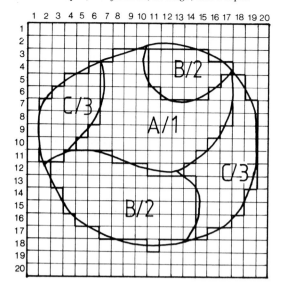

Fig. 4.1 Digitizing a simple map by grid overlay. A,B,C, original map codes; 1,2,3 integer representation of these codes.

they could represent the value of any other spatial property.

Once the grid resolution and encoding system has been decided on, each cell must be separately recorded and entered. This is usually done on a row-by-row basis, beginning at the top left hand corner, and working down the map. In our example, the rows would read as follows:

Column	1 2 3 4 5 6 7 8 9	1 1 1 1 1 1 1 1 1 1 2 0 1 2 3 4 5 6 7 8 9 0
Row		
1	0 0 0 0 0 0 0 0 0	0 0 0 0 0 0 0 0 0 0 0
2	0 0 0 0 0 0 0 0 0	0 0 0 0 0 0 0 0 0 0 0
3	0 0 0 0 0 0 0 1 1	1 2 2 2 2 2 0 0 0 0 0
4	0 0 0 0 0 3 1 1 1	1 2 2 2 2 2 2 2 0 0 0
5	0 0 0 3 3 3 1 1 1	1 2 2 2 2 2 2 1 3 0 0
6	0 0 3 3 3 3 3 1 1	1 1 2 2 2 2 1 1 3 0 0
7	0 3 3 3 3 3 1 1 1	1 1 1 1 1 1 1 1 3 3 0
8	0 3 3 3 3 3 1 1 1	1 1 1 1 1 1 1 1 3 3 0
9	0 3 3 3 3 1 1 1 1	1 1 1 1 1 1 1 3 3 3 0
10	0 3 3 3 1 1 1 1 1	1 1 1 1 1 1 3 3 3 3 0
11	0 3 3 2 2 2 2 1 1	1 1 1 1 1 3 3 3 3 3 0
12	0 0 2 2 2 2 2 2 2	2 1 1 1 3 3 3 3 3 3 0
13	0 0 2 2 2 2 2 2 2	2 2 2 2 2 3 3 3 3 3 0
14	0 0 0 2 2 2 2 2 2	2 2 2 2 2 2 3 3 3 3 0 0
15	0 0 0 2 2 2 2 2 2	2 2 2 2 2 2 3 3 3 3 0 0
16	0 0 0 0 2 2 2 2 2	2 2 2 2 2 2 3 3 3 0 0 0
17	0 0 0 0 0 2 2 2 2	2 2 2 2 2 3 0 0 0 0 0
18	0 0 0 0 0 0 0 0 0	2 0 0 0 0 0 0 0 0 0 0
19	0 0 0 0 0 0 0 0 0	0 0 0 0 0 0 0 0 0 0 0
20	0 0 0 0 0 0 0 0 0	0 0 0 0 0 0 0 0 0 0 0

These data could be typed into a text file, which could be examined for errors, and if necessary, edited interactively before the file was read into the GIS. The reader will note two important procedural problems. The first is that the accuracy of the representation is directly dependent on grid cell size; we shall return to this problem of accuracy in Chapter 6. The second is that of the sheer volume of the data. In the example, 400 numbers had to be entered to represent the map in a grid cell size of *c.* 5 mm. The data volumes are inversely proportional to the square of the cell size. For example, consider a grid encoding of a soil map measuring some 60 × 40 cm at a resolution (cell size) of 0.5 mm. 960 000 cells must be encoded, which, using 2 byte per integer, requires almost 2 Mbyte of memory. If all the data had to be punched onto cards in the format of row, column, and value, with, let us say a maximum of eight cells per card, 120 000 cards would be required: these would occupy a volume of more than a third of a cubic metre and would require an encoding time of perhaps 10 weeks! Fortunately, today there are better ways to input and encode data that allow large volumes of data to be entered and stored more easily.

Run-length codes. Considerable time can be saved when recording and entering grid data if they are input in the form of 'run-length codes'. The same idea can also be used to save considerable amounts of space in the database—see Chapter 2. Run-length coding relies on the fact that for many kinds of maps, particularly thematic (choropleth) maps, many adjacent cells have the same value. Consequently, it is only necessary to enter the data for each row, or run, specifying a cell value and the column numbers where that value begins and ends. For example, our simple map would be encoded as shown on p. 59: each 'run' is given by a triplet of numbers indicating starting column, end column and value.

In this example, the gridded map pattern has been encoded in 243 numbers instead of 400, a saving of nearly 40 per cent. Still more space can be saved if all 'empty' areas are assumed to be coded by zero (here 108 numbers or 27 per cent). Run-length coding is most effective at saving time and space for thematic maps having few separate delineations; the more complex the map, the less advantageous run length coding will be. For example, a simple digital elevation model (DEM—see Chapter 3) encoded in raster format permits each grid cell to have a unique value. In this case, the run-length codes would take up three times as much space as simple gridding.

ow	Column ranges (from, to, value)						
1	1,20,0						
2	1,20,0						
3	1, 7,0	8,10,1	11,15,2	16,20,0			
4	1, 5,0	6, 6,3	7,10,1	11,17,2	18,20,0		
5	1, 3,0	4, 6,3	7,10,1	11,16,2	17,17,1	18,18,3	19,20,0
6	1, 2,0	3, 6,3	7,11,1	12.15,2	16,17,1	18,18,3	19,20,0
7	1, 1,0	2, 6,3	7,17,1	18,19,3	20,20,0		
8	1, 1,0	2, 6,3	7,17,1	18,19,3	20,20,0		
9	1, 1,0	2, 5,3	6,16,1	17,19,3	20,20,0		
10	1, 1,0	2, 4,3	5,15,1	16,19,3	20,20,0		
11	1, 1,0	2, 3,3	4, 7,2	8,14,1	15,19,3	20,20,0	
12	1, 2,0	3,10,2	11,13,1	14,19,3	20,20,0		
13	1, 2,0	3,14,2	15,19,3	20,20,0			
14	1, 3,0	4,14,2	15,18,3	19,20,0			
15	1, 3,0	4,14,2	15,18,3	19,20,0			
16	1, 4,0	5,14,2	15,17,3	18,20,0			
17	1, 6,0	7,14,2	15,15,3	16,20,0			
18	1,10,0	11,11,2	12,20,0				
19	1,20,0						
20	1,20,0						

When gridded data are input in the form of run-length codes, they may be entered directly into a database, or they may first be transformed into a conventional grid file by a simple program. This program can also be used to carry out simple error checking, such as ensuring that the run-length codes do not miss any cells, or that they do not double-code a cell. If the gridded files are in ASCII format, they can be displayed on a screen and edited interactively by some of the better, modern interactive full-screen file editors.

(iii) *Digitizing*

The enormous labour of writing down coordinates and then typing them into a computer file can be greatly reduced by using a digitizer to encode the X and Y coordinates of the desired points, lines, areas or grid cells. A digitizer is an electronic or electromagnetic device consisting of a tablet upon which the map or document can be placed. Figure 4.2 displays various kinds of digitizers that have been or are currently in use. The most common types currently used for mapping and high quality graphics are either the electrical-orthogonal fine wire grid or the electrical–wave phase type. Both kinds of digitizer can be supplied in formats ranging from 11 × 11 in. (27 × 27 cm) to at least 40 × 60 in. (*c.* 1 × 1.5 m), as table or free-standing models, with or without backlighting. Generally speaking, the smaller digitizers are used to choose computer graphics commands from a menu; these digitizers are called tablets. Menu areas can also be defined on the larger tables used for digitizing maps and plans.

The coordinates of a point on the surface of the digitizer are sent to the computer by a hand-held mag-

netic pen, a simple device called a 'mouse' or a 'puck'. For mapping, where considerable accuracy is required, a puck consisting of a coil embedded in plastic with an accurately located window with cross-hairs is used. The coordinates of a point are digitized by placing the cross-hairs over it and pressing a control button on the puck.

Most pucks are equipped with at least one button for point digitizing, but it is now common practice to find manufacturers offering pucks with 4, 12, 16 or more additional buttons. These buttons can be used for additional program control, so that the operator can change from digitizing points to lines, for example, without having to look up, or to move the puck from the map. The buttons can also be used to add identifying labels to the points, lines or cells being digitized so that non-spatial data can later be associated with them.

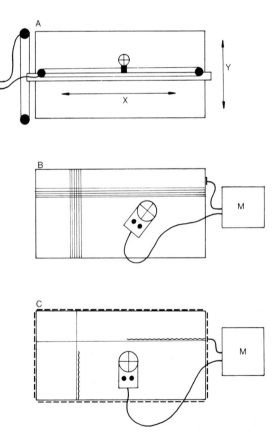

Fig. 4.2 Various kinds of digitizers. (a) Wires connected to digital encoders; (b) wire grid embedded in tablet top; (c) Electrical wave phase. M—microcomputer for control.

The principal aim of the digitizer is to input quickly and accurately the coordinates of points and bounding lines. The map to be digitized is secured to the digitizer surface with tape. The scale of the map must be entered to the computer, followed by two digitizes at the extreme left-hand bottom (X-min, Y-min) and right-hand top (X-max, Y-max) to define the area being used. The absolute coordinates of X-min, Y-min, and X-max, Y-max must then be typed in. All subsequent digitizes within these coordinates can then be automatically adjusted for alignment and scale. Lines can be digitized in two ways, known respectively as stream and point digitizing. In stream digitizing, the cursor is placed at the beginning of the line, a command is sent to the computer to start recording coordinates at either equal time intervals or equal intervals in the X or the Y direction and the operator moves the cursor along the line taking care to follow as closely as possible all the bends and undulations. At the end of a line or at a junction, the computer is told to stop accepting coordinates. The rate at which coordinates are recorded is dependent on the computer program, and for time digitizing, the density of points along the line is dependent on the speed with which the operator can trace the line. Usually, in stream digitizing, fewer coordinates will be recorded for straight line sections, where the operator can move fast, and more will be recorded for bends and other intricate parts. For equal intervals, too few points may be recorded in intricate places. The main disadvantage with stream digitizing is that if the operator does not work at the rate expected, too many coordinates may be recorded, which must later be filtered out or rejected, usually by a semi-automatic computer program (Douglas and Peuker 1973; Opheim 1982). For this reason, particularly when the operator has sufficient skill to be able to choose the best places to digitize, many persons prefer point digitizing. In this mode the operator must tell the computer to record every coordinate by pushing a button on the puck.

The digitizer can be used to input vector data, that is points, lines, and the boundaries of areas, by just entering the coordinates of these entities. In combination with the appropriate programs, the digitizer can also allow the operator to input text or special symbols at the places selected by the digitizers. The digitizer can also be used to enter data from the thematic maps as run-length codes that can be converted to full raster or vector format. The digitizing operator scans over one row of data (from left to right) at a time with the digitizer cursor with the Y-axis value held constant. Each time there is a change along the X-axis the operator records a code value for the area just passed through. The XY coordinates of the point are simultaneously recorded as a run length code. The amount of work involved is related to the resolution required. The conversion to a vector or full raster database is done by a post-processing program.

Vector-to-raster conversion. Today, it is unlikely that maps will be encoded cell-by-cell for systems that use a raster database. Instead, the digitizer is used to encode the polygons by digitizing the arcs (boundaries). These sets of arcs can be easily converted into a raster form at any resolution required, by using appropriate programs. Pavlidis (1982) provides a comprehensive discussion of these algorithms and of their advantages and disadvantages. Note that any conversion from a vector representation to a raster representation inevitably results in a loss of information because pixels on or near the digitized boundary may be misallocated or miscoded. This loss of accuracy is proportional to both the size of the grid cell and the wiggliness of the boundaries. The topic of information loss is discussed fully in Chapter 6.

Irrespective of the post-processing necessary to convert digitized data into a desired format, manual digitizing should never be done as a 'blind' exercise without the opportunity to see, and correct if necessary, the patterns of points and lines that are being sent to the computer (see pp. 68-9 on data editing). Digitizer accuracy is limited by the resolution of the digitizer itself and by the skill of the operator. There is no point in buying a digitizer more accurate than needed; for example, a digitizer of cartographic quality having a specified resolution of 0.001 in. (0.0254 mm) is a factor of 10 too accurate if one needs only to digitize hand-drawn boundaries that have been traced with a 0.4 mm pen. The actual resolution of a digitizer is never exactly that specified, but lies mostly within $\pm$ 1-2 of the specified resolution elements. Trials of digitizer accuracy suggest that the greatest deviations of a digitizer should not exceed $\pm$ 3-6 resolution elements (Johanssen 1979; OEEPE 1984). This means that for a digitizer having a resolution of 0.025 mm the deviation should not exceed ± 0.07-0.15 mm.

Greater locational errors are to be expected in stream digitizing than point digitizing simply because in stream digitizing the operator has less time to position the cursor accurately. Digitizing fatigue will also affect performance and it is not wise to spend more than 4h per day behind a digitizer if consistent work is to be maintained.

It is not necessary that the digitizer be connected to

the host computer. Digitizing is usually a task requiring little processing and can be done off-line using a microcomputer or personal computer for job control and data storage.

Once a map has been digitized it can be stored indefinitely on tape for future use. As computer cartography increases in importance, more and more standard topographic maps and thematic maps of soil, geology, land-use, etc. are being captured in digital form. It is becoming increasingly possible in many Western countries to obtain an already digitized copy of the map of interest. Digitizing, in spite of modern table digitizers, is time-consuming and enervating work: a drudge. It may take nearly as long to digitize a map accurately as it takes to draw it by hand. The average digitizing speed is approximately 10 cm min^{-1} and a detailed map may have as much as 200 m line detail. Put another way, it may take some 20–40 person hours to digitize the boundaries on a 60×40 cm size 1:50 000 soil map.

Contour maps, particularly those of mountainous terrain, may require much greater investments of time and labour, and more automated methods have been developed, as explained in the next section.

(iv) *Automated scanning*

Many organizations are not only concerned with producing maps in digital form as part of their normal production service, but they may have hundreds of existing, conventional map sheets, containing data of all kinds, that could be transformed into digital form. Proponents of digital maps and geographical information systems have often claimed that much of the information locked away in conventional maps could be made available for a wider range of users if the existing maps were in digital form. Possible users in this context range from the geomorphologist, who would be freed from having to trace stream patterns off the topographic survey map, to military organizations that wish to put digital terrain models into the computers of cruise missiles. While the geomorphologist is probably quite happy to trace his streams with a digitizer instead of a pencil and tracing paper, major governmental agencies have been forced to consider acquiring much quicker alternatives to manual digitizers for digitizing existing maps. These alternatives are to be found in the expensive pieces of equipment known as scanners.

Scanners can be separated into two types, those that scan the map in a raster mode, and those that can scan lines by following them directly. The former type is usually operated in conjunction with programs to convert the raster image to vector form when used for scanning topographic maps or the polygon outlines of soil or geological maps (see Chapter 2).

Raster scanners

The raster scanner works on the simple principle that a point on any part of a map may have one or two colours, black or white. The scanner incorporates a source of illumination (usually a low power laser) and a television camera with a high resolution lens. The camera may be equipped with a special sensor known as a charge-coupled device or CCD (see below). The scanner is mounted on rails and can be moved systematically backwards and forwards over the surface of the source document, as shown in Fig. 4.3. In some other versions, the scanner head moves in one direction only; movement in the other direction is achieved by mounting the document to be scanned on a rotating drum (Tomlinson 1967; Johannssen 1979), as shown in Fig. 4.4. The step size, which controls the cell or pixel size, is very small on modern, high-quality scanners (c. 25–50 μm); on some scanners the step size can be chosen from a range of sizes to suit the application (Leberland and Olson 1982). The resulting raster data is a huge number of pixels, registered as 'black' or 'white'. These data must be further processed to be turned into useful map images, such as contours, roads or cadastral details. To give the reader a little idea of the volumes of data generated, the scanned bit file of only the contours on a 30×50 cm topographic map sheet of a mountainous land such as Norway or Switzerland can occupy as much as two 2400-ft magnetic tapes, which at a density of 1600 BPI (bits per inch) represents some 92×10^6 bits of data. Although Leberland and Olson (1982) claim that the contours on a 1:50 000 topographic sheet can be scanned and vectorized in an hour, actual experience in production suggests that, depending on complexity, it can take from 0.2 to 8 h on a fast minicomputer such as a VAX-780 before the vector representation of the contours can be seen. Even with the best possible scanners and excellent software, the resulting digital image will be far from perfect, for it will contain all the smudges and defects of the original map plus mistakes caused by contours close together being run into fat lines instead of several thin lines, and so on (Fig. 4.5). The digital image will then need to be cleaned up interactively and contour heights must be added to reproduce the contour lines properly. The results of standard tests (OEEPE 1984) suggest that automated methods are 7 times faster than manual methods for contours, and at least twice as quick for planimetry.

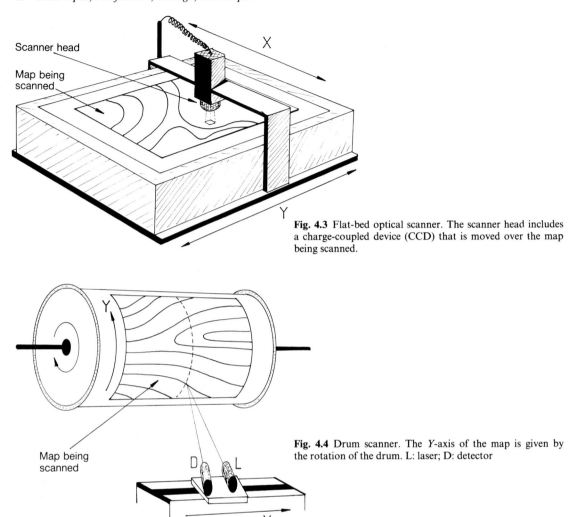

Scanner head

Map being scanned

X

Y

Fig. 4.3 Flat-bed optical scanner. The scanner head includes a charge-coupled device (CCD) that is moved over the map being scanned.

Y

Map being scanned

D   L

X

Fig. 4.4 Drum scanner. The *Y*-axis of the map is given by the rotation of the drum. L: laser; D: detector

Most maps that people want to scan contain not just black and white information, in the form of continuous lines, but also colours, text, dashed lines, and grey tones. The colour problem can be got around by scanning the colour print masters, which are usually black–white lithographics. Text can be reproduced as text images by most competent systems, but the author is unaware of any system that has yet been able to extract any intelligence from the scanned text. Dashed lines were once a problem, but this now seems to have been overcome by some companies that have invested in clever software that can look ahead or scan around to see if similar dashes occur nearby. By the same token, lines of different width on the same document are now less troublesome than a few years ago.

Charge-coupled devices

The CCD, where CCD stands for charge-coupled device, is an elegant semiconductor device that is able to translate the photons of light falling on its surface into counts of electrons (Almelio 1974). A typical CCD is very small, a square 10 × 10 mm with a resolution of up to 250 000 pixels (Kristian and Blouke 1982). The CCD can be fitted into the 35 mm camera and can be equipped with normal lens systems to produce a highly sensitive light collection instrument. Because the CCD actually counts photons the line information can be obtained by filtering out all signals that do not reach, or that exceed a certain level. The resulting line patterns can be vectorized, or transformed to another kind of raster structure for direct input to the GIS.

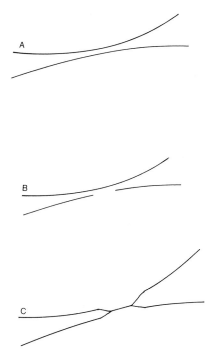

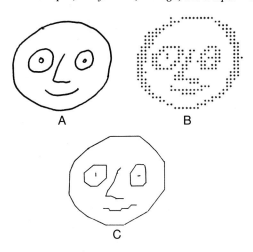

Fig. 4.6 Vectorizing a scanned image. (a) original image; (b) array of pixels resulting from the scanning; (c) fitted lines after vectorizing and 'weeding'.

Fig. 4.5 Examples of errors resulting from scanning and processing the close pair of contour lines (A).

Matching, scale correction, and alignment can be controlled through the use of fiducial marks on the documents which can themselves be scanned and processed automatically. The only complication is that these correction processes involve considerable computing that can best be done on specially developed image analysis equipment.

Raster-to-vector conversion

Raster-to-vector conversion algorithms are needed to convert arrays of pixels to line data. This capability is used to convert data from document scanners into text or lines, and also when raster data are output to a device such as a pen plotter. The output from a scanner consists often of a set of pixels that record the presence of an image (bit set), or no image (Fig. 4.6). The vectorizing process consists of threading a line through the resulting swarm of pixels, using what are collectively known as 'thinning' algorithms because the swarm of pixels is thinned to a line. Pavlidis (1982) provides a good introduction to the algorithms involved.

The resulting 'thinned' lines will probably contain many more coordinate pairs than is necessary (i.e. they

are overdefined) and so will take up exorbitant amounts of storage space. The excess coordinates can be removed using 'weeding' algorithms, the best known of which are by Douglas and Peuker (1973) and by Reuman and Witkam (1974). Recently, Opheim (1982) has published a new method that combines the best features of both these methods in an efficient way at a lower cost. The visual appearance of the resulting sets of straight line segments can be 'improved' by using B-splines (Chapter 8).

Vector scanners. The alternative to scanning lines using a raster device and then restoring the vector structure by using brute force computing is to attempt to scan line images directly. This is the approach developed and adopted by the English firm called Laserscan (Howman and Woodsford 1978). The Laserscan instruments are combined scanners and plotters that make use of clever optical and electronic methods to digitize lines from transparent documents, or to draw lines and text on diazo microfilm. The first version of the Laserscan, the HRD-1, had a screen digitizing area of 70 × 100 cm with 35 000 × 50 000 addressable points. The transparent copy of the map to be digitized is projected onto a screen in front of the operator. Using a light cursor, the operator guides a laser beam to the starting point of a line. The laser beam then follows the line until it arrives at a junction, or back at its starting point, as would happen with scanning a contour envelope. Once a line has been scanned, a second laser is used to 'paint out' the line on the screen by the principle of illuminating the familiar oil spot on parchment. The operator then guides the scanning laser to the next starting point, and so on. Before the scanning laser begins, the operator has the opportunity to attach a label to the line for subsequent additions of non-spatial attributes.

The system has the great advantage that the line scanning is almost instantaneous, and the scanned data are directly in a scale-correct vector format. The greatest disadvantages are that a great deal of operator control is essential for steering the laser at junctions, and that a transparent copy of the clean map needs to be made. If the original map is a field map, then one can better digitize it directly. Consequently, the Laserscan system has found most application for scanning contour envelopes that have already been accurately scribed and as a method for making high quality microfiche prints of completed maps.

Other types of map scanners. The scanners described above have been developed largely in response to demands to digitize quickly large volumes of complex, large-format, existing printed maps. To a certain extent, the digitizing of existing maps is only a problem for the transition period from conventional to fully digital cartography. Where new data are gathered it is only sensible to ensure that they are immediately recorded in digital form and at an appropriate level of resolution. For many thematic maps, for example, there is just no need to work at the high levels of accuracy demanded by large scale topographic sheets and engineering plans.

Video digitizers. Several simple instruments have been developed to capture boundaries interpreted from photographs or to rasterize a whole aerial photograph cheaply. They consist of a video camera connected to a 'framegrabber' (i.e. a microelectronic device) that turns an analogue television picture into a rasterized digital image. These simple video digitizers are being increasingly used to enter road and other line patterns from aerial photographs into image analysis systems used for processing remotely sensed data e.g. see Plates 1 and 2.

Analytical stereo plotters. The stereo plotter is the photogrammetric instrument used to record the levels and positions of contour lines directly from stereo pairs of aerial photographs. Originally, these instruments were manually operated; they were connected to a mechanical drawing table on which the contours, as seen by the operator through the optical system of the instrument, were drawn directly on paper. The first step in automating the data capture

from these instruments was to put electro-mechanical X, Y, and Z recorders on the mechanical drawing table and connect their output to a paper tape device. The stereo plotter was then immediately transformed into a three-dimensional digitizer. Since these first attempts, completely new stereo plotters have been developed in which not only are the raw X, Y, Z coordinates recorded electronically, but they can be processed for scale and cartographic distortions by an inbuilt microcomputer that writes the results into a file on a magnetic medium such as tape, floppy disk, or removable hard disk in a format for direct processing. These kinds of highly accurate stereo plotters are being used increasingly in topographic mapping agencies. They can be interfaced directly to integrated mapping systems (Hobbie 1984).

(v) Spatial data already in digital raster form

All satellite sensors and multispectral sensing devices used in aeroplanes for low-altitude surveys use scanners to form an electronic image of the terrain. These electronic images can be transmitted by radio to ground receiving stations or stored on magnetic media before being converted to visual images by a computer system.

The scanned data are retained in the form of pixels (picture elements). Each pixel has a value representing the amount of radiation within a given bandwidth received by the scanner from the area of the earth's surface covered by the pixel. This value can be represented visually by a grey scale or colour. Because each cell can only contain a single value, many scanners are equipped with sensors that are tuned to a range of carefully chosen wavelengths. For example, the scanners on the original LANDSAT 1 were tuned to four wavebands (Band 1, 0.5–0.6 μm; Band 2, 0.6–0.7 μm; Band 3, 0.7–0.8 μm; Band 4, 0.8–1.1 μm) in order to be able to record differences in water, vegetation, and rock.

The resolution, or the area covered by a single pixel, depends on the height of the sensor, the focal length of the lens or focusing system, the wavelength of the radiation, and other inherent characteristics of the sensor itself. Pixel sizes for terrain data vary from the non-square 80×80 m of LANDSAT 1 to a few centimetres for aeroplane-based high-resolution sensors: the reader is referred to the literature on remote sensing for further details (e.g. Swain and Davis 1978). Although scanned data from satellite and aeroplane sensors may be in pixel form, their format may not be compatible with the format of a given GIS and they may need various kinds of preprocessing (Nagy and Wagle 1979).

Preprocessing may involve adjusting the resolution, the pixel shape (both for skewness and squareness), and the cartographic projection in order to ensure topological compatibility with the database (Snijder 1978; Williamson 1977). One special problem, particularly with early, low resolution LANDSAT images, is in achieving good spatial alignment with topographic map data such as roads and boundaries. Although the latter can often be inferred from the LANDSAT images, their exact location often cannot be deduced because of the coarseness of the pixel size. Preprocessing may also involve several kinds of data reduction process such as inferring and classifying leaf area index, or land use, by combining data from several wavelengths via principal component or other transforms, and by semi-automated use of training algorithms. These kinds of processing are most commonly carried out inside the image analyser system that is also used to make the scanned images visible. The resulting mapped images would then be transferred to a more general GIS for use with other kinds of spatial data.

(vi) *Other sources of digital spatial data*

Interpolated data. Many investigations in soil science, hydrology, geology, and ecology rely on mathematical methods for interpolating the values of measured properties at unvisited points from observations taken at discrete (point) locations. The interpolations can be performed according to any of several methods (Chapter 8), and the results can be output either as a matrix of grid cells ('pixels') containing values of the property in question, or as sets of contour lines or boundaries.

Other data. Many other kinds of data that are used for geographical analyses within a GIS are not strictly spatially encoded, though they have a strong implicit spatial character. Examples are census data, lists of telephone numbers, numbers of schools in a town or district.

(b) *Entering the non-spatial associated attributes*

Non-spatial associated attributes (sometimes called feature codes) are those properties of a spatial entity that need to be handled in the geographical information system, but which are not of themselves spatial in kind. For example, a road can be digitized as a set of continuous pixels, or as a vector line entity. The road can be represented in the spatial part of the GIS by a certain colour, symbol or data location (overlay). Data about the kind of road (e.g. motorway or dirt track) can be included in the range of cartographic symbols

normally available. Once the user wishes also to record data about the width of the road, the type of surface, the construction method, the date of construction, the presence of manhole covers, water pipes, electricity lines, any specific traffic regulations, the estimated number of vehicles per hour, etc. all at once, then it is clear that providing all these data refer to a common spatial entity, they can be efficiently stored and processed apart from spatial data. By giving each type of data a common identifier they can be efficiently linked in any way desired. Similarly, for points and areas, whether displayed spatially in raster or vector format, associated spatial data referring to unique geographic entities or areas can be stored apart so that they can be processed easily.

(c) *Linking spatial and non-spatial data*

Although feature codes and identifiers can be attached to graphic entities directly on input, it is not efficient to enter large numbers of complex non-spatial attributes interactively. Linking the spatial data to the already digitized points, lines, and areas can better be done using a special program that requires only that the digital representations of the points, lines, and areas themselves carry unique identifiers. Both the identifier and the coordinates are thus stored in the database. Manual entering of simple identifiers as part of normal digitizing is easy and should not seriously slow down digitizing times, though it is not so easy to combine with stream digitizing.

For a map that has been produced by raster scanning, however, there is so far no way to read a unique identifier and automatically to associate it with the geographical entity. The attachment of unique identifiers must be done manually, usually by displaying the scanned map on an interactive work station and using a light pen or similar device to 'pick up' the graphical entities and attach the identifiers to them.

Unique identifiers can only be directly attached to graphic entities that can be generated directly in the particular computer system that is being used. For systems making use of polygon networks, however, the polygons must first be created (see Chapter 2). Once the polygons have been formed they can be given unique identifiers, either by interactive digitizing using an interactive work station, or by using 'point-in-polygon' algorithms to transfer identifier codes from already digitized points or text entities to the surrounding polygon.

Figure 4.7 summarizes the steps needed to digitize a set of boundaries and non-spatial attributes and link them together to form a topologically linked database

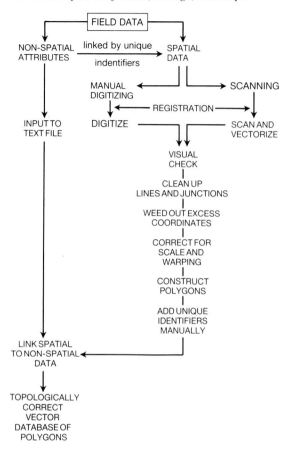

Fig. 4.7 Steps in creating a topologically correct vector polygon database.

of polygons. The particular set of steps will vary, depending on the type of mapping operation involved, on the volume of data to be processed, and on the availability or otherwise of scanners of the appropriate quality (see also Marble *et al.* 1984).

Once both the spatial and the non-spatial data have been input, the linkage operation provides an ideal chance to verify the quality of both spatial and non-spatial data. Screening routines can check that every graphic entity receives a single set of non-spatial data; they can also check that none of the spatial attributes exceed their expected range of values, or that nonsensical combinations of attributes or of attributes and geographical entities do not occur. All geographical entities not passing the screening test can be flagged so that the operator can quickly and easily repair the errors. Assigning contour heights to digitized contours is less difficult. The contour lines are displayed on an

interactive display screen, and the operator uses the cursor to draw a temporary straight line perpendicularly across a number of contours. The lowest and highest contours crossing the line get their heights manually and intermediate contour heights are assigned automatically (Leberl and Olson 1982).

Data verification, correction, and storage

Errors can arise during the encoding and input of spatial and non-spatial data. These errors can be grouped as follows:

1. spatial data are incomplete or double;
2. spatial data are in the wrong place;
3. spatial data are at the wrong scale;
4. spatial data are distorted;
5. spatial data are linked to the wrong non-spatial data;
6. the non-spatial data are incomplete.

Besides errors, the data may be overdefined, and may need to be reduced in volume. This commonly occurs with lines entered by stream digitizing or obtained from scanner input.

1. Incompleteness in the spatial data arises through omissions in the input of points, lines or cells in manually entered data. In scanned data the omissions are usually in the form of gaps between lines where the raster-vector conversion process has failed to join up all parts of a line. Similarly, the raster-vector conversion of scanned data can lead to the generation of unwanted 'spikes'. In manual digitizing, lines can be digitized more than once.

2. Mislocation of spatial data can range from minor placement errors to gross spatial errors. The former are usually the result of careless digitizing; the latter may be the result of origin or scale changes that have somehow occurred during digitizing, possibly as a result of hardware or software faults.

3. If all spatial data are at the wrong scale, then this is usually because the digitizing was done at the wrong scale. In vector systems, the scale can usually easily be changed by a simple multiplier.

4. The spatial data may be distorted because the base maps used for digitizing are not scale-correct. Most aerial photographs are not scale-correct over the whole of the image because of tilt of the aircraft, relief differences, and differences in distance to the lens from objects in different parts of the field. All paper maps suffer from paper stretch, which is usually greater in one direction than another. In addition, paper maps and field documents may contain random distortions

Plate 1

Plate 2

Plates 1 and 2 Overlaying a geological
interpretation of a LANDSAT image
correctly with the topographic map. The
latter has been digitized using a video
camera device. By varying the contrasts
of the two images a 'light table' effect has
been created. (Copyright/courtesy I^{2}S –
International Imaging Systems.)

Plate 3

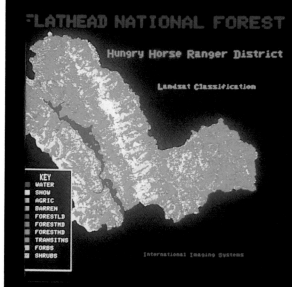

Plate 4

Plate 5

Plate 6

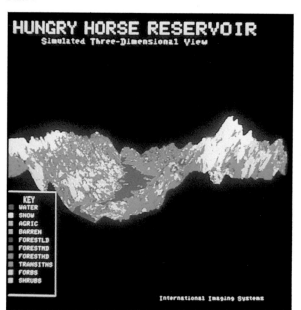

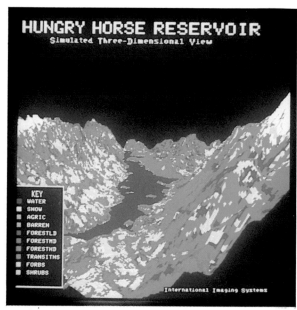

Plates 3 – 6 Land use classification of Hungry Horse reservoir in the Flathead National Forest, Montana, USA, showing superposition and projection of the thematic information on a digital elevation model. (Copyright/courtesy I²S – International Imaging Systems.)

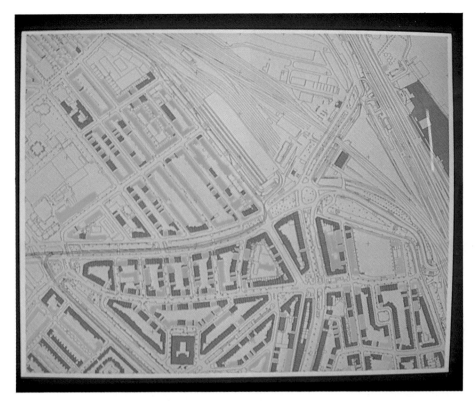

Plate 7 Very high quality raster image of part of the digital database of the City of Rotterdam showing utilities, cadastral information, and ownership details (in colours green and magenta). (Copyright/courtesy City of Rotterdam and the Computer Department, ITC, Enschede).

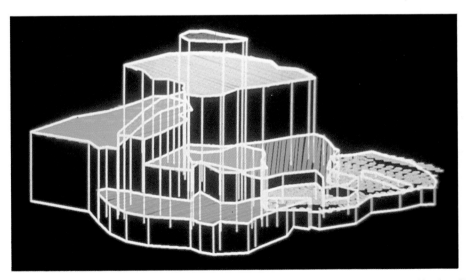

Plate 8 Three-dimensional view of a choropleth map revealing the 'stepped' character of this land use classification. Hidden line removal would greatly improve the appearance of this image. (Copyright/courtesy Computervision Europe, Rotterdam.)

Plate 9

Plate 10

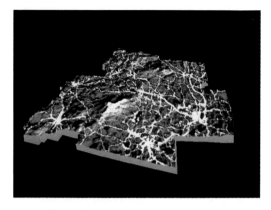

Plate 11

Plate 12

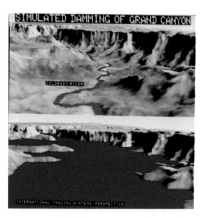

Plates 9–12 Images showing thematic information concerning the Monadnock area, New Hampshire, USA projected over a shaded relief image created from a digital elevation model. (Data Copyright/courtesy C. Steinitz and D. White, Laboratory for Computer Graphics, Harvard, Cambridge, Massachusetts – Plate 9 courtesy I²S, Plate 10 courtesy ERDAS.)

Plate 13 Three-dimensional image of the Grand Canyon obtained from LANDSAT data and a digital elevation model showing the present situation, and a simulation of the canyon dammed full of water. (Copyright/courtesy I²S – International Imaging Systems.)

Plate 14 Digital elevation model of Hungry Horse Reservoir showing trail lines superimposed on a digital elevation model. (Copyright/courtesy I²S – International Imaging Systems.)

as a result of having been exposed to rain, sunshine, coffee, beer or frequent folding.

Transformations from one coordinate system to another, for example, to the Universal Transverse Mercator (UTM), may be needed if the coordinate system of the database is different from that used in the input document or image.

5. Incorrect links between spatial and non-spatial data are usually the result of incorrect identification codes being entered to the spatial data during digitizing, or during the interactive 'touch identification' of polygons after scanning, vectorization, and polygon forming.

6. Non-spatial data can be incomplete or wrong because of typing errors or field encoding errors.

Table 4.1 lists the most common GIS capabilities for data maintenance and manipulation that are used for data verification and correction.

Rubber sheet transformation and warping

The idea behind these is that the original, faulty map can be thought of as an elastic sheet that can be stretched in all directions. This map is compared with an accurate base map and a number of points on the original map are linked by vectors to the correct positions on the base map (Fig. 4.8). The rubber sheeting algorithms then stretch and compress the original map until the linking vectors have shrunk to zero length and the tie points are registered with each other. It is then assumed that all the other points on the original map have been relocated correctly.

Rubber sheeting cannot be used for rasterized data because of the rigidity of the fixed grid and the structure of the data. Simple mathematical algorithms can

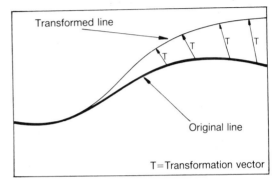

Fig. 4.8 Transformation vectors for 'rubber sheeting'.

Table 4.1 Common GIS capabilities for data maintenance and manipulation

ADD/DELETE/CHANGE	Interactive editing of the alignment, length, text, text font, and attributes of graphic entities (points, lines and areas as appropriate)
MOVE/ROTATE	Move an entity (point, line, polygon, or group of pixels) to a new position
STRETCH/RECTIFY	Adjust coordinates to fit a true base
TRANSFORM SCALE	Adjust coordinates to match a given scale
TRANSFORM PROJECTION	Adjust coordinates to match a given projection
ZOOM/WINDOW	Enlarge/reduce area of attention
CLIP	Cut out area of attention as a separate part
JOIN/EDGE MATCH	Join two or more adjacent maps ensuring continuity of line and text information across the join
POLYGON OVERLAY AND MERGE	Intersect two polygon networks to create a new polygon network
3-DIMENSIONAL PROJECTION	Create a three-dimensional view of the data (block diagram, usually with hidden line removal)
RASTER TO VECTOR	Convert (scanned) raster data to a set of lines (vectors)
VECTOR TO RASTER	Convert line and polygon data to pixels
GENERALIZATION AND SMOOTHING	Data reduction algorithms for changing data structures with scale (e.g. polygon to a point) Removal of excess coordinates in digitized lines
DATA RETRIEVAL AND REPORTING	Simple routines for counting items, reporting areas and perimeters, simple distances, etc. Simple Boolean search. Results are often written to a text file for further processing

be used for vector data but transforming or rotating raster data requires a different approach because any simple mathematically defined rubber sheeting means a distortion of the original grid.

The problem is solved by assuming that the gridded data are discrete samples from a continuous statistical surface. A new set of pixels is obtained by using an interpolation technique to convert data from the original array to the new. This process is known in image analysis terminology as 'convolution'. It is a very intensive computing problem because every output pixel must be addressed separately and have a value that is interpolated in some way from its neighbours. Consequently, warping or transforming large raster images can take very considerable amounts of computer time when done using standard FORTRAN or PASCAL software run on conventional computers. Recent technological developments have led to this process being speeded up many hundreds of times through the use of specially designed hardware (Adams *et al.* 1984). Adams and his colleagues report that their hardware board can rotate a 512 × 512 pixel image in less than 2 s compared with the tens of minutes or hours usually required on conventional computers.

The hardware warper has two separate processes. The first is the computation of the addresses of the output pixels relative to the input data matrix. The general equation for a first order warp (translation, rotation, scale) given by Adams *et al.* (1984) is:

$$u = a_0 + a_1 a_2 x + a_1 a_3 y$$
$$v = b_0 + b_1 b_2 x + b_1 b_3 y \qquad (4.1)$$

where x, y are the original pixel coordinates, u, v are the new coordinates, a_0 and b_0 are translation values, a_1 and b_1 are x and y scale values respectively, and a_2, b_2 and a_3, b_3 are dependent on the angle of rotation θ as given by

$$a_2 = \cos\theta \qquad b_2 = -\sin\theta$$
$$a_3 = \sin\theta \qquad b_3 = \cos\theta. \qquad (4.2)$$

For warps that are not coplanar, such as in the problem of fitting satellite imagery to the curved surface of the earth to match a conventional map projection such as the Universal Transverse Mercator, higher order warps must be used.

Interpolation can be achieved by several local techniques. The simplest, and most limited, is to interpolate the new pixel cell from its closest neighbour. A better alternative is a bilinear interpolater in which the new value is computed from the four input pixels surrounding the output pixel (Fig. 4.9). The best interpolater is probably the cubic convolution (Fig. 4.10)

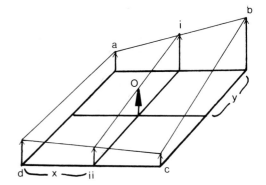

Fig. 4.9 Bilinear interpolation from four input pixels (a–d) to compute output value (O).

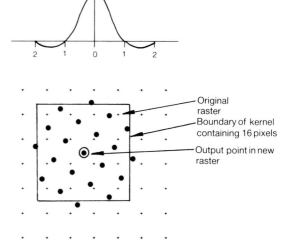

Fig. 4.10 Cubic convolution using the sinc function (Sin x/x).

which uses a neighbourhood of 16 pixels and a weighted sum approach based on a two-dimensional version of the sinc x (sin x/x) function. The overlays and 3D displays in Plates 1–6 and 13–14 were made using these methods.

Data verification

The best way to check that the spatial data have been correctly digitized is to get the computer to draw them out again, preferably on translucent, or in any case, thin paper, at the same scale as the original. The two maps can then be placed over each other on a light table and compared visually, working systematically from left to right and up and down across the map.

Missing data, locational errors, and other errors should be clearly marked on the printout with a bold felt pen. Certain of the better vector systems can also be commanded to print out the identification codes attached to each graphic entity. These too should be checked. If the map is a unique drawing, locational errors need only be considered within the map boundary; if the map is one of a series covering a larger area, or the digitized data must link up with map data already in the computer, then the spatial data must also be examined for spatial contiguity across map edges. Certain operations, such as polygon formation, may also indicate errors in the spatial data.

Non-spatial data can be checked by printing out the files of non-spatial data and checking the columns by eye. A better method is to scan these data files with a computer program that can check for gross errors such as text instead of numbers, numbers exceeding a given range, and so on. The programs that link spatial and non-spatial data can also be used to check that all links have been properly made. The programs should be written in such a way that they flag only the errors.

Using patience and common sense, all major errors can easily be spotted in the data. It is much more difficult to spot errors in non-spatial data when the values are syntactically good but incorrect.

Data editing

Most data editing of geographical information is a time-consuming, interactive process that can take as long, or longer than the data input itself (Nagy and Wagle 1979; OEEPE 1984). The portion of the map containing the errors is displayed at an enlarged scale (zooming in) on a graphics CRT controlled by a keyboard and a small digitizer tablet.

Attribute values and spatial errors in a grid map must be corrected by changing the value of the faulty cells. This can often be done by a simple command that requests the row and column number of the cells and the correct attribute value. If large numbers of cells are wrong, the new information could be digitized and simply written over the existing values.

Minor locational errors in vector databases can be corrected by keying in new data, indicating their position on the digitizer tablet, or by using computer commands to move, rotate, erase, insert, stretch or truncate the graphical entities as required.

Whereas editing a raster database usually has little chance of a 'knock-on' effect causing difficulties in other parts of the database, some vector editing operations cannot be used in isolation but must be followed by checks or operations to ensure the coherency of the

database. For example, in networks in utility mapping (e.g. telephone lines) editing the line B–C into two lines with a branch B′–B may require that the pointers indicating the flow of signals from A to C must be rebuilt.

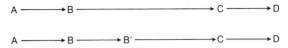

In polygon networks, if a line X–Y is moved or changed the polygon areas must be recomputed.

Data updating

Many geographical (spatial) data are not inviolate for all time and are subject to change. Few of these changes are so deterministic that they can be performed automatically. For example, political boundaries may change with the whims of parliament, land use and field boundaries may change as the result of re-allotment, soil boundaries change as a result of land improvement or degradation. Change in the landscape implies that the resident database is faulty and needs to be edited, and in fact, the basic operations just described for editing are also equally applicable for updating. Updating is rather more than just modifying an ageing data base; it implies resurvey and processing new information. Organizational problems can arise when planning a survey to update a database, because one has to be able to refer to the contents of the existing database to know what has changed. Some aspects of the earth's surface, such as rock types, change slowly, and important changes are few, so updating remains a small problem. But there are other kinds of geographical data where it may be more cost-effective to resurvey completely every few years rather than attempt to update old databases. By comparison, updating the non-spatial data is trivial, provided the one-to-one links between non-spatial data records and the spatial entities remain unaltered.

Data back-up and storage

Building a digital database is a costly and time-consuming process and it is essential that the digital map information is transferred from the local disk memory of the computer to a more permanent storage medium where it can be safely preserved. Digital databases for topographic, cadastral, and environmental mapping can be expected to have a useful life of 1–25 yr and it is essential to ensure that they can be preserved in mint condition.

In most cases, digital data are stored invisibly on magnetic media such as magnetic disk or tape. The high costs of permanently mounted disk-storage systems and the high handling risks associated with exchangeable disks mean that they are little used for archiving. Instead, magnetic tape is much used, predominantly in the form of 0.5-in.-wide nine-track tapes written at 800 BPI or 1600 BPI (bits per inch), or, more recently, with densities as high as 6250 BPI.

Because one cannot see the data on the tape, some people have expressed doubts about the stability of the records and the best procedures for storing them. The recommendations for data archiving received from the tape manufacturers Memorex, Scotch, BASF, and Nashua, and from the English Ordnance Survey, the Canada Land Information System, the United States Department of Agriculture Soil Conservation Service and the United States Geological Survey EROS Data Center (Burrough 1980) are explained below.

Current practice for handling tapes varies greatly between those organizations that rewrite tapes frequently to those that find that no rewriting necessary over a period of up to seven years. For example, the Ordnance Survey, which in 1971 began building an archive that exceeds 10 000 plans, follows strict backup procedures laid down by British Government Codes of Practice (Central Computing Agency, no date). These procedures involve keeping multiple copies of each plan on given tape; for data banking two copies of the tape are made. One of these tapes is then copied to produce a third, and these three first generation tapes are later supported by one still valid. After six months they are cleaned and rewound; after twelve months they are copied to produce a fresh data bank tape (Arnold 1979). On the other hand, the EROS Data Center does not rewrite 0.5-inch tapes at all because the staff have experienced no data degradation over a seven-year period. They find it sufficient to clean and rewind archived tapes on a tape certifier/ cleaner apparatus before reading them on the computer. However, they stress the importance of a proper environment in both the computer and storage area for maintaining tape quality (Thompson 1979). The procedures followed by the Canada Land Information System fall somewhat between those of these two organizations (Switzer 1979).

The costs of using data on both working and archival tapes are divided between the initial costs of data acquisition and those of maintenance. The inability to rewrite stored data could have minor or catastrophic consequences. But if tapes must be frequently cleaned and rewritten the data value can also be reduced through too high handling and maintenance costs.

Clearly, there are large differences in the maintenance costs incurred by the organizations mentioned above and one should be certain of the best course to follow.

According to manufacturers' specifications (cf. 3M Company 1968) the magnetic particles on the tape do not lose their signals over time; the information is essentially permanent unless altered by an external magnetic field. However, the polyester tape backings are more sensitive to damage from dirt during recording or playback, or bad handling of the tape spools (Holder 1977). Fire or nuclear radiation are also possible hazards.

Tape preparation is the most important part of data storage. The tape unit must be kept properly adjusted by the manufacturer or service bureau, and the operators must ensure that the tape heads, rollers, pinch wheel or other surfaces that come into contact with the tape are scrupulously clean. These surfaces can be cleaned easily with cotton buds and iso-propyl alcohol. They should never be touched with the fingers. The manufacturers, the Canada Land Information System, and the EROS Data Center stress that smoking and eating should not be allowed in computer rooms or storage areas because of the dangers of cigarette ash or food particles contaminating the tape or tape heads. Once tapes have been written, they should be rewound completely to ensure even spooling at a constant tension. Tape reels should be handled by the hub, and not by one flange only. Flanges on tape reels must not be bent or distorted. Once the tape has been written and rewound, the end of the tape should be held down by a strip of vinyl plastic (not sticky tape!!) and a piece of sponge plastic to exclude dust, and the tape placed in its box. Tape boxes are preferred to edge strips because they support the reel by its hub and protect it from physical damage. Boxed tapes should be stacked vertically in racks in metal cupboards. Tapes can be kept horizontally but not in such a way that the reels become distorted through the pressure of the overlying reels or books. The storage environment should be as similar to that in the computer room as possible, and certainly within the temperature limits 7–32°C and of 40–60 per cent humidity. These conditions should prevent the tapes becoming sticky or flaking, and should also prevent fungal growth. Annual cleaning and rewinding prevents physical deterioration from these causes.

The storage environment should be such that the magnetic flux near the tapes is less than 50 Oe. This means that tapes should not be placed within 10 cm of a source of magnetic field (such as an electric motor) having a field inside it of 1500 Oe. In practice, this means that tapes placed inside metal storage cup-boards will never be subjected to damaging magnetic fields. According to studies reported by Holder (1977), magnetic storage media (including credit cards, tapes, floppy and rigid disks, etc.) are really quite safe from all kinds of stray magnetic influence such as airport metal detectors and microwaves.

Investigations also suggest that magnetic media are not very susceptible to nuclear radiation. Scotch Tape (3M Company 1968) affirm that magnetic tape 'will be unaffected by Nuclear Radiation until the dosage approaches a level of 200 000 times greater than that which would cause death in 50 per cent exposed humans'. At such levels no one would be left to read the tapes anyway.

Fire is the greatest risk in storage because it affects the physical properties of the plastic in the tape. Prop-erly wound tapes are less of a fire risk than loosely wound ones because air is excluded. Table 4.2 presents manufacturers' data on temperature susceptibilities of magnetic tape. Clearly, valuable tape records must be protected from excessive heat and fire risk.

Table 4.2 Temperature susceptibilities of magnetic tapes

Temperature (°C)	Result
125	Backing distortion
160	Softening of both backing and binder with some adhesion of adjacent layers
290	Darkening and embrittlement of the backing and binder
530	Charring

[1]Source: 3M Company (1968).
NB Data from other manufacturers from their normal speci-fication pamphlets.

The safety and cheapness of magnetic tape are over-whelming advantages for its uses as an archiving medium. However, conventional tape has one impor-tant disadvantage when compared with disks, and that is the slow speed of data access. Mass Storage Systems (MSS), now coming into use at major computing centres, are in fact a different type of magnetic tape that permit the contents of whole disks to be quickly written on them in the same format as exists on the disk. The MSS tapes are 7 cm broad and 15–25 cm long, held in a special cassette, and they permit the storage of the order of 50 Mbyte of data. Each tape block corresponds to one disk cylinder so data can very quickly be transferred from disk to tape and vice versa without altering its format.

Because MSS devices use magnetic tape, it is likely that all the comments above concerning ordinary tapes are directly applicable, except that cleaning and re-winding should be far less onerous. MSS devices are expected to be more useful for large volumes of data (e.g. utility networks for a whole city) rather than for special-purpose thematic mapping.

Providing tape equipment is well maintained, the operating environment is kept scrupulously clean, and storage conditions operate to prevent damage from fungus, dirt, and fire, it seems clear that expensive back-up systems involving frequent copying and re-writing of tapes are not essential. Once a tape has been written and checked it appears to be sufficient to re-wind and clean it once a year and also when it is removed from the archive for use. Tape cleaning and rewinding is best done on a proper certifier/cleaner apparatus; this is essential for library management.

Digital data can also be stored and transferred using floppy disks (the magnetic disk media used in micro-computers and word processors) and tape cassettes. The latter are much used for back-up data from cer-tain graphics work stations for they are simpler, quicker and much cheaper than most reel-to-reel tape systems for limited amounts of data. As with large tapes, tape cassettes and floppy disks need to be kept clean and to be rewritten regularly.

The volume of data that can be stored in a single unit is being extended rapidly by improved technology. It has been predicted that within the foreseeable future simple, removable disks will become available that will allow between 10 and 100 Mbyte of data to be stored on a single side of a 9-in.-diameter disk that can be addressed by a microcomputer (Fox 1985). At present, these large storage volumes are only available on the larger and more expensive machines.

There are indications that the video disk technology currently used for recording music and video signals on compact disks will be developed to provide huge read-only memories (ROMs) for computers. A single-sided CDROM (compact disk read-only memory) measuring 12 cm in diameter can hold 600 Mbyte of data. A single video disk would then be able to provide a huge read-only store of maps and geographical data that could be quickly retrieved and used for further analyses. Such a system would be ideal for distributing large geographical databases containing information about spatial features that do not change quickly, or for storing large amounts of remotely sensed data. Used in combination with data about the more mut-able aspects of the area in question, CDROMs could provide a very useful source of standard data and programs for a wide variety of GIS applications in a very compact format.

Data output

Data output is the operation of presenting the results of data manipulation in a form that is understandable to a user or in a form that allows data transfer to another computer system. People-compatible output is in the form of maps, graphs, and tables; computer-compatible output may be in the form of a magnetic tape that can be read into another system, or it may involve some form of electronic data transmission over data communication networks, telephone lines or radio links. Most geographical information systems will include software for a range of data output options (Table 4.3). Output techniques in GIS rely heavily on the skills developed in the rapidly growing field of computer graphics (e.g. Foley and Van Dam 1982; Giloi 1978; Mufti 1983; Newman and Sproull 1979; Rogers and Adams 1976; Ryan 1979; Kunii 1985).

Table 4.3 Common GIS capabilities for data output

Zooming/windowing to select area for output
Scale change
Colour change
Modifications to text and line fonts, colours, dimensions, etc.
Three-dimensional display
Selection of data using layers or overlays
Plotter commands (special plotter formats)
Dump commands to output data on magnetic media
Printing commands for text file output

People-compatible output devices can be classified into those that produce ephemeral displays on electronic screens and those that produce permanent images (hard copies) on paper, mylar, or other material. The electronic displays are known as VDUs (visual display units) or graphics terminals, the hard-copy devices as plotters. Both VDUs and plotters can be further classified according to whether the display is produced by a raster scanning technique or by a vector line-drawing technique. The reader should note that the raster or vector structure of the output device is

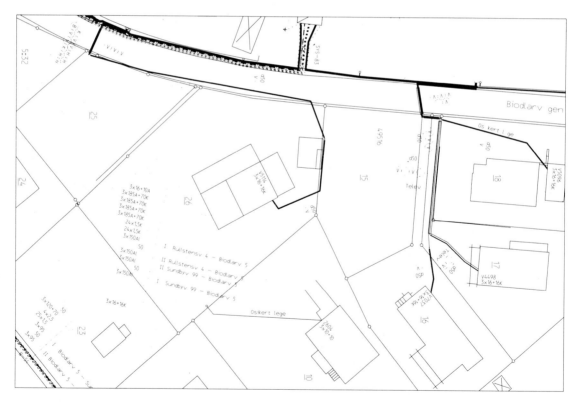

Fig. 4.11 High quality vector plot drawn on a flatbed plotter using a tangential head with a scribing tool. (Courtesy Sysscan a.s.)

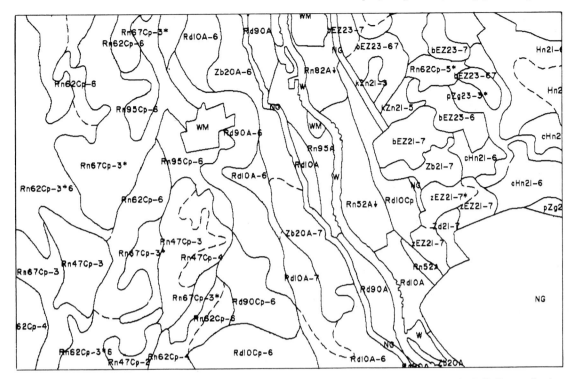

Fig. 4.12 Vector data plotted on a good quality matrix plotter. (Courtesy The Netherlands Soil Survey Institute and Versatec BV.)

usually but not necessarily the same as that of the geographical database to which the device is connected. For example, Figs. 4.11 and 4.12 show examples of maps in vector structure printed on respectively a vector plotter and on a raster device, and Fig. 4.13 shows an example of raster data drawn by a pen (vector) plotter.

Vector display devices

(a) *Pen plotters.* Pen plotters are robot draughtsmen. They are essentially a plane surface on which paper can be laid, and a pen holder that can be moved independently in the X (horizontal) and the Y (vertical) directions. In a variant, known as the drum plotter, the plane surface is replaced by a drum that can move independently in the Y direction. All information is drawn by a series of line-drawing commands: move pen to point XY, set pen down, move pen to $X'Y'$, move pen to $X''Y''$ ...., raise pen up. The moves to the XY coordinates can be indicated by either giving absolute or incremental coordinates.

The flexibility and speed of a pen plotter is determined largely by the amount of preprogrammed infor-

mation it has for drawing complex shapes such as letters and symbols. A simple plotter has to be fed with all the 'move pen' and 'pen up/down' instructions to draw every letter, whereas a 'smart' plotter will contain a preprogrammed, 'hard-wired' character and symbol set that needs only to be referenced by simple computer commands. The quality of the plotted image depends largely on the step-size of the pen-control motors, which should be not more than 0.001 in. (0.0254 mm) for good cartographic work. The highest quality plotters used for accurate map making and for preparing peel-coat colour masters can be equipped with a scribing point mounted in a tangential head (to ensure that the scriber always cuts in the same direction as the plotter head is moving), or with a light beam or a laser in place of a pen, drawing directly on lithographic film.

The Laserscan FASTRACK system uses a laser beam for writing maps directly onto diazo film in microfiche format.

(b) *Vector screens or 'storage displays'.* Vector screens operate on a similar principle to pen plotters, the main difference being that the pen is replaced by a beam of

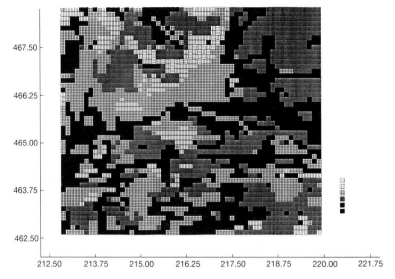

Fig. 4.13 Raster data plotter by a pen plotter. This kind of plot often costs a considerable amount of computing to prepare the plot files. (Courtesy A. Bregt, The Netherlands Soil Survey Institute.)

electrons and the paper by a green phosphor screen. Once the image has been written on the screen it remains visible until the whole screen is cleared. Consequently it is impossible to display motion on a vector screen.

A quick, semi-permanent paper copy of the image on the vector screen can be obtained from a hard-copy device. The hard-copy device is a simple thermal printer linked to the display generator of the screen, that prints the information on the screen on an A4 piece of treated paper in approximately 10 s. The hard-copy device can be a useful asset when editing parts of a map or when designing map legends and symbols.

Raster display devices

(a) *Raster plotters.* The simplest raster plotter is the lineprinter or printing terminal, and the earliest computer mapping systems were designed to use these crude, but simple and fast tools for output. The greatest drawback of the lineprinter for mapping is the non-square $1/10$ in. $\times 1/6$ in. character size, which causes a map based on a square grid cell database to be stretched in the Y direction. For a very long time, the only inadequate remedies to this problem were either to collect data on a non-square rectangular grid to match the line printer format, or to purchase a specially modified lineprinter. Fortunately, the problem has now been completely solved by the introduction of matrix printers that can be set to print square or non-square characters, or graphics symbols.

Consequently, simple maps can be obtained very cheaply, even on personal computers.

Multiple-colour printing is available on some matrix printers by use of a three-colour ribbon. The degree of resolution on matrix printers is governed by whether only the characters are used or whether every dot (*ca.* $0.05\,mm^2$) has been programmed separately.

If only the characters are used, then different grey scales must be built up by using different characters and symbols and by overprinting. The simplest way to make a coloured thematic map using a matrix printer used to be to print each map class separately as a fully black image and use the printout to make a series of lithographic colour masters. Overprinting the characters VAXO leads to a black cell, but programming each dot separately gives much better results.

Much better resolution raster printing (up to 400 dots per inch, which is 16.7 dots per mm), coupled with fast printing speeds, can be obtained from matrix plotters that make use of the electrostatic principles of xerography. They have two basic parts, a paper transport mechanism and a transverse bar carrying a large number of closely spaced, fine needles. Each needle corresponds to a grid cell in a single row from a rasterized image, and is given an electrostatic charge if the cell it represents is 'on' (i.e. black). The charge is transferred to the paper, which is moved up one row and the needles are recharged to match the bit pattern in the next row of data. The charged points on the paper are developed (i.e. they receive a spot of ink) to produce the image. The main advantage of matrix plotters is their speed.

Typically, a 40 cm × 60 cm soil map would be drawn in approximately 30 s on a matrix plotter, a task that would take from between 30 min to 2 h on a pen plotter. The plot time on a matrix plotter is also not dependent on detail, though the preprocessing needed to produce the raster image may be. Matrix plotters using the xerographic principle can now produce colour plots. Colour printing is also possible with the ink-jet plotter in which the cells in the data array are used to guide electrostatically charged ink drops onto paper. Expensive ink-jet plotters have a high resolution (*c*.10–12 dots/mm) and can reproduce *c*. 4000 colours. Low resolution (*c*. 3–5 dots/mm) ink-jet plotters that can give reasonable quality plots are now available for modest prices. By using clever dot programming, continuous colours are possible (e.g. Kubo 1985).

Optical film writers. Very high quality output of rasterized data is achieved in colour or in black and white by using a special film recorder. The principle is very similar to that of the drum scanner except that the light source is focussed and modulated to expose a point on the surface of a photographic film mounted on a high-speed revolving drum. The optical carriage is stepped in the *X*-direction after each rotation by a distance that can be adjusted to 25, 50, 100, or 200 μm. 256 discrete, repeatable levels per primary colour can be used. The resulting images are difficult to distinguish from high quality photographs (cf. Fig. 3.15).

(b) *Raster display screens.* The simplest raster display screens use conventional television technology in the sense that the image is built up from lines scanned across the screen. The difference with conventional television comes from the fact that the strength of the scanning electron beam (which controls the brightness) is not controlled by an analogue or continuously variable signal but by a bit pattern in a special computer memory called a frame buffer. The frame buffer is a large matrix in which each cell may take the value 0 or 1 to control whether the electron beam is off or on over a particular part of the screen. The size of the matrix or memory needed can be estimated from the resolution or cell size. For example, the European television standard is 625 lines. To represent the whole screen at this resolution would require 625 × 625 × 4/3 = 520.833 bits (where 4/3: is the width/height ratio of the screen) or 65 kbyte (a byte is 8 bits). To represent the whole screen at half this resolution would require only 16 kbyte. It was not until these large memories

could be made cheaply that the raster display device became possible.

Because each cell in the frame can be addressed and read separately, and because the whole screen is scanned (or 'refreshed') 30 times a second, simply writing new values to the frame buffer can cause a picture to move over the screen. The simplest frame buffers allow only single bits per cell and so the resulting image is in monochrome (the various monochrome colours such as black and white, green or orange are a result of the screen phosphor). Grey tones and colours can be generated by adding 'bit-planes' to the frame buffer. For example, if each cell in the frame buffer can contain 4 bits instead of one, $2^4 = 16$ different grey scales or colours can be referenced at once. Most commercial systems have at least 8 bit planes (256 possibilities) while 12 and 24 are becoming increasingly common, together with a spatial resolution of 1024 × 1024 pixels (see Plate 7). The information from the bit planes is used to control the red, green, and blue electron guns of the monitor tube look-up tables, and look-up tables can be programmed to use standard Munsell colours (Hue, Value, and Chroma), or rectangular colour coordinates, allowing 'continuous colour' graduations to be used on a map (Harvard University 1982; Dutton 1982; Sibert 1980) c.f. Plates 11–12.

Hard copies of the coloured images produced by raster screens can be obtained photographically using special devices. Because most photos taken directly from the television screen suffer from reflections, special photo-display devices are available with which 35 mm cameras or large-format Polaroid films can be used e.g. Plates 3–6, 9–12. The best results are obtained by using these film plotters, but low-cost colour ink-jet printers are gaining favour as a quick, reliable printing technique.

The interactive graphics workstation

The interactive graphics workstation is a suite of hardware for controlling a computer mapping or design system. It is used for interactive design work, for detailed editing and for checking the map before it is committed to the printer. The workstation usually comprises a keyboard and visual display unit for entering computer commands, a small digitizer or tablet for entering frequently used computer commands, text or labels and one or two high resolution raster or vector display screens. The idea of the two screens is that one can show an overview of the whole map while details are displayed on the other. Although most interactive graphics workstations used with CAD/CAM systems interface with a vector database, current commercial developments favour the use of high-resolution colour raster displays in place of the former, monochrome, green storage displays. Some systems use a combined vector/raster screen on which the vector screen displays fixed information and the raster display, which is in another colour, allows an operator to see how lines and symbols can be moved around. These combined screens can be very useful when editing.

Graphics software for output

Until recently, most graphics software has been device-dependent, which is to say that every time a new output device was added to a system, the programs had to be modified. Some unofficial device standards have been common for some time (notably CALCOMP standards for pen plotters and TEKTRONIX standards for graphics screens, or more recently the set of protocols used to link matrix printers to the IBM personal computer) but they were neither universally defined nor accepted. Because of the costs associated with rewriting graphics software to meet non-standard hardware, there have been international demands for real standards that would enable all graphics software to become device-independent. This has now been achieved through the design and implementation of the Graphic Kernel System—GKS (Waggoner 1985; Rawlins 1985).

The Graphic Kernel System is the result of efforts by the German Standardization Institute DIN to produce a universal graphics software standard. The German effort has been influenced by many national and international organizations and has been accepted as an ANSI and as an international standard (Bono *et al.* 1982; Waggoner 1985).

The Graphic Kernel System provides the programmer with a subroutine library of two-dimensional graphics primitives (basic units) that can be accessed through a consistent interface in high-level computer languages such as FORTRAN-77. The basic drawing primitives in vector mode are called the polyline, the polymarker, and text units. The polyline primitive draws a set of connected straight lines (i.e. a 'chain' or a 'string'); the polymarker is similar, except that it places symbols at each specified point and draws no lines. The text primitive draws text strings at any desired position and angle.

In raster mode, GKS supports fill and cell array primitives. Drawing primitives are available for special symbols. The GKS also allows attributes concerning line signature and colour to be attached to the output primitives. Sets of primitives can be defined and handled as single entities. The GKS supports the concept of multiple work-stations, providing support for interactive control through the use of digitizing tablets or light pens. It can be supported fully on modern, intelligent work-stations, so that they can operate efficiently and independently of a host computer.

The single most important feature about GKS is that all program output from the program modules to the display devices is routed through a program known as a virtual device interface (VDI). The VDI is device specific, but its function is to make any given graphic output device look just like any other. The idea is similar to the device code used in FORTRAN to write text to a screen, a line printer or a disk file, except the output is graphics. Consequently, with GKS/VDI software, expensive graphics software can be directed to many different devices without the need for expensive revision. It is anticipated that this facility should greatly benefit programmer productivity.

Data presentation

Most users of GIS seem to want the graphical output from the system to be very similar to conventional map products. Smooth contour lines or coloured or shaded choropleth maps produced to all the standards of hand cartography are the products that are mostly required e.g. Plates 1, 2, 7. All maps produced by the computer should be clearly laid out; they should have a sensible legend or set of class intervals (see Chapter 7), a title, an orientation indicator (north arrow or coordinate marks) and a scale or scale bar. Note that a scale bar is more suitable when maps are zoomed on the screen or reproduced at different scales. The choice of colours or grey scales is also very important if the map is to convey its message clearly, and it is in these aspects of GIS that the cartographer can play an important role. Often, users of expensive GIS systems fail to communicate properly because of lack of knowledge of the arts of graphical communication. The reader is advised to consult one of the many excellent books on map presentation (e.g. Campbell 1984; Davies 1974; Dent 1985; Dickinson 1974; Hodgkiss 1981; Keates 1973; Robinson *et al.* 1978) for advice on these matters.

The concentration on standard cartographic products, and the rejection by cartographers of the line-printer cell map, has meant that there has been relatively little work done on developing new methods of cartographic expression that match the new computer techniques. True, colour graphics displays have made new visual effects possible, but it is only recently that these images could be easily turned into hard copies. The DOT-MAP program (Dutton 1978) presents interesting possibilities for experimenting with various kinds of normal and fuzzy line types and shading; Eyton (1984) has presented a set of methods for raster contouring using a high resolution electrostatic plotter that allows many kinds of display possibilities, including stereoscopy, not possible by hand. The combination of displaying thematic data over block diagrams or shaded relief images, discussed in Chapter 3, has also resulted in some very powerful visual images, which if combined with the data analysis capabilities of the GIS, can be used to dramatic effect. There are tremendous possibilities to be explored for combining the power of current computer graphics techniques (e.g. van Dam 1984) with geographical information processing.

Summary

There is a very wide range of commercially available output devices that range from the very cheap to the hideously expensive. As a rough guide, cost is a function of the square of the linear dimensions of the device and its function; for example, at the time of writing the prices of pen plotters can range from *ca.* US $400 for a small, low quality device to more than US $100 000 for a large, quality flat bed plotter.

The advantages and disadvantages of raster versus vector display devices can be summarized as shown in Table 4.4.

User interfaces

All geographical information systems are made up of complex programs that are capable of many different kinds of operation. It is very cumbersome for a user to run a complex system by simply entering a series of data in response to READ statements issued from the computer. Consequently, properly designed, modern systems use one or more conversational and interactive ways in which the user can enter commands.

Menus

The simplest method for easy command selection is by way of a 'menu', or list of possible command names. This is displayed on the terminal so that the user may make a choice, either by entering a number or letter corresponding to the desired action, or via the cursor control buttons ($\uparrow\downarrow\rightarrow\leftarrow$) on the keyboard. Alternatively, the cursor on the screen may be controlled by a mouse and digitizing tablet, or a light pen or tracker ball. The menu commands are written in natural language so that the user can easily understand what the

Table 4.4 Comparison of raster and vector display devices

Device	Type	Advantages	Disadvantages
Plotters	Matrix	Quick, cheap. Only low quality hardcopy at present except for ink-jet	Printing process means that stable materials can be used only with most expensive systems
		Good at space-filling, shading	Line/text quality poor to moderate Interfacing may require expensive software
	Pen	High quality lines in all ink colours	Shading slow and costly Slower than matrix plotters
		All plotters can use stable base material	Mechanical parts wear out, affecting accuracy
		Interfacing is easy	Very high quality apparatus is expensive
Display tube	Refresh	Uses cheap, mass technology from televisions Colour, motion	Low quality hard-copy from screen
	Storage	High resolution large memories	Monochrome only Tubes very expensive, high voltage supplies

programs can do. In complex programs menus may be hierarchically nested so that a command sequence can be built up to allow many possible permutations. For example, a main menu might have four options:

1. ENTER
2. OUTPUT DATA
3. TRANSFORM DATA
4. EXIT

Choosing item 1 from this menu could call up a second:

1. ENTER POINT
2. ENTER LINE
3. ENTER POLYGON
4. ENTER CIRCLE
5. ENTER TEXT
6. RETURN

Choosing 2 might result in a menu with the following choices:

1. HORIZONTALLY
2. VERTICALLY
3. PARALLEL TO
4. FREE
5. RETURN

Choosing 3 would mean that the user had chosen to enter a line parallel to a line in the database that has yet to be identified. This identification would almost certainly be done interactively, with the element in question being 'picked up' by placing the cursor close to it on the screen and asking the computer to identify the chosen line.

Command language interpreters

Hierarchical menus are ideal for users who make occasional use of a system and who do not wish to remember all possible commands and their functions. More highly skilled users and users of systems in which a very large range of options exist are better served by a command language interpreter or CLI. The idea is that the commands needed to call up, run, and modify programs can be written in a form of English (or other natural language) in a way that can be understood both by user and machine. These 'very high level languages' must have strict rules of grammar and syntax in order to avoid ambiguities.

Essentially, a command language consists of three components: verbs, nouns, and modifiers. The verbs refer to actions that the system must perform, such as INPUT, MOVE, ROTATE, DELETE or CHANGE, that are common to a great many operations. The nouns refer to the kinds of database elements that are being acted upon. For graphic data, nouns would include POINT, LINE, POLYGON, CIRCLE, TEXT, etc. Non-graphic attributes might also be directly referable by name. The modifiers, as the name implies, are used to fine-tune the action of the verb on the noun. The set of commands selected via the menu example above could be entered as:

INPUT	LINE	HORIZONTALLY:
verb	noun	modifier

The : terminates the command and tells the computer to stop accepting characters from the keyboard and to expect data to be sent from the digitizer.

The allowable list of verbs, nouns, and combinations is held in sets of look-up tables in the computer.

As a verb or a noun is typed in, the computer checks to see if it is allowed (i.e. that it can be 'understood'); if both verb and noun are acceptable, the combination must be checked. An allowed combination is cross-referenced with the starting address of the required program module. The modifier or modifiers (there can be more than one) is used by the program to control the execution of the command.

The command language interpreter is much more powerful than the simple menu. Frequently used verb–noun combinations can be grouped into menu commands that can be called up by a single digitize in the defined area of a small digitizing tablet attached to the graphics workstation. So the user can have the simplicity of the menu system combined with freedom from having to type commands, thereby eliminating the chance of typing mistakes. These easy-to-use menus that can be operated from a digitizer are regarded as essential for interactive working with graphic design and mapping systems. But the CLI also allows a user to write programs that consist of series of verb–noun commands that together will perform a complex set of operations. These programs can be used to good advantage when multistep analyses or transformations must be carried out in the same way on more than one data set.

A file containing such an executable series of commands written in the command language is often called a 'MACRO' or a 'BATCH' file. In more sophisticated systems, the MACRO facilities may allow the user to include statements from a programming language such as BASIC or PASCAL, so that still more complex tasks can be carried out. These MACRO programs are subject to the grammar and syntax of both the CLI and the programming language, and may themselves be compilable (translated into machine mode) to provide 'supercommands'. With these facilities a skilled user can develop specialized application software without having to write out the basic subroutines for manipulating the geographical data. They provide an ideal way of creating software modules that can be used for data analyses and transformation (see Chapter 5).

Defaults

With so many options to choose from, the user may become bewildered as to which modifier or modifiers should be used for a given task. The system should be designed in such a way that if the user does not specify exactly what is required (either via the menu or the CLI modifiers) it will use sensible default values of the parameters in the programs. Because the appropriate default values may vary from application to application, the user should be able to set the default values as required. For example, for one application it may be desirable to input text in a particular font (or style), and of a particular size. Instead of repeating the modifiers for font and size every time as in,

INPUT TEXT FONT ******* SIZE ********:

the defaults can be first set with

SET TEXT DEFAULT FONT ****** SIZE ******

followed by simple INPUT TEXT: commands.

Instead of allowing every user the freedom to alter defaults, it may also be desirable to define all system defaults in a control file that is directly accessed by the system. This control file is set up by the system manager for the work in hand and cannot be accessed by normal users.

Help facilities

Even the most experienced user cannot expect to know everything about a complex system and the casual user will be even more at sea. All systems must be well documented (software without good documentation is worse than useless), but most users resent having to consult a library of computer manuals in order to find the answer to simple problems. It is becoming increasingly common that systems include HELP files that can be called up interactively to render on-line aid. HELP files can often be referenced directly in a menu by typing a certain code, or in a CLI, by entering a ? at the beginning or end of the verb–noun combination. On-line HELP files should be written in such a way as to get the user out of most difficulties. Unfortunately, HELP files take up program and disk space and in smaller systems there may well have to be a trade-off between the detail of HELP that can be provided and the space available.

Windows

In the interactive graphics systems used for geographical information systems, the displays cannot show all the visual detail of a complex database at full resolution. Consequently, most graphics systems allow the user to zoom in and display an enlarged part of the database. Zooming may also be combined with other operations, such as isolating or cutting out a part of the database for special analysis, display or updating.

Many systems make it possible for the user to have more than one 'window' through which to view the database. Some interactive graphics systems use two screens for this, with one to display the enlarged, active image and the other to give the overview. Other systems combine several windows on one screen. The windows need not necessarily be just different displays of the graphical data, they can be used to display separate tasks that are being executed concurrently (Kay 1984).

User interaction: conclusion

Proper, easy interaction between user and GIS requires a well-thought-out menu system, a CLI, or both. It is only recently that much development has been done on making the user's task easier, and to a large extent, this work has only been made possible by the availability of large, cheap memory space. When the computer had only just enough space for the code containing the algorithms no one paid much attention to user interaction. Today, user interaction is rightly considered to be very important, and the code needed for 'user friendliness' may well be a large part of a computer program.

References

Adams, J., Patton, C., Reader, C., and Zamora, D. (1984). Fast hardware for geometric warping. In *Proc. 3rd Australasian Remote Sensing Conf.* Queensland.

Almelio, C. F. (1974). Charge-coupled devices. *Scient. Am.* **230**(2), 22–31.

Arnold, I. K. G. (1979). Personal communication. Ordnance Survey, Southampton, England.

Bono, P. R., Encarnacao, J. L., Hopgood, R. A., and ten Hagen, P. J. W. (1982). GKS—the first graphics standard. *IEEE Comp. & Appl.* **2**, 9–23.

Burrough, P. A. (1980). Het opbergen van digitale kartografische gegevens (in Dutch). *Kartogr. Tijdschr.* **6**(2), 23–5.

Campbell, J. (1984). *Introductory cartography.* Prentice-Hall, Englewood Cliffs, NJ.

Central Computing Agency (no date). Recommended procedures for the care and maintenance of magnetic tapes. Central Government Code of Practice No. 14. London.

Dam, A. van (1984). Computer software for graphics. *Scient. Am.* **251**, 102–13.

Davies, P. (1974). *Data description and presentation.* Oxford University Press, Oxford.

Dent, B. D. (1985). *Principles of thematic map design.* Addison-Wesley, Reading, Mass.

Dickinson, G. C. (1974). *Statistical mapping and the presentation of statistics.* Arnold, London.

Douglas, D. H. and Peuker, T. K. (1973). Algorithms for the reduction of the number of points required to represent a digitized line, or its caricature. *Can. Cartogr.* **10**, 112–22.

Dutton, G. (1982). Land alive—an algorithm for 4-color hill shading. *Perspect. Comput.* **2**(1), 26–39.

Eyton, J. R. (1984). Raster contouring. *GeoProcessing* **2**, 221–42.

Foley, J. D. and van Dam, A. (1982). *Fundamentals of interactive computer graphics.* Addison-Wesley, Reading, Mass.

Fox, B. (1985). Optical memories for home computers. *New Scient.* **11**, (April).

Gilio, W. K. (1978). *Interactive computer graphics.* Prentice-Hall, Englewood Cliffs, NJ.

Harvard University (1982). Context—an introduction to the work of the laboratory for computer graphics and spatial analysis. President and Fellows of Harvard University, Massachusetts.

Hobbie, D. (1984). Planicomp-Intergraph interface. In *Proc. Intergraph Seminar on Digital Mapping*, Barcelona, Spain, 29–30 March 1984.

Hodgkiss, A. G. (1981). *Understanding maps.* Dawson, Folkestone, UK.

Holder, C. (1977). Caring for magnetic media. *Data Mgmt* October 1977, 26–30.

Howman, C. and Woodsford, P. A. (1978). The Laserscan fastrack Automatic Digitizer System. In *Proc. 9th Conf. International Cartographic Association, Maryland.*

Johannsen, Th. M. (1979). How to get cartographic data in computer systems. In *Proc. International Cartographic Association Commission III—Conference on Computer-Assisted Cartography*, Nairobi 6–11 November 1978, 37–85.

Kay, A. (1984). Computer software. *Scient. Am.* **251**(Sept.), 41–7.

Keates, J. S. (1973). *Cartographic design and production.* Longman, Harlow, UK

Kristian, J. and Blouke, M. (1982). Charge coupled devices in astronomy. *Scient. Am.* **247**(4), 48–56.

Kubo, S. (1985). Continuous colour presentation using a low-cost ink-jet printer. In Kunii (1985), pp. 344–53.

Kunii, T.L. (ed.) (1985). *Frontiers in computer graphics.* Springer-Verlag, Tokyo.

Leberl, F. W. and Olson, D. (1982). Raster scanning for operational digitizing of graphical data. *Photogramm. Engng. Rem. Sens.* **48**(4), 615–27.

Marble, D. F., Lauzon, J. P., and McGranaghan (1984). Development of a conceptual model of the manual digitizing process. *Proc. Int. Symp. on Spatial Data Handling.* 20–24 August, Zurich, 146–71.

Mufti, A. A. (1983). *Elementary computer graphics.* Reston Publishing, Reston, Va.

Nagy, G. and Wagle, S. (1979). Geographic data processing. *Comput. Surv.* **11**(2), 139–79.

Newmann, W. M. and Sproull, R. F. (1979). *Principles of Interactive computer graphics.* McGraw-Hill, New York.

OEEPE (1984). *Test of digitising methods.* European Organisation for Experimental Photogrammetric Research. Official Publ. No. 14. Institut für Angewandte Geodäsie, Berlin.

Opheim, H. (1982). Fast reduction of a digitized curve. *GeoProcessing* **2**, 33–40.

Pavlidis, T. (1982). *Algorithms for graphics and image processing.* Springer-Verlag, Berlin.

Rawlins, M. G. (1985). A standards solution to your graphics problems. In Kunii (1985), pp. 375–84.

Reumann, K. and Witkam, A. P. M. (1974). Optimizing curve segmentation in computer graphics. *Int. Computing Symp. 1973.* North-Holland, Amsterdam, pp. 467–72.

Robinson, A. H., Sale, R., and Morrison, J. (1978). *Elements of cartography* (4th edn). Wiley, New York.

Rogers, D. F. and Adams, J. A. (1976). *Mathematical elements for computer graphics.* McGraw-Hill, New York.

Ryan, D. L. (1979). *Computer-aided graphics and design.* Marcel Dekker, New York.

Sibert, J. L. (1980). Continuous-color choropleth maps. *GeoProcessing* **1**, 207–16.

Snijder, J. P. (1978). The space oblique Mercator projection. *Photogramm. Engng. Rem. Sens.* **44**(5), 585–96.

Swain, P. H. and Davis, S. M. (1978). *Remote sensing: the quantitative approach.* McGraw-Hill, New York.

Switzer, W. (1979). Personal communication. Canada Land Data Systems Division, Ottawa, Canada.

Thompson, R. J. (1979). Personal communication. United States Department of the Interior. Geological Survey EROS Data Center, Sioux Falls, South Dakota.

Tomlinson, R. F. (1967). An introduction to the Geo-Information system of the Canada Land Inventory. Ministry of Forestry and Rural Development, Ottawa.

Tomlinson, R. F. (1980). The handling of data for natural resources development. In *Proc. Workshop Information Requirements for Development Planning in Developing Countries.* ITC Enschede.

Waggoner, C. N. (1985). GKS, a standard for software OEMs. In Kunii (1985), pp. 362–74.

Williamson, A. N. (1977). Corrected LANDSAT images using a small computer. *Photogramm. Engng. Rem. Sens.* **43**(9), 1153–9.

3M Company (1968). The handling and storage of computer tape. *Computer Talk* Vol. 1, No. 1, 1–7, 3M Company, St. Paul, Minnesota.

5. Methods of Data Analysis and Spatial Modelling

Introduction

The major difference between geographical information systems and systems for computer-assisted cartography is the provision of capabilities for transforming the original spatial data in order to be able to answer particular queries. Some transformation capabilities, such as those necessary for data cleaning or updating, or for changing scales or projections, will be common to both geographical information systems and computer-assisted cartography. These transformation methods were discussed in Chapter 4. Geographical information systems, however, provide a very much larger range of analysis capabilities that will be able to operate on the topology or spatial aspects of the geographical data, on the non-spatial attributes of these data, or on non-spatial and spatial attributes combined. These analysis capabilities will, in most geographical information systems, be provided in such a way that a user can work interactively in order to perform the analyses and syntheses required.

Figure. 5.1 presents a hierarchical overview of the main kinds of capabilities that can be used for data utilization and analysis in geographical information systems. These capabilities range from simple methods for retrieving subsets of information from the database, through univariate and multivariate methods of statistical analysis to spatial analyses using neighbourhood functions and interpolation methods. Because interpolation methods and statistical methods of classifying data are more complex than many of the other data analysis techniques used, they are described in more detail in Chapters 7 and 8. Furthermore, as we shall see, spatial modelling methods can be used to create an almost unlimited range of capabilities for data analysis by stringing together sets of simple analysis capabilities, or by writing special simulation programs.

The general problem of data analysis is stated in Fig. 5.2. The user has a particular problem or query. The database contains information in the form of maps that can be used to answer the user's problem.

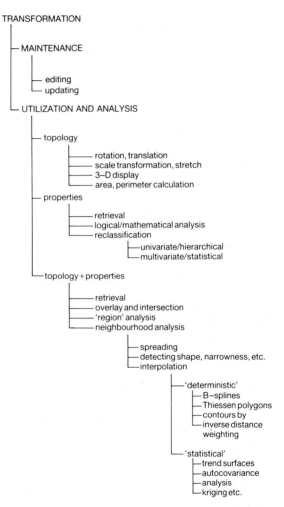

Fig. 5.1 Schematic overview of the hierarchy of data transformation operations in geographical information systems.

All that is necessary is to establish a link between database and output that will provide that answer in the form of a map, tables, or figures. The link is any function that can be used to convert data from one or

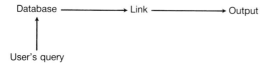

User's query

Fig. 5.2 The general statement of the data analysis problem.

Table 5.1 Truth table for Boolean operators

A	B	NOT A	A AND B	A OR B	A XOR B
1	1	0	1	1	0
1	0	0	0	1	1
0	1	1	0	1	1
0	0	1	0	0	0

NB 1 implies 'true'; 0 implies 'false'.

more input maps into an output map. This chapter is about how links can be defined and used.

Definition of the database

Before going further it is as well to define clearly the nature of the geographical database that will provide the information required. In most geographical information systems it is assumed that the information in the database is present in the form of points, lines, and areas and their associated attributes. While it is not essential for the user to know whether the spatial extents of the data are encoded in a vector or a raster form, certain operations will be easier in the vector form, and others will be easier in raster form.

Simple data retrieval

If the data have been encoded in a vector system using an overlay or layer structure (see Chapter 2), then the data that have been grouped together on that layer can be very simply retrieved. For example, if a system allows 64 different layers to be used, and if major roads have been entered into layer 1, minor roads on layer 2, railways on layer 3, rivers on layer 4, and so on, it is trivial to be able to display only major roads, or minor roads and rivers, simply by calling up the appropriate layers. These layer facilities were very common on the early CAD–CAM turn-key systems and are ideal for situations where there are few different kinds of graphical elements in the database. In geographical databases these methods are hardly appropriate because of the large number of attributes that each element may have. Besides, the simple layer system requires that data be classified for a particular layer before input, which has to be done manually; this is not feasible for a large database.

Boolean logic

The alternative procedure is to retrieve data by using the rules of Boolean logic to operate on the attributes and spatial properties. Boolean algebra uses the operators AND, OR, XOR, NOT to see whether a particular condition is true or false (Table 5.1). Simple Boo-

lean logic is often portrayed visually in the form of Venn diagrams (Fig. 5.3). If set A is the set of items having attribute a, and set B is the set of items having attribute b, then the statements

A AND B, A OR B, A XOR B, A NOT B,

will return items that have attribute combinations covered by the shaded portions of the respective Venn diagrams. For example, in a database of soil mapping units, each mapping unit may have attributes describing texture and pH of the topsoil. If set A is the set of

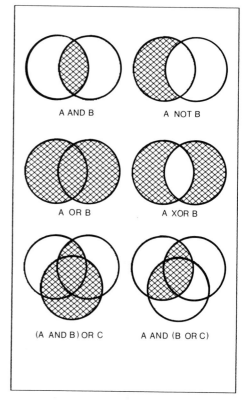

Fig. 5.3 Venn diagrams showing the results of applying Boolean logic to the intersection of two or more sets. In each case, the shaded area is 'true'.

all mapping units for which the topsoil has a clay loam texture, and if set B is the set of all mapping units for which the top soil pH exceeds 7.0, then the logical retrieval statements will work as follows:

X = A AND B finds all mapping units that have topsoil texture clay loam and a pH > 7.0 combined,

X = A OR B finds all mapping units that have either a topsoil texture of clay loam or a pH > 7.0, either separately or in combination,

X = A XOR B finds all mapping units that have either a topsoil texture of clay loam, or a pH > 7.0, but not in combination with each other.

X = A NOT B finds all mapping units that have a topsoil texture of clay loam in which the pH is 7.0 or less.

Note that unlike arithmetic operations, Boolean operations are not commutative. The result of A AND B OR C depends on the priority of AND with respect to OR. Parentheses are usually used to indicate clearly the order of evaluation (Fig. 5.3). In the example, if set C is all mapping units of poorly drained soil, then X = (A AND B) OR C returns all mapping units with a topsoil texture of clay loam combined with a pH > 7.0 or all poorly drained soil. This retrieval is not very specific. On the other hand, X = A OR (B AND C) returns all mapping units with the combination of pH.7.0 and poor drainage or those with a topsoil texture of clay loam.

Boolean operations should not be thought of as being only applicable to the attributes of the geographical elements, because they can also be applied to the spatial properties. For example, find all mapping units with clay loam texture in combination with a pH > 7.0 that exceed 5 ha in area. More complicated searches may involve the shapes of areas, the properties of the boundaries of areas or the properties of neighbouring areas. For example, in a land-use database, one might want to know all areas of woodland bordering urban areas, or in a visual classification of landscape to retrieve all open areas that have a particular shape and are bounded by a certain kind of hedgerow (cf. Buitenhuis *et al.* 1982).

Reclassification and display

Once the geographical data have been retrieved, it is usually necessary to reclassify them and to redisplay them so that the visual presentation reflects the new data structure as perceived by the user. When the data are polygons in vector format, reclassification procedures must ensure that when two or more adjacent polygons receive the same new name, the lines between them are dissolved and a new polygon network is con-

structed to obtain the statistics of the new map and for a clean map image (Figs 5.4, 5.5).

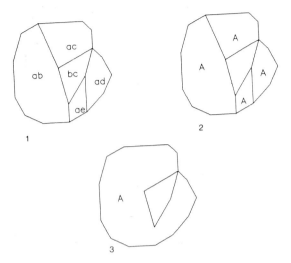

Fig. 5.4 When a source map (1) is reclassified and adjacent polygons receive the same code (2), it is necessary to dissolve the unnecessary boundaries and recompute the polygon structure (3).

Boolean operations on two or more maps

Very often the user will want to extract data from two or more maps: for example, he may want to know where a given kind of land use occurs on a particular kind of soil. The soil information will have been encoded in one map, the land-use information in another. The classical method of solving this problem is to lay transparent copies of each map on a light table and to trace off the corresponding areas (c.f. Plates 1–2). This is a time-consuming and inaccurate process, so one of the first requirements of many geographical information systems has been the ability to intersect two polygon networks so that Boolean logic can be applied to the results. Figure 5.6 shows the results of overlaying two simple maps, each containing six polygons. In this example, the resulting network contains 15 polygons. The number of polygons on the final map is not only dependent on the numbers of polygons on the initial maps, but also on the form of the boundaries. The more convoluted the boundaries on the source maps, the more derived polygons can be expected.

The problem of how to overlay two or more polygon networks occupied the attentions of computer cartographers for many years. The major stumbling block was how to deal with the very large number of small and seemingly unimportant polygons that resulted

Fig. 5.5 A soil series map (a) and its derivatives (b–d). The symbols on map (a) are the Netherlands Soil Survey map unit codes, which indicate from left to right, topsoil characteristics (*small letters*), soil family (*capital letter*), drainage class (*small letter*), texture class (*numbers*) and lime content (*A or C*). Units with 'As' in code are complexes. (b) is a derived map showing the first stage of generalization to soil families, with common lines removed. (c) shows the same map after interactive editing to improve the map image. (d) shows a derived map resulting from the Boolean classification algorithm 'polygon should be classed as "GOOD" IF soil family is "R" AND drainage is "d" AND if polygon area > 12 ha.' (Courtesy The Netherlands Soil Survey Institute.)

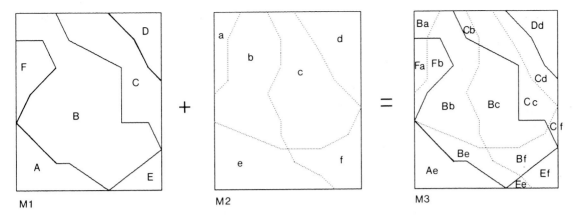

Fig. 5.6 The result of overlaying two simple maps to create a third. Many small, new polygons are created.

when lines on the two maps were almost but not quite, identical. These 'nonsense' areas must be filtered away or merged with the adjacent larger polygons in order to give a satisfactory map image of clean polygon outlines, a procedure that may lead to loss of information or to the creation of misinformation. The problem of the errors that can occur when polygons are overlaid is discussed more fully in Chapter 6. Another major problem with polygon overlay in vector format was the very heavy computing demands when searching for intersections of the boundary lines on the two maps, reconnecting the lines and building the new polygon network together with its associated attributes. The first major breakthrough was made by the Laboratory of Computer Graphics (White 1977) and is incorporated in the ODYSSEY program (Laboratory for Computer Graphics 1983). Now many other commercial geographical systems include polygon overlay software.

A general approach to map overlay

The intersection of two or more polygon nets by overlay is a special case of a much larger set of operations that can be used to analyse area data. In order to generalize it is useful to construct the following conceptual model of the geographical database.

A region is defined as a set of loci sharing a particular attribute or a certain value of a particular attribute. The loci are defined in terms of sets of X and Y coordinates. The simplest region is a point, having only one XY coordinate pair; the most complex encloses many loci. Note that a region may consist of one or more polygons or may be perforated by regions of another kind (cf. Fig. 2.1 (d, e))

An attribute is a given geographical variable or property. Attributes can be expressed on binary, nominal, interval, or ratio scales. Each attribute can be thought of as defining a separate overlay.

An overlay is a set of mutually exclusive contiguous regions associated with a particular area. Each overlay is defined by a given attribute.

Note that this model has a structure that is very similar to that used for raster representations of spatial data described in Chapter 2. In fact, the only difference is that in the raster database structure space is necessarily quantized into regular, usually square cells, whereas in this model no quantization is implied. Put another way, the raster database is a discrete approximation to the structure proposed here.

It is also assumed that for every locus on a map, a new attribute can be generated as a function of attributes on the overlays already present in the database. So, for every locus, with coordinates X, Y, a value of a new attribute can be expressed as:

$$U = f\{A, B, C, \ldots\} \qquad (5.1)$$

where $A, B, C, \ldots$ are the values of the attributes defining the first, second, third ... overlays, and f is a function that has yet to be defined (Fig. 5.7). The idea behind this function is of course the same as that behind the 'link' that was used in Fig. 5.2.

Classes of transformation functions: points, regions, and neighbourhoods

There are three major classes of transformation that can be used to control the transformation functions suggested by eqn (5.1). The first group of functions

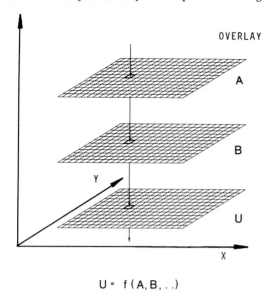

$$U = f(A, B, ..)$$

Fig. 5.7 A general approach to map overlay and transformation.

operates only on the values of all the attributes relating to each locus, (the vertical vectors of attribute values). In other words, the function or operation is independent of the effects of the values of attributes at neighbouring loci, and of general properties of the regions or sets to which the loci may also belong (Fig. 5.8(a)).

The simplest of these purely 'point' transformations are the mathematical operations of addition, subtraction, multiplication, division, exponentiation, taking logarithms, and evaluating trigonometrical functions. Just as simple are the finding of extremes or averages or applying Boolean logic. The value of the attribute on the new overlay could be a class value or name, or it could be the result obtained from a principal component analysis or a clustering algorithm. The function for computing the value on the new overlay could also be a simulation program designed to compute a single output value as a function of several input values, that in this model of geographical data would be obtained from the other overlays. Table 5.2(a) lists a number of the more commonly used 'point' functions. Note that the intersection of two polygon networks described above is essentially a simple logical operation for combining two overlays.

Most geographical information systems, particularly commercial systems, include methods for performing some 'point' operations, even if these are usually mainly limited to Boolean logic and reclassification.

The value of these methods in spatial analysis is often more the result of spatial autocovariance (loci close together are more likely to have similar values than loci that are far apart) than of any deliberate attempt to model spatial interactions.

The second class of functions relates to properties of the region or set to which a given locus belongs. These properties might be those of length, area, perimeter or shape, or they might relate to the number of loci having a certain value on one overlay that occur within the area defined by a region on another. For example, one may wish to produce a new map in which administrative areas are coded according to the number of schools within their boundaries from an overlay of administrative areas and school locations. Alternatively, one may wish to calculate a new value for a locus according to the properties of the boundary of the region in which the point lies. An example from landscape mapping was quoted above. These 'region' operations are summarized in Table 5.2(b); some are illustrated in Fig. 5.8 (b and c).

The third class of functions relates the point to its neighbours. These are all functions that explicitly make use of some kind of spatial associations in order to determine the value for the locus on the new overlay. These may include whether or not neighbouring points have the same value as the point in question, or the distance on a given overlay from the point in question to a point having a different value. Neighbourhood functions also include the calculation of a value representing a weighted average, maximum value, minimum value, measure of diversity or rate of change of a part of the statistical surface represented by the overlay in an area around the point, and so on. Some of these functions, such as computation of slope, aspect, and ridge and valley lines were described in Chapter 3. Others, such as methods of spatial interpolation, will be discussed in Chapter 8. Neighbourhood operations are summarized in Table 5.2(c) and some are illustrated in Fig. 5.8 (d–h).

A fourth class of operations in geographical information analysis concerns variations in spatial patterns over time. Most geographical information systems in current use treat the database as a static model of the landscape. A given analysis proceeds in one direction from database to the end product desired. A classic example is the production of land suitability maps from existing soil maps. But there are many situations where the landscape changes rapidly over time as a result of processes of erosion, salinization, deforestation, urban growth, lowering or raising the groundwater level, and so on. In these situations, analyses

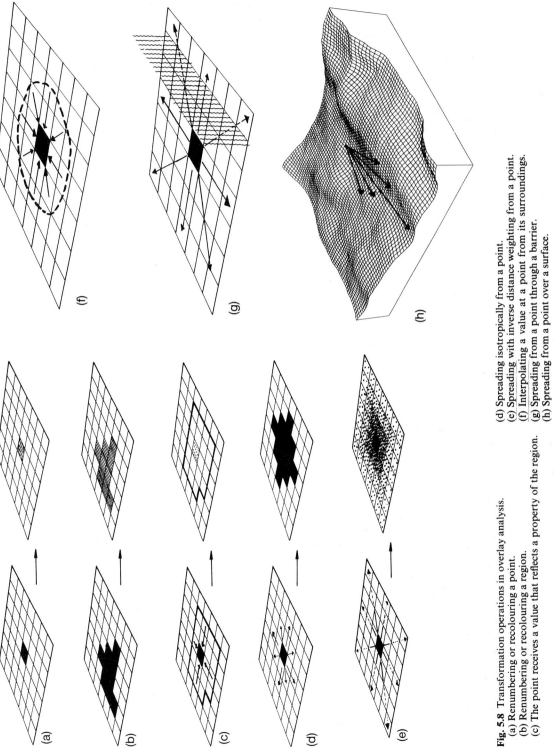

Fig. 5.8 Transformation operations in overlay analysis.
(a) Renumbering or recolouring a point.
(b) Renumbering or recolouring a region.
(c) The point receives a value that reflects a property of the region.
(d) Spreading isotropically from a point.
(e) Spreading with inverse distance weighting from a point.
(f) Interpolating a value at a point from its surroundings.
(g) Spreading from a point through a barrier.
(h) Spreading from a point over a surface.

Table 5.2   Overlay analysis capabilities
(a) Point operations

Operation	Keyword	Modifiers	Summary description
Summation	ADD	Weighting	Over all loci add values of two or more attributes to give new value
Subtraction	SUBTRACT	Weighting	Subtract
Multiplication	MULTIPLY	Weighting	Multiply
Division	DIVIDE	Weighting	Divide
Exponentiation	EXPONENTIATE	Weighting	Raise to power
Trig. functions			Convert to trig. function
Log. functions			Convert to log. function
Square root			Convert to square root
Averaging	AVERAGE		Take (weighted) average of two or more values to give new value
Covering	COVER	—	Cover one map with non-zero cell values of second map to give third map
Boolean combination	CROSS	AND/OR/NOT/XOR	Combine two or more discrete or continuous maps into a third using Boolean logic on attributes to yield a new map
Finding extremes	MAXIMIZE MINIMIZE	—	Find maximum/minimum values of attributes in two or more overlays and write to output overlay
Extraction or isolation	EXTRACT		Select specified values and/or ranges of values from one overlay to make a new overlay
Determine frequency distribution	HISTOGRAM		For whole overlay or selected area, compute histogram
Match frequency distribution to theoretical distribution	DISTRIBUTION STRETCH		For whole map or part of area, recompute image so that Z-values match theoretical distribution
Assign a constant value to an overlay	CONSTANT	—	Assign the constant value to all loci on an overlay
Divide range of cell values into equal classes	SLICE	—	Divide the range of values of a continuous or discrete attribute into equal number of intervals and assign new value to loci according to the interval in which it falls

Table 5.2 (a) continued

(a) Point operations

Operation	Keyword	Modifiers	Summary description
Two-way comparison of two overlays	SCORE	Average Total Maximum Minimum Median Majority Minority Diversity Deviation Overlap	Cross tabulate attribute values from two maps on a point-by-point basis. Resulting summary statistic yields a new map
Multivariate operations and class allocation	PCOMP		Principal component transform of cell values on *n* overlays (bands) PC scores written to output overlays
	CLUSTER		Perform cluster analysis
	ALLOCATE	Nearest neighbour Class mean Parallelepiped Maximum likelihood	Allocate unit to a class on output map according to a classification and allocation criteria.
Fourier transforms + filtering	FOURIER		Compute two-dimensional Fourier transforms and apply filters for high or low components. Recompute map by universal Fourier transform.

(b) 'Region' or legend unit operations

Operation	Keyword	Modifiers	Summary description
Reclassify or renumber legend units	RENUMBER		Assigns new values to specified units or legend values or ranges of values on map. Can also be used to enhance contrast in an image
Determine	REPORT SIZE AREA PERIMETER LENGTH Number of separate occurrences	Lines Regions	Compute or read from database the appropriate data about regions and display or write to file
Determine shape of region and/or holes	EULER		Determine the shape or form of a given region and the number of separate occurrences of region on an overlay
Reclassify regions according to area	SIZE		Compute area of each region and rename accordingly to give discrete output map

Table 5.2 (b) continued

(b) 'Region' or legend unit operations

Operation	Keyword	Modifiers	Summary description
Overlay/intersect two polygon nets	OVERLAY		Lay two polygon networks over each other and produce new polygon net (vector or raster)
Boolean search on regions			As for points
Classify region according to inclusions			As for points

(c) Neighbourhood functions/operations

Operation	Keyword	Modifiers	Summary description
Continuity of adjacent units	CLUMP	Distance criterion or 'friction criterion'	Create a new map by uniquely identifying contiguous groups or 'clumps' of units. Contiguity may be specified by a distance criterion
	SCAN	Distance Average Total Maximum Minimum Median Majority Minority Diversity Deviation Proportion	Summarize value for each unit on a map according to statistics of neighbouring units within/beyond a given distance to create a new continuous map (pixels/points)
	SPAN	Distance	Compute a value for each pixel on a discrete map according to the distance from that cell to a cell in another class
Find sites within distance and/or range of values of a given target	DSEARCH	Distance Range Direction	Select points within a specified distance or range on a continuous or discrete map and create new map
Functions of a continuous surface	SLOPE	Average Maximum	Differentiate overlay representing a continuous surface to give gradient map as output
	ASPECT		Idem, but for orientation of slopes
	PROFILE		Analyse type of slope profiles

Table 5.2 (c) continued

(c) Neighbourhood functions/operations

Operation	Keyword	Modifiers	Summary description
Functions to make a continuous surface from point data (INTER-POLATION)	SPREAD	Distance	Renumber all loci with a value reflecting their distance from a given starting point or line
		Over Uphill Downhill Through	Modify spreading/interpolate by using a continuous or discrete map to determine spreading pathways. The 'substrate' map may also include barriers
Contouring	CONTOUR		Create isopleth map from gridded data
Interpolate	TREND		Compute trend surface and map it as continuous overlay
	INVERSE		Compute weighted average value for each pixel and map as a continuous overlay
	OPTIMAL		Use covariance functions to aid interpolation (KRIGING etc.)
Functions to look over a continuous surface or find shortest path	VIEW	Over	Allocate output cells to one of two classes according to whether they can be 'seen' from a target point on one overlay looking over a continuous three-dimensional surface on another
	STREAM	Over	Find shortest route between two points on a continuous surface
	PATHWAY		Find shortest path along network in terms of time, cost distance, etc.
Point in polygon	PPOINT		Find the area containing a given point

based on a database that has been built up with a philosophy of semi-permanence cannot hope to produce relevant answers. Given that the variation of a process over time is understood, however, there is no reason why dynamic elements should not be incorporated into the analysis of geographical data.

Cartographic modelling using natural language commands

The user of a geographical information system is not necessarily interested in knowing exactly how the various point, region or neighbourhood operations are programmed, nor in the exact methods used for organizing the data in the computer. He or she is much more likely to have a good general knowledge of arithmetical and logical processes and would prefer to use these existing skills for the geographical analyses that must be done. Ideally, the user would like to be able to express his thoughts in a language that is also very similar to that used in his daily work. The great popularity of spreadsheet programs, on business microcomputers for example, is a striking example of how users respond to computer systems that are designed specifically to cope with their needs in terms they can easily understand. So, if a planner wants to create a buffer zone around a set of roads, he does not really want to have to digitize the buffer zone interactively around all the roads he has displayed on a screen, but he would much rather be able to say to the computer something like 'SPREAD ROADS TO X METERS' in order to create the required *x*-metre wide zone. The planner may then want to know how many houses there are in this zone, and in natural language he would say 'COUNT HOUSES IN BUFFER ZONE'. He might also want to determine the average density of houses in different parts of the buffer zone, in which case he would like to be able to say something like 'MAP HOUSING DENSITY IN BUFFER ZONE INTO FIVE EQUAL-VALUED CLASSES'. In other words, if a user can express the action in words that he wishes to perform on the geographical data, why should he not be able to express that action in similar terms to the computer?

Dana Tomlin, now of Harvard, made a great step towards turning a set of computer programs into a useful interactive tool-chest when he proposed a method for defining what he called a 'map algebra', and then wrote an experimental computer program to implement his ideas (Tomlin 1983a, b). The program is called the Map Analysis Package (MAP). Tomlin developed his ideas together with J. K. Berry of Yale and Carl Steinitz of Harvard. Tomlin's program uses ideas similar to those discussed for command language interpreters in Chapter 4. Each overlay in MAP represents a separate attribute and it is referred to by a unique name. Each spatial analysis operation is called up by a verb, the action of which may be controlled by an appropriate modifier. Table 5.2 also includes the appropriate verbs (keywords) and modifiers for each of the operations listed (NB the terms used here include some extensions to Tomlin's originals).

Just as in normal language verbs act on nouns, so in Tomlin's algebra the verbs act on one or more overlays. So the syntax of the Map Analysis Package allows a user to tell the computer to

ADD OVERLAY1 TO OVERLAY2 FOR OVERLAY3

when he wants to sum the values of two attributes over all loci covered by the map. If a user wants to convert a soil series map to a land quality map, then he can say

RENUMBER SERIES FOR LANDQUALX

followed by a definition of the correspondence between the soil series classes on overlay 'SERIES' and the required land quality *X* that will be produced on overlay 'LANDQUALX'.

Most of the other point and region operations given in Table 5.2 will be self-explanatory from the descriptions given, but some of the neighbourhood functions such as SCAN and SPREAD may require a little more explanation.

When a user wishes to compare a site with its surroundings he scans around to take note of the vicinity in which it is situated. So it is necessary to specify just what is meant by 'vicinity' and also to specify the kind of comparison that is to be made. The statement

SCAN OVERLAY1 AVERAGE WITHIN D FOR OVERLAY2

requests the computer to compute for every locus on OVERLAY2 a value that is the average of the values of all points within distance *D* of that locus on OVERLAY1. It is a way of specifying a local smoothing function. The statement

SCAN OVERLAY1 DIVERSITY WITHIN D FOR OVERLAY2

asks the computer to write a measure of the number of different values found within the circle radius *D* centred on the locus in OVERLAY1 to OVERLAY2. This version of the command results in an output overlay that displays the spatial complexity of the input overlay.

Very many neighbourhood operations involve the transfer of material or energy over topographical surfaces or over surfaces in which the third dimension represents travel time or construction costs. Material may spread uphill or downhill or may be affected by the presence of filters and barriers. As material spreads through a filter the incremental costs in energy or dollars may be increased by the nature of the 'friction' in the filter. Take for example, the travel times associated with travelling by car into the inner city area. The travel time (or cost) is a function of the 'friction' imposed on movement by the inner city jams. So a planner wishing to study travel times, if he had prepared an overlay detailing the locus of his starting point and an overlay of traffic density, could simply prepare a travel cost map by giving the command

SPREAD STARTPOINT THROUGH TRAFFIC TO D FOR TRAVELCOST

where *D* is the distance from the starting point over which the analysis is required.

A rural planner might be more interested in the area that can be irrigated by gravity flow from a dam. In this case he would want to prepare two overlays, one the dam site, the other a digital elevation model. The command

SPREAD DAMSITE DOWNHILL OVER TOPO
TO D FOR IRRIGATION

would give him the required result. He could then place dams at other locations and compare the results.

Linking command sequences into cartographic models

By linking the 'primitive' point, region, and neighbourhood commands together in sequence, so that the output overlay from one command is the input to the next, Tomlin, Steinitz, and colleagues have shown that it is possible to create an unlimited number of tailor-made map-processing capabilities that can be used to tackle many analytical problems in geographical information processing. They call these command sequences 'cartographic models', and the process 'cartographic modeling'. The idea is that the user when confronted by a problem should not immediately rush to the nearest available keyboard but should first attempt to work out for himself the data needed in order to provide the answer. The next step is to work out using clear logic how one should proceed from the data to the required answer. This means setting up a flow chart in which all the necessary steps are clearly shown. This is followed by translating the processing steps into the language of the MAP commands (or the language of the system being used if it is not the Map Analysis Package). Only when this line of reasoning has been clearly thought out and translated should the user go to the computer.

The easiest way to appreciate how such a system of cartographic modelling and map 'algebra' can be used for analysing geographical data is to follow through a number of simple examples that illustrate clearly the principles involved.

Three examples of cartographic modelling applied to land evaluation in a developing country

These three examples use data collected from a small study area in Kisii District in Kenya (Legis 1983) for an experimental geographical information system analysis using the Map Analysis Package. The Kisii District was used as a training area for students of Tropical Soil Science by the Agricultural University, Wageningen from *c.* 1974–1982 for soil survey and land evaluation. Compared with many developing countries, therefore, there is a considerable amount of detailed information about many aspects of the area, which has been brought together by Wielemaker and Boxem (1982). The actual study area covers some 1406 ha (3750×3750 m) lying within the area covered by the 1:12 500 detailed soil survey of the Marongo area, Kisii District (Boerma *et al.* 1974). This small area was chosen for its wide variety of parent material (seven major geological types), relief (altitude ranges from 4700 to 5300 ft above sea level—1420–1600 m) and soil (12 mapping units). The detailed soil survey included information about parent material, soil series, soil depth to weathered bedrock, stoniness, and rockiness. Each of these attributes was digitized as a separate overlay on to a 60×60 array of cells. Each cell covered some 0.39 ha. The contour map was also digitized to yield a digital elevation model (see Chapter 3), which is shown in Fig. 3.6. Information about the climate, the chemical status of the soil, the land use, and cultural practices was also available (Wielemaker and Boxem 1982.) Other information about roads, streams, and the location of settlements and infrastructure such as the coffee factory were digitized from the topographical map on to separate overlays. The lengths of the slopes (needed for estimating erosion) were interpreted from stereo aerial photographs and digitized as a separate overlay. Besides the mapped data, information was also available relating the soil series to sets of land qualities that could be used for determining the suitability of the area for various kinds of land use, or in the terminology of FAO land evaluation, 'land utilization types'. These data were available in the form of conversion tables.

Example 1. Prepare a suitability map for smallholder maize cultivation, using the FAO Land Evaluation Methodology (FAO 1976; McRae and Burnham 1981).

The FAO land evaluation methodology proceeds by converting land characteristics, or primary land attributes that are recorded by a soil survey, into a set of land qualities that are relevant for the land utilization type under consideration (in this case smallholder maize). Four land qualities are important for determining the physical land suitability for growing maize; these are nutrient supply, oxygen supply, water supply and erosion susceptibility. These land qualities can be ranked according to the following classes:

(a) No limitation;
(b) Moderate limitation;
(c) Severe limitation.

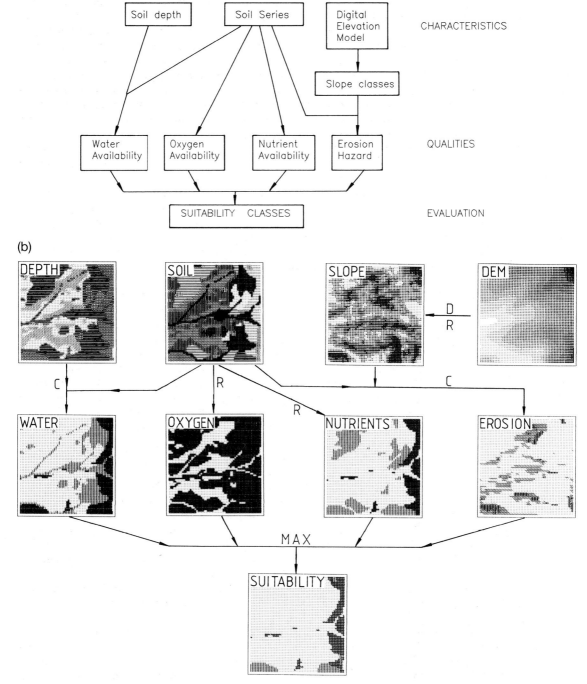

Fig. 5.9 Flowchart of the operations needed to create a map of suitability classes for maize using FAO Land Evaluation procedures.

C = CROSS operation; R = RENUMBER operation;
D = DIFFERENTIATE operation; MAX = MAXIMIZE operation. Darker tones on all maps except 'SOIL' indicate 'more' or 'better'.

Key to maps: DEPTH = soil depth classes; SOIL = soil series; SLOPE = slope classes; DEM = digital elevation model; WATER = land quality map of water supply for roots; OXYGEN = idem for oxygen supply; NUTRIENTS = idem for nutrients; EROSION = susceptibility to erosion under maize; SUITABILITY = final result.

Each land quality is determined by assessing the appropriate land characteristics. Water availability is a function of soil depth and soil series; oxygen availability and nutrient availability can be derived directly from the soil series information, and the erosion susceptibility or hazard can be considered to be a function of slope gradient and soil series. The actual values of the conversion functions are given in Wielemaker and Boxem (1982).

Figure 5.9 shows a flow chart of operations that could be used to determine the land suitability. The soil series overlay is converted into oxygen and nutrient availability overlays by using the RENUMBER operation twice. The digital elevation model is differentiated to yield a gradient model that is then classified using the RENUMBER operation again. The resulting slope classes are combined with the soil series overlay by the CROSS operation. The CROSS operation is also used to obtain classes for water availability from the overlays of soil depth and soil series. In each case, the resulting land quality overlays are coded with the values 1, 2, or 3 to indicate no limitations, moderate or severe limitations.

The resulting land suitability at each locus in the area is determined by the worst case of the four land quality overlays. This can be found easily by using the MAXIMIZE operation, which gives the required end result. This map is then made ready for presentation by presenting a suitable legend and display symbolism. Once the flowchart has been set up, the analysis proceeds automatically and equally for all parts of the survey area. No mistakes are made because a conversion code for a particular area was misread or omitted, as can sometimes happen when the analysis is done by hand. It costs no more than a few minutes to implement this kind of analysis on even a small computer, and it is simple to repeat using other values of the conversion factors relating soil to the land qualities. On the other hand, the result is no better than the data and the insight in the land evaluation procedure allow.

Example 2. Estimate the suitability of the study area for smallholder maize for a time 40 years hence, assuming that in the interim period the farmers have been growing maize over the whole of the area simply to feed the population, which in 1985 was growing at more than 4 per cent per annum. Investigate which simple conservation methods the farmers can implement themselves in order to protect the soil from erosion, and determine in which parts of the area these conservation methods are most likely to be successful.

This problem is an example of a common type of situation in land evaluation. Data exist for the present situation, or for some time in the recent past. The landscape will change, the data will become obsolete, and the changes will be complex and not totally predictable. We can gather insight into what might happen in the future by working with 'scenarios'—plausible models that can be applied to the digital database in order to explore quickly and easily what might happen. Rather than letting land-use planners loose in situations in which they have little or no experience (and the increasing pressures on land in developing countries is giving rise to situations that few have the necessary expertise to handle) it is surely preferable to train them on digital models of the landscapes. Just as pilots learn to fly on flight simulators, and architects and road designers build maquettes in order to broaden their experience and develop their ideas, so the land use planner can learn from 'mistakes' made on digital landscape models before irrevocable errors are made in the landscape itself.

The approach adopted for this problem was to assume that erosion was likely to be the greatest problem for continuing success with maize growing, in spite of the fact that erosion is not a serious problem in the Kisii area today. It is well known, however, that erosion is often a result of intensifying agriculture, and in the Kisii area the local farmers had already been encouraged to make use of maize stalks to construct 'trash lines' along the contours in order to reduce soil losses (Wielemaker and Boxem 1982). So the main problem is one of how to estimate soil losses. This was done by including an empirical erosion model in the land evaluation procedure in order to estimate (a) how soil depths might be reduced by erosion, (b) absolute rates of erosion, and (c) the benefits of the trash lines. The information about new soil depths, rates of erosion, and the benefits of trash lines could be incorporated into a new, future 'soil conditions for maize' overlay that would replace the erosion overlay used in the previous example. At the same time, the intersection of the new depth and the soil series maps could give new estimates of the nutrient availability, oxygen availability, and water availability (Fig. 5.10).

Two empirical erosion models were used to simulate the soil losses, namely the Universal Soil Loss Equation (USLE) developed by Wishchmeier and Smith (1978) and the Soil Loss Estimation Model for Southern Africa (SLEMSA) developed by Stocking (1981). These empirical methods were used because they are well-known, easy to compute, and the data for both

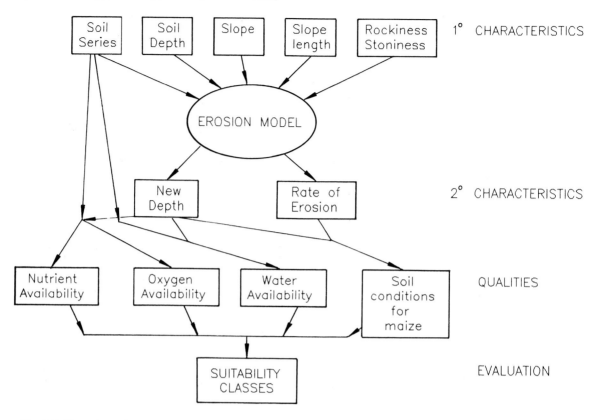

Fig. 5.10 Flow chart of the operations used to estimate the suitability of the area for maize 40 years hence.

were already in the database. The disadvantage of these empirical models is that they are a grosss over-simplification of the real problem of estimating erosion (e.g. see de Ploey 1983), but specialist models are often location-specific or require data that are not to be found in general purpose databases.

Although it is possible to use the Map Analysis Package commands to compute the USLE or SLEMSA, it is not efficient to perform specialist analyses within a general purpose package and so a special computer program was written. This program was able to accept output from the Map Analysis Package as input, and its output could be immediately read in to MAP.

The erosion models were used as point operations, i.e. they computed the soil loss per cell without taking into account the soil losses and gains over neighbour-ing grid cells. The effects of simple terracing using trash lines on the erosion were estimated by reclassi-

fying the slope length overlay and repeating the si-mulations. In all, the simulations resulted in 12 new overlays, of new soil depth, of new rockiness and rate of erosion for both models with and without the effects of the trash lines. For a given model, subtract-ing the overlay of the rate of erosion with trash lines from the overlay estimated using no trash lines gives a map showing where terracing will have most benefit. Subtracting the overlays of the rates of erosion esti-mated under the same conditions by each of the two models yields an overlay of the difference in estimates provided by the models (Fig. 5.11). Note the large absolute differences in erosion estimated by the two models.

The results of the simulations suggest that there will be a slow degradation of the landscape's suitability for maize over the period—class a) areas decline from 14.1 per cent to 11.6 per cent, and marginal areas from 51.3 per cent to 50.6 per cent over the 40 years. The

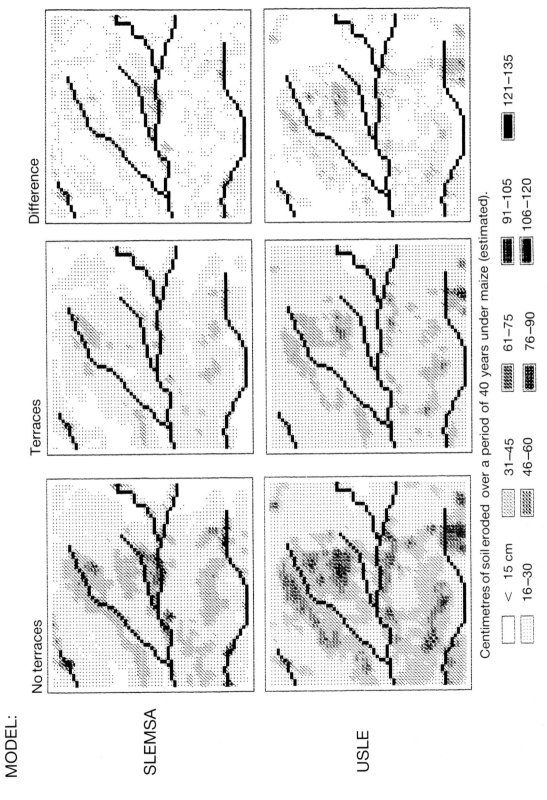

Centimetres of soil eroded over a period of 40 years under maize (estimated).

Fig. 5.11 Estimating erosion under maize in Kisii, Kenya.

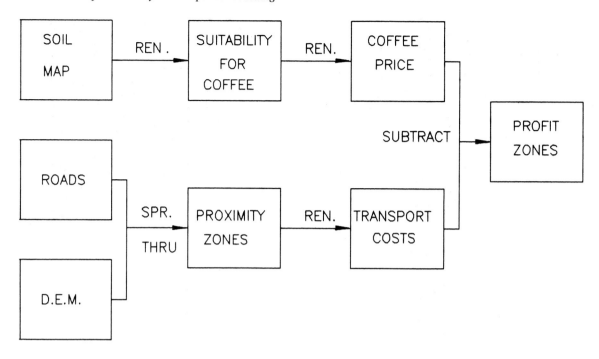

Fig. 5.12 Flowchart of the operations used to estimate the profitability of growing coffee.

simulations suggest that erosion will be concentrated in certain areas, and that in some of these the degree of erosion will be little modified by trash lines. The sensible conclusion would be to use these areas for some other, more permanent crop that would support the local population in other ways.

At first sight, the results seem quite convincing and realistic, but we have no way of knowing if they are anywhere near the truth. It is well known that empirical equations cannot easily be transported from one country to another, in spite of the many efforts that have been made to find truly 'universal' models. It is essential that all models are properly calibrated by reliable field work in the areas where they are used.

Example 3. Given that the coffee factory is located near a hilltop in the north-east of the area, and that

the area is crossed by roads along which coffee can be transported to the factory, evaluate the suitability of the various parts of the area for growing coffee.

The suitability of the various parts of the area for coffee depends on (a) the physical suitability of the soil for growing coffee, and (b) the proximity of that site to transportation facilities. We shall assume that all coffee beans must be carried by labourers from the coffee trees to the roads. Consequently, transport costs will increase both with distance from a road and with the relative elevation of site and road.

Figure 5.12 is a flowchart of the operations necessary. The evaluation of the physical suitability for coffee is similar to that for maize, involving a simple translation of the soil series overlay into land qualities, which are then combined into suitabilities. A further renumbering converts coffee suitability into the price

Coffee price

▨	20
▨	40
▨	60
▨	80

Fig. 5.13 Expected returns for coffee based on physical suitability.

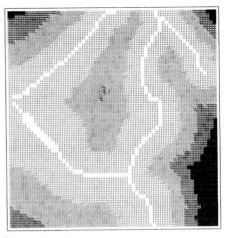

Transport costs

☐	0
▨	10
▨	15
▨	20
▨	25

Fig. 5.15 Transport cost zones.

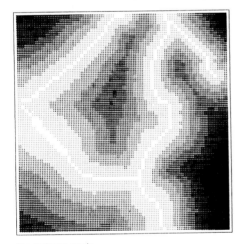

Proximity to roads

Fig. 5.14 Proximity to roads as a function of distance and altitude.

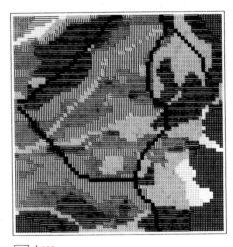

☐	Loss
▨	No profit or loss

Increasing profit

Road

Fig. 5.16 Expected profits for coffee as a function of physical suitability and proximity to transport.

expected for coffee beans, excluding transport (Fig. 5.13). The evaluation of the spatial suitability requires the use of neighbourhood analyses in order to assess the effect of proximity to a road. The road proximity can be assessed by creating an asymetric buffer zone along the road, in which the width of the buffer is initially determined by distance. This can be achieved by regarding the topography as a 'filter' or barrier through which the coffee must be carried (Fig. 5.14). These distance zones can be converted to costs simply by renumbering in terms of the prices the labourers have to be paid (Fig. 5.15). Subtracting the transport costs map from the expected prices yields the map of expected profits (Fig. 5.16). Using the price units adopted here shows that while some areas are clearly quite profitable, farmers on other parts of the area not very far removed from the good sites would operate at a loss. The total expected profit for the area as a whole, could of course be obtained by simply integrating over the whole map.

Advantages and disadvantages of cartographic modelling in land evaluation and planning

The examples presented above offer only a limited introduction to the possibilities for 'cartographic modelling' that are offered by a generic tool kit for spatial analysis such as the Map Analysis Package, or the other analytical geographical information systems currently being used and developed. The same or similar techniques have been used in many projects in landscape planning, particularly in North America, and many case studies have been published for applications ranging from simulating the effects of regional planning on spatial development to the utilization of deer habitats (see for example, Steinitz 1979; Steinitz 1982; Steinitz and Brown 1981; Teicholz and Berry 1983; Tomlin *et al.* 1983).

In October 1983, the Map Analysis Package had been acquired by 71 University departments (10 outside North America), 38 public agencies and government research institutes and 35 private organizations (Berry 1983). So far there have been fewer applications of cartographic modelling in Europe than in North America, but the techniques are gaining ground, particularly in West Germany (e.g. Arnold *et al.* 1982 for resolving land-use conflicts between highway routes and nature reserves), Yugoslavia (e.g. Marusic 1982 for regional planning) and in The Netherlands for local authority and ecological planning (e.g. van den Berg *et al.* 1984; van den Berg and Blom 1985). Similar

techniques are also incorporated into a number of commercial packages.

There are several important advantages to using a system of spatial analysis such as that described above. The first is that the user very quickly learns how to use the geographical information system when he or she can communicate with the computer in terms not too far removed from those used in daily practice. The author's experience of using the Map Analysis Package in both undergraduate and post-academic teaching courses bears out the ease with which students can begin to use spatial analysis techniques without first having to undergo boring computer courses.

A major advantage of 'cartographic modelling' compared with conventional methods of land evaluation and planning, at least as carried out in some countries and in some disciplines, is the need to define the problem clearly and to decide on the data required to solve it. The need to develop a clear, logical flowchart using well-defined spatial operations that can be linked together forces the user to think clearly about the steps needed to solve the problem and to make his methodology open to examination. The ease with which a number of options or scenarios can be compared, linked to the possibilities for the simulation of processes over time permits 'what if?' analyses that are simply not possible without a geographical information system. These kinds of analyses are usually easier to carry out in systems using a raster overlay database structure, though some, such as finding the shortest path through a network, are naturally easier in vector structures. The graphical quality of these raster analyses should not be judged from the simple lineprinter graphics used here to illustrate the results of cartographic modelling because recent hardware developments have made the quality of raster images approach that of vector plotters for comparable prices (see Chapter 4).

The main disadvantages of cartographic modelling are associated not so much with the lower spatial resolution of raster database structures but with the deterministic assumptions of the 'algebra' and the spatial algorithms. Current systems often use integer numbers to represent all kinds of information on the overlays, even though the original data may have been encoded on nominal or ranked scales. The user needs to be well aware that mathematical operations (e.g. ADD or SUBTRACT) have no meaning when used for nominal or ranked variables, though Boolean logical operations on such variables are quite legitimate. A second, major problem is that the modelling steps implicitly assume that all information encoded on the overlays is absolutely correct and contains no error components whatsoever. It is tacitly assumed that there is no propagation of errors from one stage in the modelling to the next. A third problem is that most of the spatial analysis operations listed in Table 5.2 are noncommutative, so the user must be especially careful about the order in which transformations are carried out. As with all tools and instruments, good and skilful use comes with practice, and the new user of spatial analysis tools such as the Map Analysis Package is advised to pay particular attention not only to the way in which the program runs on the computer, but to the organizational and intellectual opportunities it affords.

References

Arnold, F. Brocksieper, R., Rijpert, J. M. S., and Winkelbrandt, A., (1982). Umweltverträglichkeitsprüfung zur geplanten Bundesautobahn A 46. *Natur u. Landschaft* **57**, 458–63.

Berg, A. van den, Bijlholt, A. G., Germeraad, P. W., van Lith-Kranendonk, J., and Roos-Klein Lankhorst, J., (1984). Landschapsanalyse Boxtel: onderzoek naar de bruikbaarheid van het computerprogramma MAP voor planvorming op gemeentelijke niveau. Rapport No. 364 Rijksinstituut voor Onderzoek in de Bos- en Landschapsbouw 'De Dorschkamp', Wageningen.

——and Blom, R., ed. (1985). MAP-studiedag. In *Proc. Workshop over the Applications of the MAP Program*, 10 May 1985. Rijksinstituut voor Onderzoek in de Bos- en Landschapsbouw 'De Dorschkamp', Wageningen.

Berry, J. K. (1983). *MAP-NEWS*. The newsletter of Map Analysis Package (MAP) users, Vol 1, No. 1. Yale University School of Forestry and Environmental Studies, Connecticut, USA.

Boerma, P. N., Henneman, G. R., Kauffman, J. H., and Verwey, H. E. (1974). Detailed soil survey of the Marongo area. Preliminary report No. 3. Training project in Pedology, Agricultural University, Wageningen.

Buitenhuis, A., Burrough, P. A., and de Veer A. A. (1982). Het gebruik van het Informatiesysteem Landschapsbeeld voor de herziening van het Streekplan Twente. Report No. 1470, Netherlands Soil Survey Institute, Wageningen.

FAO 1976. A framework for land evaluation. Soils Bulletin No. 32. FAO Rome and ILRI, Wageningen, Publication No. 22.

Laboratory of Computer Graphics (1983). The ODYSSEY system summary. Laboratory of Computer Graphics and Spatial Analysis, Harvard University.

Legis, R. P. L. (1983). Computer mapping techniques for assisting land evaluation and assessment of erosion hazards in Kisii, Kenya. M.Sc. Thesis, course in Soil Science and Water Management, Agricultural University, Wageningen.

McRae, S. G. and Burnham C. P. (1981). *Land evaluation*. Oxford University Press, Oxford.

Marusic, I. J. (1982). Landschaftsplanung auf Computerbasis—Erstellung eines umfassenden Landschaftsplans für das gebiet von Ljubljana. *Natur u. Landschaft* **57**, 441–6

Ploey, J. de (ed.) (1983) Soil erosion. *Catena* Special Number No. 3.

Steinitz, C. (1979). Simulating alternative policies for implementing the Massachusetts Scenic and Recreational Rivers Act: the North River Demonstration Project. *Landsc. Plan.* **6**, 51–89.

—— (1982) Die Monadnock-Region von New Hampshire, Planung in Hinblick auf eine starke Landschaftsveränderung. *Natur u. Landschaft* **57**, 429–32.

—— and Brown, H. J. (1981). A computer modelling approach to managing urban expansion. *GeoProcessing* **1**, 341–75.

Stocking, M. (1981). A working model for the estimation of soil loss suitable for underdeveloped areas. Development Studies Occasional Paper No. 15, University of East Anglia, UK.

Teicholz, E. and Berry, B. J. L. (1983). *Computer graphics and environmental planning*. Prentice-Hall, Englewood Cliffs, NJ.

Tomlin, C. D. (1980). The Map Analysis Package (draft manual). Yale School of Forestry and Environmental Studies, Connecticut.

Tomlin, C. D. (1983a). Digital cartographic modelling techniques in environmental planning. Ph.D. dissertation, Yale University, Connecticut.

—— (1983b). A map algebra. In *Proc. Harvard Computer Conf. 1983*, 31 July–4 August, Cambridge, Mass.

—— Berwick, S. H., and Tomlin, S. M., (1983) Cartographic analysis of deer habitat utilization. In *Computer graphics and environmental planning* (ed. E. Teicholz and J. K. Berry) pp. 141–50. Prentice-Hall, Englewood Cliffs, NJ.

White, D. (1977). A new method of polygon overlay. In *Proc. Advanced Study Symp. on Topological Data Structures for Geographic Information Systems*, Harvard.

Wielemaker, W. G. and Boxem, H. W. (1982) Soils of the Kisil area, Kenya. Agricultural Research Report No. 922, PUDOC/Agricultural University, Wageningen, The Netherlands.

Wischmeier, W. H. and Smith, D. D. (1978) Predicting rainfall erosion losses. *Agricultural Handbook 537,* USDA, Washington, DC.

6. Data Quality, Errors, and Natural Variation

Geographical information systems are powerful but expensive tools. The expense arises not only from the cost of the hardware, software, and trained personnel, but also from the not inconsiderable costs of data collection, data capture, and processing. These latter costs may amount to a large proportion of total project costs—for example, some years ago, Bie and Beckett (1970) estimated that the costs of collecting soil survey field data were more than 50 per cent of total project costs. Data collection via remote sensors may be cheaper than field survey in pounds or dollars per square kilometre, but because of the volumes of data now being processed, costs of data input and verification are more than simply non-negligible budget items. It is implicit in the whole business of geographical resource information processing that the collection and processing of environmental data leads to improvements in environmental management and control. This can only be so if the data that are collected, entered, stored, and processed are sufficiently reliable and error-free for the purposes for which they are required.

The cartographic processes discussed in Chapter 5 made the implicit assumption that all the data used for the cartographic modelling were totally error-free. By 'error-free' is meant not only the absence of factually wrong data caused by faulty survey or input, but also statistical error, meaning free from variation. In other words, the cartographic operations of adding two maps together by means of a simple overlay imply that both source maps can be treated as perfect, completely deterministic documents with uniform levels of data quality over the whole study area.

There can be a false lure about the attractive, high-quality cartographic products that cartographers, and now computer graphics specialists, provide for their colleagues in environmental survey and resource analysis. As Chrisman (1984a) has pointed out 'we have developed expectations, such as smooth contour lines, which are not always supported by adequate evidence'. Blakemore (1984) has also recently drawn attention to the naïve claims of some adherents of computer cartography that computer-assisted cartographic products are necessarily accurate to the resolution of the hardware used to make them. He points out that a few critical authors, such as Boyle (1982), Goodchild (1978), Jenks (1981) and Poiker (1982) have drawn attention to the problems of errors in geographical information processing but that in general there has been inadequate investigation into how errors arise and are propagated.

Many soil scientists and geographers know from field experience that carefully drawn boundaries and contour lines on maps are elegant misrepresentations of changes that are often gradual, vague, or fuzzy. People have been so conditioned to seeing the variation of the earth's surface portrayed either by the stepped functions of choropleth maps (sharp boundaries) or by smoothly varying mathematical surfaces (e.g. Figs. 1.1, 1.2, 3.6) that they find it difficult to conceive that reality is otherwise. Besides the 'structure' that has been modelled by the boundaries or the isolines, there is very often a residual unmapped variation that occurs over distances smaller than those resolvable by the original survey. Moreover, the spatial variation of natural phenomena is not just a local noise function or inaccuracy that can be removed by collecting more data or by increasing the precision of measurement, but is often a fundamental aspect of nature that occurs at all scales, as the proponents of fractals have recently pointed out (see Mandelbrot 1982; Burrough 1983a, b, 1984, 1985; Goodchild 1980; Mark and Aronson 1984).

It is remarkable that there have been so few studies on the whole problem of residual variation and how errors arise, or are created and propagated in geographical information processing, and what the effects of these errors might be on the results of the studies made. This chapter gives first an overview of the basic issues involved, and then examines some aspects of error propagation in more detail.

Table 6.1 shows three main groups of factors governing the errors that may be associated with geographical information processing. The word 'error' is

Table 6.1 Sources of possible error in GIS

I. *Obvious sources of error*
 1. Age of data
 2. Areal coverage—partial or complete
 3. Map scale
 4. Density of observations
 5. Relevance
 6. Format
 7. Accessibility
 8. Cost

II. *Errors resulting from natural variations or from original measurements*
 9. Positional accuracy
 10. Accuracy of content—qualitative and quantitative
 11. Sources of variation in data:
   data entry or output faults
   observer bias
   natural variation

III. *Errors arising through processing*
 12. Numerical errors in the computer:
   the limitations of computer representations of numbers
 13. Faults arising through topological analyses:
   misuse of logic
   problems associated with map overlay
 14. Classification and generalization problems;
   methodology
   class interval definition
   interpolation

used here in its widest sense to include not only 'mistakes' but also to include the statistical concept of error meaning 'variation'. Group I errors include topics that are most obvious and easy to check on; Group II contains more subtle sources of error that can often only be detected while working intimately with the data. Group III is perhaps the most important because it includes the mistakes, errors, and misapprehensions that can arise as a result of carrying out certain kinds of processing. Group III errors are the most difficult to spot because they require an intimate knowledge of not only the data, but also of the data structures and the algorithms used. Consequently, they are likely to evade most users.

I. Obvious sources of error

1. Age of data

It is rare that all data are collected at the same time for a given project, unless that project is a specific piece of research. Most planners and environmental agencies are forced to use existing published data in the form of maps and reports, filled in as necessary by more recent remote sensing imagery (including aerial photographs) and field studies. Mead (1982) comments

that 'with the exception of geological data, the reliability of data decreases with age'. Although this may be broadly true in the sense that geology changes much more slowly than soil, water regimes, vegetation or land-use, it is also possible that old data are unsuitable because they were collected according to systems of standards that are no longer used or acceptable today. Many attempts to capture old data, using hand-written field sheets and out-of-date terminology, have had to be abandoned simply because of the enormous costs involved.

2. Areal coverage

It is desirable that the whole of a study area, be it an experimental field or a country, should have a uniform cover of information. Frequently this is not the case, however, and the user of resource data must make do with partial levels of information. It is quite common, even in developed countries, for there to be no complete cover of soil information over a study area, except at scales that are too small for the purpose required. Many countries still have fragmentary coverage of soil maps at scales of 1:25 000–1:50 000. Moreover, during the 30–40 years that soil survey has been taking place, the concepts and definitions of soil units, the ways they should be mapped, and the surveyors themselves have changed. This historical fact can lead to inconsequential map units along map sheet boundaries, that are difficult to resolve without further survey.

If coverage is not complete, decisions must be made about how the necessary uniformity is to be achieved. Options are to collect more data, or to generalize detailed data to match less detailed data. Note that it is extremely unwise to 'blow up' generalized or small-scale map data to obtain the necessary coverage.

3. Map scale

Most geographical resource data have been generated and stored in the form of thematic maps, and only in recent years with the development of digital information systems has it been possible to have the original field observations available for further processing. Large scale maps not only show more topological detail (spatial resolution) but usually have more detailed legends (e.g. a soil map of scale 1:25 000 and larger usually depicts soil series legend units, while a soil map of scale 1:250 000 will only display soil associations— see Vink 1963 for details). It is important that the scale of the source maps matches that required for the environmental study—small-scale maps could have insufficient detail and large scale maps may contain too much information that becomes a burden through the sheer volume of data. Many survey organizations provide their mapped information at a range of scales and the user should choose that which is most appropriate to the task in hand.

4. Density of observations

Much has been written about the density of observations needed to support a map (e.g. Vink 1963; Beckett and Burrough 1971; Webster and Burgess 1984), yet there are still many organizations that produce maps without giving any information whatsoever about the amount of ground truth upon which it is based. This attitude is changing—The Netherlands Soil Survey Institute provides its contract survey clients with maps showing the location and classification of all soil observations; the Land Resources Development Centre in London publishes maps showing the density and location of sample points and transects in surveys (see for example the Reconnaissance Soil Survey of Sabah, Acres *et al.* 1976).

Although the actual density of observations may be a reasonable general guide to the degree of reliability of the data, it is not an absolute measure, as statistical studies of soil variation have shown. A rough guide to the density of observations needed to resolve a given pattern is given by the 'sampling theorem' originating from electronic signal detection, that specifies that at least two observations per signal element need to be made in order to identify it uniquely. Webster (1977) and Nortcliff (1978) have shown how nested sampling techniques can be used to identify the spatial dimensions of soil patterns. The nested sampling techniques use a variance analysis to estimate the distances over which major increases in variance occur. Figure 6.1 presents some results of such a reconnaissance study conducted in The Netherlands (Burrough *et al.* 1983) in a complex landscape in which the lateral variation of the subsoil cannot be easily discerned either from landform or from aerial photographs. The landscape in question is built up from a Miocene clay substrate that has been partially covered by boulder clay. The boulder clay has itself been eroded by meltwaters and then covered by aeolian coversands of varying thickness. The results of the nested sampling suggested that decreasing sample spacing from 200 m to 20 m would result in a very limited improvement in the quality of a map displaying textural variations in the coversands. On the other hand, the spatial patterns of the boulder clay can only be resolved by sampling at intervals of less than 20 m.

There has also been considerable interest recently in

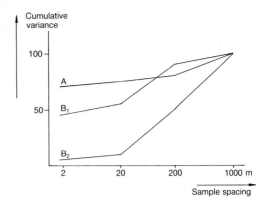

Fig. 6.1 Results of nested analysis of variance for some soil properties in the Hupselse Beek catchment area, The Netherlands, showing the clearly separated spatial structures of the late-Pleistocene coversand (A) and the underlying subsoil boulder clay (B_1, B_2).

using information from autocovariance studies to estimate the number of samples necessary to map an area or to estimate average values of areas to given levels of confidence (see for example, Burgess and Webster 1980; McBratney and Webster 1983; Webster and Burgess 1984). The results suggest that much can be gained by using the techniques of geostatistical spatial analysis providing that there is sufficient information to estimate the spatial relations (usually using the semivariogram) and that the assumptions of the methods used are valid. Interpolation methods will be explored in Chapter 8. As noted in Chapter 3, there has also been considerable work in photogrammetry to estimate the densities of observations that need to be made from aerial photographs in order to support reliable digital terrain models (Makarovic 1975; Ayeni 1982).

In short, sample density is only a rough guide to data quality. It is also important to know whether the sampling has been at an optimum density to be able to resolve the spatial patterns of interest.

5. Relevance

Not all data used in geographical information processing are directly relevant for the purpose for which they are used, but have been chosen as surrogates because the desired data do not exist or are too expensive to collect. Prime examples are the electronic signals from remote sensors that are used to estimate land use, biomass or moisture, or observations of soil series based on soil morphology that are used to predict soil fertility, erosion susceptibility or moisture supply. Provided that the links between the surrogates and the desired variables have been thoroughly established then the surrogates can be a source of good information.

The calibration of surrogates is a major part of remote sensing technology. Briefly, an apparently 'homogeneous' group of pixels on the image is selected for use as a 'training set'. The variation of reflectance of each frequency band recorded is displayed in the form of a histogram; the practice is to select a training set of pixels that return narrow, unimodal distributions. These training set pixels are calibrated by 'ground-truth' observations so that the set of pixels can be equated with a crop type. a soil unit or any other definable phenomenon. The remaining pixels in the image are then assigned to the same set as the training set, using allocation algorithms based on discriminant analysis (minimum distance in multivariate space of the original frequency bands), maximum likelihood or parallelepiped classifiers (see for example, Estes *et al.* 1983).

Maps of desired properties can sometimes be made by establishing statistical correlations with other, cheaper to measure properties, using regression analysis, co-spectral analysis or co-kriging (e.g. Davis 1973; McBratney and Webster 1983). In all cases, the quality of the map will always be less than that made using the desired data. The reader must not be swayed by the visual beauty of the presentation. Nevertheless, it may be more efficacious to use surrogates, simply because of the cost and difficulty of measuring the original property.

6. Format

There are three kinds of data format of importance. First there are the purely technical aspects of how data can be written on magnetic media for transfer from one computer system to another. These include such considerations as the kind of magnetic medium (tape, cassette, floppy disk, data line), the density of the written information (tape block lengths, number of tracks—usually nine—and the density of bits per inch—usually 800, 1600, or 6250 BPI), the type of characters used (ASCII, EBCDIC, or binary), and the lengths of records. For data lines, it is essential that the speed of transmission (in bauds) of the two computers is matched.

The second kind of format concerns the way the data are arranged, or in other words, the structure of the data themselves. Are mapped data encoded as points, as boundary codes (vectors) or as rasters? If the areas are coded in raster format, what is the size of each pixel? Is the organization of the data tied to a particular computer system that makes exchange difficult without conversion? For example, many turn-key graphics systems have their own internal data structures that make direct data exchange difficult. Standards do exist, however, (e.g. the IGES standard or the Graphics Kernel System standards), and are used increasingly. For example, many systems can output graphical data in the CALCOMP or TEKTRONIX standards to a wide range of plotting and display devices, respectively.

The third kind of format is most concerned with the data themselves, their scale, projection, and classification. Scale and projection conversions can usually be accomplished quite easily by using appropriate mathematical transformations ón the coordinate data (e.g. Maling 1973). Matching classifications can be very difficult, as anyone will know who has tried to classify soil profiles according to several systems of classification (e.g. de Bakker 1979).

To summarize, data exchange often requires that data be reformatted to a lowest common denominator format that can be read by many systems easily. These formats are not necessarily the most compact nor the most efficient but are expedient. Surprisingly enough, though there are standard data formats for satellite data, and there are format standards within countries for topographic data (e.g. in the UK for Ordnance Survey Maps, in The Netherlands and Germany for topographic mapping), international standards for cartographic data exchange have yet to be fully developed. This state of affairs reflects the rapid growth and development of digital geographical information processing.

7. Accessibility

Not all data are equally accessible. Data about land resources might be freely available in one country, but the same kind of data could be a state secret in another. Besides the military aspects of data for geographical information systems (here one thinks immediately of digital terrain models) inter-bureau rivalries can also obstruct the free flow of data. Costs and format problems can also seriously hinder data accessibility. In recent years a new kind of middleman, the information broker, has sprung up to assist the seeker of data from digital archives. Details about information services can be obtained from government or international agencies (e.g. Euronet DIANE News, the newsletter of the Directorate General for Information Market and Innovation, Commission of the European Communities, Luxemburg).

8. Costs

Collection and input of new data or conversion and reformatting of old data cost money. For any project, the project manager should be able to assess the costs and benefits of using existing data as compared with initiating new surveys. Digitizing costs may be especially high for inputting detailed hand-drawn maps or for linking attributes to spatial data. Scanners may offer savings for data input of contour lines and photographic images. It may be cheaper for a survey agency to contract out digitizing work to specialist service bureaux than to do the work in-house using staff who can be better used for more skilled work. Similarly, if an agency only occasionally needs to perform certain kinds of data transformations or to output results to expensive devices such as flat-bed plotters of high quality, it may be cheaper to make use of service bureaux.

II. Errors resulting from natural variation or from original measurements

1. Positional accuracy

The importance of the positional accuracy of geographical data depends largely on the type of data under consideration. Topographical data are usually surveyed to a very high degree of positional accuracy that is appropriate for the well-defined objects such as roads, houses, land parcel boundaries, and other features that they record. With modern techniques of electronic surveying the position of an object on the earth's surface can now be recorded to decimetre accuracy. In contrast, the position of soil or vegetation unit boundaries often reflects the judgement of the surveyor about where a dividing line, if any, should be placed. Very often, vegetation types grade into one another over a considerable distance as a result of transitions determined by microclimate, relief, soil, and water regimes. Changes in slope class or groundwater regime are also unlikely to occur always at sharply defined boundaries.

Positional errors can result from poor field work, through distortion or shrinkage of the original paper base map or through poor quality vectorizing after raster scanning. Local errors can often be corrected by interactive digitizing on a graphics workstation, while general positional errors can be corrected by various kinds of transformation, generally known as 'rubber sheeting' techniques, that have been described in Chapter 4.

The success of rubber sheeting methods depends largely on the type of data being transformed, and the complexity of the transformation. Many methods work well for simple linear transformations but break down when complex shrinkages must be corrected. The methods do not necessarily work well when the original map consists largely of linked, straight-line segments. For example, some years ago, attempts were made at The Netherlands Soil Survey Institute to use rubber sheeting methods to match a digitized version of an early nineteenth century topographic map to a modern 1:25 000 topographical sheet for the purpose of assessing changes in land use. The road pattern of the area in question was similar to that of a rigid girder structure. When submitted to the rubber sheeting process, the road lines were not stretched but the structure crumpled at the road intersections, in much the same way that a bridge or crane made from Meccano might crumple at the joins!

2. Accuracy of content

The accuracy of content is the problem of whether the attributes attached to the points, lines, and areas of the geographical database are correct or free from bias. We can distinguish between qualitative accuracy, which refers to whether nominal variables or labels are correct (for example, an area on a land-use map might be wrongly coded as 'wheat' instead of 'potatoes') and quantitative accuracy which refers to the level of bias in estimating the values assigned (for example, a badly calibrated pH meter might consistently estimate all pH values one unit high).

3. The sources of variation in data

Variations ('errors' in the broadest sense), can occur in geographical data in several ways. Errors resulting from mistakes in data entry are trivial in the sense that they can in principle be corrected. These kinds of mistakes can most easily be detected when they lead to unexpected values in the data; if they result in allowed values then detection is very difficult.

Measurement errors. Poor data can result from unreliable, inaccurate or biased observers or apparatus. The reader should clearly understand the distinction between accuracy and precision. Accuracy is the extent to which an estimated value approaches the true value, i.e. the degree to which it is free from bias. In statistical terminology, precision is a measure of the dispersion (usually measured in terms of the standard deviation) of observations about a mean. Precision also refers to the ability of a computer to represent numbers to a certain number of decimal digits.

Field data

The surveyor is a critical factor in the quality of data that are put in to many geographical information systems. Well-designed data collection procedures and standards help reduce observer bias. Even so, the user of environmental data obtained from field surveys should realize that some observers are inherently more perceptive or industrious than others;

the quality of soil surveyors varies from the two-minute job of an irresponsible aerial photo interpreter to that of the surveyor whose sampling plan suggests that he is planting onions (Smyth, quoted in Burrough 1969).

Very large differences in the appearance of a map can result from differences in surveyor or from mapping methods as studies by Bie and Beckett (1973) for soil survey and Salomé *et al.* (1982) for geomorphology have clearly demonstrated.

In large survey organizations it should be possible to determine and record the qualities of each surveyor, an extra attribute that could be stored with the data themselves. Such a procedure would almost certainly be strenuously resisted by the staff, however, as an attempt to reduce personal privacy, or to cast a slur on professional expertise and an introduction of policing. It is unlikely that any major survey organization in a democratic country could easily introduce a regular observer quality rating into its data-gathering methodology. A wiser approach for improving observer quality would be to improve all aspects of the data-gathering process, such as standardizing observational techniques, data recording forms, and by developing a joint commitment between survey management and staff to work to the highest possible standards.

Laboratory errors. Intuitively, one expects the quality of laboratory determinations to exceed those of field observations. Although determinations carried out within a single laboratory using the same procedure may be reproducible, the same cannot be said of analyses performed in different laboratories. The results of a recent world-wide laboratory exchange program carried out by the International Soil Reference and Information Centre in Wageningen (van Reeuwijk 1982, 1984) showed that variation between laboratories for the *same soil samples* could easily exceed ±11 per cent for clay content, ±20 per cent for Cation exchange capacity (±25 per cent for the clay fraction only), ±10 per cent for base saturation and ±0.2 units for pH. The implications for classification and standardization are enormous!

Spatial variation and map quality. Many thematic maps, particularly those of natural properties of the landscape such as soil or vegetation, do not take into account local sources of spatial variation or 'impurities' that result from short-range changes in the phenomena mapped. This problem has been the subject of much recent research, particularly in soil survey, soil physics and groundwater studies (e.g. Beckett and Webster 1971; Bouma and Bell 1983; Bouma and Nielsen 1985). The studies have concentrated on describing the level of variation and how quantitative methods for classifying and interpolating can aid survey and understanding. Chapter 8 is devoted to studying these quantitative methods in more detail.

Originally, systematically surveyed soil maps were estimated to contain no more than 15 per cent 'impurities' within the units delineated (Soil Survey Staff 1951). Impurities were defined as observations that did not match the full requirements as specified in the map legend. Many studies (e.g. Beckett 1971; Burrough *et al.* 1971; Marsman and de Gruijter 1985; Wilding *et al.* 1965) have shown that not only was the 15 per cent a wild guess, but that the concept of 'impurity' had little meaning. By varying the legend, the definition of just what was a matching observation, and so the purity, could be manipulated at will.

Much subsequent work (e.g. Beckett and Burrough 1971; Marsman and de Gruijter 1984) has focused on the within-map unit variance as a criterion of map quality, and at least one soil survey organization (The Netherlands Soil Survey Institute) has taken active measures to estimate map unit variance as a part of systematic soil survey (de Gruijter and Marsman 1985). The approach in many studies of map unit variance has been to regard the map unit classes as defining units in a one-way analysis of variance in which the value of a property Z at a point x is given by:

$$Z(x) = \mu + \alpha_j + \varepsilon \qquad (6.1)$$

where μ is the overall mean of Z for the entire map, α_j is the difference between μ and the mean of unit j, and ε is a normally distributed random residual variation or 'noise', otherwise known as the 'pooled within-class variance'.

In reality, the pooled within-class variance is insufficient to describe the residual variation within mapping units. This is because:

(a) for the same property different mapping units often have different levels of residual variation;

(b) the level of the residual variance very often has a power law relation to the size of the area mapped (e.g. Beckett and Webster 1971; Burrough 1983a,b; Mandelbrot 1982);

(c) the variation of the value of a property within a mapping unit is often not 'random' in the true statistical sense, but may often vary in a spatially correlated way that could be mapped out by using interpolation methods or by surveying at a larger scale.

The problem of classification and spatial variation will be discussed further in Chapters 7 and 8. Here it is important to realize that spatial variation within map units can contribute greatly to the relative and absolute errors of the results produced by map overlay analysis. More details about how to estimate the errors propagated in the overlay analyses are given later in this chapter.

III. Errors arising through processing

1. Numerical errors in the computer

As well as the problems inherent in the data indicated above, there are other sources of unseen error that can originate in the computer. The most easily forgotten, yet critical aspect of computer processing is the ability of the computer to be able to store and process data at the required level of precision. The precision of the computer word for recording numbers has important consequences for both arithmetical operations and for data storage.

Many people do not appreciate that use of computer variables and arrays having insufficient precision can lead to serious errors in calculations, particularly when results are required that must be obtained by subtracting or multiplying two large numbers. For example, the 'shorthand' or 'desk' method of estimating the variance of a set of numbers involves adding all the numbers together, squaring the result and dividing by the number of numbers. This 'constant' is then subtracted from the sum of the squares of all the numbers to obtain the sum of squared deviations. If many large numbers are involved, large rounding errors will almost certainly occur when the number of bits in the computer word is insufficient to handle the precision required.

Rounding errors are unlikely to be a problem when performing statistical calculations in large computers when the programming language allows double-precision variables and arrays to be defined. They are likely to be troublesome in 8-bit and 16-bit microcomputers, however, particularly if 'shorthand' methods of calculation are used. In the above example, it is much wiser first to calculate the average of the set of numbers, then to calculate the deviation of each number from the average and then sum the squared deviations. This method of estimating the sums of squares is not only closer to the original method of defining variance, but avoids rounding errors in the subtraction process.

There is a simple, and very revealing test of calculation precision that can demonstrate just how computer word length can affect the results of calculation (Gruenberger 1984). The number 1.0000001 is squared 27 times (equivalent to raising 1.0000001 to the 134 217 728th power). Table 6.2 shows the results of performing this calculation on an IBM personal computer using Advanced Basic with 8-digit or 16-digit precision. After 27 squarings the eight-digit result has acquired a cumulative error of more than 1200 per cent! The DEC Rainbow personal computer gives exactly the same result as the IBM Personal Computer Basic with 8-digit precision, but the BBC micro (which has a different processor and BASIC interpreter) does rather better. Clearly, the programmer must avoid situations in which the results of a calculation depend on accuracies of representation that exceed the number of digits available for representing the numbers.

In many systems used for raster processing, data are coded as integers. The problems of accurately estimating areas and perimeters of polygons in raster format were noted in Chapter 2. Franklin (1984) has explored the problem of data precision for other GIS operations, such as scaling and rotation, when the results of arithmetical operations are truncated to the nearest integer. As Fig. 6.2(a) shows, scaling a simple triangle by a factor of three results in the point P being moved outside the triangle. Rotating point P (Fig. 6.2(b)) moves it inside the circle.

The obvious answer is to increase the precision with which the computer represents numbers, i.e. to work with real numbers with a decimal representation. As Franklin demonstrates, this merely pushes the problem to another level; it does not go away. The problem is one that is intimately linked with the way the computer represents numbers and it is possible to find real numbers for which computer implementations of simple arithmetic violate important real number axioms of distributivity, associativity, and commutativity.

For example, associativity:

$$(A+B)+C=A+(B+C)$$

This rule is violated in a computer that stores fewer than 10 significant digits for $A=1.E10$, $B=-1.E10$, $C=1$. Franklin shows that these problems can be corrected by using different methods of computation,

Table 6.2 Rounding errors in some microcomputers: results of multiple squaring of 1.0000001

	BBC Micro	FORTRAN-77	IBM personal computer		
	BASIC		BASIC		
No.of Squares	Single precision	Single precision	Single precision	Double precision	BASIC single– double per cent difference
1	1.0000002	1.000000	1.000000	1.00000020000001	0.0000038
2	1.0000004	1.000000	1.000001	1.00000040000006	0.0000077
3	1.0000008	1.000000	1.000001	1.00000080000028	0.0000154
4	1.0000016	1.000000	1.000002	1.00000160000120	0.0000307
5	1.0000032	1.000000	1.000004	1.00000320000496	0.0000615
6	1.00000641	1.000010	1.000008	1.00000640002016	0.0001229
7	1.00001281	1.000020	1.000015	1.00001280008128	0.0002459
8	1.00002563	1.000030	1.000031	1.00002560032640	0.0004917
9	1.00005126	1.000060	1.000061	1.00005120130818	0.0009833
10	1.00010252	1.000120	1.000122	1.00010240523794	0.0019663
11	1.00020506	1.000240	1.000244	1.00020482096271	0.0039312
12	1.00041016	1.000490	1.000488	1.00040968387704	0.0078565
13	1.00082048	1.000980	1.000977	1.00081953559496	0.0157137
14	1.00164164	1.001950	1.001955	1.00163974282851	0.0314297
15	1.00328598	1.003910	1.003913	1.00328217441356	0.0628688
16	1.00658276	1.007840	1.007841	1.00657512149601	0.1257719
17	1.01320885	1.015740	1.015744	1.01319347521471	0.2517049
18	1.02659216	1.031740	1.031735	1.02656101821766	0.5040405
19	1.05389147	1.064480	1.064478	1.05382752412407	1.0106168
20	1.11068724	1.133110	1.133113	1.11055245060146	2.0314411
21	1.23362614	1.283940	1.283944	1.23332674553692	4.1041535
22	1.52183344	1.648510	1.648513	1.52109486125669	8.3767437
23	2.31597703	2.717600	2.717595	2.31372957694150	17.4551843
24	5.36374959	7.385320	7.385325	5.35334455521391	37.9572042
25	28.7698096	54.543000	54.543020	28.65829792683842	90.3219043
26	827.701947	2974.940000	2974.941000	821.29804006343120	262.2242807
27	685090.513	8850270.000000	8850273.000000	674530.47061203350000	1212.0642262

(a)

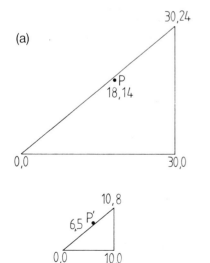

(b)

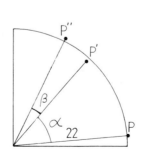

Fig. 6.2 Scaling (a) and rotation (b) can lead to topological errors when rounding occurs in integer arithmetic and the grid size is too coarse.

which themselves bring extra problems of complexity and the need to develop or use special subroutines for arithmetical operations.

Chrisman (1984b) has examined the role of current hardware limitations in another problem in geographical information systems; namely, that of storing geographical coordinates to the desired level of precision. Whereas 16-bit machines have presented few problems for storing the coordinates of low-resolution, single-scene LANDSAT images, the high accuracy required by cadastral systems, or the sheer range of coordinates required to cover a continent result in numbers that are too large to be recorded in a single computer word.

For example, with the 32-bit word used in many computers currently used for GIS, spatial dimensions can be recorded with the following precision:

Maximum dimension (metres)	Maximum precision attainable
10 000.00	dddd.dx
100 000.0	ddddd.x
1 000 000	dddddx

where d means good data, and x is the excess precision needed to avoid most of the topological dilemmas of the kind shown in Fig. 6.2. While it is unlikely that a user will require a precision better than 10 m for an area of 1 000 × 1 000 km, the impending arrival of the French satellite SPOT with its 10 m resolution, which may be used to supply data for the resource inventory, means that the 32-bit floating point representation in the GIS is stretched to the limit. Moreover, it may be necessary in the inventory to refer to ground control points that have been located with much greater precision.

As Chrisman (1984b) and Tomlinson and Boyle (1981) point out, the problem of locational precision is critical when the user wishes to interface different kinds of data sets that have been acquired at different scales and to different levels of precision. These problems are greater when working with established inventories than when all data must be collected for specific projects, because often in the latter case the data are collected from scratch.

There are several possible solutions to the problems posed by the length of the computer word. One is to work with double-precision words in order to have more significant digits available (Table 6.3). This solves the problem, allowing coordinates for the whole earth (some 40 000 km in circumference) to be recorded to a very high precision:

100 000 000.000 000 0 metres, or ddddddddd.ddxxxxx.

This goes too far the other way, allowing sufficient precision for locating viruses accurately in a world database! The cost is of course, a doubling of the size of the computer memory and data storage areas, and the need for special software for double-precision arithmetic.

An alternative is to work in 32-bit integers, having first converted all distances to centimetres or millimetres. A third, and potentially the most useful solution, is to adopt a nested approach (Grothenn and Stanfenbiel 1976). The area is divided into tiles that can be defined at a coarse level of resolution and for which the origins can be established exactly using limited precision. Within each tile all coordinates are measured at the next level of detail with reference to the local origin. The nesting can be repeated if necessary. Single-word storage can then be used throughout with the exception of control points, and double-precision arithmetic may only be necessary when sewing tiles together. Because a tile will usually contain as much data as a user can reasonably see on the screen

Table 6.3 The relation between computer word length and digital range and precision

Number of bits	Number of significant digits (decimal)	Approximate decimal range
16 integer	4	$-32768 \leqslant \times \leqslant +32767$
32 integer	9	$-2 \times 10^9 \leqslant \times \leqslant 2 \times 10^9$
64 integer	18	$-9 \times 10^{18} \leqslant \times \leqslant 9 \times 10^{18}$
80-bit packed decimal	18	$-99\ldots99 \leqslant \times \leqslant +99\ldots99$ (18 digits)
Short real 32 (single precision)	6–7	$8.43 \times 10^{-37} \leqslant \times \leqslant 3.37 \times 10^{38}$
Long real 64 (double precision)	15–16	$4.19 \times 10^{-307} \leqslant \times \leqslant 1.67 \times 10^{308}$

at any one time, the nesting is not a limiting factor when using a local processor.

2. Faults associated with topological analyses

The problems arising in geographical data processing caused by topological map overlay and through applying particular algorithms to variable data that are assumed to be 'uniform', are so numerous that they are dealt with more fully in the second part of this chapter. Most procedures commonly used in geographical information processing assume implicitly that (a) the source data are uniform, (b) digitizing procedures are infallible, (c) map overlay is merely a question of intersecting boundaries and reconnecting a line network, (d) boundaries can be sharply defined and drawn, (e) all algorithms can be assumed to operate in a fully deterministic way, and (f) class intervals defined for one or other 'natural' reason necessarily are the best for all mapped attributes. These ideas result from the traditional ways in which data were classified and mapped. They have presented large technical difficulties for the designers of geographical information systems but rarely have these problems been looked at as a consequence of the way in which the various aspects of the world have been perceived, recorded, and mapped.

3. Classification and generalization

Many irregularities in the data entered to geographical information systems can also be attributed to the methods used for classification and for interpolating from point data to areas. Classification and interpolation are such large topics that they are dealt with separately in Chapters 7 and 8.

Problems and errors arising from overlay and boundary intersection

Many operations in geographical information processing involve the procedure of overlaying one or more spatial networks. The spatial networks may be composed of lines, of regular grids or of irregular polygons. The overlay may be for the purposes of data conversion, such as converting a vector representation of a polygon net to raster form by overlaying a grid of given resolution, or for the purposes of data combination, such as when two or more raster maps are overlaid or when two polygon networks are intersected. The aim of the overlay can be a purely topological manipulation, or a manipulation solely on the properties of the cells or polygons, or both, as was

described in Chapter 5 on geographical data manipulation.

In the following section we shall consider the possible errors that can result from (a) representing a vector polygon net as a set of grid cells on a raster, (b) from logical and arithmetic operations on two or more overlaid grid cell or polygon networks, and (c) from overlaying and intersecting two polygon networks. Finally we shall consider some aspects of the problem of using boundaries to describe the spatial variation of natural phenomena.

Errors resulting from rasterizing a vector map

Errors can arise in two ways when a choropleth map is represented by an array of grid cells. The first, and most obvious source of error is that because each grid cell can only contain a single value of an attribute, it is only the mean value that is carried in the cell. In the original LANDSAT imagery, in which each cell had a size of some 80×80 m, the signature of the pixel was a mean value of the reflectance averaged over the area of the whole cell. If part of the cell covered a highly reflecting surface such as a road or a sandy beach, this could so weight the mean reflectance as to give an over-representation of the area of 'road' or 'beach' in the whole image. These kinds of classification error typically occur when the size of the grid cell is larger than the features about which information is desired. It is a problem particularly when large-area grid cells are used to record many features in a complex landscape (Fig. 6.3).

Besides the problem of coding the features occurring within a grid cell there is also the problem of topological mismatch when a polygon map is approximated by a grid. We shall first describe ways of estimating

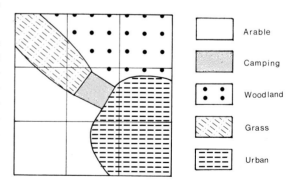

Fig. 6.3 Grid cells that are too large to resolve spatial details present coding problems. How should the central cell be coded?

how large this kind of mismatch is likely to be and then we will examine some of the practical consequences of the problem.

Frolov and Maling (1969) considered the problem of error arising when a grid cell is bisected by a 'true' boundary line. They assumed that the boundary line could be regarded as a straight line drawn randomly across a cell. The mean square area of the cut-off portion of each bisected boundary cell i (the error variance) can be estimated by

$$V_i = aS^4 \qquad (6.2)$$

where V is the error variance, S is the linear dimension of the (square) cell and a is a constant. Frolov and Maling calculated the value of a as 0.0452 but subsequent work reported by Goodchild (1980) suggests that a better value is $a = 0.0619$.

The error variance in an estimate of area for any given polygon is given by a summation of all the errors from all the bounding cells. If m cells are intersected by the boundary, the error variance will be

$$V = maS^4 \qquad (6.3)$$

and the standard error

$$SE = (ma)^{1/2}S^2 \qquad (6.4)$$

assuming that the contribution of each cell are independent. Goodchild (1980) suggests that this assumption should not always be regarded as valid.

The number of boundary cells, m, can be estimated from the perimeter of the polygon. It can be shown (see Frolov and Maling 1969), that m is proportional to $\sqrt{N}$, where N is the total number of cells in the polygon. The standard error of m is estimated by $kN^{1/4}a^{1/2}S^2$. Because the estimate of polygon area $A = NS^2$, the standard error as a percentage of the estimate is proportional to $N^{-3/4}$ (Goodchild 1980), i.e.

$$e = ka^{1/2}N^{-3/4}. \qquad (6.5)$$

If the variable is cell side S instead of cell number N, the percentage error is dependent on $S^{3/2}$. Goodchild (1980) reports studies that have verified these relationships empirically.

The constant k depends on the polygon shape, long thin shapes having more boundary cells than a circular form of the same area. Frolov and Maling (1969) give values of k for various standard shapes, using the independent straight line hypothesis.

Switzer's method

Switzer (1975) presented a general solution to the problem of estimating the precision of a raster map that had been made from a polygonal thematic map. His analysis does not deal with observational or location errors, but assumes that error is solely a result of using a series of points located at the centres of grid cells to estimate an approximate grid version of the original map. Switzer's method deals essentially with ideal choropleth maps, i.e. thematic maps on which homogeneous map units are separated by infinitely thin, sharp boundaries. The method assumes that a 'true' map exists, against which an estimated map obtained by sampling can be compared. Realizing that the 'true' map is often unknown or unknowable, Switzer showed that by applying certain assumptions and by using certain summary statistics, errors of mismatch could be estimated from the estimated or gridded map itself.

The analysis begins by assuming that a map M has been partitioned into k homogeneous map units, or colours. Each of the k map units may be represented on the map by one or more sub-areas. This 'true' map is estimated by laying an array of n basic sampling cells over the map. Here we shall only consider the situation where the array of sampling cells is regular and congruent, and each cell is defined by a single sampling point at the cell mid point. The map units on the 'true' map are denoted M_1, M_2, ... M_k, and on the estimated map by M_1, M_2, ... M_k. Each cell on the estimated map is allocated to a map unit M_i if the sampling point in the cell falls within map unit M_i on the 'true' map. This is the procedure commonly used when converting a vector polygon network to raster format. For the purposes of this analysis we shall, like Switzer, assume the total area of the map is scaled to unity, i.e. $A(M) = 1$.

The error of the map estimation or rasterizing process is given as

$$L_{ij} = A(M_i \cap M_j)\, i <> j \qquad (6.6)$$

where L_{ij} is the area of the map that truly belongs to map unit i but which is represented as map unit j on the estimated map. The total area of incorrectly mapped portion of map unit M_i is then given by

$$L_i = \sum_{j <> i} L_{ij}\ (i\ \text{fixed}) \qquad (6.7)$$

and the total mismatch for the whole map is given by

$$L = \sum_{i=1}^{k} L_i. \qquad (6.8$$

The total and partial mismatch is easy to calculate if the original or 'true' map exists in digital form. Very often, however, the 'true' map does not exist, the rasterizing having been done by laying a grid over a map or aerial photograph, or by using a scanner, so the degree of mismatch must be estimated from the estimated or grid map itself.

The degree of mismatch of the estimated map is a function of two independent factors, (a) the complexity of the true map, and (b) the geometrical properties of the sampling net. Considering first the complexity of the map, we can define a quantity $P_{ij}(d)$ as the probability that a random point is in true map unit i and that the cell centre point is in true map unit j when the points are separated by distance d.

Switzer proposed that if $P_{ij}(d)$ can be thought of as an infinite, differentiable function, it can be approximated by a Taylor expansion of its derivatives P_{ij}' and P_{ij}''. The Taylor's series expansion states that any function $f(x)$ about a point $x=a$ that possesses a continuous derivative $f^{(n)}\{x\}$ in the interval (a,b) can be approximated by the infinite series of polynomials (e.g. Sokolnikoff and Sokolnikoff 1941).

$$f(x)=f(a)+f'(a)(x-a)+\{f''(a)(x-a)^2\}/2!+\dots$$
$$+f^{(n)}(a)(x-a)^n\}/n!+\dots \quad (6.9)$$

If $a=0$, the expansion reduces to

$$f(x)=f(0)+f'(0)x+\{f''(0)x^2\}/2!+\dots$$
$$+f^{(n)}.x^n/n!+\dots \quad (6.10)$$

Rewriting eqn (6.9) for the $P_{ij}(d)$ results in

$$P_{ij}(d)=P_{ij}(0)+P_{ij}'(0).d+(P_{ij}''(0).d^2)/2+\dots \quad (6.11)$$

Because, in general, $P_{ij}(d=0)=0$, and the derivative $P_{ij}'d$ at $d=0$ is strictly positive, it can be shown that the mismatch area can be approximated by using the first derivative

$$L_{ij}=P_{ij}'\sum_{h=1}^{n}A(S_h).D_h \quad (6.12)$$

where n is the number of sampling points, $A(S_h)$ is the area of cell S_h and D_h is the mean distance between a random point in sampling cell S_h and the datum point of the cell. In the case of all sample cells having the same shape and the datum point at the centre of the cell, eqn (6.12) reduces to

$$L_{ij}=P_{ij}'.D \quad (6.13)$$

where D is a value characteristic of the sample net. So, estimation of the mismatch involves finding suitable estimations of P_{ij}' and D.

Estimating D. For a rectangular net, D is given by:

$$D=n^{(-1/2)}\{2\sqrt{(r+r^{-1})}+r^{-3/2}\ln(r+\sqrt{(1-r^2)})$$
$$+2r^{3/2}\ln(r^{-1}+\sqrt{(1+r^{-2})})\}/12 \quad (6.14)$$

where r is the ratio of the cell sides.

When $r=1$ (square net), $D=0.383n^{-1/2}$

When $r=0.6$ (a rectangular net corresponding to the dimensions of normal lineprinter characters), $D=0.417n^{-1/2}$ (9 per cent worse than square).

When $r=0.25$, $D=0.532n^{-1/2}$, (39 per cent worse than square), and when the net is hexagonal then $D=0.377n^{-1/2}$. If the datum points were located at random in the cells then the value of $D=0.520n^{-1/2}$ (35 per cent worse than centre-point square).

To summarize: a square grid with datum points located at cell centres gives errors that are only 1.6 per cent worse than the most efficient hexagonal sampling scheme. Elongating the cells results in greater mismatch as does using randomly located datum points in the cells.

The local linear approximation in eqn (6.13) is adequate for comparing the efficiencies of sampling designs, but for actual mismatch estimations it is improved by including a quadratic term of order d^2. The reason is because the second derivative of $P_{ij}(d=0)$, P_{ij}'' at $d=0$ is strictly negative when the map domain is two-dimensional or higher. Hence the linear approximation can never be exact, whereas a negative d^2 coefficient could be. This also implies that the linear approximation overestimates mismatch. The estimate for the mismatch area now becomes:

$$L_{ij}=P_{ij}'\sum_{h=1}^{n}A(S_h)D_h+\tfrac{1}{2}P_{ij}''\sum_{h=1}^{n}A(S_h)D_h^* \quad (6.15)$$

where D_h^* is the mean squared distance between a random point in the sampling cell S_h and the datum point in the cell. For a completely congruent sampling pattern and large n, eqn (6.15) simplifies to:

$$L_{ij}=P_{ij}'.D+\tfrac{1}{2}P_{ij}''.D^*. \quad (6.16)$$

For a square grid net with sample points at cell centres, eqn (6.15) becomes:

$$L_{ij}=0.383n^{-1/2}P_{ij}'+0.083n^{-1}P_{ij}'' \quad (6.17)$$

The problem now is to estimate the P_{ij}' and the P_{ij}'' functions at the value of $d=0$. Switzer suggests that this can be done by calculating the frequency ratios $P_{ij}(n^{-1/d})$, $P_{ij}(2n^{-1/d})$ of cell pairs on the estimated map in which at distances of d, $2d$, etc. the cells fall in different map units i and j. The estimated derivatives can be obtained for a square grid from these cell frequency counts by:

$$P'_{ij} = \tfrac{1}{2}n^{1/2}\{4P_{ij}(n^{-1/2}) - P_{ij}(2n^{-1/2})\} \quad (6.18)$$

$$P''_{ij} = \tfrac{2}{3}n^{1/2}\{2P_{ij}(n^{-1/2}) - P_{ij}(2n^{-1/2})\}$$

so that for an estimated map based on a square set of grid cells,

$$L_{ij}\,(\text{quadratic}) = 0.60P_{ij}(n^{-1/2}) - 0.11P_{ij}(2n^{-1/2}). \quad (6.19)$$

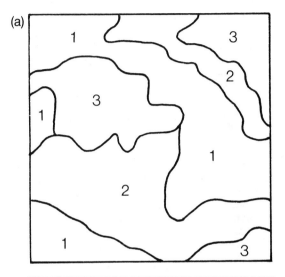

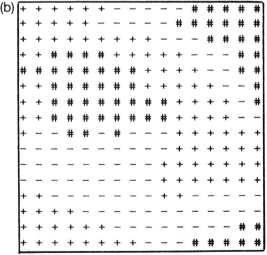

Legend   class 1 +
           class 2 −
           class 3 #

[Note that the values of the coefficients differ from Switzer's published formula; the corrections are given by Goodchild (1980)].

The $P_{ij}(n^{-1/2})$ and $P_{ij}(2n^{-1/2})$ probabilities are estimated from a frequency count as follows:

1. Estimate the total number of cell pairs at distance $d = 1$ cell width. The total number of pairs at a given distance is equal to

$$NPAIRS = 4 \times (P \times Q) - 2 \times d \times (P + Q)$$

where P = number of rows, Q = number of columns in the grid, and the second term is a correction for the cells on the edge of the grid.

2. For each pair of mapping units i and j, count the number of cell pairs along and up and down the grid that lie in different mapping units ($TALLY_{ij}$)

3. Compute $P_{ij}(n^{-\frac{1}{2}})$ as $TALLY_{ij}/NPAIRS$.

4. Repeat steps 1–3 with $d = 2$ cell widths to estimate $P_{ij}(2n^{-1/2})$.

5. Calculate L_{ij} from eqn (6.19).

6. Calculate total mismatch for each mapping unit L_i as the sum of the L_{ij}s, remembering that the mismatch of $L_{ji} = L_{ij}$.

7. Calculate total mismatch as the sum of the L_is.

An example. Figure 6.4(a) shows a simple thematic map depicting a soil or geological pattern of three mapping units. Assuming that this is a true map, what will be the relative mismatch errors arising from digitizing it using grid rasters of different sizes? Two estimates of the original map will be tested, using respec-

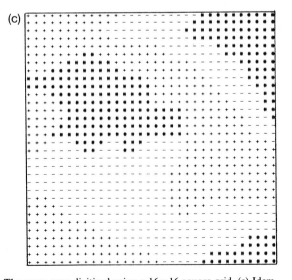

Fig. 6.4 (a) Original vector polygon map of three regions. (b) The same map digitized using a 16 × 16 square grid. (c) Idem, but digitized to a 32 × 32 square grid.

tively a 16×16 and a 32×32 cell grid (Fig. 6.4 (b and c)).

The results are presented in Table 6.4. For a grid measuring 16×16 cells, there are 960 cell-pairs at distance $d = 1$. The total number of cell pairs straddling a boundary leads to frequency estimates for each mapping unit. For a distance $d = 2$, the number of pairs is 896. Entering the frequency estimates into eqn (6.16) leads to an estimated mismatch of 8.5 per cent. Using the 32×32 cell grid leads to an estimate of 4.1 per cent, demonstrating that a fourfold increase in the number of grid cells is needed to reduce the estimation error by half. Both these estimates of mismatch compare favourably with the estimates of mismatch obtained by measuring the areas of the mapping units on the original map (Fig. 6.4a).

Errors associated with digitizing a map, or with geocoding

Switzer's method to estimate mismatch assumes implicitly that a 'true' map exists that has homogeneous (uniform) mapping units, and infinitely sharp boundaries. In practice, however, even the best drawn maps are not perfect, and extra errors are introduced by the digitizing process, as authors such as Blakemore (1984) and Poiker (1982) have pointed out. Consider the problem of boundary width and location (the problem of within-map unit homogeneity will be dealt with later) on a digital map of polygons in vector format. The digital map will almost certainly have been derived by digitizing a paper version of the map. There are two sources of potential error: (a) errors

associated with the source map; and (b) errors associated with the digital representation.

(a) Apart from the potentially correctable errors of paper stretch and distortion in the printed map or source document, errors arise with boundary location simply because drawn boundaries are not infinitely thin. A 1-mm-thick line on a 1:1250 map covers an area 1.25 m wide; the same line on a 1:100 000 map covers an area 100 m wide. A detailed 1:25 000 soil map measuring 400×600 mm may have as much as 24 000 mm of drawn lines covering an area of 24 000 mm^2 or 10 per cent of the map area! Common sense suggests that the true dividing line should be taken as the mid-point of the drawn line, but it is not being cynical to state that the area of the map covered by boundary lines is simply an area of uncertainty. When these boundary lines are converted by digitizing, extra errors arise because with hand digitizing the operator will not always digitize exactly the middle of the line, and with scanners, errors will arise with the data reduction algorithms used.

(b) The representation of curved shapes depends on the number of vertices used (Aldred 1972, p. 5). Consequently, the relative error of digitizing straight lines is much less than that resulting from digitizing complex curves. Translating a continuous curved line on a map into a digital image involves a sampling process: only a very small proportion of the infinity of possible points along a curve is sampled by digitizing as is shown in Fig. 6.5 (Smedley and Aldred 1980).

Clearly, boundaries on thematic maps should not be regarded as absolute, but as having an associated error band or confidence interval. MacDougal (1975) sug-

Table 6.4 Result of applying Switzer's method to the map in Fig. 6.4(a).

Mismatch estimates using quadratic fit on square grid

(a) 16×16 grid			(b) 32×32 grid	
Polygon pairs	**Probability estimates**			
	$P_{ij}(n^{-1}/d)$	$P_{ij}(2n^{-1}/d)$	$P_{ij}(n^{-1}/d)$	$P_{ij}(2n^{-1}/d)$
1 2	0.05104	0.09821	0.02545	0.05130
2 3	0.02188	0.04464	0.01184	0.02422
3 2	0.03438	0.05804	0.01689	0.03333
	Mismatch per polygon pair			
	$L12\ 0.020$ $L21\ 0.020$ $L31\ 0.008$		$L12\ 0.010$ $L21\ 0.010$ $L31\ 0.004$	
	$L13\ 0.008$ $L23\ 0.014$ $L23\ 0.014$		$L13\ 0.004$ $L23\ 0.006$ $L23\ 0.006$	
	Mismatch per polygon			
	$L1\ 0.028$ $L2\ 0.034$ $L3\ 0.022$		$L1\ 0.014$ $L2\ 0.016$ $L3\ 0.011$	
	Total mismatch $\% = 8.46$		Total mismatch $\% = 4.11$	

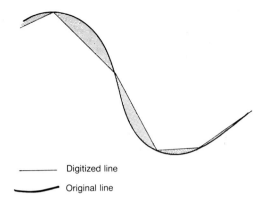

——— Digitized line

——— Original line

Fig. 6.5 Digitizing a curved line is a sampling process.

gests that the total boundary inaccuracy can be estimated by

$$H = \sum_{i=1}^{N} (h_i . l_i)/T \qquad (6.20)$$

where h_i is the horizontal error (in standard deviations) of line i, length l_i, N is the number of boundary lines on the map, and T is the total area of the map. If all boundary lines are of the same type (e.g. they are all soil boundaries) eqn (6.20) simplifies to

$$H = (h.L)/T. \qquad (6.21)$$

The total line length L can be estimated by placing a grid over the map and counting the number of crossings, K, and using the formula

$$L = (T.K)/0.6366 \qquad (6.22)$$

where 0.6366 is a constant described by Wentworth (1930).

Perkal (1966) defined an 'epsilon' distance about a cartographic line as a means of generalizing it objectively, and Blakemore (1984) has suggested that Perkal's concept can be used efficiently in reverse to indicate the width of an error band about a digitized version of a polygon boundary. Blakemore discusses the application of this concept with respect to an application of the well-known 'point-in-polygon' problem. He shows that the question 'Does point *XY* lie within polygon A?' results in five classes of answers:

   (i) definitely in
   (ii) definitely out
   (iii) possibly in
   (iv) possibly out, and
   (v) ambiguous (on the digitized border line).

These situations are illustrated in Fig. 6.6. 'Definitely in' records the core area within the error band; 'possibly in' records a point that falls within the overlap of the inner half of the confidence band and the polygon. 'Possibly out' records a point that falls in the outer half of the confidence band; technically speaking the point would be returned as falling outside the polygon, but it could actually be inside the 'true' polygon if it had been erroneously digitized or geocoded. An ambiguous point has coordinates that coincide exactly with a point on the digitized boundary—such points are rare, but do occur.

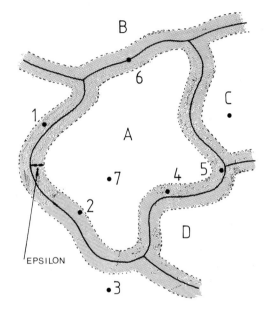

Fig. 6.6 Error zones (width epsilon) and ambiguities for point-in-polygon searches. (Adapted from Blakemore 1984.)

Blakemore (1984) illustrates the effects of these kinds of errors when dealing with problems of combining a vector polygonal net with a square grid cell network. The problem he chose was that of overlaying a UK Department of Industry 1-km-square grid database of industrial establishments on a polygonal map of 115 north-west England employment office areas. A total of 780 entries in the database geocoded to a 1-km square grid resolution was tested for their inclusion in the polygon network. The 1-km-square grid leads to an epsilon or confidence band of 0.7071 km. Table 6.5 presents Blakemore's results.

The 'possibly out' class includes data points that fell outside the polygon network of employment office areas altogether. 'Possibly in' refers to points

Table 6.5 Epsilon error results

Category	Per cent
1. Possibly out	1.5
2. Possibly in	4.4
3. Unassignable	1.4
4. Possibly in/out 2 polys.	29.8
5. Possibly in/out >2 polys.	6.7
6. Ambiguous	1.2
Subtotal	45.0
7. Definitely in	55.0
Total	100.0

falling within the inner half of the error band in polygons on the edge of the polygon net. 'Unassignable' refers to points that fell outside the error band of the outer boundaries of the outer polygons. In some circumstances the point-in-polygon routine suggested that the industry was located in the sea! 'Possibly in/out 2 polys.' refers to points that were flagged as being possibly in and possibly out of two adjacent polygons; 'possibly in/out >2 polys' refers to points that were possibly in or out of more than two polygons. 'Ambiguous' refers to those points actually occurring on the digitized polygon boundaries. The implication of the study was that only 60 per cent of the workforce in the industries in the database could definitely be associated with an employment office area. The mismatch errors and ambiguities were relatively larger for long, thin polygons and for employment areas having narrow protuberances or insets than for large, broadly circular areas. The study resulted in a considerable amount of validation and checking of the databases to ensure that the errors brought about by the grid-cell point geocoding were removed.

Errors associated with overlaying two or more polygon networks

Spatial associations between two or more thematic maps of an area are commonly displayed or investigated by laying the polygonal outlines on top of one another and looking for boundary coincidences. Before the days of digital maps, the process was achieved using transparent sheets, and the boundary coincidences were established using fat marker pens to trace the results. The onset of the digital map promised better results because all boundaries were supposed to be precisely encoded, but in fact the result of the new technology was to throw up one of the most difficult and most researched problems in computer cartography. Not only did a solution of the problem in technical terms cost many years' work but investigations have shown that the results of overlay throw up more questions about data quality and boundary mismatching than they solve.

McAlpine and Cook (1971) were among the first to investigate the problem when working with land resources data. They considered two maps of the same locality containing respectively m_1 and m_2 ($m_1 > = m_2$) initial map segments (polygons) that were overlaid to give a derived map having n segments. To simplify the problem, they experimented by throwing a single hexagon with random orientation and displacement over a mosaic of hexagons. The trials were done using sample hexagons having sides 0.5, 1, 2, and 3 times the length of the sides of the mosaic hexagons. They found that the number of derived polygons n on the derived map could be estimated by

$$n = m_1 + m_2 + 2.\{m_1.m_2\}^{1/2} \quad (6.23)$$

for two maps, which for k maps can be generalized to

$$n = [\sum_{i=1}^{k} m_i]^2. \quad (6.24)$$

McAlpine and Cook (1971) showed that map overlay gave rise to a surprisingly large proportion of small polygons on the derived map. They applied their analysis to a case study of overlaying three maps of scale 1:250 000 of census divisions, present land-use intensity, and land systems from Papua and New Guinea containing 7, 42, and 101 initial polygons, respectively. The overlay of the three maps gave 304 derived polygons (equation (6.24) estimates 368 derived polygons, but McAlpine and Cook regard this as satisfactory). The overlay process resulted in 38 per cent of the area being covered by polygons having areas of less than 3.8 km^2.

The results of the overlay were evaluated by classifying the derived polygons by size and boundary complexity (i.e. polygons bounded solely by initial mapping segments, those bounded only by land use and land system boundaries, and those bounded by all three types of boundaries). A 10 per cent random sample of derived polygons was evaluated by three colleagues to determine the measure of agreement between the initial and the derived polygon descriptions. As Fig. 6.7 shows, the lack of agreement was substantial for the smallest derived polygons, and some 30 per cent of the area of the derived map was represented by polygons that had little or no agreement with the initial descriptions!

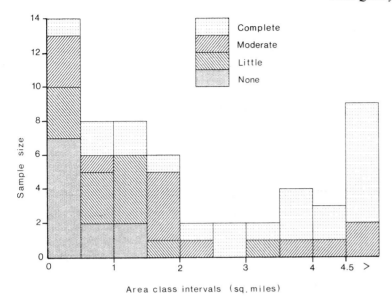

Fig. 6.7 Results of a case study test of overlaying three polygon networks. (Adapted from McAlpine and Cook 1971.)

Goodchild (1978) extended the discussion of the polygon overlay problem to show that the number of derived polygons is more a function of boundary complexity than the numbers of polygons on the overlaid maps. He showed that an overlay of two polygons having respectively v_1 and v_2 vertices could produce any number of derived polygons from three to $v_1.v_2+2$ when all Boolean operations including .NOT.A.AND.NOT.B are used. Moderate numbers of derived polygons are produced when, as in McAlpine and Cook's example, the overlaid maps show statistical independence. When the boundaries of polygons on the source maps are highly correlated, however, serious problems arise through production of large numbers of small, 'spurious' polygons. Prominent and important features, such as district boundaries or rivers, may occur as part of polygon boundaries in several maps. These several representations of the same boundary will have been separately digitized, but because of digitizing and other errors they will not exactly coincide.

The spurious polygon problem contains two apparent paradoxes. First, the more accurately each boundary is digitized on the separate maps, and the more coordinates are used, the larger the number of spurious polygons produced. Second, subjective methods of map drawing, designed to assist the eye in generalizing when using manual methods of overlay, result in large problems when working with digital maps.

Goodchild (1978) analysed the situations in which spurious polygons were most likely to occur through the conjunction of two digitized versions of the same arc, with n_1 and n_2 vertices, respectively (Fig. 6.8). Goodchild, using the statistics of runs of binary symbols, showed that the number of spurious polygons S generated by conjunction of two arcs having n_1 and n_2 vertices ranges from

$$S_{min} = 0 \qquad (6.25)$$

to

$$S_{max} = 2 \min(n_1.n_2) - 4 \qquad (6.26)$$

with a random expectation of

$$E(S) = [2n_1 n_2/(n_1 + n_2)] - 3 \qquad (6.27)$$

if symbols occur randomly in sequence along the conjoined arcs. The minimum value of S occurs when the overlap is of maps having symbols of one type occurring together; the maximum value of S occurs for maximum intermixing. By simulating five possible situations in which arcs were conjoined, Goodchild showed that eqn (6.27) overestimates the average number of spurious polygons that can occur by some 17 per cent. The actual number of spurious polygons found never exceeded 71 per cent of S_{max}. The more carefully a map is digitized, however, the larger the values of n_1 and n_2, and so the larger the number of spurious polygons will become.

Spurious polygons are in fact equivalent to the mismatch areas resulting from rasterizing a polygon. Their total area should decrease as digitizing accuracy

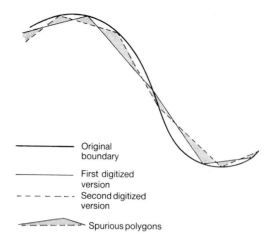

Original boundary

First digitized version

Second digitized version

Spurious polygons

Fig. 6.8 How spurious polygons occur in map overlay. Note that in this example the spurious polygons could be completely eliminated by fitting a polynomial or a spline function to *both* sets of digitized points.

increases, but the greater problem is their removal to avoid nonsense on the final map. They can be removed by erasing one side on a random basis, after screening the polygon for minimum area, or the two end points can be connected by a straight line and both sides dissolved. A more sophisticated approach is to consider all points within a given distance from the complex arc as estimates of the location of a new line, and then fit a new line by least squares or maximum likelihood methods. In all cases, it is highly likely that the complex line will be moved from its topographically 'true' position. The net result of overlaying a soil map (having not very exact boundary locations) with a county boundary map (topographically exact boundaries) may be that the topographic boundaries become distorted. To avoid this problem it is necessary to weight the topographic boundaries in such a way that they are carried through to the new map.

The nature of boundaries

The problems resulting from digitizing and overlaying boundaries really only arise because boundaries on choropleth maps are considered to be precisely defined sharp lines delineating areas of different kinds. This concept is tenable when dealing with administrative boundaries such as those around land parcels, local authority areas or countries that are, in principle at least, sharply defined. The boundaries drawn on choropleth maps of soil, vegetation, or geology are rarely

universally sharp and drawing them as thin, flowing lines often misrepresents their character. So perhaps we should not worry unduly about their exact location, or their elegant representation. If we could accept that razor sharp boundaries in soil and vegetation patterns rarely occur, we would be spared the problems of the topological errors associated with map overlay and intersection. We could treat the overlap zones as those in which our knowledge is 'fuzzy' or unclear.

Let us consider the possibility that the variations in natural phenomena usually represented by boundaries are rarely, if ever, sharp or smooth. To take the case of soil boundaries, at least three kinds are recognized by practising soil surveyors, though a clear distinction between them rarely occurs in the soil map or the associated report. The most easily recognizable boundaries are those associated with abrupt and large changes in the value of critical soil properties over short distances (Fig. 6.9a). These soil changes can usually be easily deduced from external features of the landscape. Such boundaries are to be found at the edges of river terraces, at the junctions between major changes in geology (an intrusion, for example) or associated with abrupt changes in relief. But although the changes may be abrupt at one scale, they will always appear to be less distinct when examined more closely. Less easy to recognize and locate are the boundaries used to divide a zone of continuous variation into compartments simply to aid classification and mapping (Fig. 6.9b); these changes typically occur as a result of climatic gradients (see Burrough *et al.* 1977, for example) or as a result of gradual soil changes resulting from differential deposition (for example, across a river flood plain from levées to backswamps). These boundaries may be very difficult to locate precisely, particularly when the trends are masked by short-range variations resulting from measurement errors or from the spatial effects of secondary processes (see Burrough 1983 a,b). The last kind of boundary occurs solely as a result of two observations being classified differently, simply because the value of a 'discriminating criterion' lies on opposite sides of a class, as distinct from a landscape barrier. As Fig. 6.9c shows, such a boundary may have absolutely no real meaning in a region where short-range variation is dominant.

The statistical nature of boundaries

Consideration of Fig. 6.9 suggests that for many environmental properties, such as those of soil, geology or vegetation, it might be better to attempt to locate

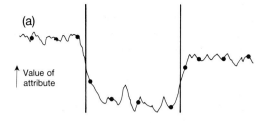

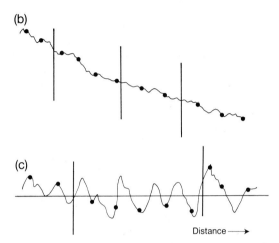

Fig. 6.9 Types of boundaries encountered when mapping natural resources. (a) abrupt; (b) dividing a trend; (c) resulting from sampling variation; ● sample sites.

boundaries from a statistical consideration of the way in which the value of critical properties change with distance, particularly in situations where there are few clear external indications, such as landform or aerial photo appearance. The concept of a 'boundary' is related to that of an edge, i.e. a location where the average rate of change of value of a property is a maximum.

Webster and Wong (1969) proposed a method for detecting soil boundaries along regularly sampled one-dimensional transects. Their idea was to lay a double window over the transect that covered equal numbers of sampling points on both sides (Fig. 6.10).

The average values of a property, x' and x'', in the two halves of the window were computed and compared using the Student's t-test, with the assumption that the variances s'^2 and s''^2 on both sides of the window are reasonably homogeneous. The value of t was computed in the usual way as

$$t = \frac{|x' - x''|}{s} \cdot \left[\frac{n'.n''}{(n' + n'')} \right]^{1/2} \qquad (6.28)$$

where s is the pooled standard deviation, and n' and n'' are the numbers of points in the two parts of the window. If the window is symmetrical, $n' = n''$ and equation (6.28) reduces to

$$t = \frac{|x' - x''|.[n/2]^{1/2}}{s} \qquad (6.29)$$

where n is now the number of points in one half of the window. The best position of a boundary will be when t is a maximum, so by plotting the estimates of t against position along the transect, the best boundary positions can be seen.

As with most filtering techniques, the results of the t-test analysis vary with the width of the window. Narrow windows will tend to record short-range changes, suggesting the presence of too many boundaries; wider windows will incorporate too much smoothing. Webster (1973) suggested that the optimum window width could be estimated by autocorrelation analysis.

When gradual changes occur, the simple split moving window is inadequate to detect optimal boundary spacings and Webster (1978) used a window with a 'mullion' to omit sample values near the centre, thereby increasing the contrast between the two halves. Hawkins and Merriam (1973, 1974) adopted another approach, which considers the transect as a whole and attempts to find the optimal locations of a specified number of boundaries consistent with minimizing the pooled within-boundary variance. As Webster (1978) points out, this can require an immense amount of computing because of the large number of possible boundary spacings that must be examined. Both

● Sample points

Fig. 6.10 The split-moving window method of optimal boundary location. Here the window has a width of four sample points on a regular transect.

Webster (1973, 1978), Webster and Wong (1969), and Hawkins and Merriam (1973, 1974) chose to work with multivariate data; the former used Mahalonobis' distance D or D^2 on the principle component scores of the original data, (Webster 1980 gives a FORTRAN IV program of his procedure) while Hawkins and Merriam transformed their data to canonical variates.

To the author's knowledge, the above statistical boundary-location techniques have only been applied to one-dimensional analyses of field data. This is largely because field data are rarely collected on a fine two-dimensional net, or because the scientists involved have preferred to use an interpolation technique, such as trend surfaces, moving averages or kriging, that assumes a model of continuous rather than abrupt change. There is often a real need to look for discontinuities in two-dimensional spatial data because the assumptions inherent in many interpolation and contouring techniques are not flexible enough to cope with boundary situations.

In contrast to the foregoing, image analysis technology has many methods for locating edges or boundaries in digital image data. Davis (1976), Rosenfeld and Kak (1976) and Levialdi (1980) all present thorough reviews of current techniques, and Poggio (1984) gives a more popular review of the current state of the art. As in the one-dimensional methods reviewed above, the two-dimensional algorithms can be grouped according to those that make use of local windows or 'kernels' (usually to detect the slope or rate of change of a surface) and those that attempt general solutions. The more advanced methods are able to incorporate extra information from an operator or external database over the type of the object being detected, a facility that at first sight seems more appropriate for recognizing tanks or houses than soil or vegetation patterns. But it is just this kind of man-machine interaction that may well assist the soil surveyor to continue drawing a soil boundary in those difficult situations when the boundary changes from a clear feature in the landscape to a vague meander somewhere in the middle of a fuzzy continuum.

Fractals

In principle it should be possible to distinguish abrupt boundaries, boundaries placed somewhere along a continuum, and boundaries drawn only because points have been classed separately, while mapping and compiling the documents to be used for digitizing. The information about the degree of a boundary could be then incorporated into the overlay and cleaning-up processes. There are two important practical problems

associated with this idea, however. The first is that the degree of abruptness of a boundary between two soil or vegetation units may vary over its length, which may well lead to excessive complications when processing. The second problem is that the actual location and length of a boundary is very dependent on the scale at which it is mapped. Many years ago, the scientist Lewis Fry Richardson made a study of the relation between the measured length of a coastline or lake outline and the scale at which it was mapped. He found that the length of the coastline as estimated by the map increased logarithmically with increasing map scale. This is because as the scale of the map is increased, more and more previously unresolved features can be delineated. In the limit, the length of the coastline is infinite. Also, the coastline is never actually as smooth as the drawn lines would have us believe.

Richardson's findings have been taken up and incorporated into the theory of fractals, proposed by the French-American mathematician Benoit B. Mandelbrot (Mandelbrot 1982). Basically, Mandelbrot's thesis recognizes that for most naturally occurring phenomena, the amount of resolvable detail is a function of scale; increasing the map scale does not result in an absolute increase in precision, but only reveals variations that had hitherto passed unnoticed. Fractals have two important characteristics. First, they embody an idea of 'self-similarity'; that is the manner in which variations at one scale are repeated at another. Second, they are said to have the peculiar property of fractional dimension, from which they get their name.

A fractal curve, (such as a soil boundary) is strictly defined as one where a mathematical parameter, known as the 'Hausdorff–Besicovitch dimension' exceeds the topological dimension. This can be understood simply as follows: a continuous linear series such as a polynomial tends to look more and more like a straight line as the scale at which it is examined increases. Also, the distance A–B between any two arbitrarily chosen points along the curve does not change as the scale changes. Examination of a fractal series at larger scales, however, results in the resolution of more and more detail, and the distance between any two arbitrarily chosen points depends on the scale at which it is measured.

Consider Fig. 6.11. Let the line A–B in Fig. 6.11(a) be resolvable by a map scale having a minimum resolution length x, so that the distance A–B is four units. Let the scale be increased by a factor $r = 3$, to just allow resolution of the detail shown in Fig. 6.11(b). If the distance A–C is measured at the new resolution y, it will be four of the new units long. The total length

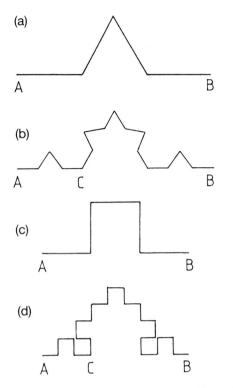

Fig. 6.11 Examples of ideal fractal curves: (a,b) $D = \ln4/\ln3 = 1.2618$; (c,d,) $D = \ln5/\ln3 = 1.4650$.

the curve is so smooth that it can be fully approximated by a polynomial; a tangent can be drawn at any point along its length. A D-value larger than 1 implies that the line has an associated band of 'fuzziness' or uncertainty that eats up a little of the second, spatial dimension. When $d = 2$, the 'fuzziness' is so large that the line has in fact become an area. For surfaces, the D-value ranges between 2 (completely smooth) and 3 (infinitely crumpled).

The variations of soil or vegetation boundaries are usually highly non-regular in form, and Mandelbrot has shown that they can be better approximated by a stochastic fractal such as the fractional Brownian motion or function fBm. The well-known random walk or Brownian motion random process (also known as the Bachelier-Wiener-Levy process), defined by

$$Z(x + \varepsilon) = Z(x) + \varepsilon \qquad (6.31)$$

has the property that for a series of randomly spaced increments ε, the differences of the value of the property Z measured at points x, $x + \varepsilon$, are given by a normally distributed Gaussian process with zero mean and variance ε. Brownian motion is a self-similar process in the sense that if the steps are divided by a positive, but arbitrary ratio r and rescaled in the ratio r^H, where $H = 0.5$, the rescaled function has a probability distribution that is identical to that of the original function. In other words, examination of the Brownian line function at a larger scale reveals a statistically equivalent Brownian function at that scale. Mandelbrot's insight was to suggest that by allowing the parameter H to vary between 0 and 1, a whole family of self-similar fractional Brownian functions could be obtained, the 'fuzziness' of which would cover the range from $D = 1$ to $D = 2$. Some of these fractional Brownian lines are shown in Fig. 6.12.

The idea of self-similarity that is embodied in the fractal concepts implies that if geographical objects such as mountains or rivers are true fractals their variations should be scalable. In other words, the variation of landforms, for example, seen over a few metres should be statistically similar to those seen over hundreds or thousands of metres when transformed by a simple scaling parameter. Geographers have reacted in different ways to these ideas. Scheidegger (1970) rejected Mandelbrot's ideas as absurd; Zonneveld (1973) independently pointed out that the real scale of geomorphological features seen on aerial photographs could not be deduced from form alone. Miller (1980) describes the application of scaling methods for studying soil-water phenomena that have allowed conceptual and analytical breakthroughs in soil physics.

A–B (in metres or miles) however, will be longer when measured in terms of y units than x units. The exercise can be repeated (in theory infinitely) to reveal successive levels of detail for each scale. Mandelbrot's most recent book (Mandelbrot 1982) contains many superb illustrations displaying the rich variety of forms that can arise from these and other simple graphical models.

By analogy, the curve A–B in Fig. 6.11 behaves similarly at all scales, so that once its properties are known at one scale they can be deduced from another merely by applying a scaling parameter. The level of variation present at all scales can be described by a single parameter, the fractal dimension, defined by Mandelbrot as

$$D = \log N/\log r \qquad (6.30)$$

where N is the number of steps used to measure a pattern unit length, and r is the scale ratio. In Fig. 6.11(a,b) $N = 4$ and $r = 3$ so $D = 1.2618$.

The value of D for a linear fractal curve can vary between $D = 1$ and $D = 2$. The value $D = 1$ implies that

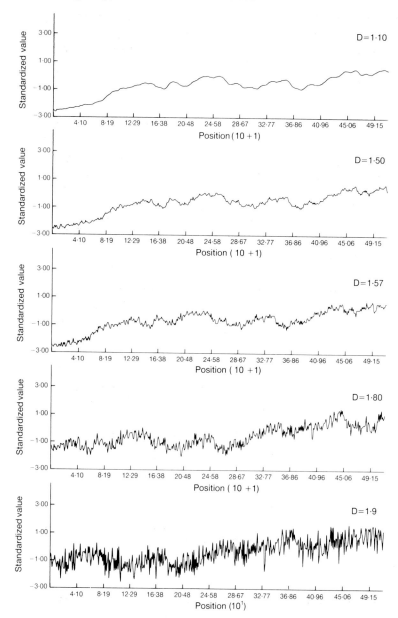

Fig. 6.12 Linear fractional Brownian function of different *D* values. The figure shows the first 512 points in simulated series of 1024 points. To facilitate comparison, all series have been standardized to zero mean and unit variance. Each of the above traces could represent a boundary at different degrees of 'fuzziness'.

Figure 6.13 shows that the idea of self-similarity and scaling also applies to the patterns of boundaries drawn on soil maps. Map (b) is an enlargement of an area falling within map (a); map (c) is an enlargement of part of map (b) and so on. The cumulative probabilities of a straight line transect on the map crossing a boundary are given in Fig. 6.14; they can all be reasonably well modelled by an exponential curve of the general type

$$P(x) = 1 - e^{-\lambda x} \qquad (6.32)$$

The parameter λ is the average boundary intensity, and on a transect length L the number of boundaries has a Poisson distribution with expectation λL. The mean boundary spacing, x, is given by $1/\lambda$. Note that the values of λ in Fig. 6.14 relate to millimetres on the map; they can be converted to metres, kilometres, or miles by a simple scaling parameter. Burgess and

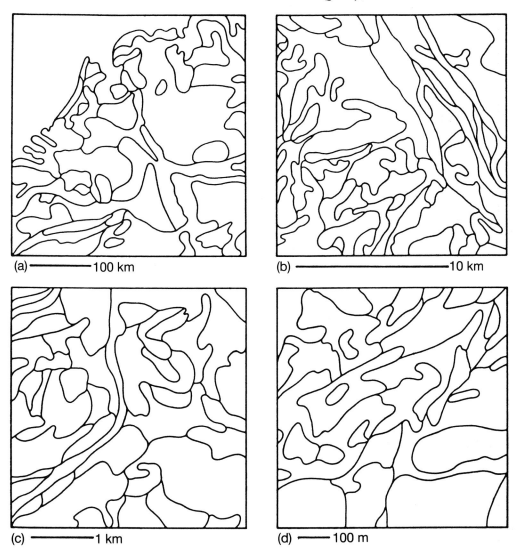

Fig. 6.13 Nested soil map patterns of north-west Europe at various scales. (Adapted from Burrough 1983a.)

Webster (1984) note that in many situations, the cumulative distribution of boundary spacings can be modelled better by the gamma distribution, for which the cumulative function is

$$P(x) = \int_0^x \frac{\lambda(\lambda y)^{(\alpha-1)}}{\Gamma(\alpha)} e^{-\lambda y} dy \qquad (6.33)$$

$\Gamma(\alpha)$ is a constant, from which the distribution gets its name. It is defined by

$$\Gamma(\alpha) = \int_0^\infty y^{(\alpha-1)} e^{-y} dy. \qquad (6.34)$$

When $\alpha = 1$, the gamma distribution reduces to the exponential distribution given in eqn (6.32).

The Weibull distribution is also similar; its cumulative function is

$$P(x) = 1 - e^{-(\lambda x)^\alpha}. \qquad (6.35)$$

It too, reduces to the exponential distribution when $\alpha = 1$. Changing α affects the shape of the distribution most near the origin; when $\alpha < 1$, the function increases more steeply than exponential; if $\alpha > 1$ the curve has a sigmoid form.

Although there are differences in the exact form of

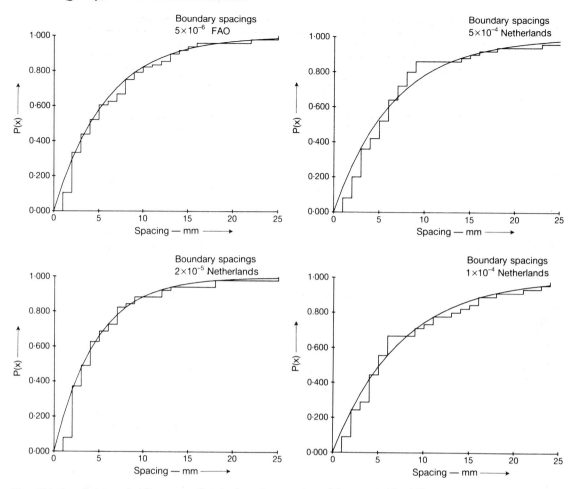

Fig. 6.14 Cumulative probability curves for the boundary spacings of the maps in Fig. 6.13.

the gamma distribution needed to describe the cumulative probability distribution of boundary spacings in a given area (cf. Burgess and Webster 1984), the fact that a simple statistical formula is generally applicable at all map scales lends credence to the tenets of the fractal theory and its application to mapped data.

If a boundary on a thematic map is considered to be a fractal, it can be modelled by a Brownian line function having an appropriate value of the fractal dimension D. An appropriate raster representation of the boundary will depend on D. Goodchild (1980) has shown that Switzer's estimate of mismatch for rasterizing polygons can be rewritten to show the dependence on both cell size and D as

$$L_{ij} = [k(D)/A] \cdot b^{(2-D)} \qquad (6.36)$$

where $k(D)$ is given by $k'[0.60 - 0.11(0.25)^{D/2}]/4$ and k' is the constant of proportionality in the equation

$n = k'b^{(2-D)}$ where n is the number of times a cell has an immediate neighbour of different colour. So, if D is known, or can be estimated, it provides a means of judging the relative benefits to be gained by using smaller grid cells or denser sampling.

Estimating the fractal dimension, D

If the fractional Brownian motion fBm is a useful model of the variation of geographical features, then they should have statistical properties that resemble those of the fBm and their fractal dimensions can be measured using the relations given by Mandelbrot (1982) for the fBm. Table 6.6 summarizes these methods; they are all easy to calculate, and in theory they should all yield straight lines on double logarithmic plots. When these methods are used to estimate D values of various geographical and geophysical phenomena they yield the results presented in Table 6.7.

Table 6.6 Summary of methods used to estimate D for geographical data

Name of method	Relation	Estimate of D
1. Length of a trail	$L(\lambda)=k\lambda^{1-D}$ λ is step size k is constant	Plot log L against log λ Slope of line is $1-D$
2. Area/perimeter relationship	$A=kP^{2/D}$ A is estimated area P is estimated perimeter k is a constant	Plot log A against log P Slope is $2/D$
3. Variance of increments or semivariance (one-dimensional transect)	$2\gamma(h)=h^{(4-2D)}$ where h is sampling interval	Plot log $\gamma(h)$ against log h Slope is $(4-2D)$
4. Power spectrum (one-dimensional transect)	$P(\omega)\simeq\omega^{-(5-2D)}$ where $P(\omega)$ is the power and ω is frequency	Plot log $P(\omega)$ against log ω Slope is $-(5-2D)$
5. Rescaled range R/S analysis	The ratio of the rescaled range $R(t,s)$ for a series over time t, to the sequential variance $S^2(t,s)$ is proportional to the lag s.	Plot log R/S against log s Graph has a slope of $(2-D)$
6. Korcak empirical relation for islands.	$Nr\,(A>a)=F'a^{-(D/2)}$ where $Nr\,(A>a)$ is the number of islands above size a, F' is a positive constant.	Plot log $Nr(Aa)$ against log a; slope is $-(D/2)$

NB Full definitions of these methods will be found in Mandelbrot (1982).

Table 6.7 Estimated D-values for some geographical data (from Burrough 1985)

Description	Apparent D (linear)
Varve data	1.02–1.5
Tree ring indices	1.22–1.45
Annual precipitation	1.13–1.36
River flows	1.02–1.52
Thickness and lithology of Palaeozoic sediments	1.25–1.45
Iron ore in rocks	1.4–1.9
Groundwater levels	1.3–1.8
Landform	1.1–1.3–1.7
Soil properties	1.5–2.0

In general it appears that some phenomena, such as the variation of landform, and fluids such as water and air tend to have small D-values, i.e. they vary smoothly, and long-range variations dominate. Conversely, the variations of soil properties and minerals in rocks tend to be dominated by noisy, short-range variation. These results match our intuitive understanding that it is better to model landforms, groundwater surfaces and air pressure by continuous (isopleth) maps. They demonstrate, however, the fuzzy, unclear nature of soil changes and show why it is unwise to pay too much attention to the exact location of a soil boundary or to represent such boundaries with a high degree of cartographic accuracy, particularly if that artificial accuracy leads to the technical problems of map intersection and overlay.

If the fractal Brownian model fitted all experimentally derived results well we would only need to know the D-value and the absolute amplitude of the variation at any given scale in order to be able to estimate the amount of sampling needed to produce a map of a given resolution at any other scale. All errors due to spatial variation could be predicted easily without sampling! Unfortunately, nature is more complex than the simple fractal Brownian model. Independent studies of the variation of landforms (Goodchild 1981; Mark and Aronson 1984), soil properties (Burrough

1984, 1985) and craters on Mars (Woronow 1981) show that the estimated value of *D* of a given data set may vary with the absolute scale at which the measurements have been made. In cases where *D*-values could be estimated from the same data using several of the methods listed in Table 6.6, different values resulted. When different processes had been at work in the same landscape to produce the outlines of the landforms that were analysed, different *D*-values were obtained. In general, it seems that in the same landscape, *D*-values increase with altitude, presumably because depositional processes operating at lower altitudes tend to lead to smoother landforms than the dominantly weathering and erosion processes found in the mountains. In some situations, the landscapes or soil properties had characteristic scales of variation, which is counter to the idea of the Brownian fractal motion, which assumes that no single scale is characteristic. For the variation of soil properties along a transect dominated by geological changes, however, Burrough (1983b) showed that they could be modelled successfully by a weighted, nested model of random variation incorporating the characteristic length scales of the landscape in question.

It is clear from all these fractal studies, however, that boundaries cannot be regarded as absolute; they are artefacts or compromises, and their statistics (length, breadth) are a complex function of the variation of the property being mapped and of the scale and mapping method.

Research in the application of fractal ideas to cartography is still in its infancy. Dutton (1981) and Armstrong and Hopkins (1983) have proposed using fractal methods to generate a required level of wiggliness from smoothly drawn lines in order to achieve a given degree of 'naturalness'; Dell'Orco and Ghiron (1983) propose a method for storing drawings that preserves 'fractality' (*sic*). No doubt more work will follow, stimulated by the striking fractal 'landscapes' produced by Mandelbrot and his colleague Richard Voss (Voss 1985) that have captured the enthusiasm of the computer graphics world. Perhaps their work will not only serve to stimulate the production of pictures for science fiction movies, but will also lead to a serious attempt to find new ways of representing the variations of natural phenomena that are better than those currently used today.

Combining attributes from overlaid maps

Having discussed the question of combining boundaries through overlay, and the associated problems that

may occur as a result of failing to realize the imperfections of real-world data, we will now consider the problem of error propagation with respect to combining the attributes from different maps. The problem is stated in Fig. 5.7 (p. 86). Given that X and Y are two independent maps that are overlaid to produce a third, U, and that the cell C_{ij} is not on or near a boundary on either map, what is the error (or magnitude of uncertainty) in the value of U as a result of variations in X and Y?

We will consider the cases when the transformation algorithm

$$u = f(x, y, \ldots) \tag{6.37}$$

expresses (a) simple arithmetical relationships ($+$, $-$, $\times$, $\div$), (b) logical relationships (AND, OR, NOT)

(a) Arithmetical relationships

Consider the situation in which the value of an attribute on map X is not exact but has an associated error term ε so that the value of the attribute cannot be better known than $x \pm \varepsilon x$. An example could be that of the value of readily available water in a soil mapping unit that was regarded as statistically homogeneous. We wish to combine a map of readily available soil water X with a map of irrigation effectiveness Y, in which the irrigation effectiveness also has a variation $y \pm \varepsilon y$. If, as in the example here, the maps of X and Y can be considered independent, then if εx and εy are each of the order of 20 per cent, the error of total available water $u = (x + y)$ will be of the order of 28 per cent. For cartographic overlay operations involving more than two steps, the increase in error can be explosive.

The propagation of errors through arithmetical operations on normally distributed variables has been long understood, but has received little attention in geographical information processing. If we consider only random, independent errors, then for a relationship

$$u = f(x_1, x_2, x_3, \ldots \ldots x_j s) \tag{6.38}$$

in which the x_js are all independent, then S*u*, the standard deviation of *u* is given by

$$Su = [\sum_{i=1}^{j} (\delta u / \delta x_i)^2 . Sx_i^2]^{\frac{1}{2}} \tag{6.39}$$

and the standard error of *u*, SE*u*, is given by

$$SEu = [\sum_{i=1}^{j} (\delta u / \delta x_i)^2 . SEx_i^2]^{\frac{1}{2}} \tag{6.40}$$

where SEx_i is the standard error of x_i (Parratt 1961).

The fractional standard deviation in u is:

$$\text{Fractional } Su = Su/u \qquad (6.41)$$

and the fractional standard error in u is:

$$\text{Fractional } SEu = SEu/u. \qquad (6.42)$$

Fractional standard deviation or fractional standard error are usually expressed in per cent.

These formulae hold when there is no correlation between the x_is. When they are correlated, the eqns (6.39) and (6.40) above must receive an extra term to express the increase in error in u due to correlation. This term is:

$$[\sum_{i=1}^{I} \sum_{j=1}^{J} \{\delta u/\delta x_i . \delta u/\delta x_j . Sx_i . Sx_j . r_{ij}\}]. \qquad (6.43)$$

Let us now consider some specific examples.

Sum or difference—no correlation. Let

$$u = x \pm y \pm \cdots,$$

then $\delta u/\delta x = 1$, $\delta u/\delta y = \pm 1$, etc.

By eqn (6.39)

$$Su = \sqrt{(Sx^2 + Sy^2 + \cdots)} \qquad (6.44)$$

For example, if $x = 10 \pm 1$ and $y = 8 \pm 1$,

$$u = 10 + 8 = 18$$

and

$$Su = \sqrt{(1+1)} = 1.4.$$

The absolute error in u is greater than either x or y, but in the case of addition, the relative error ($1.4/18 = 8$ per cent) is lower than for the original variates (10 and 12.5 per cent). For subtraction, the absolute error Su is the same, but the relative error is now much greater being ($1.4/2 = 70$ per cent). Whereas addition of two random numbers, and hence of two maps, can be thought of as a benign operation with respect to error propagation, subtraction can lead to explosive increases in relative errors, particularly when x and y are similar in value.

In the case that y is a constant, i.e. $u = x + a$, there is no difference in the variance of u and x. Adding or subtracting constants therefore has no deleterious effect on errors.

Addition of correlated variables. When the variables x_1, $x_2, \ldots$ are correlated, the term given in eqn (6.43) must be included in the computation of the error of u. Let

$u = x + y$, in which r_{xy} expresses the correlation ($-1 \leqslant r_{xy} \leqslant 1$) between x and y.

$$Su = \sqrt{\{Sx^2 + Sy^2 + 2Sx . Sy . r_{xy}\}}. \qquad (6.45)$$

In the case of $u = (10 \pm 1) + (8 \pm 1)$

$$Su = \sqrt{\{1 + 1 + 2.1.1.r_{xy}\}}$$

so that if x and y are 100 per cent positively correlated, the error in u is exactly the sum of the errors of x and y. If x and y are negatively correlated, the error in u, Su, could be less than if x and y were independent.

Product or quotient—no correlation. Let

$$u = x^a . y^b, \qquad (6.46)$$

where a and b are assumed exact constants. Then,

$$\delta u/\delta x = ax^{(a-1)} . y^b$$

and

$$\delta u/\delta y = bx^a . y^{(b-1)}$$

so by eqn (6.39),

$$Su = \sqrt{\{a^2 . x^{2(a-1)} . y^{2b} . Sx^2 + b^2 . x^{2a} . y^{2(b-1)} . Sy^2\}}. \qquad (6.47)$$

Because the partial differentiation in the Taylor expansion is done at the values of x and y, the values of x and y in this expression are taken as the mean values of x and y. Consider the case where

$$u = xy \qquad (x = 10 \pm 1, y = 8 \pm 1).$$
$$u = 8 \times 10 = 80$$
$$Su = \sqrt{\{y^2 . Sx^2 + x^2 . Sy^2\}}$$
$$= \sqrt{\{64 \times 1 + 100 \times 1\}}$$
$$= \sqrt{164} = 12.8.$$

Multiplication not only raises the absolute error, but also the relative error, in this case to $12.8/80 = 16$ per cent.

In the case of y being a constant, i.e. $u = ax$, eqn (6.47) reduces to:

$$Su = \sqrt{\{a^2.Sx^2\}}. \qquad (6.48)$$

In the case of the relation

$$u = Ax^a \qquad (6.49)$$

where A and a are constants, we must be careful because of our assumption that the variables were uncorrelated. In eqn (6.49) x is perfectly correlated with itself so that the error of u, Su, is given by

$$Su = \sqrt{\{A^2.a^2.x^{2(a-1)}Sx^2\}}. \qquad (6.50)$$

For the case $x = 10 \pm 1$, the error of u in the expression

$$u = x^2 = 10^2 = 100$$

is given by

$$Su = \sqrt{\{(2x)^2 . Sx^2\}}$$
$$= \sqrt{\{20^2 . 1\}} = \sqrt{400} = 20.$$

Not only has the absolute error increased, but the relative error ($=20/100=20$ per cent) has also doubled.

Logarithmic and other relations. Let $u = B \ln x$ (6.51)

$$\delta U / \delta x = B/x$$

so $Su = \sqrt{\{(B^2/x^2).Sx^2\}}$
$$= B.Sx/x.$$ (6.52)

Consideration of eqn (6.52) shows that the increase or decrease in error depends solely on the ratio of $B:x$.

If $u = A \sin x$
$$Su = A. Sx \cos x$$ (6.53)

where Sx and x are in radians.

Recommended strategies for arithmetic algorithms. The way in which errors in normally distributed variables are propagated by simple arithmethic led Alonso (1968) to propose a few simple rules of thumb for building or choosing algorithms or mathematical models. He suggested that one should:

(a) avoid intercorrelated variables;
(b) add where possible;
(c) if you cannot add, multiply or divide;
(d) avoid as far as possible taking differences or raising variables to powers.

We should also remember that we might be able to reduce the variances of the mapped variables by making more accurate measurements or by using better interpolation techniques.

An example. Let us now consider the effects of error propagation in one of the modelling exercises discussed in Chapter 5, namely the simulation of soil erosion in Kisii, Kenya. It will be remembered that the aim of this study was to estimate the amount of erosion that might occur in a given area under a land use scenario of smallholder maize, grown over a period of 40 years. The amount of erosion was estimated in the first instance using the universal Soil Loss Equation:

$$A = R \times K \times L \times S \times C \times P$$ (6.54)

where A is the annual soil loss in tonne ha^{-1}, R is a measure of the erosion caused by rainfall, K is the erodibility of the soil, L is the slope length in m, S the slope in per cent, C is the cultivation parameter and P

the protection measures. This equation was evaluated for every cell in the study area for a period of 40 years.

The source data for this study were limited rainfall studies and conventional choropleth maps displaying only the 'representative' values of the soil and climatic variables. Moreover, the R, L, and S factors were themselves derived through the use of several regression formulae.

The R factor. The value of R in the USLE was estimated by using the FAO formula:

$$R = 0.11 \, abc + 66$$ (6.55)

where

a is the average annual precipitation in cm,
b is the maximum day-precipitation occurring once in 2 yr in cm, and
c is the maximum total precipitation of a shower of one year occurring once in 2 y, also in cm.

The best information available for the study area (Wielemaker and Boxem 1982) suggested that reasonable values for a, b, and c were:

$$a = 172.5 \pm 20 \, cm, b = 5.41 \pm 1.1 \, cm, c = 2.25 \pm 0.5 \, cm.$$

The estimates of the standard errors are large because of the limited data for the area.

By eqn (6.55), $R = 297$ cm and by eqn (6.47), the standard error in R is ± 72 cm per year.

The K factor. For the more erodible soils, evidence from outside the study area suggested that a K value of 0.1 for an eroded soil over laterite was probable. Given the often large variability of soil properties (a CV of 50 per cent is common) a map unit standard deviation of ± 0.05 is not unreasonable.

The L factor. The slope length factor L was calculated using Wischmeier and Smith's (1978) formula of

$$L = (l/22.1)^{\frac{1}{2}}$$ (6.56)

where l is the slope length in metres. Considering a typical, long slope in the area, a length of $100 \, m \pm 20 \, m$ is reasonable; this converts to an L value of 2.13 ± 0.045.

The S factor. The slope gradient factor S was computed using the parabolic regression formula

$$S = 0.0065s^2 + 0.0454s + 0.065$$ (6.57)

where s is the slope expressed as a percentage (Smith and Wischmeier 1957). For a slope of 10 ± 2 per cent (an optimistic estimate of the standard deviation of the classes on the slope map) equations 6.57 and 6.47 yield a value of S of 1.169 ± 0.122.

The C factor. The estimated value of the cropping management factor C was 0.63. Given the uncertainty of estimating C for a crop that does not cover the soil surface for the whole year, and that Rose (1975) found that a C-value for maize varies between 0.4 and 0.9, the error in C was estimated at ± 0.15.

The P factor. The erosion control practice factor, P, was estimated at a value of 0.5 ± 0.1.

To summarize, the values of the factors of the USLE and their estimated errors are:

$$R = 297 \pm 72$$
$$K = 0.1 \pm 0.05$$
$$L = 2.13 \pm 0.045$$
$$S = 1.169 \pm 0.122$$
$$C = 0.63 \pm 0.15$$
$$P = 0.5 \pm 0.1,$$

which yields an annual soil loss rate of 23 ± 14.8 tonne yr^{-1}, corresponding to a soil surface lowering of 0.23 ± 0.15 cm yr^{-1}, or 9 ± 6 cm in 40 years. In other words, the variation in predicted soil loss, given the integrity of the model, was that 95 per cent of cells having the climate/slope/soil regime specified here would have a soil loss ranging between 3 and 21 cm.

The large margin of error resulting from the use of multiplicative models, (such as the USLE) with data that cannot be more accurately specified, led Alonso (1968) to remark that in situations where data are poor we are better off with simple, additive models than with complex regression models using multiplication and powers, simply because the error propagation is lower. The large error margins obtained above are in addition to any systematic errors caused by the USLE or any other model being inappropriate or badly calibrated for the area. In fact, with such large error margins, discussions about which models are good, and which are bad become irrelevant. We may seek to improve the quality of our predictions by using better models, but unless at the same time we attempt to reduce the variance of the data used in the models, the results may be worse than useless.

(b) Logical relationships (AND, OR, NOT)

In data retrieval or in map overlay, it is implicit in the use of Boolean logic that the description of set A necessarily includes all items in the set and that description applies to all of them. In many resource survey legends we use classification hierarchies in which class membership is often very rigidly defined (see for example the USDA Soil Taxonomy). But when we map areas of the earth's surface and then wish to associate these areas with the classes of *point* observations we find that although a class name only includes profiles of a certain type, the delineated area

very often contains impurities or exceptions. Instead of a closely defined set in which the set name applies to all parts of the area given that name, we have a set with a well-defined *central concept*, surrounded by a less well-defined cloud of observation points that, like Blakemore's loci in the polygon-grid overlay problem (see Fig. 6.6) are possibly in or possibly outside the class.

The reasons for the doubtful points are several, as Webster (1968) pointed out in his critique of the USDA Seventh Approximation (later Soil Taxonomy). They include the problems of errors in determining the exact value of discriminating criteria (criteria used to allocate an individual to a class), the problems of short-range variation within the basic unit mapped that causes the set of observation points to be less homogeneous than the set of classification points, and other errors introduced by map generalization caused by scale reduction or conversion to raster format.

Given that we have two maps, X and Y and we wish to evaluate the logical expression

$$U = f(A, B) \tag{6.58}$$

for two sets of grid cells or areas, A on map X and B on map Y, where A and B are sets with a clear central concept but which are known to include impurities, a satisfactory procedure will not only look for topologically congruent sites, but will also examine the sites to see how closely they match the central set concepts. Clearly, simple Boolean logic is unable to cope with this problem, but by using developments in fuzzy set theory, currently finding research applications in language processing and information retrieval, answers may be at hand.

In the map overlay problem, suppose that set A contains 20 per cent of impure cells, and set B contains 10 per cent, simple Boolean combination (e.g. $U = A \cap B$) would result in a set U that contained some 22 per cent impurities, but we would not know which. In fuzzy set theory, we define a *membership function* to express the degree to which a cell or area is a member of the set. The membership function is a very useful device that allows one to model linguistic vagueness or the map unit impurities described above (Kaufmann 1975; Zadeh 1965). Using the fuzzy set approach allows one to use linguistic quantifiers that are less precise than strict, hierarchical logic allows ('most', 'some', 'a few'), but which are often very well suited to map overlay problems in resource assessment.

Salton and McGill (1983) describe the application of fuzzy set theory to information retrieval, and what follows here is an attempt to apply their reasoning to the problem described above. Consider the result of overlaying maps X and Y to give U, where U is a set of cells. In particular, consider a single cell, CELL, on map U. If A denotes the 'concept' or mapping class of all cells denoted by A, then the membership function of cell CELL in set A may be denoted as fA(CELL). In the usual terminology, fA(CELL) represents the weight of term A in the allocation of cell CELL. Given a number of concept classes A, B, C, ... Z (representing various map overlays) it is now possible to identify each cell by giving its membership function with respect to each overlay, i.e.

$$D = (fA(\text{CELL}), fB(\text{CELL}), \dots fZ(\text{CELL})). \quad (6.59)$$

The similarity of two cells may be obtained as a function of the differences in the membership functions of the two items in corresponding concept classes. Specifically, given T different concept classes, the *fuzzy distance* between cells CELL′ and CELL″ might be computed as

$$d(\text{CELL}',\text{CELL}'') = \sum_{x \in \tau} (fX(\text{CELL}') - fX(\text{CELL}|)) \quad (6.60)$$

or alternatively as

$$d(\text{CELL}',\text{CELL}'') = \sqrt{[\sum (fX(\text{CELL}') - fX(\text{CELL}''))^2]} \quad (6.61)$$

Ranked allocation to the final output map would be achieved by retrieving the cells in order of increasing fuzzy distance from the combined central concept.

Salton and McGill (1983) point out that one attractive feature of the fuzzy set approach is the possibility of extending the definition of the membership function to include combinations of terms. Given the membership functions of cell CELL with respect to map units A in overlay X and B in overlay Y, then

$$f(A \text{ AND } B) (\text{CELL}) = \min(fA(\text{CELL}), fB(\text{CELL}))$$
$$f(A \text{ OR } B) (\text{CELL}) = \max(fA(\text{CELL}), fB(\text{CELL}))$$
$$f(\text{NOT} A) (\text{CELL}) = 1 - fA(\text{CELL}). \quad (6.62)$$

The fuzzy set rules given in eqn (6.62) satisfy the normal rules of Boolean algebra when fA(CELL) and fB(CELL) are restricted to the values 0 and 1. The fuzzy set model is thus an extension to the rules of Boolean logical combination in situations where weighted identifiers can be applied to the cells.

Fuzzy set theory seems to have much to offer in situations where sets of classified cells need to be overlaid and combined. At the time of writing, however, the author is unaware of any work currently being done to apply fuzzy set theory in mapping. As Salton and McGill (1983) point out, 'A number of attempts have been made to use fuzzy set models in [information] retrieval ... however, the resulting systems have never been evaluated.'

Conclusions

This chapter has reviewed the main sources of error and variation in data that can contribute to unreliable results being produced by a geographical information system. Many kinds of error can be detected before data are input to the system, or can be caught during data entry. The more subtle, and therefore potentially damaging, errors can arise through data processing operations such as digitizing and map overlay; these errors often escape the naïve user of geographical information systems.

Natural spatial variation in the original data is probably the major source of unseen errors. Current practices of thematic mapping tend to hide natural variation behind a smokescreen of smoothly drawn lines and homogeneously presented mapping units. The user of the map document often has only qualitative statements about within-map unit variation on which to judge the quality of the map. When data are highly variable, the results obtained from mathematical models (particularly those using expressions with multipliers and powers) may have such large error margins as to be useless. In these situations, one should try to adopt new strategies for improving the ways in which environmental data are collected, analysed, and mapped. These ways require an improved awareness of the nature of geographical variation, and in particular:

(a) better and more appropriate classification techniques;

(b) improved interpolation techniques to avoid having to use class averages and 'representative' sites as the basis for statements about larger areas; and

(c) reducing measurement errors in field determinations known to be particularly error prone or subject to bias.

Some answers to these points will be discussed in the next chapters.

References

Acres, B. D., Bower, R. P., Burrough, P. A., Folland, C. J., Kalsi, M. S., Thomas, P., and Wright, P. S. (1976). *The soils of Sabah* (5 vols). Land Resources Division, Ministry of Overseas Development, London.

Aldred, B. K. (1972). *Point-in-polygon algorithms*. IBM, Peterlee, UK.

Alonso, W. (1968). Predicting best with imperfect data. *J. Am. Inst. Plan.* (APA Journal). July 1968, 248–55.

Armstrong, M. P. and Hopkins, L. D. (1983). Fractal enhancement for thematic display of topologically stored data. In *Proc. AUTOCARTO 6*, Ottawa, Canada.

Ayeni, O. O. (1982). Optimum sampling for digital terrain models. *Photogramm. Engng and Rem. Sens.* **XLVIII** (11), 1687–94.

Bakker, H. de (1979). *Major soils and soil regions in The Netherlands*. Junk, The Hague/PUDOC, Wageningen.

Beckett, P. H. T. (1971). The cost-effectiveness of soil survey. *Outlook Agric.* **6** (5), 191–8.

—— and Burrough, P. A. (1971). The relation between cost and utility in soil survey IV. *J. Soil Sci.* **22**, 466–80.

—— and Webster, R. (1971). Soil variability—a review. *Soils Fert.* **34**, 1–15.

Bie, S. W. and Beckett, P. H. T. (1970). The cost of soil survey. *Soils Fert.* **33**, 203–17.

—— and Beckett, P. H. T. (1973). Comparison of four independent soil surveys by air-photo interpretation, Paphos area (Cyprus). *Photogrammetria* **29**, 189–202.

Blakemore, M. (1984). Generalisation and error in spatial data bases. *Cartographica* **21**, 131–9.

Bouma, J. and Bell, J. P., ed. (1983). Spatial variability. Special Issue, *Agric. Wat. Mgmt* **6**, Nos. 2/3.

—— and Nielsen, D. R. (1985). *Spatial analysis of soil data*. PUDOC, Wageningen.

Boyle, A. R. (1982). The last ten years of automated cartography: a personal view. In *Computers in cartography* (ed. D. Rhind and T. Adams) pp. 1–3. British Cartographic Society, London.

Burgess, T. M. and Webster, R. (1980). Optimal interpolation and isarithmic mapping of soil properties I. The semivariogram and punctual kriging. *J. Soil Sci.* **31**, 315–31.

—— and Webster, R. (1984). Optimal sampling strategies for mapping soil types. I. Distribution of boundary spacings. *J. Soil Sci,* **35**, 641–54.

Burrough, P. A. (1969). Studies in soil survey methodology. Unpublished D.Phil thesis, University of Oxford.

—— (1983a). Multiscale sources of spatial variation in soil I. The application of fractal concepts to nested levels of soil variation. *J. Soil Sci.* **34**, 577–97.

—— (1983b). Multiscale sources of spatial variation in soil II. A non-Brownian fractal model and its application in soil survey. *J. Soil Sci.* **34**, 599–620.

—— (1984). The application of fractal ideas to geophysical phenomena. *Bull. Inst. Math. Appl.* **20** (3/4), 36–42.

—— (1985). Fakes, facsimiles and fractals: fractal models of geophysical phenomena. In *Science and uncertainty* (ed. S. Nash) pp. 151–170. IBM/Science Reviews Northwood, UK.

——, Beckett, P. H. T., and Jarvis, M. G. (1971). The relation between cost and utility in soil survey, I–III. *J. Soil Sci.* **22**, 359–94.

——, Brown, L., and Morris, E. C. (1977). Variations in vegetation and soil pattern across the Hawkesbury Sandstone plateau from Barren Grounds to Fitzroy Falls, New South Wales. *Aust. J. Ecol.* **2**, 137–59.

——, Oerlemans, G., Stoffelsen, G., and Witter, J. V. (1983). Reconnaissance soil studies to determine optimum survey scales and mapping legend for soil moisture research in the Hupselse Beek Hydrological Catchment: Oost Gelderland. Report No. 1, Study Group 'Soil variability Hupselse Beek', Agricultural University, Wageningen.

Chrisman, N. R. (1984a). The role of quality information in the long-term functioning of a geographic information system. *Cartographica* **21**, 79–87.

—— (1984b). On storage of coordinates in geographic information systems. *GeoProcessing* **2**, 259–70.

Davis, J. C. (1973). *Statistics and data analysis in geology*. Wiley, New York. (Second edition 1986.)

Davis, L. S. (1976). A survey of edge-detection techniques. *Comput. Graph. & Image Process.* **4** (3), 248–70.

Dell'Orco, P. and Ghiron, M. (1983). Shape representation by rectangles preserving fractality. In *Proc. AUTOCARTO 6*, Ottawa, Canada.

Dutton, G. H. (1981). Fractal enhancement of cartographic line detail. *Am. Cartogr.* **8**(1), 23–40.

Estes, J. E., Hajic, E., and Tinney, L. R., ed. (1983). Fundamentals of image analysis: analysis of visible and thermal infrared data. *Manual of remote sensing* (ed. R. N. Colwell) Chapter 4. American Society of Photogrammetry, Falls Church, Va.

Franklin, W. R., (1984). Cartographic errors symptomatic of underlying algebra problems. In *Proc. Int. Symp. on Spatial Data Handling*, 20–24 Aug., Zurich, Switzerland, pp. 190–208.

Frolov, Y. S. and Maling, D. H. (1969). The accuracy of area measurements by point counting techniques. *Cartogr. J.* **6**, 21–35.

Gruijter, J. J. de and Marsman, B. (1985). Transect sampling for reliable information on mapping units. In *Spatial analysis of soil data* (ed. J. Bouma and D. Nielsen) pp. 150–65. PUDOC, Wageningen.

Goodchild, M. F. (1978). Statistical aspects of the polygon overlay problem. In *Harvard papers on geographic information systems* (ed. G. Dutton) Vol 6. Addison-Wesley, Reading, Mass.

—— (1980). Fractals and the accuracy of geographical measures. *Math. Geol.* **12**, 85–98.

Grothenn, D. and Stanfenbiel, W. (1976). Das Standarddatrenformat zum Austausch Kartografischer Daten. *Nachr. Karten Vermess.* Reihe I, Heft. **69**, 25–49.

Gruenberger, F. (1984). Computer recreations. *Scient. Am.* **250**(4), 10–14 (April 1984).

Hawkins, D. M. and Merriam, D. F. (1973). Optimal zonation of digitized sequential data. *Mathl Geol.* **5**, 389–95.

—— and Merriam, D. F. (1974). Zonation of multivariate sequences of digitized geologic data. *Mathl Geol.* **6**, 263–9.

Jenks, G. F. (1981). Lines, computers and human frailties. *Ann. Ass. Am. Geogr.* **71** (1), 1–10.

Kaufman, A. (1975). *An Introduction to the theory of fuzzy subsets*, Vol 1. Academic Press, New York.

Levialdi, S. (1980). Finding the edge. In *Digital image processing* (ed. J. C. Simon and R. M. Haralick) pp. 105–48. Reidel, Dordrecht.

McAlpine, J. R. and Cook, B. G. (1971). Data reliability from map overlay. In *Proc. Australian and New Zealand Association for the Advancement of Science, 43rd Congress*, Brisbane, May. Section 21—Geographical Sciences.

McBratney, A. B. and Webster, R. (1983). Optimal interpolation and isarithmic mapping of soil properties. V. Coregionalisation and multiple sampling strategy. *J. Soil Sci.* **34**, 137–62.

MacDougal, E. B. (1975). The accuracy of map overlays. *Landsc. Plan.* **2**, 23–30.

Makarovic, B. (1975). Amended strategy for progressive sampling *ITC J.* 1975 (1), 117–28.

Maling, D. H. (1973). *Coordinate systems and map projections*. George Phillip, London.

Mandelbrot, B. B. (1982). *The fractal geometry of nature*. Freeman, New York.

Mark, D. M. and Aronson, P. B. (1984). Scale-dependent fractal dimensions of topographic surfaces: an empirical investigation with application in geomorphology and computer mapping. *Mathl Geol.* **16**, 671–83.

Marsman, B. and de Gruijter, J. J. (1984). Dutch soil survey goes into quality control. In *Soil information systems technology* (ed. P. A. Burrough and S. W. Bie) pp. 127–34. PUDOC, Wageningen.

Mead, D. A. (1982). Assessing data quality in geographic information systems. In *Remote sensing for resource management* (ed. C. J. Johannsen and J. L. Sanders) Chapter 5, pp. 51–62. Soil Conservation Society of America, Ankeny, IA.

Miller, E. E. (1980). Similitude and scaling of soil–water phenomena. In *Applications of soil physics* (ed. D. Hillel). Academic Press, New York.

Nortcliff, S. (1978). Soil variability and reconnaissance soil mapping: a statistical study in Norfolk. *J. Soil Sci.* **29**, 403–18.

Parratt, L. G. (1961). *Probability and experimental errors*. Wiley, New York.

Perkal, J. (1966). On the length of empirical curves. Discussion paper 10, Ann Arbor, Michigan Inter-University Community of Mathematical Geographers.

Poggio, T. (1984). Vision by man and machine. *Scient. Am.* **250** (4), 68–78 (April 1984).

Poiker, T. K. (1982). Looking at computer cartography. *GeoJournal* **6**(3), 241–9.

Reeuwijk, L. P. van. (1982). Laboratory methods and data quality. Program for soil characterization: A report on the pilot round. Part I. CEC and texture. *Proc. 5th Int. Classification Workshop*, Khartoum, Sudan, Nov. 1982. 58pp.

—— (1984). Idem. Part II: Exchangeable bases, base saturation and pH. Int. Soil Reference and Information Centre, Wageningen, 28pp.

Rose, E. (1975). Erosion et ruissellment en Afrique de l'ouest: vingt annees de mesures en petites parcelles experimentales. Cyclo. ORSTOM, Abidjan, Ivory Coast.

Rosenfeld, A. and Kak, A. (1976). *Digital picture processing*. Academic Press, New York.

Salomé, A. I., van Dorsser, H. J., and Rieff, Ph.L (1982). A comparison of geomorphological mapping systems. *ITC J.* 1982(3), 272–4.

Salton, G. and Mcgill, M. J. (1983). *Introduction to modern information retrieval*. McGraw-Hill, New York.

Scheidegger, A. E. (1970). Stochastic models in hydrology. *Wat. Resources Res.* **6**, 750–5.

Smedley, B. and Aldred, B. K., (1980). Problems with geodata. In *Data base techniques for pictorial applications* (ed. A. Blaser) pp. 539–54. Springer-Verlag, Berlin.

Smith, D. D. and Wischmeier, W. H. (1957). Factors affecting sheet and rill erosion. *Trans. Am. geophys. Union* **38**, 889–96.

Soil Survey Staff (1951). *Soil survey manual*. USDA Handbook No. 18, US Govt. Printing Office, Washington, DC.

—— (1976) *Soil taxonomy*. US Govt. Printing Office, Washington, DC.

Sokolnikoff, I. S. and Sokolnikoff, E. S. (1941). *Higher mathematics for engineers and physicists*. McGraw-Hill, New York.

Switzer, P. (1975). Estimation of the accuracy of qualitative maps. In *Display and analysis of spatial data* (ed. J. C. Davis and M. J. McCullagh) pp. 1–13. Wiley, New York.

Tomlinson, R. and Boyle, A. R., (1981).The state of development of systems for handling natural resources inventory data. *Cartographica* **18**, 65–95.

Vink, A. P. A. (1963). *Planning of soil surveys in land development*. Publication of the International Institute Land Reclamation and Improvement, No. 10.

Voss, R. (1985). Random fractal forgeries: from mountains to music. In *Science and uncertainty* (ed. S. Nash) pp. 69–88. IBM Science Reviews, Northwood, UK.

Webster, R. (1968). Fundamental objections to the 7th approximation. *J. Soil Sci.* **19**, 354–66.

—— (1973). Automatic soil boundary location from transect data. *Mathl Geol.* **5**, 27–37.

—— (1977). *Quantitative and numerical methods in soil classification and survey*. Oxford University Press, Oxford.

—— (1978). Optimally partitioning soil transects. *J. Soil Sci.* **29**, 388–402.

—— (1980). DIVIDE: A FORTRAN IV program for segmenting miltivariate one-dimensional spatial series. *Comput. Geosci.* **6**, 61–8.

—— and Burgess, T. M. (1984). Sampling and bulking strategies for estimating soil properties in small regions. *J. Soil Sci.* **35**, 127–40.

—— and Wong, I. F. T. (1969). A numerical procedure for testing soil boundaries interpreted from air photographs. *Photogrammetria* **24**, 59–72.

Wentworth, C. K. (1930). A simplified method for determining the average slope of land surfaces. *Am. J. Sci.* Ser. 5, **20**, 184–94.

Wielemaker, W. G. and Boxem, H. W. (1982). Soils of the Kisii area, Kenya. Agricultural Research Report No. 922,

PUDOC/Agricultural University, Wageningen, The Netherlands.

Wilding, L. P., Jones, R. B. and Schafer, G. M. 1965. Variation of soil morphological properties within Miami, Celina and Crosby mapping units in West-Central Ohio. *Proc. Soil Sci. Soc. Am.* **29** (6), 711–17.

Wischmeier, W. H. and Smith, D. D. (1978). Predicting rainfall erosion losses. Agricultural Handbook No. 537, USDA, Washington, DC.

Woronow, A. (1981). Morphometric consistency with the Hausdorff-Besicovitch dimension. *Mathl. Geol.* **13,** 201–16.

Zadeh, L. A. (1965). Fuzzy sets. *Inf. Control* **8** (3), 338–53.

Zonneveld, J. I. S. (1973). Convergentie en luchfotointerpretatie. *KNAG Geogr. Tijdschr.* **VII**(1), 38–48.

7. Classification Methods

Information analysis in geographical information processing can be summed up as an exercise in resolving spatial data into patterns that we can understand, commonly called 'structure' or 'signal', and patterns that we cannot unscramble, commonly called 'noise'. The main problems arise because of the way 'structures' or 'signals' are recognized, classified, and mapped, and the inflexibility of conventional inventory methods for data extraction and quantitative analysis.

In conventional inventory and mapping, the original data are usually classified very soon after the original observations have been made. Perhaps this is nowhere so common as in soil survey. Soil profiles are described and analysed and then the appropriate soil class is worked out using the keys given in the chosen classification system, which is almost invariably hierarchically arranged. Areas of land within which there is a topographical unity and where profiles of the same class occur are delineated as units. When aerial photo interpretation is used, the procedure is a little different in that the delineation of the land units precedes the ground survey, but the net result is much the same. Areas of land are referenced to a soil unit in a hierarchical soil classification that is itself defined in terms of a number of soil properties that are considered to be of critical importance. Similar procedures have been used in integrated surveys and other natural resource surveys.

The procedure just described is unavoidable when large amounts of complex information must be reduced quickly to manageable proportions by persons who have no access to more powerful methods for processing data. Indeed, it is probably the only sensible way to proceed under those circumstances. The methodology assumes that through a proper understanding of the object of study (the landform, the soil pattern, and so on), natural units can be recognized that will serve as universal vehicles for information storage and transfer. This approach succeeds so long as the correlations between the critical or discriminating properties that are the keys in the classification and the information that a user really needs are large; if these correlations are weak or non-existent, then the classification serves little or no useful purpose.

Most conventional thematic maps that are sources of the data for many geographical information systems present their 'structure' in the form of delineated units (regions or mapping units) described by a legend. The legend describes the modal, or average values of critical properties in terms of the classification units within the boundaries of the mapping units; the spatial variations and variations in the values of the attributes of the phenomenon mapped may be alluded to only qualitatively in the legend or memoir, if at all. The original observations will have been replaced by a 'type area description', or a 'modal profile' or some other kind of 'representative' entity, that carries a class name from a national or international classification system. The result is that the original observations, including the information about all spatial structures and scales, have been superseded by an artificial line network that describes only *one* kind of structure at *one* spatial scale. All accurate quantitative information about within-map unit variation has been lost.

Although these kinds of thematic maps may present valuable overviews of spatial variation over large (that is, with respect to the map scale) areas, the information they can carry about local, within-map unit variations has been largely emasculated by the nature of the mapping process. At every stage in the hand-mapping process decisions must be made about scale, about which structures and which attributes are important. With a geographical information system, however, we do not have to digest, classify, and reduce data before they can be used for analysis. Instead, we can arrange that all the original observations are entered directly into the GIS, so that we can decide at leisure on the best classification for a given purpose, or can map individual properties separately by using appropriate interpolation methods. Instead of being forced to classify first, then interpolate using choropleth methods only, the GIS should allow the flexibility to operate on chosen subsets of the database, using the most appropriate combination of classification and interpolation methods for the task in hand.

So, the aim of the next two chapters is to describe some ways by which the user of the geographical data can extract more information from the original observations than would be possible with conventional maps by using appropriate statistical and numerical methods. In so doing, the margins of error associated with the results of the analyses and models made with the GIS should be improved.

Classification

Classification is essential for human understanding—without classification or generalization our brains become swamped by detail. Very often, we literally cannot see the wood for the trees. Also, the human brain seems to be limited in the number of classes that it can cope with, and seven classes plus or minus two per level in the hierarchy seems for many applications to be comfortable. Binary classifications, such as 'good' and 'bad' are usually considered to be insensitive and of little general value; classifications with more than 10 classes per hierarchical level, unworkable. Seven, plus or minus two is a good compromise; we recognize seven colours of the rainbow, many soil classifications recognize seven to ten major levels (e.g. USDA Soil Taxonomy has ten major taxonomic classes, the Handbook of Australian Soils (Stace *et al.* 1968) has seven major classes, each of which is split into four to nine subclasses) and many automated mapping and shading programs have automatic defaults set to handle ten classes.

Classifying the ranges of values of a single continuous variable

Simple classifications are often made in order to display continuously varying quantitative spatial properties such as population density, landform gradient, air pollution levels, and so on as easy-to-understand choropleth maps. The way in which the class intervals are chosen is critically important for the visual impression conveyed by the map. Evans (1977) made a thorough study of the problem and produced his own classification of class interval systems, from which the following is drawn.

Exogenous class intervals are fixed according to threshold values that are relevant to, but not derived from, the data set under study. Consequently, although they may be part of a standard classification system, they need not necessarily be the most appropriate for the area in question. Exogenous class intervals are widely used in soil survey and land evaluation classification systems that have been set up for national or international purposes. They have the advantage of universal applicability, but the great disadvantage that they may fail to resolve the variations in any specific area. For example, a classification of landform gradients in the classes 0–2 per cent, 3–5 per cent, 6–8 per cent, 9–16 per cent, 17–30 per cent, >30 per cent might not be sensitive enough to classify land with easily erodible soils with gradients that fell only in the range 0–8 per cent. If exogenous intervals are derived from qualitative class definitions (e.g. the range of values allowed within a given soil series definition), they may not be unique and may in fact overlap.

Arbitrary class intervals are chosen without any clear aim in mind. Very often the intervals are irregularly spaced and have been chosen without a proper examination of the data. Arbitrary class intervals may metamorphose into exogenous class intervals if used habitually for any length of time, particularly if their use is endorsed by official publications from weighty organizations.

Idiographic class intervals are chosen with respect to specific aspects of the data set. They include methods that attempt to divide the data into multi-modal groupings. As Jenks and Caspall (1971) demonstrate, the number of 'natural breaks', and to a certain extent their location, that might show the multi-modal appearance of a data set can depend very greatly on the number of classes used to plot the histogram (Fig. 7.1). Idiographic class intervals are usually not exactly reproducible from data set to data set, thereby making objective comparison difficult, if not impossible. Evans (1977) points out that some idiographic methods, such as Monmonnier's correlation-based method (Monmonnier 1975), are dangerous tools that in the hands of the unscrupulous can be used to get any result desired.

Serial class intervals have limits that are in direct mathematical relation to one another. If these limits are chosen to be independent of the characteristics of the particular data set, then results from different samples or data sets will be strictly comparable. The variable to be mapped is thought of as being represented by a 'statistical surface' which can be adequately described by:

(a) Normal percentiles—class intervals subdivide a normal distribution with mean μ and standard deviation σ into classes of equal frequency.

(b) Classes defined as a proportion of the standard deviation, with classes centred on the mean. For example, dividing a distribution into the intervals at

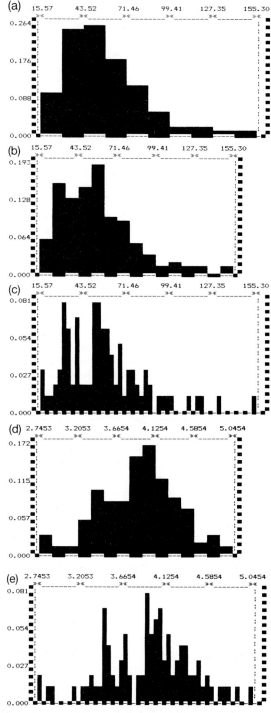

Fig. 7.1 Changing the number of classes (a–c) or changing the transformation (d–e) (here to logarithm) can considerably affect the decision to regard a data set as being composed of one or more 'natural' classes.

$\mu-1.8\sigma$, $\mu-1.2\sigma$, μ-0.6σ, μ, $\mu+0.6\sigma$, $\mu+1.2\sigma$ and $\mu+1.8\sigma$ results in eight classes. This kind of class interval may not be directly applicable for skewed data sets, or for those that contain truly multimodal distributions or a few extreme values.

(c) Equal arithmetic intervals with no variation in class width, such as are normally used for elevation contours. Whole number class intervals are easiest to understand. Many computer programs have a default option that divides the range of values in the data set into equal classes. This has the problem that class intervals may be decimal numbers and difficult to assimilate; also, because the range is an idiographic property of the data set, maps of the same variable derived from different data sets will not be strictly comparable.

(d) Equal intervals on reciprocal, trigonometric, geometric, or logarithmic scales. These scales can be used when the original data are not normally or rectangularly distributed.

Exogenous versus idiographic class intervals

In many quantitative studies of the quality of maps and classifications, such as those referred to in Chapter 6, the discussion has often been one of whether exogenous class boundaries have been adequate to resolve the variation in the data sufficiently. Very often the argument has been about whether other exogenous boundaries would be better (e.g. Lamp 1981), or whether the data possess some 'natural structure' which, if it could be revealed by some means or other, would be optimal for the data to hand.

A very widely used method of comparing the success of exogenous class limits is to use them to partition the data into classes and then to use a one-way variance analysis to estimate how much of the variance of the total data set is 'explained' by the classes. The analysis of variance model is given by

$$Z(x) = \mu + \alpha_j + \varepsilon$$

where the value of variable Z at point x in class j is given in terms of the overall mean μ, the deviation between μ and the mean of class j, α_j, and a normally distributed error term ε having mean of zero and variance σ^2. This model implicitly assumes that each 'mode' in a frequency distribution of the data can be equated with a class.

A 'good' classification is understood to be one that takes up as much of the variation in the data set as possible in terms of differences between the class means, leaving the residual error ε to be as small as possible. It is often assumed that the residual within-class variance is about the same for every class. The

Table 7.1 One-way analysis of variance

Source of variation	Degrees of freedom	Sum of squares	Mean square
Between-class means	$j-1$	$SS_b = \sum_{i=1} n_i(x_i - x)^2$	$SS_b/(j-1)$
Within classes (residual)	$N-j$	$SS_w = \sum_{i=1}^{j} \sum_{k=1}^{n_i}(x_{ik} - x_i)^2$	$SS_w/(N-j) = s^2_w$
Total	$N-1$	$SS_t = \sum_{i=1}^{j} \sum_{k=1}^{n_i}(x_{ik} - x)^2$	$SS_t/(N-1) = s^2_t$

where N is the total number of items in the sample
  j is the number of classes
  x is the mean of the whole sample
  x_i is the mean of the ith class
  n_i is the number of items in the ith class
  SS_b, SS_w, SS_t are convenient symbols for sums of squares
  s^2_w is the estimated within-class variance
  s^2_t is the estimated total variance.

analysis is performed as shown in Table 7.1 (Webster 1977, Snedecor and Cochran 1967).

A simple method of estimating the effectiveness of a classification is to calculate the ratio s^2_w/s^2_t, sometimes known as the relative variance. The term s^2_w estimates the pooled within-class variance or ε; s^2_t estimates the variance of the whole population before classification has been carried out. So

$$1 - (s^2_w/s^2_t)$$

estimates the proportion of variance accounted for by classification. Exogenously defined classifications can be compared in terms of relative variance, and the one that returns the lowest value for a given purpose will be the best.

The success of exogenous classifications depends greatly on the data, on the area from which the samples have been taken and on the relation between the kind of properties and the discriminating criteria used. Beckett and Burrough (1971) showed that for soil profiles sampled in three areas in the English Midlands, classified by the Soil Survey of England and Wales, relative variances for chemical and physical properties ranged from an exceptionally low value of 0.06 through 0.20 to 0.94 with a median value of 0.60. Yost and Fox (1981) published results showing that for Andepts (volcanic soils) on Hawaii, the United States Soil Taxonomy returned relative variances of chemical properties of 0.40–0.50 at the first category. Yet not all standard national classification systems have been so successful. Lamp (1981) reported a study

of 17 chemical properties from nearly 2000 soil profiles in West Germany in which the pedogenetically defined main and sub-horizon designations returned median relative variances of 92 per cent and 84 per cent respectively; a simple one-stage classification based on parent material returned a median relative variance of 57 per cent.

Visual appearance and information content in choropleth maps

The choropleth map is the visible result of cutting the data set by a number of horizontal planes, the positions of which are set by the class boundaries. As Evans (1977) and Jenks and Caspall (1971) have rightly pointed out, the map maker has an enormous range of possibilities to choose from in order to produce the map he thinks is required. Jenks and Caspall calculated that for a data set of 102 values of gross farm products for the State of Ohio, 101 different two-class choropleth maps could be made, 5050 three-class maps, 166 650 four-class, 4 082 925 five-class, 79 208 745 six-class, and 12 677 339 920 seven-class maps! These numbers do not include maps based on the properties of the frequency distribution, such as means and standard deviations. There is clearly 'an opportunity for the map-author to select a map which suits a known or unknown bias' (Jenks and Caspall 1971, p. 222); 'a skilled cartographer can manipulate his map like a musician does his instrument, bringing out the quality he wants' (Schultz 1961).

Many thematic maps are used as data sources for geographical information systems; they are not just the products of data analyses and classification. The knowledge that these maps can be so easily manipulated must warn us about the dangers of attempting to do clever manipulations with pre-digested data. It is always best where possible to enter the original data into the GIS, or at least to reject all sources of classified data that are not supported by reliable information about within-class means and deviations.

Multivariate analysis and classification

Ordination. In many environmental surveys we are dealing with not one, but many properties that have been measured at the set of data points, and it is necessary to reduce these complex multivariate data in order to bring understanding. Because many environmental variables are quite often correlated with each other, it is possible that the data could be simplified by looking for sets of related variables. Principal component analysis is the most commonly used method of examining data measured on ratio scales for intercorrelations. Other methods of ordination, such as reciprocal averaging (also known as correspondence analysis—Hill 1973, 1974) and principal coordinate analysis are used when the data include binary (presence-absence) and nominal data. Webster (1977) gives a full description of principal component analysis, and another useful description of the method is given by Davis (1973).

Principal component analysis is a mathematical technique for examining the relations between a number of individuals n, each having a set of properties, m. The original data are transformed into a set of new properties, called principal components, that are linear combinations of the original variables. The principal components have the property that they are orthogonal (independent) of each other. So,

$$PC1 = \alpha_1 V_1 + \beta_1 V_2 + \gamma_1 V_3 \ldots \omega_1 V_m$$
$$PC2 = \alpha_2 V_1 + \beta_2 V_2 + \gamma_2 V_3 \ldots \omega_2 V_m \qquad (7.2)$$

and so on to PCm. The α_1s, β_1s etc. give the contribution of each original variate to each principal component.

Although principal component analysis is only a rotation and projection of the data along new axes, it often happens that the various components are capable of physical interpretation. The principal component scores (the value of each principal component for every data point) can be treated as a set of new variables. Very often a large part of the variation of a data set containing 20–40 original variables (some 70–80 per cent, say) is contained in the first six principal components, which can represent a very useful data compression. Just as with the original variables, the principal component scores can be mapped. If a given principal component can indeed be interpreted physically, then the map of its distribution may reveal important aspects of the data set. Webster and Burrough (1972) showed that an isarithm (contour) map of the first principal component scores computed from a set of 126 soil profiles on a 100 m 6×21 grid sampled on the Berkshire Downs in England matched the pattern of soil series closely. Figure 3.6 (p. 45) is a block diagram of the first principal component scores of soil data computed from a 6×25 grid spaced at 125 m sampled in an area near Follonica, Italy (Kilic 1979). The 'terrain model' shown in Fig. 3.6 very closely resembles the actual landform, for the upper river terrace and the valley of the Pecora river can be easily recognized in the computer plot of the condensed soil data.

Nortcliff (1978) used principal component analysis in conjunction with the technique of nested analysis of variance in order to search for spatial structure in soil data from Norfolk, England. McBratney and Webster (1981) preferred to transform their data to canonical variates before embarking on a spatial analysis of soil data in Scotland; Burrough *et al.* (1977) used principal component analysis to transform soil data, and reciprocal averaging to transform vegetation presence/absence data in a spatial study of climate, vegetation and soil interrelationships in New South Wales.

Clearly, data ordination techniques such as principal component analysis, canonical variance analysis, and reciprocal averaging can be useful tools for reducing data sets to manageable proportions in order to map complex data. The scientific users of a GIS that has been set up for environmental or ecological research should expect to be able to have access to these, and other statistical techniques as an important part of their system.

Cluster analysis. Although ordination may bring about a considerable reduction in the complexity of a large, multivariate data set, many people wish to reduce the complexity still further by reducing the data to a set of multivariate-defined classes. Very often, after ordination, the values of the principal component scores at the data points are plotted not in geographical space, but in the space defined by the principal component axes. This scattergram, as it is often called, may show apparent groupings or clusters of data points that have similar values on both axes. It would reduce the complexity of the data set still further if these clusters could be referred to a unit or class in a classification system. Furthermore, because these clusters are derived wholly from an analysis of the original data, they would represent 'natural' groupings that should be more representative of reality than exogenous, hierarchical classes imposed from without.

In the late 1960s and early 1970s there was a considerable amount of effort devoted to the development and application of numerical methods of classification (numerical taxonomy) to natural resource data, soil profiles, vegetation data) and so on. Webster (1977) has given a thorough description of the methodology and the applications in soil science, and the reader is referred to his text for details. (See also Sokal and Sneath 1963; Lance and Williams 1966; Williams *et al.* 1966.) Today, cluster analysis is a standard technique that is available on most large computers (e.g. CLUSTAN, Wishart 1977); it is usually not difficult to send point data from the GIS to clustering programs.

Although clustering techniques are objective and reproducible in the sense that they can always be repeated in exactly the same way with the same data, there is a multitude of ways in which clustering can be done and, as with the problem of classifying univariate data for choropleth maps, there are many possible ways of proceeding. To start with, there are divisive systems and agglomerative systems. Divisive systems consider the whole data set first, and then examine the best ways to subdivide into groups. Agglomerative systems examine the similarities between individual data points before fusing them into groups. The similarity between a pair of data points in the m-dimensional data space can be estimated in several ways. All methods use a concept of 'distance' in the variable space as a measure of similarity. The closer the data points in m-dimensional space, the more similar the data points. One can choose the intuitive Euclidean distance or dissimilarity, which is defined as

$$d_{ij} = \sqrt{\left\{ \sum_{k=1}^{m} (X_{ik} - X_{jk})^2 \right\}} \qquad (7.3)$$

where X is the value of property k at data points i and j.

The Euclidean distance has the disadvantage in that it is sensitive for the scales on which the variables have been measured. For this reason, Euclidean distances are usually computed for data that have first been transformed to principal components computed from the correlation matrix. These principal components are scaled to zero mean and variance σ^2. The original data can also be scaled directly to zero mean and unit variance if preferred. Euclidean distances are also sensitive to extreme data values or outliers.

The Canberra metric,

$$d_{ij} = \frac{1}{m} \sum_{k=1}^{m} \left[\frac{|X_{ik} - X_{jk}|}{X_{ik} + X_{jk}} \right] \qquad (7.4)$$

gives a value of dissimilarity in the range 0-1. Similarities are given by $1 - d_{ij}$.

Other measures can be used, e.g. the City Block Metric

$$d_{ij} = \sum_{k=1}^{m} |X_{ik} - X_{jk}| \qquad (7.5)$$

or Mahalonobis's D^2, which is defined as

$$D_{ij} = (X_i - X_j)' \sum^{-1} (X_i - X_j). \qquad (7.6)$$

Here $\sum$ is the pooled within-groups variance–covariance matrix, and X_i, X_j are the vectors of scores for data points i and j. Mahalonobis's D^2 has the advantage that it allows for correlations between variables. The other measures work better with independent variables.

One or other of these distance measures is used to build a similarity or dissimilarity matrix of size $\frac{1}{2}N(N-1)$, where N is the number of items in the data set. This used to be a problem with the computers of the 1960s and early 1970s because of limitations of the size of the memory in the central processor. Today's computers with virtual memories are limited only by disk space, but a data set of 1000 items would require approximately 2 Mbyte for 32-bit representation of the similarity matrix alone.

Once the similarity matrix has been computed, the next stage is linking the individuals into groups. The obvious first step is to find pairs of points that are closest in the space defined by the variables. This is easy; it just means searching the similarity matrix. But it is not so easy to decide how the third and subsequent points should be added to an existing cluster, or how existing clusters should be fused. In the single linkage method, a point is allocated to the group that its nearest neighbour belongs to. In the centroid method, an item is fused with the group to which the distance from it to the group centre is least. After every item is added, the group centroid must be recalculated. In Ward's method, an item is added to the group that produces the least increase in the total sum of squared deviations between individuals in groups and group means. The steps with which the items are fused into groups can be plotted as a 'dendrogram' or linkage tree.

The range of methods for calculating similarities and for establishing linkages between items and groups leads to a large number of possible classification strategies. Ideally, if the data are well-structured, then different methods should yield similar results. The truth is often otherwise. Figure 7.2 shows two dendrograms resulting from applying clustering methods to a data set of 64 soil profiles. Twenty soil properties were measured at each profile, and the data were first transformed to principal components. In both cases, the dissimilarity matrix was calculated using the Euclidean distance metric. Only the linking strategy differed; Fig. 7.2(a) shows the results obtained using the single linkage method and Fig. 7.2(b) those obtained using Ward's method. The results are not quite so different as they at first appear, but they suffice to show the way in which the one technique (Ward's method) can be used to give the impression of clear, well-defined clusters, while the single linkage method gives an impression that the clusters are almost non-existent.

The next problem when using cluster analysis is to decide on the number of clusters that should be used to summarize the results. Webster (1977) describes the

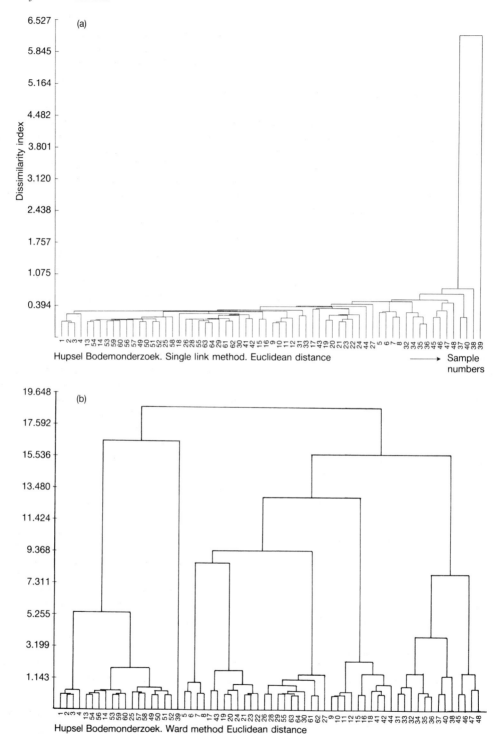

Fig. 7.2 The clustering strategy can severely affect the visual appearance of the dendrogram; (a) Single-linkage clustering; (b) Ward's method. Both methods applied to the same data with similarity computed by Euclidean distance. Soil profile data from the Hupsel study (Burrough *et al.* 1983, p. 133).

use of a statistic known as Wilks's criterion for this purpose.

We should also expect that the classification methods should lead to a map that will show where the various class members are located. Webster and Burrough (1972a, b) attempted to map the results of cluster analyses that had been applied to soil data, but the results were never satisfactory. The resulting maps were always too spotty, too noisy to be useful. Even the addition of spatial location into the data set or the use of local spatial forcing functions failed to improve the results greatly. De Gruijter (1977) adopted a slightly different tactic. He first interpolated the original data to a finer grid and then used an allocation method to match grid cells with classes that had been determined from the original sample data. The mapped results were more acceptable than those produced by Webster and Burrough but they were still not ideal. On the other hand, researchers at the UK's Institute of Terrestrial Ecology have used clustering techniques together with allocation methods to produce small-scale maps of landscape and vegetation for planning studies, and these maps have not suffered greatly from the spottiness found in the soil studies (County of Cumbria 1978).

A final problem with clustering methods is that they are idiographic; the results are dependent on the exact characteristics of the data set. Consequently, classifications derived for data from neighbouring areas are unlikely to be exactly comparable, even when the clustering strategy is the same throughout. It is often very difficult to make an interpretation in physical terms of a cluster obtained by these analyses, and consequently they have found little favour for routine surveys.

Allocating individuals to existing classes

For many users of geographical information systems the problem is often not one of creating new classifications, but of allocating individuals to classes in existing classifications in the best possible way. The problem is that many classes are defined on the basis of the values of more than one attribute (i.e. they are multivariate) and even though the defined limits of the classes may not overlap, there are definite grey areas where multivariate classes overlap and merge. In these cases what should the user do?

The classic answer to the classification problem is to establish a hierarchy of attributes that are referenced by a key—examples are the plant and animal taxonomies, or the methods adopted for the main kinds of soil classification in most countries. Unfortunately,

(and it seems to be particularly acute in soil survey), the standard method of classification used for one purpose often seems to cut right across the classification requirements of another purpose, and so the user following the rules ends up feeling dissatisfied with the results.

The problem of allocating individuals to classes has been central to the analysis of satellite images. Here, the problem is easy to analyse because there are usually only a few attributes defining the multivariate space (e.g. 4, 7, or 16 wavebands) and there are no pre-existing taxonomies to bias discussions. Consider Fig. 7.3(a), which shows four clusters of points in a two-dimensional space defined by two attributes X and Y. There are at least three different ways in which a new individual can be allocated to an existing cluster. In Fig. 7.3(b), the class boundaries are defined by the extreme values of the attributes X and Y; this is known in image analysis as a 'parallelepiped' classification, but it is the same principle that is used in classic hierarchical classification using simple Boolean logic. Because the clusters are not spherical, but elongated, and thus overlap, a point such as that represented by the black dot with the white star cannot be allocated unambiguously. An alternative strategy is shown in Fig. 7.3(c), in which a point is to be allocated according to the group for which the distance from the point to the group centroid is the smallest. Again, because of non-spherical clusters, misallocation is possible. The third option is shown in Fig. 7.3(d). Here, bell-shaped zones of probability have been calculated for each group; an individual is then allocated to the class for which the probability of membership is greatest. These kinds of methods are known as maximum likelihood classifiers.

Maximum likelihood methods can be extended by using Bayesian algebra to weight a class according to the *a priori* probability or anticipated likelihood of occurrence for an item in a class and according to the cost of misclassification (Haralick and Fu 1983). The weights are used to minimize the costs of misclassification, resulting in a theoretically optimal classification. Maximum likelihood methods are the most discriminating of the methods discussed here; their disadvantage is that they require considerably more computing than the simpler methods.

Expert systems for geographical information systems

A main use of classification and allocation procedures is to enable users to retrieve items from a complex database. If the items have been classified before input

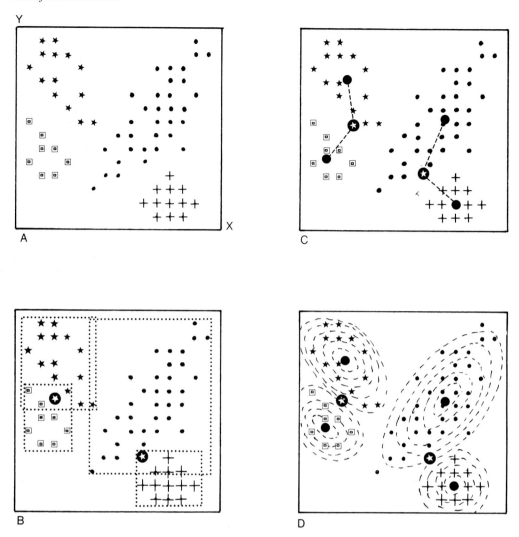

Fig. 7.3 Cluster shape and orientation in multivariate space affects the results of classification algorithms. (a) Naked clusters. (b) Parallelepiped classification—the classification of the points represented by black circles and white stars is ambiguous. (c) Distance to centroid method—classification is still ambiguous. (d) Maximum likelihood—the contours are lines of equal probability.

then the task is trivial. Increasingly though, large amounts of unclassified data are being put into information systems and the user is then required to define both classification and allocation algorithms in order to get out what is required. As was shown briefly above, this can be no easy matter, and the results may not be entirely satisfactory. Also, a casual user of a system, or a non-specialist in a particular area of work may not exactly know how to formulate his requests. Because the experts who can do this are few, it seems sensible to attempt to incorporate their knowledge in a computer system in such a way that casual users can make full use of it. Systems that can make use of this kind of acquired information or experience and make it available to others are known as 'expert systems'.

Figure 7.4 shows a simple overview of an expert system. The principle is that the expert, (i.e. the person who has a deep and thorough understanding of a problem area) makes his knowledge available to a computer program. This phase is known as 'knowledge acquisition'. The knowledge acquired is converted into sets of rules for recognizing or describing

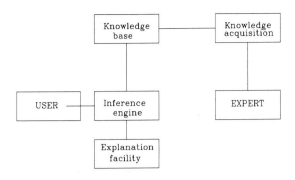

Fig. 7.4 Overview of an 'expert system'.

certain entities that may exist in the knowledge base that the system can access. Initially, knowledge was coded in the form of formal logical statements, but humans use much more sophisticated methods, such as analogy, when confronted by a problem. Modern developments in artificial intelligence are proceeding towards the formulation of systems that can capture more aspects of the human thought processes (Lenat 1984; Nilsson 1980).

The user, who wants to get information out of the knowledge base, enters his queries through a program known as an 'inference engine'. This module has the task of converting the user's requirements into sets of formulated queries that can be used by the acquired knowledge to process the knowledge base. The inference engine also has an explanation facility which can tell the user why it is searching for particular kinds of entities.

Expert systems have been developed and used in several fields, notably medicine, geological exploration, and military fields. It would be interesting to apply expert systems to the problems of land evaluation. Good soil and water experts are few, and very often they have intensive experience in only a few lands. The establishment of international soil and land evaluation classification systems using the rules of formal logic has been less successful than had been expected because in each different land there is always a different combination of factors that needs to be taken into account. The second-rate expert continues to use his knowledge and classification learned in country X for problems in country Y. The true expert, confronted by a new situation, adapts his knowledge. In principle an expert system could be used to pool information from the real experts on a world-wide, or continent-wide basis so that local extension and development officers, instead of following inappropriate methods, could benefit from the best advice available.

Summary—classification methods in geographical information systems

Classification methods are essential parts of any geographical information system. Many current systems, however, do not provide classification facilities that are any more sophisticated than simple Boolean logic, and so allow only exogenous, arbitrary, and equal interval classifications. Image analysis systems will have multivariate classification methods for pattern recognition and feature recognition while geographical information systems for scientific research may well include, or have access to, multivariate methods of numerical taxonomy. Expert systems offer interesting prospects for the future.

The following rules for classification are suggested:

1. *Don't classify* (a) if you have complete spatial coverage of an area (e.g. with pixels) and the original data values must be used for further processing.

(b) if you have data collected at a set of sample points. Use interpolation techniques first to apply the data to the whole area and then classify if necessary.

2. *Classify* if data are multivariate and if identification of a cluster with an 'object' or a 'type' is essential for further analysis. Identification could make use of information that is available to the user but that is outside the current database.

3. *Classify* for display and presentation of spatial data but not for data storage. Don't use arbitrary scales and treat exogenous scales warily. Idiographic scales may sometimes be useful, but use objectively defined serial scales when at all possible.

References

American Photogrammetric Society (1983). *Manual of remote sensing* (2nd edn). American Photogrammetric Society, Falls Church, Va.

Beckett, P. H. T. and Burrough, P. A. (1971). The relation between cost and utility in soil survey. IV. Comparison of the utilities of soil maps produced by different survey procedures, and to different scales. *J. Soil Sci.* **22**, 466–80.

Burrough, P. A. (1983). Multiscale sources of spatial variation in soil. I. The application of fractal concepts to nested levels of soil variation. *J. Soil Sci.* **34**, 577–97.

—— and Webster, R. (1976). Improving a reconnaissance classification by multivariate methods. *J. Soil Sci.* **27**, 554–71.

—— Brown, L. and Morris, E. C. (1977) Variations in vegetation and soil pattern across the Hawkesbury Sandstone Plateau from Barren Grounds to Fitzroy Falls, New South Wales. *Aust. J. Ecol.* **2**, 137–59.

County of Cumbria (1978). An ecological survey of Cumbria.

Cumbria County Council and Lake District Special Planning Board/Institute of Terrestrial Ecology, Structure Working Plan, Working Paper No. 4.

Davis, J. C. (1973) *Statistics and data analysis in geology.* Wiley, New York. (Second edition 1986.)

Evans, I. S. (1977). The selection of class intervals. *Trans. Inst. Br. Geogrs* (N.S.) **2**, 98–124.

Gruijter, J. J. de (1977). *Numerical classification of soils and its application in survey.* PUDOC, Wageningen.

Haralick, R. M. and Fu, K.-S. (1983). Pattern recognition and classification. *Manual of remote sensing* (2nd edn). American Photogrammetric Society, Falls Church, Va.

Hill, M. (1973). Reciprocal averaging: an eigenvector method of ordination. *J. Ecol.* **61**, 237–49.

—— (1974). Correspondence analysis: a neglected multivariate method. *Appl. Stat.* **23**, 340–54.

Jenks, G. F. and Caspall, F. C. (1971). Error on choroplethic maps: definition, measurement, reduction. *Ann. Ass. Am. Geogr* **61**, 217–44.

Jones, T. A. and Baker, R. A. (1975). Determination of important parameters in a classification scheme. *Geol. Soc. Am. Mem.* **142**, 317–31.

Kilic, M. (1979). M.Sc. Thesis Soil Science and Soil Water Management Course, Agricultural University, Wageningen.

Lamp, J. (1981). Morphometric analyses of pedon data. In Girard, M.-C. (ed). In *Proc. ISSS Working Group on Soil Information Systems Meeting No. 5*, (ed. M. C. Girard) Sept. 1981, Paris, pp. 87–94. Departement des Sols. Institut National Agronomique, Paris-Grignon.

—— (1983). Habilitation thesis, Christian-Albrecht University, Kiel.

Lance, G. N. and Williams, W. T. (1966). Computer programs for hierarchical polythetic classification ('similarity analyses'). *Comput. J.* **9**, 60–4.

Lenat, D. B. (1984). Computer software for intelligent systems. *Scient. Am.* **251** (3), 152–60.

McBratney, A. B. and Webster, R. (1981). Spatial dependence and classification of the soil along a transect in North-East Scotland. *Geoderma* **26**, 63–82.

Marriott, F. H. C. (1974). *The interpretation of multiple observations.* Academic Press, London.

Monmonnier, M. S. (1975). Class intervals to enhance the visual correlation of choroplethic maps. *Can. Cartogr.* **12**, 161–78.

Nilsson, N. (1980). *Principles of artificial intelligence.* Tioga, Palo Alto, Calif.

Nortcliff, S. (1978). Soil variability and reconnaissance soil mapping: a statistical study in Norfolk. *J. Soil Sci.* **29**, 403–18.

Schulz, G. M. (1961). An experiment in selecting value scales for statistical distribution maps. *Surv. Map.* **21**, 224–30.

Snedecor, G. W. and Cochran, W. G. (1967). *Statistical methods* (6th edn). Iowa State University Press, Ames, Iowa.

Sokal, R. R. and Sneath, P. H. A. (1963). *Principles of numerical taxonomy.* W. H. Freeman, San Francisco.

Stace, H. C. T., Hubble, G. D., Brewer, R., Northcote, K. H., Sleeman, J. R., Mulcahy, M. J., and Hallsworth E. G. (1968). *A handbook of Australian soils.* Rellim, Glenside.

Webster, R. (1977). *Quantitative and numerical methods in soil classification and survey.* Oxford University Press, Oxford.

—— and Burrough, P. A. (1972a). Computer-based soil mapping of small areas from sample data: I. Multivariate classification and ordination. *J. Soil Sci.* **23**, 210–21.

—— and Burrough, P. A. (1972b). Computer-based soil mapping of small areas from sample data: II. Classification smoothing. *J. Soil Sci.* **23**, 222–34.

Williams, W. T., Lambert, J. M., and Lance, G. N. (1966). Multivariate methods in plant ecology. V. Similarity analyses and information analysis. *J. Ecol.* **54**, 427–45.

Wishart, D. (1977). CLUSTAN user manual. University College, London.

Yost, R. S. and Fox, R. L. (1981). Partitioning variation in soil chemical properties of some Andepts using soil taxonomy. *Soil Sci. Soc. Am. J.* **45**, 373–77.

8. Methods of Spatial Interpolation

When polygons on a choropleth map cannot be more finely divided into smaller spatial entities, we cannot say anything more precise about what is happening within their boundaries than a general average or a 'representative' value allows. So, in these situations, reference to a pixel or polygon class would find the best predicted value for an unvisited point. Very frequently, however, we have point observations at our disposal, a data set derived from a set of localities arranged either at random, or on a regular lattice over the area of interest. These points may be associated with a particular area unit, just as soil profile observations can be associated with a given map unit delineation, or they may have been collected without any kind of area stratification of the landscape in mind. Whatever is the case, it is possible that such a spatial array of data points may enable us to make more precise statements about the value of properties of interest at unvisited sites than is possible by using mapping-unit means. This procedure of estimating the value of properties at unsampled sites within the area covered by existing point observations is called *interpolation*. Estimating the value of a property at sites outside the area covered by existing observations is called *extrapolation*.

The rationale behind spatial interpolation and extrapolation is the very common observation that, on average, points that are close together in space are more likely to have similar values of a property of interest than points further apart. Two observation points a few metres apart on a single hill are more likely to have a similar value for altitude than points on two hills some kilometres apart. When a given area has been classified and delineated as a 'homogeneous' unit on a geological, soil, or vegetation map, we have discarded all the information about the way in which any given property varies within that area. If we could find ways of modelling this variation by using interpolation techniques, we may expect that our estimates of the value of any given property at unvisited sites could be greatly improved. Maps so constructed should result in smaller errors when used for overlay

analyses in the geographical information system. This section describes some of the most commonly used methods for interpolation, and suggests some ways in which these interpolation techniques can be of help when attempting to bring points and areal data to a common spatial framework for map overlay and cartographic modelling.

The available methods for interpolation

We are all familiar with the contours on a topographic map that have been constructed by following lines of equal height by examining aerial photographs stereoscopically on a stereoplotter. On the aerial photographs, or in the landscape itself, it is possible to see or visit all parts of the topographic surface in order to construct or verify the contours that have been drawn from the real surface before us. With point observations of soil, groundwater, temperature, and many other environmental variables, the actual pattern of variation cannot be seen but can only be sampled at a set of points. The value of a property between data points can be interpolated only by fitting some plausible model of variation to the values at the data points and then calculating the value at the desired location. The problem of interpolation is thus a problem of choosing a plausible model to suit the data.

Interpolation is a problem that has occupied the geographers and earth scientists for a very long time, and is one that still commands a great deal of attention. Important reviews of interpolation techniques have appeared in many separate disciplines; for example, Ripley (1981), Matheron (1971), Journel and Huijbregts (1978), Agterberg (1982), Lam (1983), and Webster (1984) have all written major reviews of interpolation techniques and their applications.

Interpolation by drawing boundaries

The simplest method of interpolation is to use external landscape features to delineate 'landscape units'. These are the units drawn on most choropleth, thematic maps of soil, geology, vegetation, or land-use. Parallel

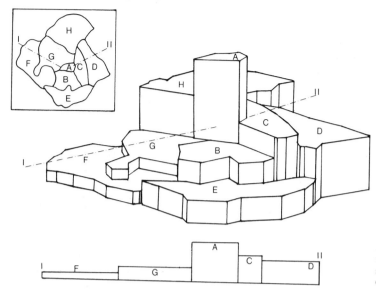

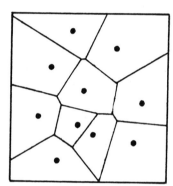

Fig. 8.1 The choropleth map is 'stepped' model of the landscape. (Based on a screen image, courtesy Computervision Corporation, The Netherlands.)

techniques are the edge-seeking algorithms used in image analysis. These techniques assume that all important variation occurs at boundaries; within boundaries, the variation is homogeneous and isotropic, i.e. is the same in all directions, and leads to a 'stepped' model of the landscape (Fig. 8.1). Of course, we can always divide up an existing area entity or polygon by drawing new boundaries within it (e.g. see Beckett 1984), but this approach may not be the most appropriate, particularly when the variation to be resolved is gradual rather than abrupt in nature.

Another method of interpolation using boundaries is that employed by Thiessen polygons (also known as Voronoi polygons or Dirichlet cells). The idea is that given a two-dimensional array of sampling points, the 'best' information about an unvisited point can be gleaned from the data point nearest to it. This is an idea that all who use climatic data will intuitively accept; in the absence of local observations, one uses the data from the nearest available weather station. Thiessen polygons divide a region up in a way that is totally determined by the configuration of the data points. If the data lie on a regular square grid, then the Thiessen polygons are all equal, regular squares of side equal to the grid spacing; if the data are irregularly spaced, then an irregular lattice of regions results (Fig. 8.2).

Green and Sibson (1978) have produced a well-known algorithm for computing these cells, and Ripley (1981) has provided a mathematical discussion of the principles of tesselation involved. From the point of view of the user wishing to interpolate a value at un-

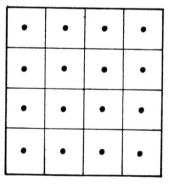

Fig. 8.2 Thiessen (or Dirichlet) polygons with irregular and regular sample point searching.

sampled points, the method has several drawbacks, however. First, the size and shape of the areas depends on sample layout; this can lead to polygons having a strange shape, particularly at edges. Second, the value of the property of interest in each cell is estimated by a sample of one, which is useless for gaining any idea of the error margins to be placed on that estimate. Third, computation of a value at an unsampled point becomes a point-in-polygon problem; it has nothing to do with our intuitive ideas that points close together are more likely to be similar than points far apart. Sibson (1980) has described a method called 'natural neighbourhood' interpolation that attempts to overcome some of these problems by using weighted averages that are proportional to the tile areas (see Ripley 1981, p. 41). Thiessen polygons are probably best for qualitative (nominal) data because other interpolation methods are inapplicable.

Interpolation models embodying ideas of gradual change

In contrast to the discrete techniques described above, almost all other methods of interpolation embody a model of continuous spatial change that can be described by a smooth, mathematically defined surface. They include techniques such as spline functions, least-square trend surfaces, Fourier series, and moving averages including kriging. These methods may be divided into global (universal) and local fitting techniques. With global techniques, a model is constructed from all observations of the property of interest at all points in the study area—examples are trend surface analysis and Fourier series. It is characteristic of these models that local features are not well accommodated and so they are most often used for modelling long-range variations, such as the relation between major aspects of landform and groundwater levels, for example. Local fitting techniques such as splines, and moving averages estimate values from the neighbouring points only; consequently, local anomalies can be accommodated without affecting the value of interpolation at other points on the surface.

Global methods of interpolation

Trend surface analysis

The simplest way to describe gradual long-range variations is to model them by polynomial regression. The idea is to fit a polynomial line or surface, depending on whether our data are in one or two dimensions, by least squares through the data points. It is assumed that the spatial coordinates X, Y are the independent variables, and that Z, the property of interest, is the dependent variable.

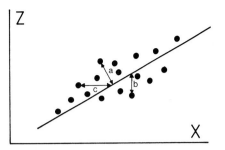

Fig. 8.3 Linear best-fit regression line to the variation of property Z with distance X. In trend analysis, the regression line is fitted so as to minimize the sums of squares $\Sigma\,(\hat{Z}_i - Z_i)^2$—distance b in the figure—rather than distance from the point to the regression line (a) or the squared deviation in distance (c).

Consider the value of an environmental property Z that has been measured along a transect at points X_1, $X_2, \ldots X_n$. Assume that Z increases monotonically with X as shown in Fig. 8.3. The long-range variation of Z can be approximated by the regression line

$$Z = b_0 + b_1 X \qquad (8.1)$$

where b_0 and b_1 are the polynomial coefficients known respectively as the intercept and the slope in simple regression. The regression line is fitted such that the sum of the deviations

$$\sum_{i=1}^{n} (\hat{Z}_i - Z_i)^2$$

is minimized over the n sampling points.

In many circumstances Z is not a linear function of X but may vary in a more complicated way, as illustrated in Fig. 8.4. In these situations quadratic or still-higher-order polynomials such as

$$Z = b_0 + b_1 . X + b_2 . X^2 \qquad (8.2)$$

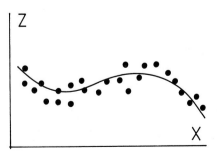

Fig. 8.4 Higher-order polynomials are needed to fit non-linear distribution of points.

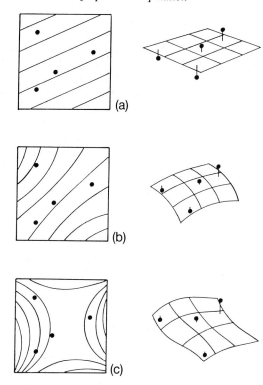

Fig. 8.5 Trend surfaces in two spatial dimensions. (a) Linear, (b) quadratic, (c) cubic.

can be used. By increasing the number of terms it is possible to fit any complicated curve exactly.

In two dimensions the polynomials are surfaces of the form

$$f\{(X,Y)\} = \sum_{r+s\leq p} (b_{rs}.X^r.Y^s) \qquad (8.3)$$

of which the first three are:

$$b_0 \qquad\qquad \text{flat}$$
$$b_0 + b_1.X + b_2.Y \qquad\qquad \text{linear}$$
$$b_0 + b_1.X + b_2.Y + b_3.X^2 + b_4.XY + b_5.Y^2 \quad \text{quadratic}$$

Examples are shown in Fig. 8.5. The integer p is the order of the trend surface. There are $P = (p+1)(p+2)/2$ coefficients that are normally chosen to minimize

$$\sum_{i=1}^{n} \{Z(\mathbf{X}_i) - f(\mathbf{X}_i)\}^2$$

where $\mathbf{X}_i$ is the vector notation for (X, Y). So a horizontal plane is zero-order, an inclined plane is first-order, a quadratic surface is second-order, and a cubic surface with 10 parameters is third-order.

Finding the b_i coefficients is a standard problem in multiple regression, and is thus easy to do. Davis (1973) presents a simple FORTRAN program for trend surface analysis, but the reader should note that many of Davis's programs compute sums of squares by the 'desk' or 'shorthand' method, which may lead to serious rounding errors, particularly when implemented on microcomputers (see Chapter 6). Ripley (1981) warns that polynomial regression is 'an ill-conditioned least squares problem that needs careful numerical analysis'. He recommends that all distances be rescaled in the range $-1 < 0 < 1$ to avoid extremely large or small values of $f\{(X, Y)\}$.

Trend surfaces can be displayed by estimating the value of $Z(x)$ at all points on a regular grid. The grid can be that used for line printer output (Davis 1973 has examples), colour raster screen or plotter, or a data grid used to overlay maps in raster databases. Contour threading algorithms can be used to prepare output for a pen plotter.

The advantage of trend surface analysis is that it is a technique that is superficially easy to understand, at least with respect to the way the surfaces are calculated. Broad features of the data can be modelled by low-order trend surfaces, but it becomes increasingly difficult to ascribe a physical meaning to complex, higher polynomials. Second-order and higher surfaces may reach ridiculously large or small values just outside the area covered by the data. Because they are general interpolators, the trend surfaces are very susceptible to outliers in the data. Trend surfaces are smoothing functions, rarely passing exactly through the original data points unless these are few and the order of the surface is large. It is implicit in multiple regression that the residuals from a regression line or surface are normally distributed, independent errors. The deviations from a trend surface are almost always to some degree spatially dependent; in fact one of the most fruitful uses of trend surface analysis has been to reveal parts of a study area that show the greatest deviation from a general trend (e.g. see Burrough *et al.* 1977; Davis 1973). The main use of trend surface analysis then, is not as an interpolator within a region, but as a way of removing broad features of the data prior to using some other local interpolator.

The significance of a trend surface

The statistical significance of a trend surface can be tested by using the technique of analysis of variance to partition the variance between the trend and the

Table 8.1 Analysis of variance

Source	Sums of squares	Degrees of freedom	Mean square	Variance ratio
Regression	SS_r	m	MS_r	MS_r/MS_d
Deviation	SS_d	$n-m-1$	MS_d	
Total	SS_t	$n-1$	MS_t	

residuals from the trend. Let n be the number of observations, so there are $(n-1)$ degrees of variation associated with the total variation. The degrees of freedom for regression, m, are determined by the number of terms in the polynomial regression equation, excluding the b_0 coefficient. For a linear regression,

$$Z = b_0 + b_1 X + b_2 Y \qquad (8.4)$$

the degrees of freedom for regression $m=2$. The degrees of freedom for the deviations from the regression are given by $(n-1)-m$. The analysis of variance is set out as shown in Table 8.1.

The regression line or surface can be considered to be analogous to the classes in the usual analysis of variance methods. The variance ratio, or 'F-test', estimates whether the amount of variance taken up by the regression differs significantly from that expected for an equivalent number of sites with the same degrees of freedom, drawn from a random population. Just as 'relative variance' estimated how much of the variance remained after classification, so a regression relative variance can also be calculated as:

$$RV_r = MS_d/MS_t \times 100. \qquad (8.5)$$

A comparative study using relative variance could be used to compare choropleth (or classificatory) mapping with trend surfaces.

Fourier series

Fourier series can be used to describe one- or two-dimensional variation by modelling the observed variation by a linear combination of sine and cosine waves. One-dimensional Fourier series have been used to analyse time series (see Chatfield 1980) and there have been many applications in studies of climatic change. Two-dimensional Fourier series have proved useful in sedimentary geology. Davis (1973) provides a readable introduction to the complex equations involved. They have been almost totally neglected as tools for interpolation in the landscape mapping sciences, though Kratky (1981) describes their use in photogrammetry. In fact, Fourier series have been used more for structural analysis than mapping. Ripley (1981) lists a few examples of two-dimensional

Fourier analysis; other applications in soil and landscape are Burrough *et al.* (1985), Webster (1977b), and McBratney and Webster (1981). Fourier series have not been explored to any great extent for interpolation in soil survey, though Fourier analyses are used in image analysis to enhance either short-range or long-range pattern components (cf. Billingsley *et al.* 1983). In general, it would appear that most surface features of the earth, excepting such obviously periodic features as ripples and sand dunes, are too complex to show strict periodic variations unless the variations are man-made, and thus trivial, and so other methods of interpolation are preferred.

Local interpolators

Splines

Before computers could be used to fit curves to sets of data points, draftsmen used flexible rulers to achieve the best locally fitting smooth curves by eye. The flexible rulers were called splines. Weights were placed at the data points, which had a peg over which the spline could be fitted, and so held in place while the line was drawn (Pavlidis 1982). The more modern equivalent is the plastic-coated flexible ruler sold in most office equipment shops. It can be shown that the line drawn along a spline ruler is approximately a piecewise cubic polynomial that is continuous and has continuous first and second derivatives.

Spline functions are mathematical equivalents of the flexible ruler. They are piecewise functions, which is to say that they are fitted to a small number of data points exactly, while at the same time ensuring that the joins between one part of the curve and another are continuous. This means that with splines it is possible to modify one part of the curve without having to recompute the whole, which is not possible with trend surfaces or Fourier series (Fig. 8.6).

The general definition of a piecewise polynomial function $p(x)$ is:

$$p(x) = p_i(x) \quad x_i < x < x_{i+1}$$
$$i = 0, 1, \ldots, k-1 \quad (8.6)$$

$$p_i^{(j)}(x_i) = p_{i+1}^{(j)}(x_i) \quad j = 0, 1, \ldots, r-1;$$
$$i = 1, 2, \ldots, k-1. \quad (8.7)$$

The points $x_i, \ldots x_{k-1}$ that divide an interval x_0, x_k into k sub-intervals are called 'break points' and the points of the curve at these values of x are commonly called 'knots' (Pavlidis 1982). The functions $p_i(x)$ are polynomials of degree m or less. The term r is used to denote the constraints on the spline. When

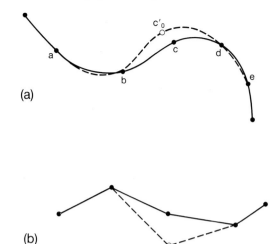

(a)

(b)

Fig. 8.6 The local nature of splines. When one point is displaced, four intervals must be recomputed for a quadratic spline (a) and two for a linear spline (b).

$r=0$, there are no constraints on the function; when $r=1$ the function is continuous without any constraints on its derivatives. If $r=m+1$, the interval x_0, x_k can be represented by a single polynomial, so $r=m$ is the maximum number of constraints that leads to a piecewise solution. For $m=1$, 2, or 3, a spline is called linear, quadratic, or cubic. The derivatives are of order 1, 2, $m-1$, so a quadratic spline must have one continuous derivative at each knot, and a cubic spline must have two continuous derivatives at each knot. For a simple spline where $r=m$ there are only $k+m$ degrees of freedom. The case of $r=m=3$ has particular significance because it was for the cubic piecewise polynomial functions that the term 'spline' was first used. The term 'bicubic spline' is used for the three-dimensional situation where surfaces instead of lines need to be interpolated.

Because of certain mathematical difficulties of calculating simple splines over a wide range of separate sub-intervals, such as might be the case with a digitized line, most practical applications use a special kind of spline called a B-spline. B-splines are themselves the sums of other splines that by definition have the value of zero outside the interval of interest (Pavlidis 1982). B-splines, therefore, allow local fitting from low-order polynomials in a simple way.

B-splines are often used for smoothing digitized lines for display, such as the boundaries on soil and geological maps, where cartographic conventions expect smooth, flowing lines. Pavlidis notes that complex shapes, such as those occurring in text fonts, can be

more economically defined in terms of B-splines than in sets of data points. The use of B-splines for smoothing polygon boundaries, however, can lead to certain complications, particularly when computing areas and perimeters. If the area of a polygon is calculated from digitized data points using the trapezoidal rule, it will be different from the area that results from smoothing the boundaries with B-splines. Another problem may arise when high order B-splines are used to smooth sinuous boundaries that also include sharp, rectangular corners (Fig. 8.7).

A problem with using splines for interpolation is whether one should choose the break points to coincide with the data points or to be interleaved with them. Different results for the interpolated spline may result from the two approaches (Fig. 8.8). Note that with splines the maxima and minima do not necessarily occur at the data points.

Splines can be used both for exact interpolation (the spline function passes through all data points) or for smoothing. The latter is a sensible procedure when it is known that there is an experimental error associated with the values at the data points. Dubrule (1983, 1984) describes an application for fitting a smoothing spline surface to data when it is desired to obtain contour lines that are as 'smooth' as possible and it is suspected that the data contain a source of random error, i.e.

$$y(x_i) = z(x_i) + \varepsilon(x_i) \qquad (8.8)$$

where z is the measured value of an attribute at point x_i, and ε is the associated random error. The spline function $p(x)$ should pass 'not too far' from the data values and so the smoothing spline is the function f that minimizes

$$A(f) + \sum_{i=1}^{n} w^2_i [f(x_i) - y(x_i)]^2. \qquad (8.9)$$

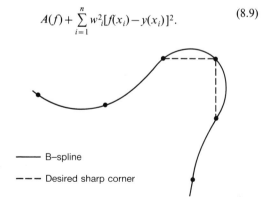

——— B–spline

– – – Desired sharp corner

Fig. 8.7 Splines can be inconvenient when used for boundaries that contain both flowing curves and sharp corners unless guiding points are used to 'fix' the corners.

(a)

(b)

□ Break points
● Data points

Fig. 8.8 The form of a spline often depends on the location of the break points. (a) linear interpolating spline with break-points located at the data points; (b) linear interpolating spline with two break points located mid-way between data points. The relative locations of the data points are the same in both cases.

The term $A(f)$ represents the 'smoothness' of the function f, and the second term represents its 'proximity' or 'fidelity' to the data. The weights w_i^2 are chosen to be inversely proportional to the error variance;

$$w_i^2 = \frac{p}{\mathrm{Var}[\varepsilon(x_i)]} = \frac{p}{s_i^2}. \tag{8.10}$$

The value of p reflects the relative importance given by the user to each characteristic of the smoothing splines.

Advantages and disadvantages of splines

Because splines are piecewise functions using few points at a time, the interpolation can be quickly calculated. In contrast to trend surfaces and weighted averages (see next section), splines retain small-scale features. Both linear and surficial splines are aesthetically pleasing and can produce a clear overview of the data quickly.

Some disadvantages of splines have already been mentioned. Others are that there are no direct estimates of the errors associated with spline interpolation, though these may be obtained by a recursive technique known as 'jack-knifing' (Dubrule 1984). Practical problems seem to be the definition of

'patches' and how patches can be sewn together to create a complete surface in three-dimensional interpolation without introducing anomalies that were not present in the original surface (e.g. see Fig. 3.1).

Methods using moving averages

One of the most often used methods of interpolating a value of a variable Z at an unvisited point x, is to compute an average value from a local neighbourhood or 'window'. In its simplest form, for regularly spaced data along a transect, the moving average for a point x in the centre of the symmetrical window is computed as

$$\hat{Z}(x) = 1/n \left[\sum_{i=1}^{n} Z(x_i) \right]. \tag{8.11}$$

In two dimensions, the same formula would apply, with the sites x_i replaced by the coordinate vector $\mathbf{X}_i$.

The size of window has a definite effect on the form of the smoothed output. Narrow windows will emphasize short-range variations and broad windows will reduce short-range variations in favour of longer range effects.

Weighted moving averages. As we have already noted, observations located close together tend to be more alike than observations spaced further apart, even if they happen to be within the same delineation of the same mapping unit. It is natural to feel that the contribution that a given sample point makes to an average interpolated value at an unvisited site should be weighted by a function of the distance between that observation and the site. So we can compute a weighted moving average

$$\hat{Z}(\mathbf{x}) = \sum_{i=1}^{n} \lambda_i Z(\mathbf{x}_i) \qquad \sum \lambda_i = 1 \tag{8.12}$$

where the weights λ_i are given by $\Phi(d(\mathbf{x}, \mathbf{x}_i))$.

A requirement is that $\Phi(d) \to \infty$ as $d \to 0$, which is given by the commonly used reciprocal or negative exponential functions $d^{(-r)}$, $e^{-(\alpha d)}$ and $e^{-(\alpha d^2)}$. Perhaps the most common form of $\Phi(d)$ is the inverse squared distance weighting

$$\hat{Z}(\mathbf{x}_j) = \frac{\sum_{i=1}^{n} Z(\mathbf{x}_i).d_{ij}^{-2}}{\sum_{i=1}^{n} d_{ij}^{-2}} \tag{8.13}$$

where the x_j are the points at which the surface is to be interpolated; usually these points lie on a regular grid.

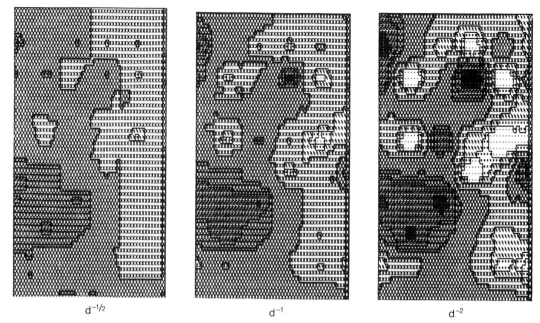

$d^{-1/2}$ d^{-1} d^{-2}

Fig. 8.9 The effect of varying the value of r in inverse distance weighting (d^{-r}) for interpolating by moving averages, using a constant window size.

The surface resulting from weighted average interpolation depend on the function, or on the parameters of the function used, and on the size of the domain or window from which the sample data points are drawn (Fig. 8.9). Ripley (1981) points out that the values estimated by moving averages are susceptible to clustering in the data points, and also to whether or not the observations are affected by a planar trend. He describes some ways of avoiding these drawbacks using methods of distance-weighted least squares.

The size of the domain not only affects the average value estimated at a point, but also controls the amount of computer time required for interpolation. Usually, the size of the domain or window is set to include a certain minimum and maximum number of data points in an effort to balance computational efficiency against precision. The number of points used, n, may vary between 4 and 12, but is usually in the range 6–8, particularly if the original data lie on a regular grid. Alternatively, one may be able to fix the number of data points used to compute the average. This will make no difference to estimates from data on a regular grid, but when data are irregularly distributed, each interpolation will be made using a window of different size, shape, and orientation.

The clumping problem with irregularly spaced data can be ameliorated by giving reduced weights to those data points that are screened from the interpolation point by other data points. This can be done by diminishing the weight given to the farther point in proportion to the cosine of the angle between the data points and the interpolated point (Shepard 1968).

Because moving average methods are by definition smoothing techniques, maxima and minima in the interpolated surface can occur only at data points. Some authors feel this to be undesirable and apply a correction whereby the slope of the interpolated surface is computed at each data point and used to project the form of the surface, rather in the manner used in B-splines. Other methods employ a local fitting of Hermitian polynomials (Giloi 1978). These methods assume that a smooth surface is both a required and a reasonable representation of the data. Very often the data may be so irregular or noisy that the interpolated surface will not pass through the data points. In these situations, the data point value is often written directly to the output file, resulting in a pit or a spike in the surface.

The interpolated values at the grid points can be displayed directly as grey-scale raster maps or on a colour raster screen or printer. The interpolated grid cell values can be used as an overlay in a raster database for cartographic modelling. Alternatively, another computer program can be used to thread isolines (lines of equal value) through the interpolated surface, and these isolines can be drawn with a pen plotter.

Optimal interpolation methods using spatial autocovariance

The local weighted moving average interpolation methods discussed above provide reasonable results in many cases, but they leave a number of important questions open. In particular, the methods generate the following important uncertainties:

(a) how large should the domain or window be?

(b) what shape and orientation should it have for optimum interpolation?

(c) are there better ways to estimate the λ_i weights than as a simple function of distance?

(d) what are the errors (uncertainties) associated with the interpolated values?

These questions led the French geomathematician Georges Matheron (1971) and the South African mining engineer D. G. Krige to develop optimal methods of interpolation for use in the mining industry. The methods have recently found use in groundwater mapping, soil mapping, and related fields.

An optimal policy is a rule in dynamic programming for choosing the values of a variable so as to optimize the criterion function (Bullock and Stallybrass 1977). The interpolation methods developed by Matheron are optimal in the sense that the interpolation weights λ_i are chosen so as to optimize the interpolation function, i.e. to provide a Best Linear Unbiased Estimate (BLUE) of the value of a variable at a given point.

The method rests on the recognition that the spatial variation of any geological, soil, or hydrological property, known as a 'regionalized variable', is too irregular to be modelled by a smooth mathematical function but can be described better by a stochastic surface. The interpolation proceeds by first exploring and then modelling the stochastic aspects of the regionalized variable. The resulting information is then used to estimate the λ_i weights for interpolation.

The success of 'kriging', as optimal interpolation is often known, rests on the validity of certain important assumptions about the statistical nature of the variation. These assumptions, that are the basis for kriging, are contained in regionalized variable theory.

Regionalized variable theory assumes that the spatial variation of any variable can be expressed as the sum of three major components. These are (a) a structural component, associated with a constant mean value or a constant trend; (b) a random, spatially correlated component; and (c) a random noise or residual error term. (NB Purists will note that the original formulation of the theory did not include the residual

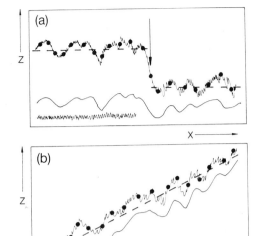

Fig. 8.10 The major components of spatial variation.

\- \- \- \- A 'structural' value that may change abruptly at a boundary (a), or vary with a constant trend (b).

~~~~ Spatially correlated random variation $\varepsilon'(x)$

wwww Spatially uncorrelated random variation ε'' (noise). Both $\varepsilon'(x)$ and ε'' are assumed to have uniform statistical properties over the whole of the sample area.

● Sample sites, at which only a part of the true variation is observed.

error but it is included here to make the discussion clearer.) Let **x** be a position in 1, 2, or 3 dimensions. Then the value of a variable Z at **x** is given by

$$Z(\mathbf{x}) = m(\mathbf{x}) + \varepsilon'(\mathbf{x}) + \varepsilon'' \qquad (8.14)$$

where $m(x)$ is a deterministic function describing the 'structural' component of Z at **x**, ε' (**x**) is the term denoting the stochastic, locally varying, spatially dependent residuals from $m(\mathbf{x})$, and ε'' is a residual, spatially independent Gaussian noise term having zero mean and variance σ^2 (Fig. 8.10).

The first step in kriging is to decide on a suitable function for $m(\mathbf{x})$. In the simplest case, where no trend or 'drift' is present, $m(\mathbf{x})$ equals the mean value in the sampling area and the average or expected difference between any two places **x** and **x** + **h** separated by a distance vector **h**, will be zero:

$$E[Z(\mathbf{x}) - Z(\mathbf{x} + \mathbf{h})] = 0. \qquad (8.15)$$

Also, it is assumed that the variance of differences depends only on the distance between sites, **h**, so that

$$E[\{Z(\mathbf{x}) - Z(\mathbf{x} + \mathbf{h})\}^2] = E[\{\varepsilon'(\mathbf{x}) - \varepsilon'(\mathbf{x} + \mathbf{h})\}^2]$$
$$= 2\gamma(\mathbf{h}) \qquad (8.16)$$

where $\gamma(\mathbf{h})$ is a function known as the semivariance.

The two conditions, stationarity of difference and variance of differences, define the requirements for the intrinsic hypothesis of regionalized variable theory. This means that once structural effects have been accounted for, the remaining variation is homogeneous in its variation so that differences between sites are a merely a function of the distance between them.

If the conditions specified by the intrinsic hypothesis are fulfilled, the semivariance can be estimated from sample data:

$$\hat{\gamma}(\mathbf{h}) = \frac{1}{2n} \sum_{i=1}^{n} \{ Z(\mathbf{x}_i) - Z(\mathbf{x}_i + \mathbf{h}) \}^2 \qquad (8.17)$$

where n is the number of pairs of sample points separated by distance h. Sample spacing h, is also called the lag. A plot of $\hat{\gamma}(\mathbf{h})$ against $\mathbf{h}$ is known as the sample semivariogram. It is an essential step on the way to determining optimal weights for interpolation.

An example

Figure 8.11 shows a typical experimental semivariogram of soil data computed from field estimates of the per cent clay content of the topsoil (0–20 cm) at sites located on a 6×25 square sampling grid. The grid, the long axis of which lay NNW–SSE, was situated in a small study area near Follonica in Italy (Kilic 1979). The grid spacing was 125 m in both directions; 136 of the possible 150 points were sampled by auger but 14 points could not be sampled because of obstacles in the field and so were recorded as missing values. The study area covered two geomorphologically distinct landscape units, namely a well-drained Pleistocene terrace and a less well-drained Holocene flood plain. A

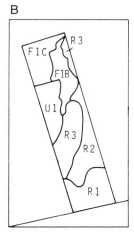
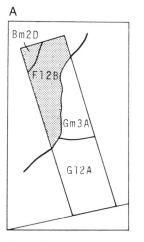

Fig. 8.12 Two conventional soil maps of the study area near Follonica: (a) Mapping scale 1:50 000; (b) Mapping scale 1:25 000. The upper (Pleistocene) terrace is shown by the shaded area in (a). The Pecora river runs close to, and parallel to the boundary between the two terraces.

reconnaissance soil survey based on aerial photo interpretation and ground survey corresponding to a mapping scale of 1:50 000 delineated four units and a later more detailed ground survey at a scale of 1:25 000 classified the area into six units (Fig. 8.12). The area is drained by the Pecora river which flows NNE–SSW along the long axis of the study area.

The semivariogram of these data shows a characteristic pattern; at short lags (here $h = 125$ m) the semivariance is small, but rises with sampling interval to a maximum at a lag of 4 or 5 sampling units. Thereafter, the semivariance remains at a broadly constant level, though in this case, average values dip a little at sampling intervals between 7 and 10 lags.

The reader will note that two curves have been fitted through the experimentally derived data points shown in Fig. 8.11. These curves are mathematical models that have been fitted to the experimentally derived semivariances in order to be able to describe the way in which semivariance changes with the lag. Consider first the curve drawn with the solid line. This curve displays several important features. First, at large values of the lag, h, it levels off. This horizontal part is known as the sill; it implies that at these values of the lag there is no spatial dependence between the data points because all estimates of variances of differences are invariant with distance. Second, the curve rises from a low value of $\gamma(h)$ to the sill, reaching it at a value of h known as the range. This is a critically important part of the semivariogram because it describes at what distance inter-site differences become

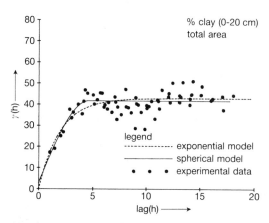

Fig. 8.11 The form of a typical semivariogram in which a spherical model (— — —) and an exponential model (- - - -) have been fitted to the experimentally estimated values of semivariance.

spatially dependent. Within the range, usually denoted by the symbol a, the closer together the sites, the more similar they are likely to be. The range gives us an answer to the question posed in weighted moving average interpolation about how large the window should be. Clearly, if the distance separating an unvisited site from a data point is greater than the range, then that data point can make no useful contribution to the interpolation; it is too far away.

The third point shown by Fig. 8.11 is that the fitted model does not pass through the origin, but cuts the Y-axis at a positive value of $\gamma(h)$. According to equation 8.17 the semivariance must be zero when $h=0$. The positive value of $\gamma(h)$ $h \to 0$ in the model is an estimate of ε'', the residual, spatially uncorrelated noise. ε'' is known as the 'nugget' variance; it combines the residual variations of measurement errors together with spatial variations that occur over distances much shorter than the sample spacing, and that consequently cannot be resolved.

The spherical model is:

$$\gamma(h) = c_0 + c_1 \left\{ \frac{3h}{2a} - \frac{1}{2}(h/a)^3 \right\} \quad \text{for } 0 < h < a \quad (8.18)$$
$$= c_0 + c_1 \qquad \qquad \text{for } h > a$$
$$\gamma(0) = 0$$

where a is the range, h is the lag, c_0 is the nugget variance and $c_0 + c_1$ equals the sill. In this example, the values of the parameters of the fitted spherical model are $a = 4.598$, nugget variance $c_0 = 2.959$ per cent clay^2, and sill $= 41.744$ per cent clay^2. The values of these parameters were obtained by weighted least-squares (cf. Cressie, in press); some authors (e.g. Burgess and Webster 1980) prefer to fit the model using the method of maximum likelihood.

Although the spherical model often seems to describe the form of the experimental semivariograms of soil data well, it is by no means the only possibility. Other often used models are:

(a) the exponential model

$$\gamma(h) = c_0 + c_1 \left\{ 1 - \exp\left(\frac{-h}{a}\right) \right\} \quad (8.19)$$

The dashed curve in Fig. 8.11 is a fitted exponential model. The value of its parameters are $a = 1.942$, $c_0 = 0.023$ and $c_0 + c_1 = 42.957$.

Semivariogram models having a clear range and sill are known as 'transition' models because the statistical nature of the spatial variation changes as the lag exceeds the range.

(b) the linear model

$$\gamma(h) = c_0 + bh \quad (8.20)$$

where b is the slope of the line. The linear model is used in situations where the semivariogram does not appear to have a sill (for example, as in the case of the semivariogram of Brownian motion) or when the magnitude of the range far exceeds the distances over which one wishes to interpolate. Linear models are also used in the technique called universal kriging (see below).

In some cases, the nugget variance ε'' so dominates the variation that the experimental semivariances show no tendency to increase with the lag. In these situations it is not appropriate to fit any model; the interpretation is that the data are so noisy that interpolation is not sensible. In these situations, the best estimate of $Z(x)$ is the usual mean computed from all sample points in the region of interest without taking spatial dependence into account. At this point any attempts to interpolate should stop as the results will not be any better than can be achieved by conventional choropleth mapping.

Directional effects in spatial variation

So far it has been assumed that the variation of the property under study is much the same in all directions. If this is so, the spatial variation is said to be isotropic. In very many situations, however, it can be expected that there is a 'grain' or preferred direction to the local, spatially dependent component of variation $\varepsilon'(x)$, and this can be examined by estimating the form of the semivariogram in different directions, for example N–S and E–W. The resulting semivariograms will then provide an answer to the question about the shape and orientation of the window from which sample points should be drawn for interpolation.

Because of the fluvial geomorphological history of the sample area near Follonica, it might be expected that variation perpendicular to the Pecora river would have a different spatial scale than that in directions parallel with the stream. Figure 8.13 shows that this is indeed so; the semivariogram calculated for east–west directions on the sampling grid (roughly perpendicular to the stream) rises more steeply than that in the north–south direction (parallel to the stream). Because of the short transects (6 points) in the east–west direction, the semivariogram cannot be estimated for more than 5 lags. Consequently it is not known whether the variation reaches a sill, so it is appropriate here to use the linear model to describe the semivariograms. The linear models fitted to these data are:

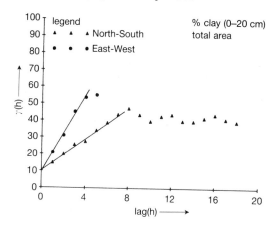

Fig 8.13 Semivariograms for the per cent clay (0–20 cm) calculated for the Follonica data in two directions: ●—across
short axis of grid; ▲—along long axis of grid. Linear models
have been fitted to the first few data points.

(a) East-west $\gamma(h) = 10.0 + 10.90h$
(b) North-south $\gamma(h) = 10.0 + 4.79h$ (8.21)

The effects of anisotropy can be incorporated in a
single semivariogram model by considering that the
variation in the north–south direction is just a
'stretched' version of that in the east–west direction.
The linear semivariogram can be written using polar
coordinates as

$$\gamma(h, \theta) = c_0 + u(\theta)|h|$$ (8.22)

where $u(\theta) = [A^2 \cos^2 (\theta - \phi) + B^2 \sin^2 (\theta - \phi)]^{\frac{1}{2}}$ (Burgess *et al.* 1981). The parameters are ϕ, the direction
of maximum variation; A the gradient of the semivariogram in that direction; and B, the gradient in the
direction $(\phi + \pi/2)$. The proportion A/B can be
thought of as the anisotropy ratio, or the amount the
survey space has to be stretched in direction ϕ so that
the semivariogram in direction A is the same as that
in direction B.

Using the semivariogram for interpolation

Given that the spatially dependent random variations
are not swamped by uncorrelated noise, the fitted
semivariogram can be used to determine the weights λ_i
needed for local interpolation. The procedure is
similar to that used in weighted moving average interpolation except that the weights come not from any
convenient deterministic spatial function, but from a
geostatistical spatial analysis based on the sample
semivariogram. We have

$$\hat{Z}(\mathbf{x}_0) = \sum_{i=1}^{n} \lambda_i \cdot Z(\mathbf{x}_i)$$ (8.23)

with $\sum_{i=1}^{n} \lambda_i = 1$. The weights λ_i are chosen so that the
estimate $\hat{Z}(\mathbf{x}_0)$ is unbiased, and that the estimation variance σ_e^2 is less than for any other linear combination
of the observed values.

The minimum variance of $\hat{Z}(\mathbf{x}_0)$ is obtained when

$$\sum_{j=1}^{n} \lambda_j \cdot \gamma(\mathbf{x}_i, \mathbf{x}_j) + \Psi = \gamma(\mathbf{x}_i, \mathbf{x}_0) \text{ for all } i,$$ (8.24)

and is

$$\sigma_e^2 = \sum_{j=1}^{n} \lambda_j \cdot \gamma(\mathbf{x}_j, \mathbf{x}_0) + \Psi.$$ (8.25)

The quantity $\gamma(\mathbf{x}_i, \mathbf{x}_j)$ is the semivariance of Z between
the sampling points $\mathbf{x}_i$ and $\mathbf{x}_j$; $(\mathbf{x}_i, \mathbf{x}_0)$ is the semivariance between the sampling point $\mathbf{x}_i$ and the unvisited
point $\mathbf{x}_0$. Both these quantities are obtained from the
model that has been fitted to the experimentally derived semi-variogram. The quantity Ψ is a Lagrange
multiplier required for the minimalization.

Kriging is an exact interpolator in the sense that
when the equations given above are used, the interpolated values, or best local average, will coincide with
the values at the data points. In mapping, values will
be interpolated for points on a regular grid that is
finer than the spacing used for sampling, if that was
itself a grid. The interpolated values can then be converted to a contour map using the techniques already
described. Similarly, the estimation error σ_e^2 can also
be mapped to give valuable information about the reliability of the interpolated values over the area of
interest.

Figure. 8.14 shows the results of interpolating the
Follonica data using the anisotropic linear models
given in eqn (8.21). Note that because the kriged surface must pass through the data points and the original data were only recorded to the nearest 5 per cent
clay, the resulting map is spotty and uneven. The map
of the error variances shows clearly how estimation
errors increase with distance from data points, especially in the neighbourhood of the missing values on
the grid.

The reader may feel that kriging is a costly technique and would like to have some indication of the
degree of improvement in prediction error the technique affords, compared with conventional mapping.
In this case, the 1:50 000 soil map resulted in mapping
units with a variance ranging between 21.62 and 60.43
per cent clay^2 with an average within-class variance of

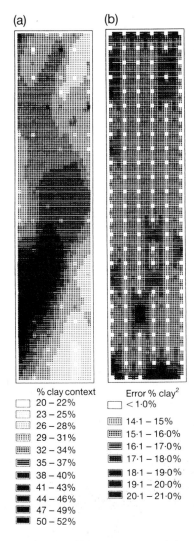

% clay context
- ☐ 20 – 22%
- ☐ 23 – 25%
- ▦ 26 – 28%
- ▦ 29 – 31%
- ▦ 32 – 34%
- ▦ 35 – 37%
- ■ 38 – 40%
- ■ 41 – 43%
- ■ 44 – 46%
- ■ 47 – 49%
- ■ 50 – 52%

Error % clay^2
- ☐ <1·0%
- ▦ 14·1 – 15%
- ▦ 15·1 – 16·0%
- ▦ 16·1 – 17·0%
- ▦ 17·1 – 18·0%
- ■ 18·1 – 19·0%
- ■ 19·1 – 20·0%
- ■ 20·1 – 21·0%

Fig. 8.14 Variation of the clay content of the topsoil (0–20 cm) over the Follonica area: (a) Map obtained by point kriging to grid cells of 37.5 × 37.5 m. (b) Map of the kriging variance.

39.32 per cent clay^2. The more detailed 1:25 000 map with 6 mapping units had variance estimates ranging between 10.80 and 41.86 per cent clay^2 with an average within-class variance of 38.92 per cent clay^2. Some of these estimates are probably not very reliable as they are based on few samples. The point kriging map has most of its area covered by error variance values that do not exceed 16 per cent clay^2, and even at the edges and near missing values do the error variances nowhere exceed 21 per cent clay^2. So kriging in this area was certainly worthwhile, returning results that are

approximately two-and-a-half times better than the choropleth maps.

Clearly, kriging fulfils the aims of finding better ways to estimate interpolation weights and of providing information about errors. The resulting map of interpolated values may not be exactly what is desired, however, because the point kriging, or simple kriging, eqns (8.24) and (8.25) imply that all interpolated values relate to an area or volume that is equivalent to the area or volume of an original sample. Very often, as in soil sampling, this sample is only a few centimetres across. Given the often large, short-range nature of soil variation that contributes to nugget variance, simple kriging results in maps that have many sharp spikes or pits at the data points. This can be overcome by modifying the kriging equations to estimate an average value of Z over a block B. This is useful when one wishes to estimate average values of Z for experimental plots of a given area, or to interpolate values for a relatively coarse grid matrix that can be used with other rasterized maps in cartographic modelling (Giltrap 1983).

The average value of Z over a block B, given by

$$Z(\mathbf{x}_B) = \int_B \frac{Z(\mathbf{x})\,\mathbf{dx}}{\text{area } B} \quad \text{is estimated by}$$

$$\hat{Z}(\mathbf{x}_B) = \sum_{i=1}^{n} \lambda_i . Z(\mathbf{x}_i) \tag{8.26}$$

with $\sum_{i=1}^{n} \lambda_i = 1$, as before.

The minimum variance is now

$$\sigma_B^2 = \sum_{j=1}^{n} \lambda_j \bar{\gamma}(\mathbf{x}_j, \mathbf{x}_B) + \Psi_B - \bar{\gamma}(\mathbf{x}_B, \mathbf{x}_B) \tag{8.27}$$

and is obtained when

$$\sum_{j=1}^{n} \lambda_j \gamma(\mathbf{x}_i, \mathbf{x}_j) + \Psi_B = \bar{\gamma}(\mathbf{x}_i, \mathbf{x}_B) \text{ for all } i. \tag{8.28}$$

The estimation variances obtained for block kriging are usually substantially less than for point kriging. When these equations are used, the resulting smoothed interpolated surface is free from the pits and spikes resulting from point kriging.

Figure 8.15 shows the results of using block kriging to estimate average values of per cent clay within

(a)   (b)

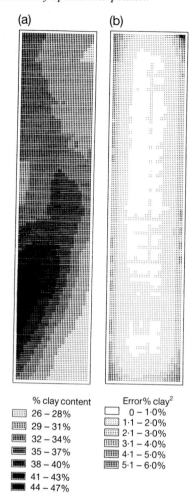

% clay content	Error% clay^2
26 – 28%	0 – 1·0%
29 – 31%	1·1 – 2·0%
32 – 34%	2·1 – 3·0%
35 – 37%	3·1 – 4·0%
38 – 40%	4·1 – 5·0%
41 – 43%	5·1 – 6·0%
44 – 47%	

Fig. 8.15 Variation of the clay content of the topsoil (0–20 cm) over the Follonica area: (a) Map obtained by block kriging over 250 × 250 m blocks to grid cells of 37.5 × 37.5 m. (b) Map of the kriging variance.

square blocks of side 250 m. The interpolation uses the same anisotropic, linear semivariograms as before. The smoothed surface now clearly shows long-range, gradual variation. The error variances now do not exceed 3 per cent clay^2 in the body of the area, and even at the corners they are less than 6 per cent clay^2. Compared with the conventional mapping, the block kriging map is estimated to be 5 to 10 times better than the conventional maps for predicting the average values of per cent clay content for 250 m × 250 m square areas.

Kriging in the presence of trends

If the data include long-range trends, the structural component $m(\mathbf{x})$ in eqn (8.14) might be modelled by a global polynomial trend surface, or by a set of class means. In these situations the original values could be transformed by subtracting them from the trend surface or corrected for class differences. The semivariograms and interpolations would then be performed on the de-trended data. Such a procedure might be appropriate in situations where there are clear climatic or relief-induced trends, but the same caveats apply here as when trend surface analysis is itself used directly for interpolation.

Very often a data set may contain local trends that are not constant over the whole survey area. These local trends may reflect different processes that have been at work in the landscape. For example, the trends in soil texture near a river levee are very often more extreme than in a backswamp area of the river floodplain, and consequently a transect lying over several components of the floodplain soil pattern will sample areas in which the soils vary spatially in different degrees. In these situations, some authors recommend the use of a technique known as 'universal kriging' in which the $m(\mathbf{x})$ term in eqn (8.14) is used to represent these local trends, or the 'drift' as it is known (Olea 1975; Royle *et al.* 1981; Burgess and Webster 1980b). Incorporating drift changes the component of spatially correlated variation $\varepsilon'(\mathbf{x})$ in eqn (8.14) so that it becomes the residual from the drift

$$\varepsilon'(\mathbf{x}) = Z(\mathbf{x}) - m(\mathbf{x}). \tag{8.29}$$

This residual should not be considered as a random error of measurement, but as a regionalized variable that is itself spatially correlated. In order to interpolate in the presence of changing drift it is necessary to be able to determine the drift at location $\mathbf{x}$ and to have an expression for the semivariances of the residuals from that drift. The problem is made more difficult because the drift cannot be estimated optimally without knowing the semivariances. So, for a given data set, the drifts could be calculated if the semivariogram was known, and the semivariogram could be calculated if the drifts were known. The way around this problem was provided by Olea (1975). It involves making reasonable assumptions about (a) analytical expressions for describing drift, (b) the form of the semivariogram, and (c) the 'sliding neighbourhood' within which the drift operates.

(a) *Drift.* Drift is defined as a systematic increase or decrease in the value of the regionalized variable in a particular direction. Drift occurs at all scales, but it is important in universal kriging for the drift to be seen to be continuous and slowly varying at the scale of working so that it can be represented by an analytical expression. So, the drift is defined by a polynomial expression,

$$m(\mathbf{x}) = \sum_{l=1}^{n} a_l f_l(\mathbf{x}) \qquad (8.30)$$

where the a_l are unknown coefficients and the $f_l(\mathbf{x})$ are integer powers of $\mathbf{x}$; n is the number of terms used to describe the drift. In practice, the drift is often represented either by a linear expression

$$m(\mathbf{x}) = a_0 + a_1 \mathbf{x} \qquad (8.31)$$

or a quadratic expression

$$m(\mathbf{x}) = a_0 + a_1 \mathbf{x} + a_2 \mathbf{x}^2. \qquad (8.32)$$

The constant a_0 cannot be calculated from the semivariogram but is not needed because the semivariogram of estimated residuals does not depend on it. The other coefficients can be calculated but they are not necessary for determining the λ_js in the kriging equations, it being only necessary to select the type of drift (Royle *et al.* 1981).

(*b*) *Choice of semivariogram model.* The linear model (eqn 8.19) is chosen to model the semivariogram of the residuals. This is because most semivariograms are linear near the origin and for interpolation it is only necessary to have information about the form of the semivariogram within one or two lag distances. For a linear drift, the slope of the semivariogram is estimated by

$$b = \frac{k-1}{k-2} \, \gamma_E(1) \qquad (8.33)$$

where k is the number of samples in the neighbourhood, and $\gamma_E(1)$ is the estimated semivariance at lag 1.

(*c*) *The size of the sliding neighbourhood.* The search area, or sliding neighbourhood, must be large enough to contain sufficient points to allow the drift and the λ_js to be estimated satisfactorily. Too large an area means redundant information and excessive computing. Practice suggests that an area containing some 12 to 15 sample points is adequate (Royle *et al.* 1981). The procedure is to calculate the theoretical semivariogram for a given drift and neighbourhood and to see how well it matches the experimental semivariogram of residuals. Matching is often done by inspecting the

results graphically. It is often not easy to judge which particular combination of drift power and neighbourhood is good and so the analysis is repeated for successively larger neighbourhoods and for both linear and quadratic drifts. This procedure is simple, but tedious when the original data are located on a regular grid; when the data are irregularly spaced then the procedure can be difficult (Royle *et al.* 1981).

Applications and limitations of universal kriging

Universal kriging can be most usefully applied to data that contain well defined local trends. Groundwater surfaces and smoothly varying landforms are examples of the sort of data that can be successfully interpolated by using this method. Soil properties, however, very often contain large, local sources of variation that shows up as the nugget variance (ε'') in many semivariograms. In these situations it is not at all easy to distinguish a true trend from the 'noise' or sampling variation. If a changing drift is assumed then the residuals will themselves have a large variance and the structural analysis linking drift power to sliding neighbourhood will be excessively complicated. Given these problems, Webster and Burgess (1980) concluded that for soil data with large nuggets little benefit over point or block kriging was to be gained from the more complicated universal kriging.

Complications with kriging

The form of the semivariogram is central to kriging, but it is not always easy to ascertain whether a particular estimate of the semivariogram is in fact a true estimator of the spatial covariation in an area. The presence of a few large values or outliers in the data may pass unnoticed in a preliminary analysis but they can have a large impact on the estimates of the semivariance provided by eqn (8.17). Cressie and Hawkins (1980) suggest a range of more robust, alternative methods. Cressie (1985) has suggested several ways in which irregularities in data can be trapped and removed, leading to improved estimates of the semivariogram. There is little reliable work published on how to estimate confidence limits to a semivariogram model, (though Burrough 1983b and Taylor and Burrough (1986) have made an attempt for the nested model of soil variation). The reasons for choosing a particular model to fit the experimental data are often difficult to explain in terms of physical processes and usually can only be rationalized in terms of a least-squares on maximum likelihood fit to the data.

To sum up: kriging is an advanced technique that relies heavily on statistical theory and on heavy computing, particularly if maps are to be made. In principle, kriging is the ideal interpolator, the steps in the estimation process demonstrate how the size and shapes of zones of spatial dependence can improve the value of local estimates, whether for points or areas. An additional bonus is that the method yields estimates of the errors associated with each interpolation, something that none of the other methods can do. Against these advantages there are the problems of removing non-stationarity from the data to achieve a situation commensurate with the assumptions of the intrinsic hypothesis. This is difficult ground, and the casual user of a geographical information system will need expert advice on how best to achieve the necessary transformations. Geographical information systems, particularly those used in mining and in soil survey, are beginning to incorporate methods of optimal interpolation. Indeed, certain geographical information systems for use in mining and mineral exploration are almost wholly geostatistical packages.

Extensions of kriging to large areas

Most published applications of kriging have been for data sets covering a small area, a few hectares maybe. Very often the sample points will all have been located within a single landscape unit, or within a single delineation of a soil unit in which the assumptions of (a) gradual change and (b) the intrinsic hypothesis have been easy to accept intuitively. Recently, McBratney *et al.* (1982) and Xu and Webster (1984) have applied the methods of optimal interpolation to data covering large tracts of land in south-east Scotland and Zhangwu county, China, respectively. Because kriging is essentially a scale-free technique, these extensions to large areas do not strain the assumptions of the theory, providing the user realizes that the variations should be related to the regional rather than the local scale. The question of statistical stationarity, or homogeneity, can be related to the kind and scale of the spatial processes operating in a landscape. If the whole of a surveyed area falls within the ambit of a single realization of a particular process, for example the geology is all sandstone, then it is likely on intuitive grounds that observations within the area will not depart too strongly from the tenets of stationarity of differences required for optimal interpolation. It seems likely that the large areas studied by Webster and his colleagues in Scotland and China were sufficiently homogeneous at the scale and sampling density at which they were studied.

Comparing kriging with other interpolation techniques

Although there are several reviews of interpolation techniques (e.g. Lam 1983; Ripley 1981) there seem to be few published studies that compare the efficacy of various methods when applied to the same data. Recently, Ripley (1981) compared the results of applying inverse distance weighting, trend surfaces and covariance models to a data set from Davis (1973) but apart from describing how the results were achieved and showing that the mapped results were visually different, he did not provide any quantitative evaluation of the success of the various methods.

Reference has already been made to Dubrule's (1983, 1984) comparison of splines and kriging in which he concluded that spline methods resulted in visually attractive maps that could be obtained with limited computing whereas kriging cost more computing time but led to quantitatively better results. Van Kuilenburg *et al.* (1982) adopted a more pragmatic approach. They compared kriging, inverse-distance weighting, and proximal mapping (Thiessen polygons) with conventional soil survey mapping (choropleth mapping) in terms of their efficacy for interpolating the value of moisture supply capacity in an area of sandy soil in the east of The Netherlands. The methods were evaluated by an independent set of test samples. This work formed part of a larger study in soil survey quality.

The study was done in a small area measuring 2×2 km near Laren in the east of The Netherlands. There were 530 original survey points, located by a stratified unaligned sampling system. The moisture supply capacity (MSC) is defined as the amount of moisture that can be supplied to a crop in a 10 per cent dry year (a year in which the potential evapotransporation deficit in the growing period from 15 April to 15 September has a probability of being exceeded only once in 10 years). The MSC was computed for each site with a computer model using climatic data for the whole area and field estimates of the water table fluctuations, thickness of the root zone, and textures, bulk densities and organic matter content of the soil horizons at each sample point. The same estimation procedure was applied to each of the 530 sample sites and also to 661 randomly located test sites.

The interpolation techniques used data from the 530 sites to estimate values at the 661 test sites. The interpolated values were compared with the observed values and for each method the root mean square (RMS) errors were calculated. The proximal technique estimated a value for a test site as that of the cell or

Table 8.2 Estimated RMS errors of interpolation methods of moisture supply capacity

Method	RMS error	95 per cent confidence limits of RMS errors	
Proximal	36.6	36.4	36.9
Weighted average	29.4	29.2	29.7
Point kriging	29.1	28.9	29.4

Soil map	Area-weighted average standard deviation within 13 mapping units	Range of values of standard deviation	
	28.6	6.6	38.3

polygon within which it fell; the inverse squared distance used the 10 nearest data points, and the point kriging method used an isotropic spherical semivariogram fitted to the experimental semivariogram with range 0.6 km, sill 1800 mm² and nugget variance 600 mm². The root mean square error of the soil map was estimated by computing the within-map unit variations of MSC from the sub-set of the 661 test borings that fell within it. Table 8.2 summarizes the results.

The results suggested that the proximal technique was least satisfactory, but for practical purposes with this attribute in this particular sample area, kriging did not outperform the simple weighted average method. Both weighted average techniques appeared to be less effective than the soil map that was based on conventional methods, which is contrary to the results obtained with the Follonica data. The reasons for this may lie in the fact that the Laren area has a particular kind of landscape structure, namely large areas of uniform aeolian sandy soils separated by clearly defined stream bottoms with poorly drained soils.

The interpolation techniques were applied without considering the landscape structure, whereas the soil survey had clearly recognized these differences. Super-position of the soil and groundwater level maps over the 530 sample points showed that there appear to be abrupt changes in the value of MSC coincident with certain soil and groundwater class boundaries (Burrough 1983b). It appeared that the different parts of the landscape would be better described in terms of separate semivariograms rather than an average semivariogram for the whole area. The presence of a few large differences in MSC over short distances leads to inefficient estimates of the semivariogram. The essen-

tial assumption in kriging that spatial variation over an area is homogeneous appears in this case to have been violated and so the quality of the results have been impaired. The conclusion to be drawn from van Kuilenburg *et al.*'s study is that if interpolation techniques are to be of real value then they should be used if possible in conjunction with, and not instead of, conventional landscape mapping methods. The same conclusion was reached by Giltrap (1983).

The value of combining landscape analysis with spatial analysis can be seen by reconsidering the Follonica data used above. Figure. 8.16 shows the results of estimating the semivariograms for the per cent clay content of the topsoil (0–20 cm) in two directions as before, but for the two terraces separately. The results are revealing. They strongly suggest that the spatial variation on the upper terrace is predominantly nugget—here there seems to be little to be gained by kriging! On the other hand, the variations on the flood plain show strong local trends that might benefit from

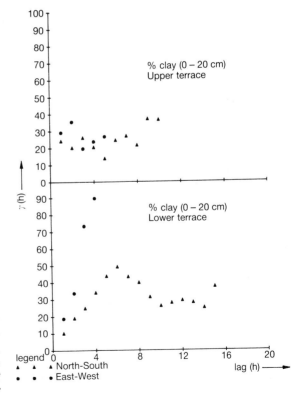

Fig. 8.16 Semivariograms of per cent clay topsoil from the Follonica area calculated separately within the main landscape units: ●—parallel with terrace boundary; ▲—perpendicular to terrace boundary. (a) Pleistocene terrace; (b) Holocene (lower) terrace.

Table 8.3   A comparison of methods of interpolation

Method	Deterministic/ stochastic	Local/ global	Transitions abrupt/ gradual	Exact interpolator	Limitations of the procedure	Best for	Output data structure	Computing load	Assumptions of interpolation model
'Eyeball'	Subjective/ deterministic	Global	Abrupt	No	Non-reproducible, subjective	Field data, aerial photo interpretation	Polygons	None	Intuitive understanding of spatial processes; homogeneity within boundaries
Edge-finding algorithm	Deterministic	Global	Abrupt	No	Often requires shapes to be defined and stored; better for man-made features than for natural landscapes	Raster images from remote sensors	Raster	Moderate	Homogeneity within boundaries
Proximal (Thiessen poly.)	Deterministic	Local	Abrupt	Yes	One data point per cell; no error estimates possible; tesselation pattern depends on data point distribution	Nominal data from point patterns	Polygons	Light/ moderate	'nearest neighbour' gives best information
Trend surface	Stochastic	Global	Gradual	No	Edge effects, outliers, complex polynomials do not necessarily have meaning; errors are rarely spatially independent.	Demonstrating broad features and removing them prior to other methods of interpolation	Points on a raster	Light/ moderate	Multiple regression— phenomenological explanation of trend surface; independent Gaussian errors
Fourier series	Stochastic	Global	Gradual	No	Not applicable to data; lacking periodicity	Periodic features such as sand dunes, ripple marks or gilgai, or man-made features	Points on a raster	Moderate	Strict periodicity in phenomenon of interest.
B-splines	Deterministic	Local	Gradual	Yes	No estimates of errors; masks all uncertainties in surface	Very smooth surfaces	Points on a raster	Light/ moderate	Absolute smoothness of variation
Moving average	Deterministic	Local	Gradual	No unless constrained	Results depend on configuration of data points and size of window; simple versions assume isotropy; no error estimates unless retrospectively calculated	Quick contour plots of moderately smooth data.	Points on a raster	Moderate	Continuous, differentiable surface is appropriate
Optimal interpolation (kriging)	Stochastic	Local	Gradual	Yes	Practical and theoretical problems of non-stationarity in data; large computing costs for mapping	Situations where the most detailed estimates and their errors are required	Points on a raster	Heavy (very heavy for universal kriging)	Intrinsic hypothesis (homogeneity of first differences); average local values can be represented by a continuous surface.

the application of universal kriging. The semivariograms for the whole area shown in Fig. 8.13 are a weighted average of those for the two terraces. They over-estimate the nugget variance for the floodplain (Fig. 8.16(b) suggests a nugget of c. 25 per cent clay^2) and under-estimate it for the Pleistocene terrace. Consequently, the original estimates for the error variances on the upper terrace shown in Figs 8.14 and 8.15 are probably much too optimistic and may give a false impression of the degree of increased precision obtained by kriging. On the other hand, kriging estimates for the lower terrace can be expected to be even more precise.

The conclusions to be drawn from these studies is that it is unwise to throw one's data into the first available interpolation technique without carefully considering how the results will be affected by the assumptions inherent in the method. Simple choropleth mapping is inadequate when there is gradual, spatially dependent variation within map unit boundaries. On the other hand, advanced techniques such as kriging, will not perform best unless the data conform to the assumptions of the method. A good geographical information system should include a range of interpolation techniques that allow the user to choose the most appropriate method for the job in hand. The interpolation methods can be used to prepare data in cell (raster) form that can then be used by the methods of overlay analysis described in Chapter 5. Table 8.3 summarizes the attributes and shortcomings of the various interpolation techniques in the hope that the user of geographical information systems will quickly be able to decide which method to use.

References

Agterberg, F. D. (1982). Recent developments in geomathematics. *GeoProcessing* **2**, 1–32.

Beckett, P. H. T. (1984). Soil information systems: the problem of developing a capacity of reappraising data for single purposes. In *Soil information systems technology* (ed. P. A. Burrough and S. W. Bie) pp. 102–11. PUDOC, Wageningen.

Billingsley, F. C., Anuta, P. E., Carr, J. L. McGillem, G. D., Smith, D. M. and Strand, T. C. (1983). Data processing and reprocessing. *Manual of remote sensing* (2nd edn), Vol 1, Chapter 17, pp. 719–92. American Society of Photogrammetry, Falls Church, Va.

Bullock, A. and Stallybrass, O. (1977). *Fontana dictionary of modern thought*. Fontana Books, London.

Burgess, T. M. and Webster, R. (1980a). Optimal interpolation and isarithmic mapping I. The semivariogram and punctual kriging. *J. Soil Sci.* **31**, 315–32.

—— and Webster, R. (1980b). Optimal interpolation and isarithmic mapping II. Block kriging. *J. Soil Sci.* **31**, 333–42.

—— Webster, R., and McBratney, A. B. (1981). Optimal interpolation and isarithmic mapping of soil properties. IV. Sampling strategies. *J. Soil Sci.* **32**, 643–59.

Burrough, P. A. (1983a). Multiscale sources of spatial variation in soil. I. The application of fractal concepts to nested levels of soil variation. *J. Soil Sci.* **34**, 577–97.

—— (1983b). Multiscale sources of spatial variation in soil. II. A non-Brownian fractal model and its application in soil survey. *J. Soil Sci.* **34**, 599–620.

—— Brown, L., and Morris, E. C. (1977). Variations in vegetation and soil pattern across the Hawkesbury Sandstone Plateau from Barren Grounds to Fitzroy Falls, New South Wales. *Aust. J. Ecol.* **2**, 137–59.

—— Bregt, A. K., de Heus, M. J., and Kloosterman, E. G. (1985). Complementary use of thermal imagery and spectral analysis of soil properties and wheat yields to reveal cyclic patterns in the polders. *J. Soil Sci.* **36**, 141–51.

Chatfield, C. (1980). *The analysis of time series*. Chapman and Hall, London.

Cressie, N. (1985). Fitting variogram models by weighted least squares. *Mathl. Geol.* **17**, 563–86.

—— and Hawkins, D. M. (1980). Robust estimation of the variogram. *Mathl. Geol.* **12**, 115–25.

David, M. (1977). Geostatistical ore reserve estimation. *Dev. Geomath.* **2**.

Davis, J. C. (1973). *Statistics and data analysis in geology*. Wiley, New York. (Second edition 1986.)

Dubrule, O. (1983). Two methods with different objectives: splines and kriging. *Mathl. Geol.* **15**, 245–55.

—— (1984). Comparing splines and kriging. *Comput. Geosci.* **101**, 327–38.

Giloi, W. K. (1978). *Interactive computer graphics—data structures, alogorithms, languages*. Prentice-Hall, Englewood Cliffs, N.J.

Giltrap, D. J. (1983). Computer production of soil maps. I. Production of grid maps by interpolation. *Geoderma* **29**, 295–311.

Goodchild, M. F. and Lam, N. S. (1980). Areal interpolation: a variant of the traditional spatial problem. *GeoProcessing* **11**, 297–312.

Green, P. J. and Sibson, R. (1978). Computing Dirichlet tesselations in the plane. *Comput. J.* **21**, 168–73.

Hawkins, D. M. and Cressie, N. (1984). Robust Kriging—a proposal. *Mathl. Geol.* **16**, 3–18.

Journel, A. J. and Huijbregts, Ch. J. (1978). *Mining geostatistics*. Academic Press, London.

Kilic, M. (1979). M.Sc. Thesis, Soil Science and Soil Water Management Course, Agricultural University, Wageningen.

Kratky, V. (1981). Spectral analysis of interpolation. *Photogrammetria* **37**, 61–72.

Kuilenburg, J. van, de Gruijter, J. J., Marsman, B., and Bouma, J. (1982). Accuracy of spatial interpolation between point data on moisture supply capacity, compared with estimates from mapping units. *Geoderma* **27**, 311–25.

Lam, N. S. (1983). Spatial interpolation methods: a review. *Am. Cartogr.* **10**, 129–49.

McBratney, A. B. and Webster, R. (1981). Detection of ridge and furrow pattern by spectral analysis of crop yield. *Int. stat. Rev.* **49**, 45–52.

McBratney, A. B., Webster, R., McLaren, R. G., and Spiers, R. B. (1982). Regional variation of extractable copper and cobalt in the topsoil of south-east Scotland. *Agronomie* **2**, 969–82.

Matheron, G. (1971). The theory of regionalized variables and its applications. Les Cahiers du centre de morphologie mathematique de Fontainebleu. Ecole Nationale Superieure des Mines de Paris.

Olea, R. A. (1975). *Optimal mapping techniques using regionalized variable theory*. Series on Spatial Analysis No. 2, Kansas Geological Survey, Lawrence, Kansas.

Pavlidis, T. (1982). *Algorithms for graphics and image processing*. Springer-Verlag, Berlin.

Ripley, B. (1981). *Spatial statistics*. Wiley, New York.

Royle, A. G., Clausen, F. L., and Frederiksen, P. (1981). Practical Universal Kriging and automatic contouring. *GeoProcessing*, **1**, 377–94.

Shepard, D. (1968). A two-dimensional interpolation function for irregularly spaced data. In *Proc. 23rd Natl Conf. Ass. Comput. Mach.* Brandon/Systems Press Inc. Princeton, NJ. pp. 517–23.

Sibson, R. (1980). Natural neighbourhood interpolation. In *Graphical methods for multivariate data* (ed. V. D. Barnett). Wiley, Chichester, UK.

Taylor, C. and Burrough, P. A. (1986). Multiscale sources of spatial variation in soil III: Improved methods for fitting the nested model to one-dimensional semivariograms. *Mathl. Geol.* **18**, 811–21.

Webster, R. (1977a). *Quantitative and numerical methods in soil classification and survey*. Oxford. University Press, Oxford

—— (1977b). Spectral analysis of gilgai. *Aust. J. Soil Sci.*

—— (1984). Elucidation and characterization of spatial variation in soil using regionalized variable theory. In *Geostatistics for Natural resources characterization* (ed. G. Verly et al.) Part 2, pp. 903–913. Reidel, Doordrecht.

—— (1985). Quantitative spatial analysis of soil in the field. *Advances in Soil Science* **3**, Springer-Verlag, New York.

—— and Burgess, T. M. (1980). Optimal interpolation and isarithmic mapping III. Changing drift and universal kriging. *J. Soil Sci.* **31**, 505–24.

Webster, R. and Burgess, T. M. (1983). Spatial variation in soil and the role of kriging. *Agric. Wat. Mgmt* **6**, 111–22.

Xu Jiyan and Webster, R (1984). A geostatistical study of topsoil properties in Zhangwu County, China. *Catena* **11**, 13–26.

9. Choosing a Geographical Information System

In the previous chapters of this book, we have explored the major aspects of the technical structures and capabilities that may be found in many modern geographical information systems. We have seen that the integration of computer technology and spatial data can provide a user with a powerful tool for environmental analysis that greatly extends the capabilities of conventional maps or of maps that are only drawn with computer assistance. We have also noted, in some detail, the problems that may arise when using the systems, particularly with less than perfect data, and we have seen that there are some developments, currently in an applied research phase, that may help to reduce some of the problems of using GIS indiscriminantly.

Having now learned about geographical information systems and having perhaps seen some of the work that has been published in scientific journals, the popular press, and the brochures of computer manufacturers, it is natural that the individual scientist, or the research institute or planning organization will want to set up a geographical information system. There are many ways of going about this and it is essential to work out in some detail exactly what system will be most suitable for a given application. First, you need to be sure that you are going to set up or purchase a system that really matches your technical requirements (and not just those the manufacturer has recognized). Second, because geographical information systems are not cheap and require specialized staff, you will need to convince the administrators that they must provide sufficient funding. Third, the kind of geographical information system adopted may have far-reaching effects on the way in which your organization works, and it is advisable to have worked out as thoroughly as possible the managerial aspects of the problem before you opt for any given system.

The problems of establishing a geographical information system were considered recently by an international committee organized by UNESCO (de Man 1984). This committee recommended a series of guidelines to be followed relating mostly to the organizational and managerial aspects of GIS. The following pages present another approach which should complement and augment some parts of the UNESCO study.

Defining the needs for GIS

1. Kind of user and user requirements

The requirements for GIS vary considerably with the kind of user. Besides the application aspect (e.g. soil survey or civil engineer or utility mapping) GIS users can be grouped according to the specificity of their task. We can distinguish the following categories:

(a) Users with an exact, defined task. The GIS is acquired for the automation of existing tasks and few changes in the procedure of data gathering, analysis, and presentation are foreseen for the immediate future. An overall improvement in efficiency over existing methods is expected.

(b) Part of the task is defined exactly, but there is a large part of the expected work that may make variable demands on a GIS. The user's information requirements are only partly known.

(c) No part of the work is defined exactly—every job may be different. Consequently, user's information requirements are unknown or variable.

Class (a) users are typical of mapping and inventory agencies and utility companies that have made enormous investments in setting up work procedures which, once set in motion, do not need to be revised frequently. This group is most attractive to computer software companies because they form a large, identifiable group with definable and solvable problems. The utility and public services mapping market probably contains most of the class (a) users and they are thought to represent some 70 per cent of the total mapping market in Europe (Computervision 1984).

Class (b) users include environmental mapping agencies that most probably have a division for systematic survey (e.g. countrywide cover of the soil pattern at 1:50 000), but which also undertake special projects and do research. Naturally they would like to be able to bring all their spatial environmental data under one system if possible. Some of their basic needs may be met by systems set up to cater for class (a) users, but special requirements will almost certainly not be met by standard systems. Because the market for these kinds of thematic mapping systems is usually small, large computer firms are not often prepared to make large investments unless the agency has the funds to pay for the special developments. The alternative is for the agency to hire its own staff to make the necessary developments.

Class (c) users are the most difficult. They include university research and teaching groups and research institutions that may be using GIS as a tool in ongoing research, or they may equally well be developing new GIS technologies.

2. Scope of application

The kind of GIS system needed depends very largely on the kind of work for which it is to be used. Besides the actual kind of work area—natural resource inventory, utility databases, mineral exploration—it is also necessary to distinguish the scope and time-scale of the application. A system that is used only for short-term project work will be geared to rapid data collection and input, analysis, and output, but will not have to include provisions for maintaining a large and complex database, as is the case for systems used for long-term inventory. In the latter situation, it is essential that the total range of geographical coordinates of the area to be surveyed can be handled easily to the accuracy required. Because of the size of the database it is unlikely that with the present technology the whole database will be accessible at any one time, although with new storage media this problem may be eased in the future. A national inventory also has to contend with data ageing and the need for resurvey and updating. National inventories also require closely controlled standards for data collection and processing. Special requirements will almost certainly require the development of special procedures which, while they might be too costly for a system used for project work, are an essential investment for a system that is to be used for many years.

Another important problem with setting up a GIS that must serve long-term applications is the technological obsolescence of computer hardware and software. Computer hardware is estimated to have a viable lifetime of about 5 years. This is partly because of physical wear in high-speed, high-accuracy components such as disk drives and plotters, but mainly because within that time span new computer technol-

ogies develop that enable formerly complex and expensive operations to be done much more easily. Computer software is to a very large extent in the same situation. Although there is a very sensible trend towards developing programming systems that can be easily transported from one computer to the other (for example by operating under operating systems such as UNIX), the reality of the current computer mapping market is that software packages (particularly turn-key systems) are specifically designed to work with a certain kind of computer and its operating system. So long as the relation between user, software, hardware, and supplier is satisfactory, the user should be able to expect that for a certain investment he will be cushioned from the shocks of excessive hardware and software change. But should the relation break down, if the user wishes to change to another supplier, then, as in the break-up of a marriage, the costs may be very high.

Every GIS has its own data structure, which is controlled by the software. If the software changes, then the data structures have to be created anew. For a national inventory this could involve a massive program of data conversion in addition to the normal back-up procedures necessary to ensure that the expensively won data are always available.

3. Technical choices—vector or raster?

As we saw in Chapter 2, GIS systems have developed along two main lines—the conceptual model, whereby the geographical entities are represented as points, lines, and areas (the *vector* model) or by a regular array of cells (the *raster* model). A third variant is the use of mathematical functions to describe spatial variations. We also saw in Chapter 4 that there is not necessarily a direct link between the database structure and the way in which the display device functions. Polygons drawn from a vector database can be drawn on a raster refresh screen, for instance. It was also shown in Chapter 2 that both the vector and raster methods of representing the spatial extents of geographical entities could be incorporated in the same database. There exist methods for converting vector format images to raster and vice versa, though the latter are much more complex and less satisfactory than the former.

So the question arises, do we need to consider a raster or a vector approach when setting up a geographical information system? Many people would say no, the question has now been made irrelevant through technological change. The reality is otherwise. While raster and vector systems should no longer be

Table 9.1 Recommendations for the use of vector and raster data structures in GIS

1. Use VECTOR data structures for data archiving phenomenologically structured data (e.g. soil areas, land-use units, etc.).

2. Use VECTOR methods for network analyses, such as for telephone networks, or transport network analyses.

3. Use VECTOR data structures and VECTOR display methods for the highest quality line drawing.

4. Use RASTER methods for quick and cheap map overlay, map combination and spatial analysis.

5. Use RASTER methods for simulation and modelling when it is necessary to work with surfaces.

6. Use RASTER and VECTOR in combination for plotting high quality lines in combination with efficient area filling in colour. The lines can be held in VECTOR format and the raster filling in compact RASTER structures such as run length codes or quadtrees.

7. Preferably use compact VECTOR data structures for digital terrain models, but don't neglect altitude matrices.

8. Use RASTER–VECTOR AND VECTOR–RASTER algorithms to convert data to the most suitable form for a given analysis or manipulation.

9. Remember that DISPLAY systems can operate either in RASTER or VECTOR modes independent of the DATA STRUCTURES that are used to store and manipulate the data.

thought of as irreconcilable alternatives it is a hard fact that certain tasks can be done better in the one mode than in the other, either because the current state of the development of algorithms, because of hardware capabilities, or because of storage requirements. The two modes should now be seen as complementary in any GIS, but the accent on a dominantly vector-based approach or a dominantly raster-based approach should depend on the type of GIS application under consideration. The relative merits of the two approaches were discussed in Chapter 2 and some recommendations concerning their use have been summarized in Table 9.1. Note that it is probably better to acquire a number of specialized modules that do a limited number of tasks well (e.g. vector mapping, raster overlay analysis, interpolation, image analysis) and link them together so that they can make use of common data sources, than to attempt to find a single universal system that can do everything.

4. *Finance available*

Both initial investment funding and continued financial support are major determinants in the success or failure of GIS. Not all potential GIS users will have

equal access to funding. Again, we can recognize three classes,

(a) Funding is generous and not limiting to acquiring any desired GIS configuration.

(b) Funding is limited to supporting well-defended and well-argued requests for a given GIS configuration.

(c) Funding is limiting—there is a danger of underfinancing leading to critical problems later.

Class (a) is a luxury that seems to be available mostly only to the military. It is to be hoped that most other potential GIS users will find themselves in class (b), but given the current situation in which commercial GIS systems are costly packages, many users, particularly those in universities, may find themselves in class (c) and they will have to consider their priorities very seriously indeed. When planning a GIS development one should first attempt to define the requirements for the job as closely as possible. Then one is in a state to consider possible hardware and software to meet these requirements within a broad budgetary framework. Actual costing comes later. Although one must certainly cut one's coat to suit one's cloth, it is better to present a well-argued case for a budget than to trim one's requirements too finely and end up with an unworkable system.

5. *Personnel available*

Just as with most other forms of complicated modern technology, GISs need to be used and operated by trained staff. Besides being trained, the staff need to be motivated to work in ways that are often quite contrary to previous manual labour. If an organization does not possess skilled labour of the right kind, then either existing staff must be retrained, or new staff must be hired. The latter option is often a great problem in government agencies at times of staff cutbacks or with elderly personnel in permanent employment.

Depending on the country and the organization, the availability of skilled labour for GIS may vary enormously. We can define *low-skilled* staff in the GIS context (and without wishing to be denigratory in any general sense whatsoever!) as those who do not have to know how the GIS works, but all they need to do is to keep it going, feed it with data, and ensure that results come out. In the sense used here, the term 'low-skilled' applies to typists, computer operators, persons digitizing maps, draftsmen working on the last stages of the final printed products, and so on. In contrast, *high-skilled* personnel can fall into four classes—managerial, liaison, technical, and scientific. Good managers are necessary both for the daily running of the GIS and for the harmonious interaction between it and the rest of the organization. Liaison personnel are needed to establish and maintain contacts with users. Technical staff include computer cartographers, programmers, system developers, and the like who know how the GIS works technically. Scientific staff include the environmental scientists and others who use the GIS for their research and application problems, and computer scientists who may be developing new GIS methods. We can identify several possible mixes of these types of personnel in an organization, as follows.

Existing staff has:

(a) Plenty of low-skilled, no high-skilled. (Comment—organization will need to acquire some high-skilled personnel or GIS will be inappropriate.)

(b) Plenty of low-skilled, some high-skilled scientific and technical staff. (Comment—organization may have to shed or intensively retrain some low-skilled staff.)

(c) Some low-skilled, and some high-skilled scientific and technical staff. (Comment—probably the ideal mix, particularly if the staff respond to retraining.)

(d) None or few low-skilled, some high-skilled scientific and technical staff. (Comment—the usual situation in universities where students are usually recruited to do some of the low-skilled work such as digitizing.)

6. Organizational aspects

Acquisition of major GIS facilities should not be done without seriously considering the way in which they will interact with the rest of the organization. It is simply not enough to purchase a computer, a plotter, a display device, and some software and to put it in a corner with some enthusiastic persons and then expect immediate returns. A serious commitment to GIS implies a major impact on the whole organization: it must be geared to different methods of data collection and processing and to different kinds of products. This means that the organization as a whole needs to plan the ways in which it expects to run its information business over a period of several years. The acquisition of GIS apparatus may mean that certain conventional operations, such as the preparation of peelcoat masters for colour printing maps, no longer need be done by hand. On the other hand, new staff and new organizational units will need to be created. For most applications of moderate size the GIS will need to be supported by a staff to give technical support at least

for the daily operation of the system, including local maintenance of hardware and software, data archiving and so on. Major hardware and software problems (i.e. those where something refuses to work as distinct from cleaning and setting up operations) will need to be covered by a service contract that has been taken up with the supplier. Service contracts cost approximately 10 per cent of the purchase price of a system and thus form an extra overhead for the organization throughout the lifetime of the system. Other organizational aspects include reliable funding and proper legal and political support.

For many organizations, GIS may appear as an exciting challenge, a new technology that will quickly remove many of the problems inherent in conventional methods of spatial data analysis. These positive aspects should not be underrated; they provide the main reasons for developing and using GIS. But new technologies bring new problems with them, and one should not be too disappointed if the new methods do not quite live up to their expectations. Indeed, at first it may appear that the GIS solution is much more expensive in the short term than the conventional methods it has replaced. The reality is that in order to survive, an organization must invest in new technology. If it does not, it will be overtaken by others who have made the investments and are organized in such a way that they can make the most of them. The skill in setting up a geographical information system is to choose a configuration that brings the greatest power and flexibility for the problem at hand for the minimum investment. And given the complex choice of computer hardware and software available, that is no easy matter.

7. The cost of GIS components and staffing requirements

The actual cost of the components necessary to set up a GIS vary greatly with the application, the size (large plotters and digitizers are much more expensive than small), and their source. Although actual costs will change rapidly with time, for the purposes of this discussion we can relate the following cost classes to the 1985 value of the US dollar:

low	< $ 10 000
moderate	$ 10 000–$ 50 000
high	$ 50 000–$250 000
very high	> $250 000.

Because GIS is so complex, it is helpful to break down the various stages of input, output, analysis, and so on, in terms of operations that can be easily iden-

Table 9.2 Investment and personnel needed for data input to GIS

| | | | Personnel | | |
| | | | | Highly skilled | |
GIS operation	Cost	Low-skilled	Technical	Scientific	Managerial
Off-line digitizing on microcomputer	low/mod.	+	−	−	(+)
On-line digitizing on interactive graphics system	high	+	+	−	(+)
Off-line scanning (high quality) + vector conversion	very high	(+)	*	−	(+)
Entering attributes in ASCII file	low	+	−	−	(+)
Building topological networks in database	low/mod.	(+)	+	−	(+)
Linking graphic and non-graphic data	low	(+)	+	−	(+)
Inputting satellite images	low	+	+	−	(+)
Geometrical transforms of satellite images	low (software) high (hardware)	+	+	−	(+)
Checking database and archiving	low/mod	+	+	(+)	+

Explanation of symbols in Tables 9.2–9.6: − not necessary;   + necessary;   * absolutely necessary;   (+) desirable, but not essential.

tified in terms of their function, their staffing requirements, and their cost magnitude. These relations have been displayed in Tables 9.2 to 9.6. The tables consider input, output, the use of a full DBMS, processing and analytical tools, interaction with the rest of the organization, and expansion/GIS research. The tables classify personnel in four classes, namely low-skilled, high-skilled managers, technical staff, and scientists. In all tables a minus sign means not necessary, a plus sign necessary, and an asterisk, absolutely essential.

Data input. Data input is not an expensive operation when done using digitizers connected to microcomputers off-line from the host computer. It is not usually cost-effective to use an expensive turn-key system for digitizing. Scanners are usually only worth purchasing for high volume digitizing of existing high quality line data, such as contours. Entering non-graphical attribute data is easiest using text files, which can also be input on a microcomputer using standard word-processing software. Linking spatial data to attributes should be done by software, as should building topological polygon networks. Projection transformation can be done at a reasonably low cost on minicomputers, but turnround times for transforming the projections of satellite images can be shortened 10–100 fold by using special array processors, which of course

increases the hardware costs. All data input operations need to be properly managed in order to obtain data from various sources, to ensure that a clean database is created and is then properly archived. It will also be a managerial task to decide which people may have access to the database, and whether that access should be limited to data extraction or whether they should be entrusted with database building and updating.

Data output. Data can be output in a wide variety of ways. It is essential for the organization and system managers to ensure that the quality of the data output matches the user's requirements. Although quick plots can be made by persons without special training, the production of a good quality product requires special skills that are acquired by a proper cartographic training. Too frequently one sees products from expensive geographical information systems that fail to please because the user was ignorant of the basic principles of visual design. Very high quality output (such as from a vector photoplotter or a high precision film recorder) may not be required very often and it may be cheaper, at least in the beginning, to hire time on them from another organization that possesses them.

Software for data analyses. Simple data retrieval is probably going to be the most frequent operation. Consequently, frequently used search routines can be

Table 9.3 Investment and personnel needed for data output from GIS

Hardware operation	Cost	Low-skilled	High-skilled		
			Technical	Scientific	Managerial
Low quality matrix plotter	low	+	−	−	−
Pen plotter (simple)	low	+	−	−	−
Ink-jet plotter (low quality)	low	+	−	−	−
Ink-jet plotter (high quality)	mod/ high	(+)	+	−	(+)
Laser microfiche	high	−	*	−	(+)
Photoplotter/ scribe	high/ v. high	−	*	+	(+)
Matrix plotter (good quality)	mod/ high	+	+	−	(+)
Matrix plotter (very good quality)	high	+	+	−	(+)
Magnetic tape	low	+	−	−	(+)
Colour graphics on screen with hard-copy device	mod/ high	+	+	(+)	(+)
Cartographic control and standards	mod/ high	−	+	*	+
High precision film recorder (colour)	high	−	+	−	(+)

Symbols: as defined below Table 9.2.

programmed as 'macro' files and run by low-skilled personnel on request from managers and scientific staff. More sophisticated retrieval systems, such as fully relational DBMS, require a period of training to use them properly, as do certain search and analysis routines in turn-key systems. Modelling, interpolation, and statistical analyses should not be carried out by staff who only know which commands to enter in order to get a result! Likewise, trained staff will be needed to use special software libraries and complex packages. If trained programmers are available, it might be cheaper and more effective to obtain a number of software libraries (e.g. NAG 1984; IMSL 1980; DISPLA; GKS) that can be used to build up the re-quired packages without having to develop all the algorithms afresh.

Planning and management. Planning and management of GIS needs to be tackled properly at all levels. Systems managers will have to be responsible for day-to-day work planning and for contacts with data suppliers and clients at a working level. They will also need to be in contact with the hardware and software suppliers to ensure that the system runs smoothly without undue technical problems. Scientists will have to manage the work that they plan to do—it should not happen that several groups wish to use large databases in a restricted system at the same time.

Table 9.4 Investment and personnel needed to use software for data analysis

GIS operation	Cost	Personnel	High-skilled		
		Low-skilled	Technical	Scientific	Managerial
Simple data retrieval	low	+	−	−	(+)
Using a relational DBMS	high	(+)	*	+	(+)
Interactive graphics system	high/ v. high	(+)	+	−	(+)
Interpolation and contouring	mod/ high	−	+	+	(+)
Map overlay	mod/ high	(+)	+	+	(+)
Statistical analyses	low/ mod	−	(+)	*	(+)
Raster processing for image analysis	mod/ high/ v. high	−	+	*	(+)
Digital terrain models	mod/ high	−	+	*	(+)
Special software	depends on type				
Software libraries	low/ mod/ high	−	+	*	(+)

Table 9.5 Investment and personnel needed for planning and management in GIS

GIS operation	Personnel	High-skilled			
	Low-skilled	Technical	Scientific	Managerial	Liaison
Planning work flow in the organization	(+)	+	+	*	−
Contacts with suppliers of data	−	+	+	*	*
Contacts with clients	−	+	+	*	*
Contacts with hardware and software suppliers	−	*	*	*	+
Contract with other mapping agencies	−	+	*	*	+

Symbols: as defined below Table 9.2

Table 9.6 Investment and personnel needed for host computers for GIS

Type of computer	Cost	Personnel			
			High-skilled		
		Low-skilled	Technical	Scientific	Managerial
Micro (Personal)	low	+	(+)	(+)	(+)
Micro (16-bit with fixed disk)	mod	+	+	(+)	(+)
Mini	high/v. high	+	+	+	(+)
Mainframe	Usually not applicable for GIS				

Symbols: as defined below Table 9.2.

Managerial and liaison staff should clearly organize the role of the GIS both within and without their organization and ensure that it gets the funding, staffing, and moral support necessary.

Host computers. Although it is possible to set up a GIS of some sort on any kind of computer, definite preferences have developed as to the size and type of host computer usually required. Current thinking suggests that a 32-bit minicomputer with 3 to 5 Mbyte of internal memory supported by disk memories of some 300–1000 Mbyte and a 1600 BPI tape drive are sufficient for many purposes, particularly turn-key systems for CAD/CAM and Image Analysis. The minicomputer will be supported by a number of 16-bit microcomputers and dedicated processors that will be used for data input, display, projection transformations, and various kinds of output. Because many GIS operations do not require particularly large amounts of calculation (excluding projection transformations and some interpolation procedures) but instead need to access frequently a large and complex database, speeds and size of disk storage are often much more critical than actual processing speeds. The problem of disk access is very often a very important factor that severely limits system performance when GIS or CAD/CAM systems are run under time-sharing on large mainframe computers. Consequently, it is not advisable to attempt to run GIS or computer cartography on mainframe computers and expect to get good interactive responses. Managers should be aware of this technical problem before they attempt to adopt the cheap solution of running an interactive GIS on the same machine that is used for administration. Of course, it may be desirable to link the GIS mini with a mainframe for exchanging data or obtaining access to software packages that cannot be supported in the GIS, but this should not be confused with the need to provide a GIS with its own stand-alone processor.

The procedure to follow when setting up a geographical information system

As has already been indicated, a great deal of careful preparation needs to go into the setting up of a geographical information system. A part of this preparation is finding out what others have done, and becoming acquainted with the enormous literature available. Publications by De Man (1984), Tomlinson *et al.* (1976), Tomlinson Associates (1980), or Teicholz and Berry (1983) are useful starting points, but they are mainly restricted to the North American situation. Given the huge choice of options available, many organizations may find it worthwhile to employ a consultant who has a recognized experience in the field.

Whether an external consultant is brought in or not, the following general procedure should ensure that no serious mistakes are made when setting up a geographical information system. The first essential is to make a detailed inventory of the existing work situation in order to define a starting point. From this base line, one then needs to be able to anticipate how future data handling needs are likely to develop in order to assess not only current requirements for computerization, but also how the system is likely to grow. The details that are likely to be required at this stage refer to the number of jobs per year to be handled, to the size and geographical extents of the databases, the accuracy and the quality of the output and the staffing required.

The following stage is to identify the kinds of hardware and software that will be necessary to satisfy the expected requirements. This is a stage where a consultant with a broad knowledge of GIS technology can be very useful. The organization that is about to set up the GIS should by this stage have a rough idea of the order of magnitude of the funding that can be expected, so that distinctions can be made between components that are absolutely essential from the beginning, those that should be acquired over a phased period, those that would be helpful but not essential (e.g. perhaps the same item could be hired for much less), and those that are essentially experimental.

The next stage is to look for suppliers of the *software* needed. Not all software can be obtained off the shelf, but there are a growing number of software houses that can provide systems that go a long way to meeting many requirements. A list of some software suppliers for GIS is given in Appendix 2. It is conceivable that different parts of a complex GIS may need to be met by several different software packages, which will need to be able to communicate with each other. Some manufacturers support a range of integrated packages; others leave the integration to the user.

Once a range of software has been found that meets the major aims, the following step is to consider the computer hardware necessary to support it. It is important to know if a given package has been designed to run on a given machine and whether it can only be run on other computers with difficulty or with a serious loss of performance. Beware especially of cheap, unsupported packages that look attractive, but which may cost your organization many man-months to get operational, for they may in the long run cost more than an expensive, quality product.

One attractive solution to the problem of hardware and software is the so-called 'turn-key' system. A turn-key system is a combination of hardware and software that has been put together by a manufacturer in order to satisfy a particular, well identified demand. So there are turn-key systems for remote sensing and image analysis, for computer aided design and manufacturing (CAD/CAM) and turn-key systems for mapping. A turn-key system might be the answer to a given organization's needs, particularly if that organization is active in a well-defined field that has an important place in the computer market. Many thematic mapping and other GIS applications are not yet so general as to have attracted sufficient investment from the turn-key manufacturers. The result is that certain turn-key manufacturers claim that their systems can be used for mapping of all kinds, when in fact they have never been properly designed for the kinds or volumes of data or the types of operations that are used in GIS. Turn-key systems, particularly those aimed primarily at the CAD/CAM market, may be less than ideal solutions for a given organization because they are expensive (you have to pay for the software you don't use as well as that which you do) and they may have hardware or software requirements that make it difficult to link them to other GIS components on other computers. On the other hand, it is only fair to say that some manufacturers of turn-key systems provide products that are very well geared to the client's requirements. The problem is one of matching requirements to capabilities in a hard commercial world.

Having identified requirements and a number of potential suppliers, the next stage is to prepare a document detailing the requirements in such a way that the suppliers can respond with serious proposals. The proposals should then be matched with the requirements and those clearly not meeting them should be rejected. The proposals remaining need to be treated very seriously, and the usual way of doing this is via the 'benchmark test'.

The benchmark test is in fact a model of the kind of work that the commissioning organization wishes to do which is given to potential suppliers. The suppliers are asked to perform the work specified in the test, very often being asked to give information about the time taken for certain operations (e.g. digitizing, polygon overlay, or projection transformation), the ease of use and the positional accuracy. Where possible, it is a good idea if the organization's own staff is present at the manufacturing site when the tests are carried out. Benchmark tests can be very thorough, examining every part of the work procedure in detail. On the other hand, they may concentrate on certain aspects of the requirements that are critical, when it is known that all the systems being tested meet certain minimum standards.

Once the benchmark tests have been carried out and evaluated the next stage is to choose a system on its price and performance. It might be that no system is suitable, in which case it may be better to wait for a few years before purchasing (Tomlinson Associates 1980). When a system has been chosen, then the finance needs to be made available. The planning procedures do not stop there because at the same time decisions have to be made about housing the new equipment, from choosing the location to installing the correct electricity supplies and air-conditioning. Staffing and staff training needs to be planned so that when the system is finally delivered it can be used to its potential as soon as possible. Even so, it is not unusual for a period of 9–12 months to elapse before the geographical information system is in full operation, and it might take longer still. Just as with all other complex tools, skills need to be developed to use them properly. One of the best ways is probably to conduct a number of small test projects to train staff and to show management what the system can do.

References

Computervision (1984). *Computervision Journal*, Europe Division News, March 1984.

DISPLA. Extensive software package of graphics routines. ISSCO, San Diego, Calif.

GKS. Graphical Kernel System. Standardized device-independent graphics software available from several computer manufacturers.

IMSL (1980). International Mathematical and Statistical Library, Houston, Texas.

Man, W. H. de, ed. (1984). *Conceptual framework and guidelines for establishing geographic information systems.* General Information Programme and UNISIST, UNESCO, Paris.

NAG (1984). National Algorithms Group Ltd, Oxford.

Teicholz, E. and Berry, B. J. L. (1983). *Computer graphics and environmental planning.* Prentice-Hall, Englewood Cliffs, NJ.

Tomlinson, R. F., Calkins, H. W., and Marble, D. F. (1976). *Computer handling of geographic data.* UNESCO, Geneva.

Tomlinson Associates (1980). *A study of forest inventory data handling systems for the province of Saskatchewan.* Tomlinson Associates, Ontario, Canada.

Appendix 1: Glossary of commonly used GIS terms

Acceptance test: A test for evaluating a newly purchased system's performance and conformity to specifications.

Access time: A measure of the time interval between the instant that data are called from storage and the instant that delivery is complete.

Accuracy: Conformance to a recognizable standard; can often mean the number of bits in a computer word available in a given system (*see* Precision). The statistical meaning of accuracy is the degree with which an estimated mean differs from the true mean. *See* Precision.

Acoustic coupler: A device that enables a computer terminal to be linked to another over the telephone system via the handset of a conventional telephone.

Addressable point: A position on a visual display unit (VDU) that can be specified by absolute coordinates.

Addressability: The number of positions (pixels) in the X and Y axes on a VDU or graphics screen.

Algorithm: A set of rules for solving a problem. An algorithm must be specified before the rules can be written in a computer language.

Aliasing: 1. The occurrence of jagged lines on a raster-scan display image when the detail exceeds the resolution of the screen. 2. In Fourier analysis the effect of wavelengths shorter than those sampled by the observation points on the form of the estimated power spectrum.

Alphanumeric code: Machine processable letters, numbers and special characters. Hence alphanumeric screen, alphanumeric keyboard for displaying and entering aphanumeric characters.

American National Standards Institute (ANSI): An association formed by the American Government and industry to produce and disseminate widely used industrial standards

American Standard Code for Information Interchange (ASCII): A widely used industry standard code for exchanging alphanumeric codes in terms of bit-signatures.

Analog (or analogue): A continuously varying electronic signal (contrast with Digital).

Application: A task addressed by a computer system.

Application program or package: A set of computer programs designed for a specific task.

Arc: A line connecting a set of points that form one side of a polygon. *See* Chain, and String.

Archival storage: Magnetic media (tapes, removable disks) used to store programs and data outside the normal addressable memory units of the computer.

Area: A fundamental unit of geographical information. *See* Point, and Line.

Array: A series of addressable data elements in the form of a grid or matrix.

Array processor: A special hardware board for high-speed processing of data encoded on a matrix.

Assembler: A computer program that converts programmer-written instructions into computer-executable (binary) instructions.

Assembly language: A low-level (primitive) programming language that uses mnemonics rather than English-like statements.

Associated data: *See* Attribute.

Attribute: Non-graphic information associated with a point, line, or area element in a GIS.

Autocorrelation, autocovariance: Statistical concepts expressing the degree to which the value of an attribute at spatially adjacent points covaries with the distance separating the points.

Automated cartography: The process of drawing maps with the aid of computer driven display devices such as plotters and graphics screens. The term does not imply any information processing.

Automatic data processing: The use of any kind of automation in data processing.

Auxiliary storage: Addressable memory devices outside the main memory of the computer such as disks and tape units.

Background processing/mode: Tasks such as printing are given a lower priority by the computer than those requiring direct user interaction.

Back-up: Making a copy of a file or a whole disk for safe keeping in case the original is lost or damaged.

BASIC: Beginner's All-purpose Symbolic Instruction Code. A simple, high-level computer programming language, originally for inexperienced computer users.

Batch processing: The processing of a group of similar jobs on the computer without operator intervention.

Baud rate: A measure of the speed of data transmission between a computer and other devices—equivalent to bits per second.

Benchmark test: A test to evaluate the capabilities of a computer system in terms of the customer's requirements.

Binary arithmetic: The mathematics of calculating in powers of two.

Binary coded decimal: The expression of each digit of a decimal number in terms of a set of bits.

Bit: The smallest unit of information that can be stored and processed in a computer. A bit may have two values—0 or 1; i.e. YES/NO, TRUE/FALSE, ON/OFF.

Bit map: A pattern of bits (i.e. ON/OFF) on the grid stored in memory and used to generate an image on a raster scan display.

Bit plane: A gridded memory in a graphics device used for storing information for display.

Bits per inch (BPI): The density of bits recorded on a magnetic tape. 800, 1600, and 6250 are common standards.

Boot up: To start up a computer system.

Bug: An error in a computer program or in a piece of electronics that causes it to function improperly.

Bulk memory: An electronic device such as disks or tapes that allow the storage of large amounts of data.

Bus: A circuit, or group of circuits that provide a communication path between the computer and peripherals.

Byte: A group of contiguous bits, usually eight, that represent a character and which are operated on as a unit. The number of bytes is used to measure the capacity of memory and storage units, e.g. 256 kbyte, 300 Mbyte.

C: A high level programming language used in graphics.

CAD/CAM: Computer-Aided Design/Computer Aided Manufacturing. Several CAD/CAM systems also include major features for GIS and automated mapping.

Cartridge disk: A type of magnetic memory disk enclosed in a plastic cartridge.

Cathode ray tube (CRT): An electronic screen for displaying information or graphics. Also called a visual display device (VDU).

Cell: The basic element of spatial information in the raster (grid) description of spatial entities.

Central processing unit (CPU): The part of the computer that controls the whole system.

Chain: A sequence of coordinates defining a complex line or boundary. *See* Arc, and String.

Character: An alphabetical, numerical or special graphic symbol that is treated as a single unit of data.

Characters per second (CPS): A measure of the speed with which a device (usually a printer or a VDU) can process data in the form of characters.

Choropleth map: A map consisting of areas of equal value separated by abrupt boundaries.

Code: A set of specific symbols and rules for representing data and programs so that they can be understood by the computer. *See* ASCII, FORTRAN, PASCAL, etc.

Colour display: A CRT capable of displaying maps and results in colour.

Command: An instruction sent from the keyboard or other control device to execute a computer program.

Command language: An English-like language for sending commands for complicated program sequences to the computer.

Compiler: A computer program that translates a high-level programming language, such as FORTRAN or PASCAL into machine-readable code.

Composite map: A single map created by joining together several separately digitized maps.

Computer graphics: A general term embracing any computing activity that results in graphic images.

Computing environment: The total range of hardware and software facilities provided by a given make of host computer and its operating system.

Configuration: A particular combination of computer hardware and software for a certain class of application tasks.

Console: A device that allows the operator to communicate with the computer.

Contour: A line connecting points of equal elevation.

Cross-hatching: The technique of shading areas on a map with a given pattern of lines or symbols.

Cursor: A visible symbol guided by the keyboard, a joystick, a tracking ball, or a digitizer, usually in the form of a cross or a blinking symbol, that indicates a position on a CRT.

Database: A collection of interrelated information, usually stored on some form of mass-storage system such as magnetic tape or disk. A GIS database includes data about the position and the attributes of geographical features that have been coded as points, lines, areas, pixels or grid cells.

Database management systems (DBMS): A set of computer programs for organizing the information in a database. Typically, a DBMS contains routines for data input, verification, storage, retrieval, and combination.

Data link: The communication lines and related hardware and software systems needed to send data between two or more computers over telephone lines, optical fibres, satellite networks, or cables.

Debug: To remove errors from a program or from hardware.

Debugger: A program that helps a programmer to remove programming errors.

Device: A piece of equipment external to the computer designed for a specific function such as data input, data storage, or data output.

Digital: The ability to represent data in discrete, quantized units or digits.

Digital elevation model (DEM): A quantitative model of landform in digital form. Also digital terrain model (DTM).

Digitize (noun): A pair of *XY* coordinates; (verb) to encode map coordinates in digital form.

Digitizer: A device for entering the spatial coordinates of mapped features from a map or document to the computer. *See also* Cursor, Puck, Mouse.

Disk: A storage medium consisting of a spinning disk coated with magnetic material for recording digital information.

Diskette: A cheap, low capacity storage medium, usually measuring $3\frac{1}{2}$, $5\frac{1}{4}$ or 8 in. in diameter. Much used in microcomputers; also known as a 'floppy' or 'floppy disk'.

Dirichlet tesselation: The process of splitting up a study area such that all points in the sample area are grouped into tiles according to the minimum distance between them and a previously sampled point. Also known as Thiessen or Voronoi polygons.

Distributed processing: The placement of hardware processors where needed, instead of concentrating all computing power in a large central CPU.

Dot-matrix plotter: A plotter of which the printing head consists of many, closely spaced (100–400 per inch) wire points that can write dots on the paper to make a map. Also known as an electrostatic plotter or matrix plotter.

Double precision: Typically refers to the use (in 32-bit word computers) of a double word of 64 bits to represent real numbers to, in this case, a precision of approximately 16 significant figures.

Drum plotter: A device for plotting maps in which the *Y*-axis movements are governed by the rotation of the drum.

Drum scanner: A device for converting maps to digital form automatically.

Edit: To remove errors from, or to modify a computer file of a program, a digitized map or a file containing attribute data.

Electrostatic plotter: *See* Dot-matrix plotter.

Element: A fundamental geographical unit of information, such as a point, line, area, or pixel. May also be known as an 'entity'.

Extrapolation: The act of extending the results of spatial sampling to points outside the area surveyed—not recommended.

File: A collection of related information in a computer that can be accessed by a unique name. Files may be stored on tapes or disks.

Filter: In raster graphics, a mathematically defined operation for removing long-range (high-pass) or short range (low-pass) variation. Used for removing unwanted components from a signal or spatial pattern.

Floppy disk: *See* Diskette.

Flatbed plotter: A device for drawing maps whereby the information is drawn by the plotting head being moved in both the *X* and *Y* directions over a flat, fixed surface. Draws with a pen, light beam, or scribing device.

Floating point: A technique for representing numbers without using a fixed-position decimal point in order to improve the calculating capability of the CPU for arithmetic with real numbers.

Floating-point board: A printed circuit board placed in the CPU in order to speed up arithmetic operations for real numbers. (The alternative is to use special software, which is usually much slower.)

Font: Symbolism used for drawing a line or representing typefaces used for displaying text.

Format: The way in which data are systematically arranged for transmission between computers, or between a computer and a device. Standard format systems are used for many purposes.

FORTRAN (FORmula TRANslation): A high-level programming language, much used in computer graphics and CAD/CAM. Recent improvements, embodied in FORTRAN 77, have made structured programming and interactive data input much easier.

Fourier analysis: A method of dissociating time series or spatial data into sets of sine and cosine waves.

Fractal: An object having a fractional dimension; one which has variation that is self-similar at all scales, in which the final level of detail is never reached and never can be reached by increasing the scale at which observations are made.

Gap: The distance between two graphic entities (usually lines) on a digitized map. Gaps may arise through errors made while digitizing or scanning the lines on a map.

Geocoding: The activity of defining the position of geographical objects relative to a standard reference grid.

GIMMS: Geographic Information Manipulation and Mapping Systems. A well-known, low-cost polygon mapping GIS.

GKS: Graphics Kernel System. A set of software primitives for allowing device-independent graphics programming.

Graphic tablet: A small digitizer (usually measuring 11×11 in.) used for interactive work with a GIS or CAD/CAM system.

Grey scales: Levels of brightness (or darkness) for displaying information on monochrome display devices.

Grid: 1. A network of uniformly spaced points or lines on the CRT for locating positions. 2. A set of regularly spaced sample points. 3. In cartography, an exact set of reference lines over the earth's surface. 4. In utility mapping, the distribution network of the utility resources, e.g. electricity or telephone lines.

Grid map: A map in which the information is carried in the form of grid cells. *See* Raster.

Hard-copy: A copy on paper of a graphics or map image originally displayed on a CRT.

Hardware: The physical components of a GIS—the computer, plotters, printers, CRTs, and so on.

Hidden line removal: A technique in three-dimensional perspective graphics for suppressing the appearance of lines that would ordinarily be obscured from view.

Hierarchical database structure: A method of arranging computer files or other information so that the units of data storage are connected by a hierarchically defined pathway. From above to below, relations are one-to-many.

High-level language: A computer programming language using command statements, symbols and words that resemble English-language statements. Examples are FORTRAN, PASCAL, C, PL/1, COBOL, BASIC.

Histogram: A diagram showing the number of samples that fall in each contiguously defined size class of the attribute studied.

Host computer: The primary, or controlling computer in a data network.

Hypsometry: The measurement of the elevation of the earth's surface with respect to sea level.

Initial Graphics Exchange Specification (IGES): An interim standard format for exchanging graphics data between computer systems.

Input: (Noun) the data entered to a computer system. (Verb) the process of entering data.

Input device: A hardware component for data entry; *See* Digitizer, Keyboard, Scanner, Tape drive.

Integer: A number without a decimal component; a means of handling such numbers in the computer which requires less space and proceeds more quickly than with numbers having information after the decimal point.

Interactive: A GIS system in which the operator can initiate or modify program execution via an input device and can receive information from the computer about the progress of the job.

Interactive graphics system: A computer system consisting of a central computer (usually a minicomputer) and a number of workstations at which an operator can draft maps and drawings interactively.

Interface: A hardware and software link that allows two computer systems, or a computer and its peripherals to be connected together for data communication.

Interpolate: To estimate the value of an attribute at an unsampled point from measurements made at surrounding sites.

Isopleth map (Isoline): A map displaying the distribution of an attribute in terms of lines connecting points of equal value; *See* contour, contrast with Choropleth map.

Jaggies: Jargon term for curved lines that have a stepped or saw-tooth appearance on a display device.

Join: (Verb) to connect two or more separately digitized maps; (Noun) the junction between two such maps, sometimes visible as a result of imperfections in the data.

Joystick: A hand-controlled lever for controlling the movements of the cursor on a graphics CRT.

Justification (right, left, or centre): The relative position of a text string or symbol on the map to the location at which it has been digitized.

Key file: In some CAD/CAM systems, a file containing the codes defining the operation of certain keyboard functions, or menu commands. In DBMS, a file containing information about search paths or indexes used to access data.

Keyboard: A device for typing alphanumeric characters into the computer. The arrangement of the keys resembles that of a typewriter, but often has more capabilities.

Kriging: Name (after D. G. Krige) for an interpolation technique using information about the stochastic aspects of spatial variation.

LANDSAT: The generic name for a series of earth resource scanning satellites launched by the United States of America.

Laser plotter: A plotter in which the information is written onto light-sensitive material using a laser.

Layer: A logical separation of mapped information according to theme. Many geographical information systems and CAD/CAM systems allow the user to choose and work on a single layer or any combination of layers at a time.

Legend: The part of the drawn map explaining the meaning of the symbols used to code the depicted geographical elements.

Library: A collection of standard, often used computer subroutines, or symbols in digital form.

Light-pen: A hand-held photosensitive interactive device for identifying elements displayed on a refreshed CRT screen.

Line: One of the basic geographical elements, defined by at least two pairs of XY coordinates.

Line follower: A semi-automatic device in which a laser beam is used to trace out lines from a source map and convert them to digital form.

Lineprinter: A printer that prints a line of characters at a time.

Look-up table: An array of data values that can be quickly accessed by a computer program to convert data from one form to another, e.g. from attribute values to colours.

Machine: A computer.

Machine language: Instructions coded so that the computer can recognize and execute them.

Macro: A text file containing a series of frequently used operations that can be executed by a single command. Can also refer to a simple high-level programming language with which the user can manipulate the commands in a GIS.

Magnetic media: Tape or disks coated with a magnetic surface used for storing electronic data.

Mainframe: A large computer supporting many users.

Map: Cartography; a hand-drawn or printed document describing the spatial distribution of geographical features in terms of a recognizable and agreed symbolism. Digital; The collection of digital information about a part of the earth's surface.

MAP: Map Analysis Package. A computer program written by C.D. Tomlin for analysing spatial data coded in the form of grid cells.

Map generalization: The process of reducing detail on a map as a consequence of reducing the map scale. The process can be semi-automated for certain kinds of data, such as topographical features, but requires more insight for thematic maps.

Mapping unit: A set of areas drawn on a map to represent a well-defined feature or set of features. Mapping units are described by the map legend.

Map projection: The basic system of coordinates used to describe the spatial distribution of elements in a GIS.

Mass storage: Auxiliary, large capacity memory for storing large amounts of data. Usually magnetic disk or tape.

Maximum likelihood: A method embodying probability theory for fitting a mathematical model to a set of data.

Menu: CAD/CAM; in interactive graphics stations a set of preprogrammed areas on the digitizing tablet. By entering a digitizer signal from one of these squares, the user can choose a particular set of commands. General interactive computing; a list of available options displayed on the CRT that the user can choose from by using the keyboard or a device such as a light-pen.

Microcomputer: A small, low cost computer (very often a single-user machine).

Minicomputer: A medium sized, general purpose single processor computer often used to control GIS.

Modelling: 1. The representation of the attributes of the earth's surface in a digital database. 2. The studying of landscape processes using mathematical algorithms written in computer code.

Modem (MOdulator-DEModulator): A device for the interconversion of digital and analog signals to allow data transmission over telephone lines.

Module: A separate and distinct piece of hardware or software that can be connected with other modules to form a system.

Mouse: A hand-steered device for entering data from a digitizer. *See* Puck, Cursor.

Multispectral scanner system (MSS): A device, often carried in aeroplanes or satellites, for recording received radiation in several wavebands at the same time.

Network: 1. Two or more interconnected computer systems for the implementation of specific functions. 2. A set of interconnected lines (arcs, chains, strings) defining the boundaries of polygons.

Network database structure: A method of arranging data in a database so that explicit connections and relations are defined by links or pointers of a many-to-many type.

Node: The point at which arcs (lines, chains, strings) in a polygon network are joined. Nodes carry information about the topology of the polygons.

Noise: Irregular variations, usually short range, that cannot be easily explained or associated with major mapped features or process.

Numerical taxonomy: Quantitative methods for classifying data using computed estimates of similarity.

Object code: A computer program that has been translated into machine readable code by a compiler.

ODYSSEY: Computer program developed at the Laboratory for Computer Graphics, Harvard, for overlaying polygon networks.

Operating system (OS): The control program that coordinates all the activities of a computer system.

Optimal estimator: An estimator for minimizing the value of a given criterion function; in kriging this is the estimation variance.

Output: The results of processing data in a GIS; maps, tables, screen images, tape files.

Overlay: 1. Programming; the process of replacing a segment of code in the computer memory. 2. Mapping; the process of stacking digital representations of various spatial data on top of each other so that each position in the area covered can be analysed in terms of these data.

Package: A set of computer programs that can be used for a particular generalized class of applications.

Paint: To fill in an area with a given symbolism on a raster display device. (*See* Cross-hatch.)

PASCAL: A high-level programming language that is been used increasingly instead of FORTRAN for scientific programming.

Pen plotter: A device for drawing maps and figures using a computer-steered pen.

Performance: The degree to which a device or system fulfils its specifications.

Peripheral: A hardware device that is not part of the central computer.

Pixel: Contraction of picture element; smallest unit of information in a grid cell map or scanner image.

Plotter: Any device for drawing maps and figures.

Polygon: A multi-sided figure representing an area on a map.

Polynomial: An expression having a finite number of terms of the form $ax + bx^2 + \ldots nx^n$.

Post-processor: A computer program that is used to convert the results of another operation into a standard format ready for further analysis.

Precision: 1. Degree of accuracy; generally refers to the number of significant digits of information to the right of the decimal point. 2. Statistical; the degree of variation about the mean.

Principal component analysis: A method of analysing multivariate data in order to express their variation in a minimum number of principal components or linear combinations of the original, partially correlated variables.

Program: A precise sequential set of instructions directing the computer to perform a task.

Puck: A hand-held device for entering data from a digitizer. (*See* Mouse, Cursor.) Usually has a window with accurately engraved cross-hairs, and several buttons for entering associated data.

Quadrant: A quarter of a circle measured in units of 90 degrees.

Quadratic polynomial: One in which the highest degree of terms is 2.

Quadtree: A data structure for thematic information in a raster database that seeks to minimise data storage.

Quantize: To divide a continuum into a series of discrete steps.

Raster: A regular grid of cells covering an area.

Raster database: A database containing all mapped, spatial information in the form of regular grid cells.

Raster display: A device for displaying information in the form of pixels on a CRT.

Raster map: A map encoded in the form of a regular array of cells.

Raster-to-vector: The process of converting an image made up of cells into one described by lines and polygons.

Real numbers: Numbers that have both an integer and a decimal component.

Real time: Tasks or functions executed so rapidly that the user gets an impression of continuous visual feedback.

Record: A set of attributes relating to a geographical entity; a set of related, contiguous data in a computer file.

Redundancy: The inclusion of data in a database that contribute little to the information content.

Refresh tube: A raster CRT in which the information is continuously refreshed or redrawn by the electron guns in a manner similar to a normal television screen. Consequently, refresh tubes can display motion.

Region: A set of loci or points having a certain value of an attribute in common.

Relational database: A method of structuring data in the form of sets of records or tuples so that relations between different entities and attributes can be used for data access and transformation.

Resampling: Technique for transforming a raster image to a particular scale and projection.

Resolution: The smallest spacing between two display elements; the smallest size of feature that can be mapped or sampled.

Response time: The time that elapses between sending a command to the computer and the receipt of the results at the workstation.

Run-length code: A compact method of storing data in raster databases.

Scale: The relation between the size of an object on a map and its size in the real world.

Scanner: A device for converting images from maps, photographs, or from part of the real world into digital form automatically.

Semivariogram: A figure relating the variance of the difference in value of an attribute at pairs of sample points to separation distance.

Simulation: Using the digital model of the landscape in a GIS for studying the possible outcome of various processes expressed in the form of mathematical models.

Sliver: A gap between two lines, created erroneously by a scanner and its raster–vector software.

Smoothing: A set of procedures for removing short-range, erratic variation from lines, surfaces, or data series.

Software: General name for computer programs and programming languages.

Source code: A computer program that has been written in an English-like computer language. It must be compiled to yield the object code before it can be run on the computer.

Spike: 1. An overshoot line created erroneously by a scanner and its raster–vector software. 2. An anomalous data point that protrudes above or below an interpolated surface representing the distribution of the value of an attribute over an area.

Spline: A mathematical curve used to represent spatial variation smoothly.

SPOT: An earth resource satellite with high resolution sensors launched by France in February 1986.

Stereo plotter: A device for extracting information about the elevation of landform from stereoscopic aerial photographs. The results are sets of X, Y, and Z coordinates.

Storage: The parts of the computer system used for storing data and programs. (*See* Archival storage, Magnetic media).

Storage tube: A CRT used for displaying maps and graphics information that retains the image continuously. Commonly green in colour, and offers higher resolution than refresh or raster screens at considerably higher price. Cannot display motion. Used for displaying vector-based maps and graphics.

String: A set of X-Y coordinate pairs defining a group of linked line segments. *See* also Chain.

SYMAP: SYnagraphic MAPping program. The original grid-cell mapping program developed by Howard T. Fisher at Harvard.

SYMVU: A program for drawing perspective views of three-dimensional data.

Syntax: A set of rules governing the way statements can be used in a computer language.

Tablet: A small digitizer used for interactive work on a graphics workstation.

Tape drive: A device for reading and writing computer files on magnetic tape.

Terminal: A device, usually including a CRT and a keyboard, for communicating with the computer.

Tesselation: The process of splitting an area into tiles. *See also* Dirichlet tesselation.

Text editor: A program for creating and modifying text files.

Thematic map: A map displaying selected kinds of information relating to specific themes, such as soil, land-use, population density, suitability for arable crops, and so on. Many thematic maps are also choropleth maps, but when the attribute mapped is thought to vary continuously, representation by isolines is more appropriate.

Thiessen polygons: *See* Dirichlet tesselation.

Tile: A part of the database in a GIS representing a discrete part of the earth's surface. By splitting a study area into tiles, considerable savings in access times and improvements in system performance can be achieved.

Time sharing: The use of a common CPU by several users in such a way that each user should be able to feel that he has the whole computer to himself. Time-sharing systems are usually not capable of supporting the massive computing demands of interactive GIS and CAD/CAM systems.

Topographic map: A map showing the topography (contours, roads, rivers, houses, etc.) in great accuracy and detail relative to the map scale used.

Topology: The way in which geographical elements are linked together.

Tracker ball: An interactive, hand-controlled device for positioning the cursor on a CRT.

Transect: A set of sampling points arranged along a straight line.

Transfer function: A mathematically defined method of transferring spatial data from one projection to another.

Transform: The process of changing the scale, projection, or orientation of a mapped image.

Tuple: A set of values of attributes pertaining to a given item in a database. Also known as a 'record'.

Turn-key system: A GIS or CAD/CAM system of hardware and software that is designed, supplied, and supported by a single manufacturer ready for use for a given class of work.

UNIX: A modern, general purpose operating system.

Utility: A term for system capabilities and features for processing data.

Utility mapping: A special class of GIS applications for managing information about public utilities such as water pipes, sewerage, telephone, electricity, and gas networks.

Vector: A quantity having both magnitude and direction.

Vector graphics structure: A means of coding line and area information in the form of units of data expressing magnitude, direction, and connectivity.

Vector display terminal: *See* Storage tube.

View port: A user-selected window through which part of the map database can be interactively accessed.

Visual display unit (VDU): A terminal with a CRT.

Weighted moving average: An average value of an attribute computed for a point from the values at surrounding data points taking account of their distance or importance.

Window: A usually rectangular area that is used to view or to transform the original map.

Word: A set of bits (typically 16 or 32) that occupies a single storage location and is treated by the computer as a unit of information.

Workstation: The desk, keyboard, digitizing tablet, and CRTs connected together as a unit for working with maps or graphics in interactive GIS and CAD/CAM.

Zero: The origin of all coordinates defined in an absolute system. Where X, Y, and Z axes intersect.

Zoom: A capability for proportionately enlarging or reducing the scale of a figure or maps displayed on a CRT.

See further:

Computervision (1983). *The CAD/CAM glossary*. Computervision, Burlington, USA.

Enticknap, N. (1979). *The Philips guide to business computers and the electronic office*. Input Two-Nine.

Meadows, A. J., Gordon, M., and Singleton, A. (1983). *The Random House dictionary of new information technology*. Random House, New York.

McGraw Hill (1984). *Dictionary of computers*. McGraw-Hill, New York.

OUP (1983). *Oxford dictionary of computing*. Oxford University Press, Oxford.

Appendix 2: A selected list of sources of information about geographical information systems

Suppliers of turn-key computer-assisted mapping and geographical information systems

a) Major systems

Applied Research of Cambridge (ARC), Wellington House, East Road, Cambridge, England.
  Suppliers of general drafting systems, digital terrain model interfaces, computer information systems and mapping and planning systems (mainly for municipal and utility work). Software runs on DEC VAX-11 and PRIME computers.

CGIS: Canadian Geographic Information System. Canada Land Data System Division, Lands Directorate, Environment Canada, Ottawa, Ontario, Canada.
  One of the largest and most sophisticated systems in existence, and the pioneering system.

COMARC Systems, 150 Executive Park Blvd, San Francisco, California, USA.
  An extensive GIS package for thematic mapping incorporating a relational DBMS. Supported on Data General, DEC, IBM, and microcomputers under UNIX.

Computervision Corporation, 201 Burlington Road, Bedford, Massachusetts, USA.
  Leading supplier of turn-key CAD/CAM systems. Mapping software is mainly oriented towards utility and municipal work.

DELTAMAP—DELTASYSTEMS, 2629 Redwing Road, Suite 330, Fort Collins, Colorado 80526, USA. (A Division of Autometric Inc., Suite 1308, Skyline 1, 5205 Leesburg Pike, Falls Church, VA 22041, USA.)
  Integrated turn-key geographical information system running on Hewlett Packard 9000 series computers under UNIX.

DIAD, Edenbridge, Kent TN8 6HS, UK.
  Low-priced turn-key system for analysis of raster-based images, mainly from satellites. Supported on a range of computers from the SAGE and STRIDE (32-bit micros) to DEC VAX-11.

DIPIX, ITS Inc., 176 Bolton Road, Vernon, Connecticut 06066–5511, USA/Linford Wood Business Centre, Sunrise Parkway, Milton Keynes, Bucks MK14 6LP, UK/120 Colonnade Road, Ottawa, Ontario, Canada K2E 7J5.
  Turn-key systems for image analysis and remote sensing based on DEC PDP-11 and VAX-11 hardware.

ERDAS Earth Resources Date Analysis Systems, Inc. Advanced Technology Development Center, 430 Tenth Street, N.W. Suite N206, Atlanta, Georgia, USA.
  Suppliers of software packages for overlay mapping and satellite image analysis running on DEC, Data General and other machines.

ESRI Environmental Systems Research Institute, 380 New York Street, Redlands, California, USA.
  Suppliers of fully integrated systems (ARC-INFO) for mainly vector-based overlay geographical information systems including DBMS capabilities. Grid-based operations and digital terrain models using TIN's are also supported.

GIMMS Limited, 30 Keir Street, Edinburgh, Scotland.
  GIMMS is a low-priced, general purpose integrated geographical processing system for producing medium to high quality thematic maps on pen plotters. A package that has stood the test of time, and that is being constantly updated.

I²S, International Imaging Systems: European office: Leuvensesteenweg 613, B-1930 Zaventem-Zuid, Belgium.
  Turn-key systems for image analysis and remote sensing. Image analysis systems includes own hardware linked to DEC PDP-11 and VAX-11 and other machines. Highly sophisticated and very powerful hardware/software for many GIS applications.

Intergraph Europe Inc. European office: Wijkmeerstraat 5/7, 2130 Hoofddorp, The Netherlands.
  World-wide producer of highly sophisticated turn-key interactive graphics systems with specialist applications in mapping.

Laboratory for Computer Graphics and Spatial Analysis, Gund Hall, 48 Quincy Street, Cambridge, Massachusetts, USA.
  The developer and supplier of programs such as SYMAP, GRID, IMGRID, DOT-MAP, ODYSSEY.

Laserscan Ltd. Laserscan Laboratories Ltd, Cambridge Science Park, Milton Road, Cambridge, England.
Manufacturers of laser line follower scanners and plotters.

MacDonald Detwyler, 3741 Shell Road, Richmond, BC, Canada V6X 2Z9.
Suppliers of systems for making orthomaps and digital terrain models directly from LANDSAT TM and SPOT digital imagery.

Quentron Digital Systems, Laser Court, 75a Angas St., Adelaide, South Australia.
Partners of CSIRO in developing and marketing digital image systems for image-based analysis of geographical data.

Raster Technologies, P.O. Box 9102, Cathedral Station, Boston, MA 02118–9990, USA.
High powered raster graphics systems for 3D-modelling and analysis of seismic data.

SPOT IMAGE, 16 bis, avenue Edouard-Belin 31030 Toulouse Cedex, France.
High Resolution satellite imagery for geographical information systems.

SYNERCOM-WILD Wild-Heerbrugg Ltd., CH-9435 Heerbrugg, Switzerland.
Turn-key system for interactive mapping produced to well-known Wild standards.

SYSSCAN P.O. Box 131, N-3601 Kongsberg, Norway.
Turn-key map information systems for utility mapping, mineral exploration, topographic and thematic mapping. Producers of a well-known scanner.

UNIRAS. 50 Mall Road, Suite 206, Burlington, MA 01803, USA/Ambassador House, 181 Farnham Road, Slough SL1 4XP, UK.
The UNIRAS line includes nine packages for various GIS applications in full colour from raster and vector mapping to kriging. These packages are written in FORTRAN and as far as possible are machine independent. They are supported on CDC, CRAY, DEC VAX and IBM machines.

b) PC-based systems

Since this book was first published there have been major developments in programming geographical information systems for personal computers. At the time of compilation (August 1987) most PC systems are designed for a hardware configuration that includes at least a 20 Mbyte hard disk, an Enhanced Graphics Adaptor and 16-colour screen and a Math Co-processor. Most systems will run on IBM (compatible) hardware using the 8086, 8088, 80286 and 80386 processors (XT, AT and 32-bit processors). The latest developments with improved graphics and 32-bit processors promise more improvements

BBC Enterprises (contact Amanda Wood/Ian Duncan at UK 01–576 0339).
The Laser Disk technology of the Domesday Project, the Ecodisk and other geographical data systems using moderately priced laser video disk technology linked to microcomputers for interactive analysis and display.

CRIES: Comprehensive resource inventory and evaluation system.
Runs on IBM XT-AT/COMPAQ with coprocessor and graphics screens. (Contact CRIES, Michigan State University, 302 Natural Resource Bldg, East Lansing, Michigan 48824–1222, USA.)

DeLORME MAPPING SYSTEMS, Lower Main Street, P.O. Box 298, Freeport, Maine 04032, USA.
CR-ROM (12 cm format) digital atlas that can be displayed and zoomed to many scales using an IBM PC/XT/AT and graphics screen.

DELTAMAP—DELTASYSTEMS, 2629 Redwing Road, Suite 330, Fort Collins, Colorado 80526, USA.
A version of DELTAMAP is available for the HP Vectra microcomputer.

ERDAS Earth Resources Data Analysis Systems, Inc. Advanced Technology Development Center, 430 Tenth Street, N.W. Suite N206, Atlanta, Georgia, U.S.A.
The ERDAS system runs on IBM and COMPAQ microcomputers that have been fitted with suitable extra processors and graphics devices.

ESRI Environmental Systems Research Institute, 380 New York Street, Redlands, California, U.S.A.
A version of ARC-INFO for the IBM-AT series of microcomputers is now available.

Golden Software Inc. P.O. Box 281, Golden, Colorado 80402, USA.
The SURFER package is an attractive, menu-driven set of programs for producing contour maps and block diagrams which runs on IBM-compatible PC's. A wide range of output devices is supported.

IDRISI

A grid-based Geographic Analysis System for 16-bit microcomputers (IBM-MSDOS). Current versions do not require a Math Coprocessor, although developments are being made. Developments are also in progress for supporting the program on the Apple Macintosh. (Contact J. Ronald Eastman, Clark University, Graduate School of Geography, Worcester, Massachusetts 01610, USA.)

Instituut voor Ruimtelijk Onderzoek, University of Utrecht, Postbus 80115, 3508 TC Utrecht, The Netherlands.
PC-GEOSTAT and PC-LANDFORM—programs for IBM PC-XT's for interpolation mapping (including kriging) and landform analysis.

GEO–EAS (Geostatistical Environmental Assessment Software). Public domain MS–DOS interactive kriging interpolation package available from the Environmental Monitoring Systems Laboratory, P.O. Box 93478, Las Vegas, NV 89193–3478.

Planning Data Systems, 1616 Walnut Street, Suite 2103, Philadelphia, Pennsylvania 19103, USA.
Suppliers of MultiMap, a low-cost IBM PC-based system using vector chain and polygons.

TYDAC Technologies Inc., 8th Floor, 220 Laurier Ave, W. Ottawa, Ontario, Canada K1P 5Z9.
Suppliers of an IBM-AT raster system using quadtree data structures. Contact Giulini Maffini.

Rijksinstituut voor Bos- en Landschapsonderzoek, 'De Dorschkamp', Postbox 23, 6700 AA, Wageningen, The Netherlands.
A user-friendly version of MAP (GEOPS) is available. Contact P. Leintjes.

Compendiums of statistical and computing software

Cable, D. and Row, B. (1983). Software for Statistical and Survey Analysis. Study Group on Computers in Survey Analysis.
This register contains 119 items of software for statistical analysis and survey of non-spatial data and the addresses of suppliers. The methods can of course be used with spatial data.

Press, W. H., Flannery, B. P., Teukolsky, S. A. and Vetterling, W. T. (1986). Numerical Recipes: the art of Scientific Computing. Cambridge University Press.
Extensive mine of theory, algorithms and program listings (in FORTRAN and PASCAL) for many aspects of numerical computing in GIS or other applications.

Roloff, L. and Browder, G. T. (1985). *Geoscience Software Directory*. 112 pp Kluwer, Dordrecht, The Netherlands.
Contains comprehensive details of more than 480 programs for geoscience applications.

Newsletters, general publications, conferences, universities, and official bodies

American Farmland Trust, 1717 Massachusetts Avenue, N.W., Washington D.C. 20036, USA.
A survey of geographic information systems for natural resources decision making. Published August 1985.

American Society for Photogrammetry and Remote Sensing (ASPRS). 210 Little Falls Street, Falls Church, Virginia 22046, USA.

AUTOCARTO.
International congresses dedicated to computer-assisted cartography and geographical information systems. Sponsored by the International Cartographic Association.

Chorley Committee Report. *Handling Geographic Information*. Report of the Committee of Enquiry chaired by Lord Chorley, Department of the Environment, (1987) HMSO, London.
Extensive and up-to-date overview of developments and applications of geographic information

EUROCARTO.
As AUTOCARTO, but in the European context.

FDC (Federal Digital Cartography) Newsletter.
A publication started in 1985 by the U.S. Federal Interagency Coordinating Committee on Digital Cartography. Contact: Larry L. Amos, 516 National Center, U.S. Geological Survey, Reston VA 22092, USA or Ann Olson, 508 National Center at Reston.

National Committee for Digital Cartographic Data Standards. The Ohio State University, 158 Derby Hall, 154 North Oval Mall, Columbus, Ohio, 43210–1318, USA.
Source of papers on digital cartographic standards for US agencies. Contact Prof. Harold Moellering.

Institut Geographique National, Service de Cartographie Aérospatiale Numérique, 2, avenue Pasteur, 94160 St-Maudé, France.

International Geographical Union.
   Commission on Geographical Data Sensing and Processing, P.O. Box 571, Williamsville, NY 14221, USA.
   Working Group on Geographical Information Systems; Joint IGU/ICA Working Group on Environmental Atlases and Maps. Contact IGU via International Council of Scientific Unions (ICSU), 51 Boulevarde de Monmorency, 75016 Paris, France.

International Journal of Geographical Information Systems.
   Published by Taylor and Francis from 1987 onward. Contact M. I. Dawes, Taylor and Francis Ltd, Rankine Road, Basingstoke, Hants RG24 0PR, UK.

International Soil Science Society. Working groups on:
A) Land evaluation information systems;
B) Soil and moisture variability in time and space;
C) Digitized international soil and terrain map.
   International workshops on the application of computer science and geostatistics to soil survey. Contact via ISSS Secretariat, International Soil Reference and Information Centre (ISRIC), Wageningen, The Netherlands.

ITC International Institute for Aerial Survey and Earth Sciences, P.O. Box 6, 7500 AA Enschede, The Netherlands.
   A range of systems for geodata processing (mainly third-world applications). M.Sc. Course on Land Information Systems.

LABLOG Newsletter of the Harvard Laboratory for Computer Graphics and Spatial Analysis, Gund Hall, 48 Quincy Street, Cambridge, Massachusetts, USA.
   The Laboratory hosted regular computer graphics conferences.

SORSA Spatialy-Oriented-Referencing Systems Association.
   An international association for promoting the development and application of spatial referencing systems. Contact address: P.O. Box 3825 Station 'C', Ottawa, Ontario, Canada K1Y 4MS.

State University of New York, Cartographic Laboratory, Buffalo, New York State, USA. Contact Dr David Mark.

Swedish Land Data Bank System, The Central Board for Real Estate Data, P.O. Box 662, S-801 Gävle, Sweden.

Technical University of Delft, Department of Geodesy, Thijsseweg 11, 2629 JA Delft, The Netherlands.
   Land Information Systems and Applied Geodesy.

UDMS Urban Data Management Symposium.
   Organizes annual symposia on the application of spatial referencing systems to urban databases. Contact: UDMS Secretariat, Thijsseweg 11, 2629 JA Delft, The Netherlands.

University of Dundee.
   Computer programs for Image Processing of Remote Sensing Data. Edited by A. P. Cracknell. Low priced computer listings issued by ERSAC Scientific Publications, Peel House, Ladywell, Livingston, West Lothian EH54 6AG, Scotland.

University of Graz, Austria.

University of Madison, Wisconsin, Department of Landscape Architecture.
   Organizes URISA congresses—contact Prof. B. J. Niemann, College of Agricultural and Life Sciences, School of Natural Resources, University of Wisconsin-Madison, Wisconsin 53706, USA.

University of Nottingham, Department of Geography, Nottingham, England.
   Computer Applications Special Issue Cartographic Drawing with computers by P. Yoeli, 138 pp together with software written in FORTRAN is a very low priced and easy introduction to automated mapping.

University of Reading/NERC Unit for Thematic Information Systems, Reading, England.

University of Utrecht, GIS Working Group, Instituut voor Ruimtelijk Onderzoek, P.O. Box 80115, 3508 TC, Utrecht, The Netherlands.

University of Zurich, Department of Geography, Winterthurerstrasse 190, CH-8057, Zurich, Switzerland.

UNESCO–GEMS (Global resource information database). Contact UNESCO, Nairobi, Kenya.

United States Geological Survey, 521 National Center, Reston, Virginia 22092, USA.

World Data Center, Boulder, Colorado, USA.
   Source of world digital databases.

Author index

Subject index